Wills
Irish Precedents and Drafting

Second Edition

Wills
Irish Precedents and Drafting

Second Edition

by **Brian E Spierin**
Senior Counsel

Bloomsbury Professional

Published by
Bloomsbury Professional
Maxwelton House
41–43 Boltro Road
Haywards Heath
West Sussex
RH16 1BJ

Bloomsbury Professional
The Fitzwilliam Business Centre
26 Upper Pembroke Street
Dublin 2

ISBN 978 1 84766 993 3

© Brian E Spierin

British Library Cataloguing-in-Publication Data
A catalogue record for this book is available from the British Library

Typeset by Pica Publishing Services, Dublin, Ireland
Printed and bound in the United Kingdom by
CPI Group (UK) Ltd, Croydon, CR0 4YY

To my mother Phyllis Spierin and In Memoriam Liam Hamilton,
Chief Justice of Ireland and my late father Denis E Spierin

CONTENTS

PREFACE TO THE SECOND EDITION

Much has happened since the first edition of this book was published early in 1999. We have changed our currency for the euro. Our Nation flew, like Icarus, too close to the sun only to fall back to earth. Civil partnerships were not on the agenda. Conveyancing law reform was an eternal twinkle in the Law Reform Commission's eye. Brussels II was in gestation, but it would take nearly six years for it to become operative in August 2004. So the timing was right for a revision, which would be worthwhile and I hope of assistance.

In the course of preparing this new edition I read again the very gracious foreword composed by the late Chief Justice of the time, Liam Hamilton. I remember clearly the day I went to his chambers, at the back of the Supreme Court, to ask if he would consider writing the foreword.

'I know why you're here,' Chief Justice Hamilton said after the exchange of usual pleasantries.

I had sat with him as Registrar for the two years before I left the High Court staff to practise at the bar. He kept a keen interest in my progress and would often seek me out in the Law Library for a chat, when he visited. I was amazed by what he said. I had never credited him with telepathy.

'You want to take your call to the inner bar,' he continued.

'No, not at all,' I protested. 'I wondered if you would write a foreword to a book I have written?'

'Of course I will do that for you,' he said with flourish of his cigarette. 'But why not take your call to the inner bar?'

The thought had not occurred to me.

'You are well able for it and ready,' he assured me. Then he paused. 'Listen,' he said. 'I will be retiring next year; would you give me the privilege of calling you to the inner bar?'

How could I refuse such a request? Subject to Government approval, ready or not I had to do it. Chief Justice Hamilton called me to the inner bar in October 1999. Little did we realise that his time with us thereafter would be so short.

During my years as his Registrar I was attending lectures in the Kings Inns at 4.30 each day. Without fail he ensured that the court would rise in time so I could make the deadline. On one occasion an urgent application caused us to sit late and on leaving the bench he bowed low to me.

'I am sorry I let you down today,' he said with a smile and a wink. 'It won't happen again.'

That was the late Liam Hamilton, Barrister, Senior Counsel, Judge, President of the High Court and Chief Justice but a human being first and last. He treated everyone he met with the same warmth and respect. He hated pretension or snobbery of any kind.

So when it came to considering whom I might include in the dedication of this edition, there was only one choice.

I would also like to remember here also, my good friend the late WG (Gerry) Kenna, Eamonn Mongey and, missed daily, Nora Gallagher. May each of them rest in peace.

I would like to thank all who encouraged me in this endeavour – Amy Hayes, in Bloomsbury Professional, for her tactful patience, Mark O'Riordan BL for his assistance in the research and Mary Henry solicitor for her wise counsel and keeping me sane.

I reiterate my heartfelt thanks to those referred to in the preface of the earlier edition. I will be ever in their debt.

Brian E Spierin SC
Law Library,

December 2012

PREFACE TO THE FIRST EDITION

Like many a good idea before it, the idea for this book was born in the bathroom, but I resisted the impulse to run around naked shouting about it. Instead I quietly started to write, or perhaps dictate would be more accurate. Over the months the book took shape and I am greatly indebted to my secretaries Angela Spierin and Terry Moran. To Angela for keying the bulk of the book and bringing it to a stage when I had to work on it thereafter myself. To Terry for keeping my other paperwork going.

At every point during the writing I was under pressure because of my practice. I longed for the luxury of going somewhere quiet and peaceful to write but maybe the absence of that luxury resulted in the book coming together more quickly than would otherwise be the case. Work on the book was confined to vacation periods. Friends were encouraging, but I think they doubted that 'the book', as it became known, would ever see the light of day. I, however, had a different view as I knew how gestation was progressing. The eventual birth brings a sense of satisfaction, but also, loss.

A wills' precedent book has not been attempted in Ireland before, which is curious when one considers that a will is probably the most important document anyone will ever sign and mistakes are not easily rectified.

Most wills in Ireland are drawn up by solicitors, and they have my sympathy. Testators will often come to them reluctantly, harbouring the superstitious notion that if they make a will they will die shortly thereafter. No other document forces us to confront our mortality more. Testators will either be vague as to what they may want to do, or be very definite as to what they require. It is for the solicitor to try to put shape on the testator's ideas and advise him or her as to the efficacy of what he or she may be suggesting. Tax considerations and planning will also be relevant, and if that was not enough the testator will mention that he or she is going on holiday the next day and would like to have 'something' in place before he or she goes!

My first introduction to wills was in the Probate Office where I commenced my working life in November 1973. One way or another I have been involved with them ever since, in the Probate Office, in the Law Society tutoring and consulting, and now in practice.

During that period I have seen a lot of wills and I believe that a book that will assist persons in drafting wills in a wide variety of situations is long overdue. Recently there has been a plethora of legislation which has a bearing on the content of wills, so the time is ripe to bring all of the law together in one volume.

I would like to thank the following persons who have been good friends to me in the course of my various careers: The Hon. Mr. Justice Liam Hamilton, Chief Justice, The Hon. Mr. Justice Peter Kelly, Eamonn Mongey B.L., Columba Ward, W.G. Kenna, Mary Finlay S.C., Mary Geraldine Miller B.L., Pauline McRandal B.L., J.G. O'Brien B.L. and Patricia Dillon B.L.

I hope that the book is of assistance and that it makes a contribution to making the practitioner's life easier.

Brian E. Spierin,
Law Library,
Four Courts,
Dublin

January 1999

FOREWORD TO FIRST EDITION

"Of comfort no man speak:

Let's talk of graves, of worms, and epitaphs;

Make dust our paper, and with rainy eyes

Write sorrow on the bosom of the earth.

Let's choose executors, and talk of wills." (*Richard II*, act 3, sc.2, 1.144)

Wills are not a comfortable subject; yet they are of near-universal interest. The efforts of mankind to direct their affairs after death are tinged with many attitudes and emotions: fear of the future, awareness of mortality, desire to care for relatives and friends, or even a simple craving to be remembered, be it in land, buildings, art, charitable work, scholarships or by one's family.

Respect for the wishes of the dead is deeply ingrained in Irish culture. Coupled with this, there has long been a popular assumption that drawing up an effective will should not be a difficult business. As a consequence, the efforts of lawyers and judges to ascertain whether a will is capable of doing what it purports to do tend to be seen in the minds of ordinary people as a prime example of 'unwarranted interference' in what would otherwise be a 'common-sense' affair. In the nineteenth and early twentieth centuries, it was common practice in many parts of the country to have the local priest or schoolmaster draw up a will for you, rather than a solicitor or an attorney. Yet this desire to keep one's affairs out of lawyers' hands often resulted in a document which gave ample scope for challenge by disaffected friends or relatives. I am reminded of the will of one Godfrey Hugh Massy Baker, dated the 27th of March, 1876. Having divided up his property as he wished, the testator concluded:

> "I have now stated my will to be best of my ability clearly, as to the disposal of my different properties; yet, in order to prevent disputes, I shall add this clause: And it is my will that all differences of opinion as to my intention shall be left to the decision of the executors, their administrators or assigns whose decision shall be final if they agree; if they do not, they shall appoint an umpire, from whose judgment there shall be no appeal. *Anyone resorting to law, I here cancel and annul every benefit they would otherwise have derived from this my will, and whatever they have forfeited shall be divided by the executors among those who had acceded to their decision.*" [emphasis added]

Ironically, it was this very clause which became the source of litigation, the result of which can be found in the report of *Massy v Rogers* (1883) 11 L.R. (Ire) 409.

Times change, and I think the importance of obtaining professional assistance in writing one's will is generally appreciated today but who will advise the advisors? I can think of no one better qualified to do so than Brian Spierin. He has spent a full quarter-century immersed in wills of all kinds; as a civil servant, a lecturer, a consultant or a barrister. But more than experience alone, he brings to this book the personal qualities which have marked his career: a flair for teaching and communication; a passion for exactness, and an infectious enthusiasm which the years have not dimmed.

This is an important, useful and groundbreaking book. Nothing like it has existed in Ireland until now, and the need has been sorely felt. To many legal practitioners – especially those taking their first hesitant steps into this area of law – it will be as though a path has suddenly opened up in the midst of a forest of brambles. Ordinary members of the public should also benefit from the clear layout, uncluttered language and myriad precedents contained in its pages.

In years gone by, when Irish law books were thin on the ground, one could safely say that any publication would become the 'standard work' in its field. Thankfully, the volume of Irish legal literature has increased beyond measure. Nonetheless, I still feel confident that Mr Spierin's opus more than justifies such a title. I wish him well, and heartily commend this book to you.

Liam Hamilton
Chief Justice
Supreme Court, Four Courts, Dublin

TABLE OF CASES

TABLE OF STATUTES

TABLE OF STATUTORY INSTRUMENTS CONVENTIONS AND EUROPEAN LEGISLATION

Chapter 1

CHECK LISTS FOR WILLS

PART I: CHECK LISTS FOR TAKING INSTRUCTIONS

[1.01] In the text that follows reference to 'the 1965 Act' is to the Succession Act 1965, reference to 'the 2009 Act' is to the Land and Conveyancing Law Reform Act 2009 and reference to 'the 2010 Act' is to the Civil Partnership and Certain Rights and Obligations of Cohabitants Act 2010.

In particular, the 2010 Act has had a major impact on testamentary freedom and anyone setting out to draft wills should be fully familiar with its contents. It confers rights, similar to those accorded to spouses, on civil partners. There are, however, subtle variations between spouses and civil partners. Further, as civil partners will always be of the same sex, only one partner will be the biological parent of any child being reared by the civil partners. The 2010 Act largely ignores this reality, and whatever one's view is of the propriety of according rights to civil partners at all, this is a regrettable lacuna.

Additionally, under the 2010 Act certain limited rights are created in favour of a surviving cohabitant.

In the chapters and pages that follow, I have endeavoured to place all of these changes, together with those wrought by the 2009 Act and case law since this book was first published 14 years ago, in context to assist any practitioner drafting a will.[1]

Since the last publication of this book, the Convention known as 'Brussels II' in relation to, *inter alia*, the recognition of divorces, separations and nullities granted in European Union member states, excluding Denmark, has come into force on the 1 August 2004. The effect of the Convention is dealt with later in this chapter.

The check lists in this chapter will be particularly useful where a practitioner is required to draft a will with some urgency, for example where a client is departing on holidays or perhaps is terminally ill. By using the check lists, the practitioner can seek to ensure that all of the testator's needs are met and that the relevant questions are asked to ensure, insofar as possible, that:

(a) the will reflects the testator's intention and instructions taking into account the testator's own particular circumstances;

(b) the practitioner will have the necessary material in his or her attendance to demonstrate later, should questions be raised, that the will of the testator is a valid one with regard to testamentary capacity; and

(c) the will is the voluntary act of the testator.

---

1. For a full commentary on the 1965, 2009 and 2010 Acts, insofar as they impact on the law of succession in Ireland and may impact on the drafting of wills, readers are referred to Spierin, *The Succession Act 1965 and Related Legislation, a Commentary* (4th edn, Bloomsbury Professional, 2011).

The primary objectives of any person drafting a will are to fairly and clearly reflect the testator's instructions and to minimise the possibility of disputes after the testator has died.

Check lists applicable to all testators

Does the testator have the requisite testamentary capacity?

[1.02] Under Irish law, for a testator to have testamentary capacity, the testator must:

(i)   be 18 years of age, or be or have been married. The 2010 Act did not amend s 77 of the Succession Act 1965 to provide that the entry into a civil partnership also conferred capacity to make a will. In order to enter into a civil partnership the parties must have attained the 18 years;[2]

(ii)   be of sound disposing mind.[3]

Most frequently, questions or disputes about testamentary capacity will arise post the testator's death. The person drafting the will should, in an appropriate case, try to anticipate any such question arising and place him or herself in the best position possible to answer any questions raised and to demonstrate that the testator had capacity.

[1.03] It goes without saying that a practitioner who believes a testator does not have capacity should not have him or her execute a will and should record why the will was not made. The attendance as to why a will was not made will be very important if expectant, but disappointed, beneficiaries query why a will was not made. If opting for making the will in a borderline case, the person drafting the will should carefully record any misgivings and the reasons why they arose.

[1.04] The test for testamentary capacity was laid down in *Banks v Goodfellow*,[4] and essentially that case provides for a threefold test. *Each element* of the test must be satisfied in order for the testator to have testamentary capacity. This test has been repeatedly applied by the Irish courts in cases involving questions of testamentary capacity. The statement of the law as set out below was endorsed by Feeney J in *In Re Flannery: Flannery v Flannery*:[5]

(a)   The testator must understand that he or she is making a will, ie, a document that will dispose of assets on death. The testator however need not understand the precise legal effect of the provisions in the will.

(b)   The testator must be capable of knowing the nature and extent of his or her estate.

(c)   The testator must be able to give consideration to those persons who might be expected to benefit from his or her estate and decide whether or not to benefit them.

---

2.   Section 59D of the Civil Registration Act 2004 as inserted by s 16 of the 2010 Act.
3.   Section 77 of the 1965 Act.
4.   *Banks v Goodfellow* (1870) LR 5 QB 549.
5.   *In Re Flannery: Flannery v Flannery* [2009] IEHC 317.

The test of mental capacity is a legal and not a medical one, and a person suffering from quite a severe mental illness may still be able to make a will if he or she is enjoying a lucid interval. Generally speaking, a person must have capacity when he or she is executing the will, but in *Parker v Felgate*[6] a testator was held to have testamentary capacity, notwithstanding that at the time of execution he was in a very debilitated physical state. He was at least able to understand that he was executing a will for which he had earlier given instructions and was therefore held to have testamentary capacity. See also the recent Irish case of *Scally v Rhatigan (No 1).*[7]

[1.05] A practitioner drawing up a will, therefore, should examine the testator in line with the threefold test laid down by *Banks v Goodfellow* and record the testator's response in a detailed attendance. If there is any doubt concerning the capacity of the testator, eg, due to old age or a psychiatric history, it would be well worthwhile having the testator examined medically to ascertain whether he or she has testamentary capacity. The results of this test should be recorded in a medical report and/or affidavit of mental capacity. While the medical evidence may not be conclusive on the issue, if it is raised, it would be of enormous assistance where a medical attendant can give a positive view as to the person's testamentary capacity.

[1.06] The medical attendant in assessing capacity might be acquainted with and have regard to the tests laid down in *Banks v Goodfellow*. A terse note saying that the testator had capacity at the time the will was made will be of limited use.

[1.07] In *Scally v Rhatigan (No 1)*,[8] Laffoy J considered the role of the practitioner and the application of the 'golden rule' in preparing a will for a person who is 'aged ... or seriously ill'. The so-called 'golden rule' was referred to by Briggs J in the case of *In Re Key Deceased.*[9] Laffoy J dealt with it as follows:

> 'In his judgment at para 7 Briggs J stated:
>
> "... the substance of the golden rule is that when a solicitor is instructed to prepare a will for an aged testator, or one who has been seriously ill, he should arrange for a medical practitioner first to satisfy himself as to the capacity of and understanding of the testator, and to make a contemporaneous record of his examination and findings ..."
>
> However Briggs J went on to say (at para 8):
>
> "Compliance with the golden rule does not, of course, operate as a touchstone of the validity of the will, nor does non-compliance demonstrate its invalidity. Its purpose, as has repeatedly been emphasised, it to assist in the avoidance of disputes, or at least in the minimisation of their scope."
>
> Those observations, in my view, represent the law in this jurisdiction. Irrespective of whether the "golden rule" or best practice is followed in a particular case, it is a question of fact to be determined having regard to all the evidence and by applying

---

6.   *Parker v Felgate* (1883) 8 PD 171.
7.   *Scally v Rhatigan (No 1)* [2010] IEHC 475.
8.   *Scally v Rhatigan (No 1)* [2010] IEHC 475.
9.   *In Re Key Deceased* [2010] 1 WLR 2020.

the eventual standard of the balance of probabilities, whether the testator was of sound disposing mind when the testamentary document was executed.'

This 'golden rule' should be borne in mind now that it has been judicially enunciated. Practitioners should satisfy themselves as to the capacity of the testator especially where the person is aged or has been seriously ill and record such findings that are made.

[1.08] In actual practice, where issues of testamentary capacity arise, it frequently amazes me how often there is little or no objective evidence of capacity at the time the testamentary document was executed. Memories fade. A doctor attending the testator at the time the will was made may not be able to recall whether or not a testator had capacity, should he or she be asked to give evidence or provide an affidavit of mental capacity, many years later.

[1.09] In the *Flannery* case, the testator was an elderly man in a hospital when the will was made. The solicitor who was drafting the will for him, and his spouse, who was also a solicitor, attended on him and acted as attesting witnesses. The testator was well-known to them both. They were satisfied that the testator had capacity. However, unknown to them, the testator had scored somewhat poorly on mental/cognitive tests to which he had been subjected in the hospital. He was, however, a reluctant participant in the tests. Feeney J believed that the poor performance was explicable in all the circumstances. The doctor who had attended him at the time did not really recollect the testator and could offer no view to the court as to the testator's capacity. The court held, on the balance of probabilities, that the testator had capacity. The court held that once due execution was proved, a presumption of capacity arose. It had not been displaced.

[1.10] In the *Rhatigan* case, Laffoy J also held that the testator satisfied all limbs of the threefold test referred to above, notwithstanding that some of the medical practitioners attending him expressed a doubt as to whether or not he had capacity.

[1.11] In the *Flannery* case, the will was of a simple type, but in *Rhatigan* the will was much more complex. The complexity of a will may have a bearing as to whether the testator could have understood same, though he or she need not understand its precise legal effect.

[1.12] Appendix 4 contains a specimen affidavit of mental capacity that might be sworn by a doctor attending a testator at the time a will was made, and left with the will. This will avoid the difficulty of trying to trace a doctor at a later time when the will may be subject to a challenge, or a doubt arises as to testamentary capacity. As Briggs J stated, the object is to avoid or minimise disputes.

[1.13] Adherence to the 'golden rule' or best practice also has a relevance in the light of the Supreme Court decision on costs in will disputes in *Elliott v Stamp*.[10] In that case, the Supreme Court stated that where information is provided to a person challenging a will, which should allay his or her fears, but the challenger proceeds notwithstanding, then this could put the challenger at risk on costs. The time to arm oneself in respect of any potential challenge is when the will is being drawn and executed. Persons drafting a will should always be alive to a potential challenge. Demonstration of adherence to the

---

10.   *Elliott v Stamp* [2008] 3 IR 387.

'golden rule' will assist in allaying the fears of potential challengers who may raise questions as to lack of capacity.

[1.14] When a will comes to be proved, an affidavit of mental capacity may be required where the person's death certificate shows that he or she died from some form of mental illness that would impair his or her cognitive function, such as Alzheimer's disease or senile decay. The Probate Office may also require an affidavit of mental capacity where the testator dies in a mental hospital. The Probate Office may initially look for an affidavit from a doctor attending the testator at the time the will was made. If there is a long lapse of time between the making of the will and the death of the deceased, the obtaining of such an affidavit may not prove possible.

The current Probate Office practice is to have regard to the surrounding circumstances. Where the will is one that a person might be expected to make, eg, one spouse/civil partner leaving all their estate to the other, and there is a reasonable lapse of time between the making of the will and the onset of any mental deterioration, an affidavit of mental capacity might not be sought. The Probate Officer can require an affidavit in any case where it is considered appropriate so to do.

In the absence of evidence from a doctor, the Probate Office *may* accept evidence from a solicitor who took instructions for the will and attended to its execution; there is a specimen of such an affidavit in **Appendix 4**.

Where there is a doubt raised concerning testamentary capacity, and no medical or other evidence is forthcoming, an application to court may be necessary to prove the will. If there is no contention concerning the proof of the will and all the persons affected are consenting, having been independently advised, such application might be made in the non-contentious Probate List in the High Court. It will, of course, be open to the Probate Judge to refer the case for plenary hearing should he or she consider that the facts of the case warrant such hearing.

[1.15] If any person, who would be prejudiced by the proof of the will, is objecting to the proof of the will on the grounds of lack of testamentary capacity, proof of the will requires a full testamentary suit by way of plenary summons in the High Court or by way of testamentary civil bill in the Circuit Court.

Therefore, the preparation of a good attendance relating to testamentary capacity and, ideally, an affidavit of mental capacity from a medical attendant could go a long way to resolving doubts concerning testamentary capacity and avoiding problems when the will comes to be proved.

Marital/civil partnership status

[1.16] Marital status may have a bearing on capacity where the testator is under the age of 18. To enter a civil partnership the parties must be 18 years of age.

Testamentary freedom

[1.17] The marital status/civil partnership status of the testator must be ascertained as it will additionally have a bearing on the advice that might be given to the testator vis-à-vis his or her testamentary freedom. Testamentary freedom has nothing to do with capacity but rather connotes the ability of the testator to dispose of his or her property without fetter.

[1.18] A person who:

•   is married;

•   has entered into a civil partnership;

•   has children (irrespective of the marital status of the testator or whether he or she is in a civil partnership); or

•   is cohabiting;

will have his or her testamentary freedom curtailed to a greater or lesser extent.

Undue influence

[1.19] In the recent case of *Darby v Shanley and others*,[11] Irvine J stated that one of the foremost duties of a solicitor in acting on instructions to draw a will for a testator was to ensure that the will was the product of the voluntary will of the testator. That is, the testator is acting free from the influence of the beneficiaries of the intended will. Irvine J stated at para 5.13 of her judgment as follows:

> '... To the forefront of those obligations, having regard to the circumstances in which they were asked to prepare Bridie Bird's will, was a requirement that they would seek to satisfy themselves that her instructions had been given independently of any influence that might have been exerted upon her by those who were to be the beneficiaries of her intended will.'

In the case of an elderly or infirm testator, the possibility of undue influence is ever present.

[1.20] There is no presumption of undue influence in the case of a will and it must be proved by the person alleging it and by cogent evidence.[12] Equally, no assumption should be made that the testator is acting freely, and the practitioner drafting the will should ensure that undue influence is not being exerted.

Where the solicitor drafting the will is a solicitor normally retained by the testator, he or she would normally know the circumstances of the testator and be in position to assess whether anyone is influencing the testator, but there is no room for complacency.

The testator should, wherever possible, be seen alone. Persons drafting wills should be particularly vigilant where the testamentary intentions of the testator change dramatically and should try to ascertain the reason therefor. It is important to ensure that the change in intentions is not being prompted by a person who may stand to benefit.

Where a testator is brought to a solicitor to whom the testator is unknown, the solicitor should be particularly wary to ensure that the testator is acting freely and voluntarily.

The solicitor's impression as to the absence of undue influence should be recorded in the attendance relating to the will.

---

11.   *Darby v Shanley and Another* [2009] IEHC 459.
12.   *Re Kavanagh: Healy v McGillycuddy and another* [1978] ILRM 175.

Foreign civil partnerships and their dissolution

[1.21] Civil Partnerships or some sort of same-sex unions were introduced in other jurisdictions prior to 2010. Some testators may have entered into a foreign civil partnership. Section 5 of the 2010 Act provides for the recognition of such civil partnerships, so practitioners should be alive to this possibility, make the relevant enquiries and advise on its recognition. Recognition is not universal and each case has to be considered in the light of the Act's provisions and the facts of the case. A ministerial order is required.

[1.22] The relationship must:

- be exclusive;

- be permanent until dissolved;

- be registered under the law of the relevant jurisdiction;

- have the equivalent rights and obligations to a civil partnership in Ireland.

The exception to recognition is where the parties are within the prohibited degrees of relationship under the 2010 Act, s 5(3).

The date of recognition as laid down in s 5(2) should be noted and it is the later of the applicable dates that is the relevant one.

[1.23] Section 5 of the 2010 Act provides as follows:

'**Recognition of registered foreign relationships**

(1) The Minister may, by order, declare that a class of legal relationship entered into by two parties of the same sex is entitled to be recognised as a civil partnership if under the law of the jurisdiction in which the legal relationship was entered into—

(a) the relationship is exclusive in nature,

(b) the relationship is permanent unless the parties dissolve it through the courts,

(c) the relationship has been registered under the law of that jurisdiction, and

(d) the rights and obligations attendant on the relationship are, in the opinion of the Minister, sufficient to indicate that the relationship would be treated comparably to a civil partnership.

(2) An order under subsection (1) entitles and obliges the parties to the legal relationship to be treated as civil partners under the law of the State from the later of—

(a) the day which is 21 days after the date on which the order is made, and

(b) the day on which the relationship was registered under the law of the jurisdiction in which it was entered into.

(3) Notwithstanding subsections (1) and (2), an order made under subsection (1) shall not be construed as entitling parties to a legal relationship otherwise recognised by that order to be treated as civil partners under the law of the State if those parties are within the prohibited degrees of relationship set out in the Third Schedule to the Civil Registration Act 2004 (inserted by section 26).

(4) Where an order is made under subsection (1), a dissolution of a legal relationship under the law of the jurisdiction in which it was entered into, or under the law of any other jurisdiction in respect of which a class of legal relationship has been declared by an order made under that subsection to be entitled to be recognised as a civil partnership, shall be recognised as a dissolution and deemed to be a dissolution under section 110, and any former parties to such a relationship shall not be treated as civil partners under the law of the State from the later of—

(a)　　the day which is 21 days after the date on which the order is made, and

(b)　　the day on which the dissolution became effective under the law of the relevant jurisdiction.

(5) Every order made by the Minister under this section shall be laid before each House of the Oireachtas as soon as may be after it is made and, if a resolution annulling the order is passed by either such House within the next 21 days on which that House has sat after the order is laid before it, the order shall be annulled accordingly but without prejudice to the validity of anything previously done under it.'

Separation/divorce/dissolution of a civil partnership

[1.24] If the testator has been married and subsequently separated, any separation agreement or court order should be perused to ascertain the position concerning the succession rights of the spouse of the testator. In particular, where there is a decree of judicial separation the order should be perused to see if orders have been made under s 14 of the Family Law Act 1995 extinguishing the succession rights of the spouse as an ancillary order to the decree. A similar order may be made under s 15A of the same Act as inserted by s 56(g) of the Family Law (Divorce) Act 1996.[13]

The 2010 Act provides for the dissolution of a civil partnership and contains many of the same provisions that relate to the dissolution of marriage, so if a civil partnership has been dissolved the order dissolving same should be examined as to its provisions and taken into account in the drafting of any subsequent will.

The position concerning the end of a cohabitation relationship, prior to the death on one cohabitant, is dealt with under the section dealing with additional considerations for persons who are cohabiting later in this chapter.

Divorce/dissolution of a civil partnership – effect on existing will

[1.25] While the 1965 Act provides that marriage and entry into a civil partnership will automatically revoke a will, unless the will is made in contemplation of that particular marriage or civil partnership,[14] neither the 1996 Act (divorce) nor the 2010 Act (dissolution of civil partnership) provide that the dissolution of the marriage or civil partnership revokes a will made either in contemplation of the marriage or civil partnership or made during the currency of the marriage or civil partnership.

13.　See **Appendix 8.**

14.　See s 85(1) of the 1965 Act as amended by s 79 the 2010 Act.

Presumably the relevant legislation provides that a will is automatically revoked by marriage or civil partnership because the entry into either state alters the status of the testator.

The dissolution surely has the same effect. It is odd, therefore, that divorce or dissolution of a civil partnership does not automatically revoke a will made prior to the divorce or dissolution.

If acting for a person who is obtaining a divorce or dissolution of a civil partnership, it would be imperative to ensure that instructions are taken and that the testator be advised of the absolute imperative of making a new will.

Foreign divorce

[1.26] If the testator has obtained a foreign divorce, the question of the recognition of the foreign divorce under Irish law should be considered. The question of recognition has paradoxically become more and not less complicated with the passage of time.

A foreign divorce will be recognised under Irish law (whenever granted) if it was granted in the court of the domicile of one of the parties to the marriage.[15]

In *G MCG v DW and Another*,[16] a divorce, obtained in England based on residence, was recognised. The case related to a divorce to which the later rules for recognition under the Domicile and Recognition of Foreign Divorces Act 1986 ('the 1986 Act') did not apply, and McGuinness J was applying common law rules.

However, in a slightly later case of *MEC v JAC*,[17] Kinlen J refused to recognise a divorce based on residence.

[1.27] In *DT v FL*,[18] Morris P was considering the recognition of a divorce obtained in the Netherlands. The divorce was granted after the 1986 Act had come into operation. Recognition was sought on the basis that the applicant was domiciled in the Netherlands or alternatively was resident there. Morris P held that the applicant was not domiciled in the Netherlands, but in fact had retained his Irish domicile of origin. The President considered the decision of McGuinness J but noted that the divorce in question there pre-dated the 1986 Act. The President does appear to quarrel with the decision of McGuinness J and does not appear to have considered the decision of Kinlen J. The President held that for divorces obtained after the 1986 Act, that Act contained the sole criteria for recognition of a foreign divorce and these did not include a divorce based on residence. As a result, the divorce was not entitled to recognition.

The Supreme Court upheld the decision of the High Court. The applicant was not entitled to rely on Brussels II to achieve recognition as the divorce was granted before Brussels II came into force and the Convention did not have retroactive effect. The Supreme Court refused to state a question to the European Court to have the matter adjudicated on.[19]

---

15. See the Domicile and Recognition of Foreign Divorces Act 1986 and the Supreme Court decision in *W v W* [1993] 2 IR 476.

16. *G MCG v DW and Another* [2000] 1 IR 96.

17. *MEC v JAC* [2001] 2 IR 399.

18. *DT v FL* [2009] IR 48.

19. *DT v FL* [2009] I IR 435.

[1.28] In *CK v JK and AG*,[20] the Supreme Court ruled that estoppel can never be raised in relation to a person's marital status. In that case, the couple were married in Ireland, had been ostensibly married for 17 years and had children. Prior to the Irish marriage the husband had been divorced in Ohio. When the Irish marriage broke down, the wife sought a judicial separation and ancillary reliefs. The divorce in Ohio would never have been capable of recognition in Ireland, and that being so, under Irish law, the Irish marriage was void *ab initio*. The 'husband' relied on the invalidity of the Irish marriage in his defence. The case came before the Circuit Court and the trial judge stated a case to the Supreme Court as to whether the husband was estopped in all the circumstances from denying the validity of the Irish marriage. The Supreme Court unanimously decided that an estoppel could not be raised where a question was raised in relation to a person's status. The court referred to the constitutional position of marriage and the family. Essentially, a person was either married or they were not. To permit the raising of an estoppel could give rise to anomalies and injustice. The court considered and refused to overrule the *dicta* of the former Supreme Court in the case of *Gaffney v Gaffney*.[21]

The recognition of divorces has become quite nuanced, and practitioners in such cases should proceed with caution and in appropriate case seek specialist advice.

Brussels II

[1.29] Brussels II provides a further basis for recognition of divorces granted within the European Union (excluding Denmark – Art 2.3) after it came into effect (Art 72 – 1 August 2004). In short, a divorce will be recognised if granted in a court of another 'member state' where either party was habitually resident/domiciled at the time of the granting of the divorce. The Convention also covers separation or nullity. In the case of the former, any order made by a court of competent jurisdiction needs to be examined to see if it deals with matters of inheritance or succession. A practitioner should not rely on what his or her client tells him or her about what any relevant court order might contain. Not to examine the order would amount to negligence in the event of an area from which loss flows. In the case of nullity, the marriage will either have been void *ab initio* or voidable. The advice of a lawyer in the relevant member state may have to be sought on whether the marriage was declared void *ab initio* or voidable under the foreign decree.

The Convention has a broader application than divorce, separation and nullity but these are the only contexts relevant to this textbook. Further, the Convention relates to recognition and enforceability of the decree of divorce, nullity or separation only. It does not apply to ancillary orders relating to property and such like.

In common with the law in most jurisdictions, the jurisdiction is founded on 'habitual residence' though the concept of 'domicile' as understood in Ireland and the United Kingdom is recognised.

---

20.   *CK v JK and AG* [2004] 1 IR 224.
21.   *Gaffney v Gaffney* [1975] IR 133.

Jurisdiction to grant a divorce, separation or decree of nullity

[1.30] The Convention provides as follows in relation to jurisdiction:

Chapter II
Jurisdiction

Section 1
Divorce, legal separation and marriage annulment

Article 3
General jurisdiction

1. In matters relating to divorce, legal separation or marriage annulment, jurisdiction shall lie with the courts of the Member State:

(a)   in whose territory:

— the spouses are habitually resident, or

— the spouses were last habitually resident, insofar as one of them still resides there, or

— the respondent is habitually resident, or

— in the event of a joint application, either of the spouses is habitually resident, or

— the applicant is habitually resident if he or she resided there for at least a year immediately before the application was made, or

— the applicant is habitually resident if he or she resided there for at least six months immediately before the application was made and is either a national of the Member State in question or, in the case of the United Kingdom and Ireland, has his or her 'domicile' there;

(b)   of the nationality of both spouses or, in the case of the United Kingdom and Ireland, of the 'domicile' of both spouses.

2. For the purpose of this Regulation, '**domicile**' shall have the same meaning as it has under the legal systems of the United Kingdom and Ireland.

The basis for jurisdiction is broad but finite. The divorce, separation or nullity must be granted in a court of appropriate jurisdiction.

The principles for recognition and grounds for non-recognition

[1.31] These are set out in Ch 3 of the Convention as follows:

Chapter III
Recognition and Enforcement

Section 1
Recognition

Article 21
Recognition of a judgment

1. A judgment given in a Member State shall be recognised in the other Member States without any special procedure being required.

2. In particular, and without prejudice to paragraph 3, no special procedure shall be required for updating the civil-status records of a Member State on the basis of a judgment relating to divorce, legal separation or marriage annulment given in another Member State, and against which no further appeal lies under the law of that Member State.

3. Without prejudice to Section 4 of this Chapter, any interested party may, in accordance with the procedures provided for in Section 2 of this Chapter, apply for a decision that the judgment be or not be recognised.

The local jurisdiction of the court appearing in the list notified by each Member State to the Commission pursuant to Article 68 shall be determined by the internal law of the Member State in which proceedings for recognition or non-recognition are brought.

4. Where the recognition of a judgment is raised as an incidental question in a court of a Member State, that court may determine that issue.

Article 22
Grounds of non-recognition for judgments relating to divorce, legal separation or marriage annulment

A judgment relating to a divorce, legal separation or marriage annulment shall not be recognised:

(a)   if such recognition is manifestly contrary to the public policy of the Member State in which recognition is sought;

(b)   where it was given in default of appearance, if the respondent was not served with the document which instituted the proceedings or with an equivalent document in sufficient time and in such a way as to enable the respondent to arrange for his or her defence unless it is determined that the respondent has accepted the judgment unequivocally;

(c)   if it is irreconcilable with a judgment given in proceedings between the same parties in the Member State in which recognition is sought; or

(d)   if it is irreconcilable with an earlier judgment given in another Member State or in a non-Member State between the same parties, provided that the earlier judgment fulfils the conditions necessary for its recognition in the Member State in which recognition is sought.

[1.32] For the purpose of the above provisions the relevant definitions are found in Art 2 of the Convention as follows:

Article 2
Definitions

For the purposes of this Regulation:

1.   the term **'court'** shall cover all the authorities in the Member States with jurisdiction in the matters falling within the scope of this Regulation pursuant to Article 1;

2.   the term **'judge'** shall mean the judge or an official having powers equivalent to those of a judge in the matters falling within the scope of the Regulation;

3.   the term **'Member State'** shall mean all Member States with the exception of Denmark;

4.　the term **'judgment'** shall mean a divorce, legal separation or marriage annulment, as well as a judgment relating to parental responsibility, pronounced by a court of a Member State, whatever the judgment may be called, including a decree, order or decision;

5.　the term **'Member State of origin'** shall mean the Member State where the judgment to be enforced was issued;

6.　the term **'Member State of enforcement'** shall mean the Member State where enforcement of the judgment is sought.

[1.33] The Convention's provisions are self-explanatory but if any issue arises in relation to the recognition of a foreign divorce, nullity or separation, whether under the 1986 Act or Brussels II, then the appropriate advice should be sought. However, should the testator be *in extremis* it is better that a will be put in place and later reviewed in the light of any advice concerning the recognition of a foreign divorce, separation or nullity.

Unworthiness to succeed – desertion, divorce a **mensa et thoro**, *murder, manslaughter and certain offences*

[1.34] The spouse/civil partner of a testator may be unworthy to succeed to the estate of a deceased person where he or she is in desertion of the spouse/civil partner for a period of at least two years *continuing* at the date of death.[22]

The Act, however, recognised the concept of constructive desertion so that if the person who is in desertion was justified in leaving, the sanction of unworthiness to succeed will not apply. The difficulty of this is that the deceased person, who has been deserted, will not be able to give evidence. The absence of cogent, independent evidence to corroborate the fact of desertion without justification will greatly hamper the ability to refute an allegation of constructive desertion. In such a case, therefore, it is essential that the practitioner drafting the will obtains and records as much information surrounding the desertion as is possible.

If the spouse/civil partner, however, seeks to assert his or her entitlement to the estate as a legal right or upon intestacy (whole or partial), then the legal personal representative of the deceased spouse/civil partner would have to assert that the spouse/civil partner is unworthy to succeed and have the matter adjudicated by the court. The onus of proving unworthiness to succeed rests on the person asserting it.

If a testator alleges that he or she has been deserted, it is essential that as much information be gathered as is possible to refute any allegation of constructive desertion after death.

[1.35] If a decree of divorce *a mensa et thoro* has been given against a spouse on the basis that that spouse was to blame for the grounds giving rise to the decree, then the spouse to blame will be unworthy to succeed.[23]

[1.36] A decree of divorce *a vinculo matrimonii* dissolves the marriage so the parties to it or to a decree dissolving a civil partnership are no longer spouses or civil partners and rights of succession are lost, except under a will, which, I have noted, will not be

---

22.　Section 120(2) and (2A) of the 1965 Act.
23.　Section 120(2) of the 1965 Act.

revoked by the dissolution. No question of unworthiness to succeed arises in this instance, and the divorce legislation and the 2010 Act provide that in certain circumstances the former spouse or civil partner can apply for provision from the estate. Such rights are usually closed off in the decree of divorce or dissolution but any relevant decree must be examined as to its contents. No assumption should be made as to its contents. Not to review the decree or order could amount to negligence; a practitioner should not rely on what the client may think the order or decree contains.

[1.37] A sane person guilty of murder or manslaughter of the deceased (be they his or her spouse/civil partner or otherwise) shall be unworthy to succeed.[24] The Act does not provide for a 'conviction'. The word 'guilty' might have to be judicially considered in the case where someone is clearly responsible for the death but has not been found guilty in a criminal court, eg, cases where one spouse kills another and then kills him or herself and there will be no criminal trial because the spouse responsible for the death is himself or herself dead. It falls to be interpreted whether the word 'guilty' in the section connotes a criminal conviction beyond a reasonable doubt or responsibility for the death as established on the civil standard of the balance of probabilities.

[1.38] Unworthiness to succeed will prevent a claim to a legal right share or a share on intestacy, either whole or partial. It will also prevent a child from maintaining a claim under s 117 of the 1965 Act. It will not defeat the right to a benefit conferred by will.

[1.39] A testator should review his or her will in the event of desertion or a decree of divorce *a mensa et thoro,* divorce *a vinculo matrimonii* or dissolution of a civil partnership.

[1.40] A testator, who is married to somebody who might be later deemed unworthy to succeed, should be advised to make a will and to keep the will under review at all times in the light of circumstances as they may change.

[1.41] It would be also advisable, in my view, for the testator to swear an affidavit setting out the circumstances in which the grounds for unworthiness to succeed may arise. This affidavit could be left with the will. A precedent is available at **Appendix 8**.

Co-owners

[1.42] In the case of co-owners of property, the murder or manslaughter by one co-owner of the other does not destroy the right of survivorship at law of the guilty co-owner. Neither does it lead to a forfeiture of his or her interest held in the property in his or her own right. In the case of *In Re Cawley,*[25] the defendant had been convicted of the manslaughter of his wife. He had accepted that he was unworthy to succeed to assets held in her sole name. As a married couple, however, they had assets real and personal in their joint names. The executors of the estate brought an application for directions as to his entitlement regarding the joint assets. The defendant, up to the date of the trial, relied on his right of survivorship and claimed that he took all of the joint assets by right of survivorship. The court held that the defendant at law took the jointly held assets by

---

24.   Section 120(1) of the 1965 Act.
25.   *Cawley and others v Lillis* [2011] IEHC 515.

right of survivorship, but that he held 50 per cent of the assets on a constructive trust for the estate of his deceased wife by reason of the fact that he had been convicted of causing her death. Of course the percentage entitlement could be changed if it could be shown that the co-owners contributed unequally to the acquisition of the property. Laffoy J in the *Cawley* case floated the idea of legislative reform to deal with the situation where one co-owner is responsible for the death of the other. Interestingly, the couple in the *Cawley* case owned a property in France jointly and the court there held that Mr Lillis was not entitled to take the property on the death of his wife, because he was criminally responsible for that death. The French property passed to her heir, her only child.

Nullity

[1.43] It would also be prudent to execute a new will where there is a decree of nullity. A marriage or civil partnership may be void *ab initio* or voidable. Arguably, where the marriage is void *ab initio* any previous will would not stand revoked. But to avoid all doubt or question arising in relation to the status of the will it would be prudent to execute a new will after a decree of nullity. In any event, the intention of the testator may have changed.

Extent of the testator's estate

[1.44] A check list should be made of the testator's assets and particular regard should be had to the principal assets of which the testator is owner.

The testator's mind should be specifically directed to what he or she wishes to do with individual assets, unless the testator has indicated that he or she wishes all of his or her estate to go to a particular person. The consequences of any such bequest and the possibility for dispute or contention should be adverted to, as should any tax considerations.

Care should be taken to draw up a list of the assets and a list of the persons who will become entitled to those assets under the will of the testator. The list should be cross-checked item by item with the testator to ensure that no asset is left out of account. While every will should contain a residuary clause, which will capture any assets not specifically disposed of, disputes may arise as to whether the testator intended to leave an asset to a particular party and then failed to do so. The more comprehensive the list, the less chance there will be of a dispute.

A practitioner may be sued in negligence for failing to have regard to the disposition of a particular asset. In the case of *In Re Collins O'Connell and another v Governor of the Bank of Ireland*,[26] a widowed testatrix solemnly told her husband's godson and the godson's wife that she was leaving them her house. The night before she made her will the testatrix confided this intent to a neighbour. The neighbour told her to ensure that the contents of house were also left to them, because she knew of a case where contents were not mentioned and there had been a dispute. When the will emerged after the death of the testatrix only the contents of the house were left of the intended beneficiaries. The will made no mention of the house, which fell in the residue; this in turn was left to a charity. The case before the court sought to have the mistake in the will rectified, which

---

26.   *Re Collins – O'Connell and Another v Governor of the Bank of Ireland* [1998] 2 IR 596.

both the High and Supreme courts declined to do. The solicitor who drafted the will was later successfully sued in negligence.

In this respect it must be borne in mind that the practitioner drafting the will owes a duty of care not only to the testator but also to the potential beneficiaries under the will.[27]

List of pecuniary legacies and legatees – with alternative provisions in the event that the legatee predeceases the deceased, if required

[1.45] Note the provision of s 98 of the 1965 Act in relation to bequests to children or issue of the testator who may predecease the testator, themselves, leaving issue. The effect of this provision, often misinterpreted, should be discussed with the testator and its operation excluded, if that is what the testator wishes. Section 98 provides that if there is a bequest to a child (or issue) of the testator who predeceases the testator leaving children (or issue), then the bequest shall not lapse but take effect as if the child had survived the testator and died immediately after him. This does NOT mean that the children will take their parent's share, but rather that the benefit intended for the child of the testator will form part of his or her estate to be disposed of in accordance with his or her will or intestacy as the case may be. If the testator wants the share of any predeceased child to pass to his or her children (or otherwise) then the will must clearly state this.

List of specific legacies and devises and legatees and devisees – with alternative provisions in the event that the specific legatee or devisee predeceases the deceased, if required[28]

[1.46] Note that in absence of an alternative provision, the specific devise or legacy will fall into the residue if the initial bequest fails.[29]

A **legatee** is a person taking a benefit of personal property.

A **devisee** is a person taking a benefit of real property (including chattels real, ie, leaseholds).

A **specific bequest** is one where a specific item of property is left to the beneficiary; eg, 'a painting from my collection of paintings' is a general legacy, while 'my painting by Jack B Yeats entitled *The Liffey Swim*' is a specific legacy.

Ademption

[1.47] Ademption can arise in a number of guises (see further under the doctrine of satisfaction). In this context, we are concerned with a situation where a will contains a specific bequest, but the subject matter is not part of the estate at the date of death. The distinction between a specific bequest and a general bequest is important because in the event of the testator disposing of an item specifically bequeathed during his or her life, the legacy will be adeemed and the beneficiary will take no substitutional benefit. A will is ambulatory in effect and the testator should not feel inhibited after making a will in disposing of his or her property. If, therefore, a person disposes of a significant

---

27.   See *Wall v Hegarty* [1980] ILRM 124 and *Darby v Shanely and Another* [2007] IEHC 459.

28.   See above concerning s 98.

29.   Section 91 of the 1965 Act.

element of his property, eg, selling his or her house, then the person's will should be immediately checked to see if it requires revision in the light of the disposal. Testators should be advised to review their wills if they make a specific disposal of property. Frequently, I have been asked to advise where a will makes a specific bequest and the subject matter is later sold. In many instances, the same solicitor will have acted in the making of the will and subsequent disposal but the will was not adverted to or revised. There is a potential for a negligence claim at the suit of the disappointed beneficiary.

Abatement

[1.48] Abatement arises where there are insufficient assets to meet the bequests contained in the will. In relation to the doctrine of abatement, specific bequests will be the last to abate, while general legacies will abate first. Abatement arises where there are insufficient assets to discharge all the general bequests contained in a deceased's will.

A list of any demonstrative legacies, if required

[1.49] A demonstrative legacy is a legacy where the amount payable is designated to be paid out of the specific fund, eg, '1,000.00 euro from my account with the Governor and Company of the Bank of Ireland at the branch at Baggot Street, Dublin'.

Ademption

[1.50] The advantage of a demonstrative legacy is that, for the purposes of the doctrine of ademption, it is treated like a general legacy; so if the testator does not have an account with the Governor and Company of the Bank of Ireland at Baggot Street at the date of his or her death, the legacy will still be payable out of the testator's general estate.

Abatement

[1.51] On the other hand, for the operation of the doctrine of abatement, the demonstrative legacy is treated as a specific legacy and therefore will abate only after all of the general legacies have abated.

The residuary estate

[1.52] It is useful to make a check list of what the residuary estate comprises and to discuss this with the testator. This will obviate the difficulty of the testator failing to leave a particular asset to a particular beneficiary if that is what he or she intends.[30] If the testator has a large estate of varying assets, it could be quite easy for the testator, through inadvertence, to fail to leave a particular asset to a particular beneficiary. If the residuary estate is identified for him or her, then he or she can indicate whether he or she is happy that the residue comprises what he or she intends it to comprise.

The residuary clause is a very important clause in any will, because it will catch all assets not disposed of and bequests which lapse or fail.[31]

---

30.   See In *Re Collins – O'Connell and Another v Governor of the Bank of Ireland* [1998] 2 IR 596.
31.   See s 91 of the 1965 Act.

It is also important because, generally speaking, where the executor is unable or unwilling to act, the person entitled to the residue will be entitled to prove the will.

Care should be taken, therefore, to try to leave the residue to a specific person or persons, rather than an entity or organisation. If the residue is being left to a particular person who has a connection with the testator, such as a friend or relative, then no difficulty arises in this regard; but where a testator intends to leave the property, say, to a charitable organisation, it would be best to leave the residue to the treasurer or other officer for the time being at the date of death of the particular charity, so that the treasurer for the time being can then apply for a grant of representation should that need arise.

[1.53] If the residue is instead left to a particular organisation and that organisation is not a trust corporation within the meaning of s 30(4) of the Succession Act 1965, then it may be necessary to bring a court application in order to raise representation to the estate of the testator. In order to avoid this, it is better that a named person or office holder be appointed residuary legatee and devisee on trust for the particular charitable entity, rather than to leave the residue to that entity itself.

> **Example 1**
>
> 'I give, devise and bequeath the rest, residue and remainder of my property to the Treasurer for the time being at the date of my death of the Dublin branch of the Samaritans at 112 Marlborough Street in the City of Dublin, upon trust for the charitable purposes of that organisation.'

The above is the more desirable way of dealing with such a bequest.

[1.54] Example 2

> 'I give, devise and bequeath all the rest, residue and remainder of my property to the Dublin branch of the Samaritans at 112 Marlborough Street in the City of Dublin.'

A bequest in this form would require a court application where there is no executor available to prove the will and it is necessary to appoint some person to administer the estate.

[1.55] Generally speaking, testators are inclined to leave the residue of their property as a complete entity, but it is possible for a testator to leave his or her residuary personal property to one person or organisation and leave his or her residuary real property to another person or organisation. In this case, the beneficiary of the personal estate will be the residuary *legatee* and the beneficiary of the real estate will be the residuary *devisee*. In this particular instance, it would be even more important for a check list of what the residue comprises to be compiled so that if any dispute arises about what the testator intended, there would be evidence of that intention.

Appointment of executors

[1.56] The testator should, in his or her will, appoint executors. While there is no difficulty about one executor being appointed, the appointment of more than one executor is often advisable. Firstly, it ensures that if a particular executor is unable to act or has predeceased the deceased, there is another executor able to act in his or her stead. Also, if a particular executor has become untraceable, it will be possible for the remaining executor to extract a grant, while reserving the rights of the missing or untraceable executor.

Secondly, where the will creates a settlement and the testator leaves real property then a trust of land as defined by Pt 4 of the 2009 Act arises and trustees of the trust should be appointed. Regard should be had to the provisions of the Act, which are set out in full in **Appendix 12, Pt 1**.[32]

Consideration should be given to appointing two or more executors, with a possible maximum of four. The executors should be persons who are likely to outlive the testator. It is also wise to appoint persons who might have an interest in the estate of the deceased so that they have an interest in the expeditious administration of the estate. Where, however, a settlement is created by a will or where there is a discretionary trust, it is perhaps advisable that the executors be independent persons without an interest in the settlement or trust so that they can exercise an independent judgment in respect of the administration of the trust, rather than having a conflict of interest.

It might also be prudent in the case of executors who are of a similar age to the deceased to appoint substitutional executors in the event that the executors appointed in the will predecease the deceased.

Revocation of earlier wills and other testamentary dispositions

[1.57] The testator should be asked whether he or she has made a previous will or any other testamentary document. The revocation clause in the will should take care to revoke not only all previous wills but also other testamentary documents. If, however, there is a previous will that the testator wishes to keep alive, eg, a will dealing with property abroad, care should be taken to ensure that the revocation clause is not so general as to have the unintentional effect of revoking this will.

Tax considerations

[1.58] Detailed tax considerations are outside the scope of this work, but the testator should be advised in relation to the tax implications of the dispositions contained in his or her will.

It would be useful for the practitioner to ask the testator whether he or she has made any gifts *inter vivos* to any beneficiary in the proposed will during his or her lifetime. Testators may not be aware that all gifts received by persons from whatever source after 5 December 1991 must be aggregated in order to ascertain a beneficiary's capital acquisitions tax liability.

If there have been substantial gifts made by the testator *inter vivos* to beneficiaries, or a benefit received from some other source, this may have a bearing on the tax that a beneficiary may have to pay and therefore may have a bearing on the tax planning aspect of the will.

---

32. See also **Ch 5**.

Additional consideration for unmarried persons, not in a civil partnership or cohabiting

Non-marital children

[1.59] Up until 14 June 1988 (the operative date of the relevant sections of the Status of Children Act 1987 ('the 1987 Act')), unmarried persons enjoyed complete testamentary freedom. Where, however, an unmarried person has non-marital children, if he or she dies intestate, his or her non-marital children will be entitled to the entire of his or her estate, and if he or she dies testate failing to make provision or make adequate provision for them, the non-marital children will have the right to bring an application pursuant to s 117 of the 1965 Act, which provides that where a parent fails in his or her moral duty to make proper provision for a child in accordance with his or her means, then the court shall make such provision for the child as to the court may seem just.

If the unmarried testator has children, consideration should be given as to what provision has been made for the non-marital child during the course of the testator's life and what provision might be made in the will.

It should be noted, however, that if the non-marital child has been legally adopted, then the Status of Children Act 1987 specifically provides that the child from the date of the adoption order becomes the child of the adoptive parents and no other person. In those circumstances, therefore, the adopted child could not bring a claim under s 117 of the 1965 Act against the unmarried testator's estate.

In reality, where the unmarried testator is the father of the child, the chances are that he may not have provided for the child properly in accordance with his means and therefore the child could have quite a strong claim under s 117 of the 1965 Act. Where the unmarried testator is the mother, the chances are that the mother will have looked after and reared the child during the course of the child's life, so therefore while the child would have some claim on the mother's estate, it might be less strong, particularly where the mother has provided well for the child and established the child in life.

It should be noted that where there has been an affiliation order made in respect of the child, that will be conclusive evidence vis-à-vis the child's paternity. If there is any doubt concerning paternity and the testator believes that he is not the parent of a person who might claim to be his child, then there may have to be a hearing concerning paternity prior to the initiation of any s 117 proceedings. In those circumstances, it would be worth the testator's while giving as much evidence as possible to show that the person who might claim to be his child is not his child, and directions might be given for the retaining of a blood or tissue sample after the death of the deceased for the purposes of DNA testing.

While many unmarried persons will benefit their next-of-kin, an unmarried testator will sometimes wish to leave property to persons who are strangers in blood or perhaps to a charity or other organisation, thereby disinheriting persons who might be expecting to benefit from the unmarried testator's estate. The potential for a dispute or challenge from persons disappointed is much greater.

[1.60] In one such case, where a bachelor testator made a very significant change in his will thereby disinheriting a previous beneficiary, I asked the solicitor who drafted both wills the reason for the change. He told me that he did not consider that any of his business. However, I would argue that in order to protect the person who might benefit in such circumstances it is of enormous assistance for the attendance to record the reason for any such change.

In such circumstances, detailed instructions should be taken concerning the testator's intentions and the reasons why he or she is adopting the course that he or she is taking. Disappointed relatives may often try to challenge a will. If detailed instructions are taken as to why the testator adopted the course he or she did, this may assist in preventing or addressing such a challenge.

An unmarried person, who has not entered a civil partnership, who has not children and who has not cohabited, has complete testamentary freedom.

Tax considerations

[1.61] These may be more important than in the case of a married person as tax thresholds of beneficiaries will be lower.

Additional considerations for persons who are married or in a civil partnership

[1.62] The testamentary freedom of a married testator or of a person who has entered into a civil partnership is curtailed by the provisions of Pt IX of the 1965 Act[33] and will be restricted to a greater extent where the testator is married or has entered a civil partnership and additionally has children.

In many situations where the testator and his or her spouse/civil partner are happily married or partnered, the likelihood is that the testator will be leaving the entire of his or her estate to his or her surviving spouse/civil partner, with perhaps alternative provisions over if the spouse/civil partner does not survive for a specified period or dies simultaneously with the testator.

Where the testator's spouse is the parent of any children of their union then a universal bequest to the spouse cannot be upset by any of the children bringing an application under s 117 of the 1965 Act.

Different considerations apply in the case of civil partners, which will be dealt with later in this section.

[1.63] If the testator does not wish to leave the bulk of his or her estate to his or her spouse or civil partner, or wishes to leave something less than the spouse or civil partner would be entitled to under Pt IX of the 1965 Act, then regard must be had to the provisions of Pt IX and the testator advised accordingly.[34] Concisely, at minimum the spouse or civil partner will be entitled to half the estate if there are no children and one-third if the testator has children.

In this regard, it should be noted that as civil partners will always be of the same sex only one of the partners can be the biological parent of any child being reared by the civil partners. This being so, one party to the partnership will have greater testamentary freedom than the other.

---

33. As amended by the 2010 Act.
34. See **Appendix 6**.

[1.64] Practitioners' tendency with couples is to advise them in relation to their wills together. But practitioners should be aware of potential conflicts of interest that might more likely arise in the case of civil partners, where there are children involved, or in the case of married persons who perhaps have re-married and one spouse is not the biological parent of some or all the children involved. In such a case, it might be better to have the spouses or civil partners independently advised, though with the consent of the persons involved the practitioners might liaise, without compromising their independence.

[1.65] Where the testator dies leaving a spouse or civil partner and no children, the spouse or civil partner will be entitled to a legal right share of one-half of the estate.[35]

[1.66] Where the testator dies leaving a spouse or civil partner and children, the spouse or civil partner will be entitled to a one-third share of the estate.[36]

[1.67] If the testator makes no provision at all for his or her spouse or civil partner, then the spouse or civil partner will be automatically entitled to the legal right share. The legal right share will vest in the surviving spouse on death.[37] The deceased spouse or civil partner will not be required to do anything to claim his or her entitlement. It should be noted that the *O'Dwyer* case involved spouses, but as the amendments inserted by the 2010 Act yield identical provisions concerning civil partners, the same interpretation of the 1965 Act's provisions (as amended) would apply.

If, on the other hand, the testator confers some benefit on his or her spouse or civil partner, the spouse or civil partner will be required to elect between the benefit granted in the will and the legal right share. In this regard, it has been held that the right of election[38] is personal to the spouse or civil partner. If it is not exercised prior to the death of the spouse, it will not be exercisable by his or her personal representatives on his or her behalf.[39] If acting for a spouse or civil partner where an election arises, it would be important that an election be made as soon as possible, especially if he or she is elderly or ill. While the Act provides for the mandatory notification of the spouse or civil partner of the right of election,[40] the right of election can be exercised prior to notification. Failure to make an election in appropriate case could amount to negligence.

[1.68] In the case of a spouse or civil partner who is of unsound mind, the court can elect on his or her behalf or in the case of a ward of court the court may elect.[41] In my experience, the court generally approaches an election in purely economic terms making an election that will most benefit the spouse or civil partner. A spouse or civil partner capable of making an election might bring other considerations to bear.

---

35.   Sections 111(1) and 111A(1) of the 1965 Act.
36.   Sections 111(2) and 111A(2) of the 1965 Act.
37.   *O'Dwyer and Another v Keegan and Others* [1997] 2 IR 585.
38.   Conferred by s 115 of the 1965 Act as amended by the 2010 Act.
39.   *In Re Urquhart* [1974] IR 197; *Reilly v McEntee* [1984] ILRM 572.
40.   Section 115(4) of the 1965 Act, as amended.
41.   Section 115(5) of the 1965 Act, as amended.

[1.69] A spouse or civil partner, who is an executor or personal representative, may require to be independently legally and indeed financially advised in relation to his or her election.

[1.70] In addition to the legal right share, the spouse or civil partner of the testator will have a right of appropriation in respect of the dwelling house in which the surviving spouse or civil partner is ordinarily resident at the date of death of the testator by virtue of s 56 of the 1965 Act as amended by the 2010 Act. This right of appropriation can be exercised in respect of any benefit accruing to a spouse or civil partner, that is to say, a benefit under a will, a legal right share or a right accruing on intestacy.

[1.71] In addition, the spouse or civil partner may appropriate the household goods and chattels with the dwelling and may appropriate the share of any person who is a minor with an interest in the estate of the testator.

[1.72] While there is no authority directly in point it is likely that the right of appropriation would also be regarded as a personal right, which could not be exercised posthumously. Once again, in an appropriate case, it would be important to act with alacrity.

[1.73] The testator should be advised that after his or her death, his or her legal personal representatives will be required by the 1965 Act to give notice to the surviving spouse or civil partner of the entitlement to elect as between any benefit given by the will and the legal right share and further in relation to exercising the right of appropriation. It would appear, however, that where no benefit is conferred on the spouse or civil partner there is no obligation on the executors to give notification of the entitlement to the legal right share. It is up to the spouse or civil partner to assert that right. Of course, as the right vests automatically in the spouse or civil partner, the legal personal representatives cannot administer the estate without having regard to that right. If there is a question mark over the spouse's or civil partner's worthiness to succeed to that right, then, unless the spouse or civil partner accepts that they are unworthy to succeed, the legal personal representatives would have to take steps to have the spouse or civil partner deemed unworthy to succeed in an appropriate case.

[1.74] The divorce legislation also provides for a claim being brought by a former spouse of the deceased against his or her estate.[42] A similar provision arises where there is dissolution of a civil partnership.[43] As part of the court order dissolving the marriage or civil partnership, this right can be blocked. In the context of drafting a will, where such decree exists the practitioner drafting the will should ask to see the actual court order and not rely on what the testator may believe to be the situation: failure to examine the decree of divorce or dissolution could amount to negligence.

[1.75] If the married testator has a spouse and children, and he or she leaves the entire of his or her estate to his or her spouse, who is also the parent of his or her children, the children will have no right to bring a claim under s 117 of the 1965 Act.[44]

---

42. See the Family Law (Divorce) Act 1996 and **Appendix 6**.
43. See s 127 of the 2010 Act.
44. See s 117(3).

[1.76] If, on the other hand, the estate is left to the spouse and he or she is not the parent of the children, then the children would have a right to bring an application pursuant to s 117 of the 1965 Act.

[1.77] As noted, civil partners will always be of the same sex. Therefore, only one of the civil partners can be the biological parent of any child of the partnership. There is no provision in the 2010 Act for the adoption of the child of one civil partner by the other, and this has been a subject of some discontent amongst same sex civil partners. If the civil partner who dies is not the biological parent of the child, then the child has no entitlement to the estate of the deceased civil partner. If the civil partner who dies is the biological parent and has not or has not properly provided for his or her child in accordance with his or her (the parent's) means then the child will have a right to apply for provision under s 117 of the 1965 Act in the ordinary way. The legal right share of the civil partner cannot be interfered with on such application.

[1.78] If the deceased spouse had marital and non-marital children, while the marital children might be excluded from bringing a claim under s 117 by virtue of s 117(3), the non-marital children may be entitled to bring such a claim, if the surviving spouse is not the parent of the non-marital child.

[1.79] Under s 117 of the 1965 Act, a child of a testator is not entitled to any specific share in the estate of the deceased. The child must establish that the parent has failed in his or her moral duty to make proper provision for the child in accordance with the parent's means. The onus of proving the failure rests on the claiming child. The Supreme Court has decided that a positive failure in the moral duty must be proved.[45] If a court is satisfied that there has been a failure, then the court may make such provision for the child as to the court might seem just. The court, therefore, has an absolute discretion to make provision for the child as it thinks proper.

[1.80] Because the decision in a s 117 claim rests with the individual judge, it can be very difficult to advise a testator, at the time of making his or her will, who may wish to exclude a child or limit provision for him or her. Judges vary in finding whether there has been a failure on the part of the parent. Further variations arise where there is such failure as to what provision might be made.

[1.81] In *Re ABC decd, XC & Ors v RT & Ors*,[46] Kearns J (as he then was) took the opportunity to distil the principles that had been established up to 2003. This compendium of principles may be of assistance in advising a testator as he or she is making his or her will. The principles as summarised by Kearns J are as follows:

> Counsel on both sides were agreed that the following relevant legal principles can, as a result of these authorities be said to derive under s 117:
>
> (a)   The social policy underlying s 117 is primarily directed to the protection of those children who are still of an age and situation in life where they might reasonably expect support from their parents, against the failure of persons who are unmindful of their duties in that area.

---

45.   *In re IAC* [1990] 2 IR 193.
46.   *Re ABC decd, XC & Ors v RT & Ors* [2003] IR 250 at 262.

(b)   What has to be determined is whether the testator, at the time of his death, owes any moral obligation to the children and if so, whether he has failed in the obligation.

(c)   There is a high onus of proof placed on an applicant for relief under s 117, which requires the establishment of a positive failure in the moral duty.

(d)   Before a court can interfere, there must be clear circumstances and a positive failure in moral duty must be established.

(e)   The duty by s 117 is not absolute.

(f)   The relationship of parent and child, does not, itself and without regard to other circumstances, create a moral duty to leave anything by will to the child.

(g)   Section 117 does not create an obligation to leave something to each child.

(h)   The provision of an expensive education for a child may discharge the moral duty as may other gifts or settlements made during the lifetime of the testator.

(i)   Financing a good education so as to give a child the best start in life possible and providing money, which, if properly managed, should afford a degree of financial security for the rest of one's life, does amount to making 'proper provision.'

(j)   The duty under s 117 is not to make adequate provision but to provide proper provision in accordance with the testator's means.

(k)   A just parent must take into account not just his moral obligations to his children and to his wife, but all his moral obligations, eg to aged and infirm parents.

(l)   In dealing with s 117 applications, the position of any applicant child is not to be taken in isolation. The court's duty is to consider the entirety of the testator's affairs and to decide upon the application in the overall context. In other words, while the moral claim of a child may require a testator to make a particular provision for him, the moral claims of others may require such provision to be reduced or omitted altogether.

(m)   Special circumstances giving rise to a moral duty may arise if a child is induced to believe that by, for example, working on a farm, he will ultimately become the owner of it, thereby causing him to shape his upbringing, training and life accordingly.

(n)   Another example of special circumstances might be a child who had a long illness or exceptional talent which it would be morally wrong not to foster.

(o)   Special needs would also include physical and mental disability.

(p)   Although the court has very wide powers both as to when to make provision for an applicant child and as to the nature of such provision, such powers must not be construed as giving the court a power to make a new will for the testator.

(q)   The test to be applied is not which of the alternative courses open to the testator the court itself would have adopted if confronted with the same situation but, rather, whether the decision of the testator to opt for the course he did, of itself and without more, constituted a breach of moral duty to the plaintiff.

(r)   The court must not disregard the fact that parents must be presumed to know their children better than anyone else.

[1.82] When advising a testator who is not benefiting or is limiting a benefit to a child or children, regard should be had to the above principles and a statement or affidavit drawn up with the will whereby the parent sets out his or her reasons for not benefiting or limiting the benefit to a child. If a s 117 application is intimated after death, the affidavit could be proffered to answer the threat. In my experience, a failure to make any provision at all for a child can be foolhardy, unless the child is manifestly not in need of provision.

[1.83] The view of the testator will not be conclusive of the question as the court is required by s 117 to consider all of the circumstances from the point of view of a prudent and just parent. After such analysis, the court, therefore, may not necessarily agree with the view of the testator. However, as noted by Kearns J and the Supreme Court, parents must be presumed to know their children best.

The testator's view expressed in affidavit form may assist a court in reaching its conclusion.

[1.84] In the context of s 117,[47] a claiming child need not be a child who is dependent upon the testator. Provision has been made by the courts for children who have long since become independent of the testator but where, nevertheless, the testator, in the view of the court, failed in his or her moral duty to make proper provision for the child in accordance with his or her means. Some need on the part of the claiming child must, nevertheless, be established.[48]

[1.85] In relation to a married testator, regard should be had to any separation agreement, decree of divorce *a mensa et thoro* or decree of divorce *a vinculo matrimonii* (whether Irish or foreign) to ascertain how this may impact upon the rights of any former or existing spouse of the testator. Regard should also be had as to whether the foreign divorce would be recognisable by an Irish court or whether the person to whom the testator was married would still be regarded as a spouse under Irish law and therefore entitled to his or her rights under Pt IX of the Succession Act 1965.

Tax considerations

[1.86] These may be less important as since 1985 there is no capital acquisitions tax between spouses. The fall in property values and corresponding reduction in tax thresholds for children should also be borne in mind.

Additional considerations for testators who are civil partners

[1.87] While for the most part similar considerations arise in relation to spouses and civil partners, the failure of the 2010 Act to recognise the possibility of children being brought up in a civil partnership potentially gives rise to problems. I foresee much litigation and judges calling for reform of the legislation before the position is clarified. In a number of respects, a surviving civil partner is vulnerable where the deceased civil partner is survived by children of whom the deceased civil partner is the biological

---

47. For a full analysis and commentary on s 117 see Spierin, *The Succession Act 1965 and Related Legislation, a Commentary* (4th edn, Bloomsbury Professional, 2011).

48. *EB v SS and Another* [1998] 4 IR 527.

parent. The legislation had, of course, to provide for the rights of the children but the legislation appears to lack balance. I am of the view that this is because the legislation adopted not even a half-baked approach to addressing the difficulties that could potentially arise.

For this reason, I highlight below additional considerations that should be borne in mind when drafting the will of a civil partner who has children of whom he or she is a biological parent.

Children of a civil partner who dies intestate

[1.88] It is important to realise another important distinction between a spouse and children of a deceased person on the one hand and the civil partner and children of a deceased person on the other in the case of intestacy.

[1.89] In the case of the former, where there is spouse and children and the deceased dies intestate then the rights are fixed in law and cannot be interfered with, the spouse takes two-thirds of the estate and the children take one-third between them. The children cannot apply to court for any greater provision, even if the surviving spouse is not their parent and therefore owes no moral duty to them.

[1.90] In the case of a civil partner and children, however, the child or children in the case of intestacy can apply to have the share of the civil partner reduced so that additional provision is made for them.[49] The Act provides that the child cannot receive any greater benefit than he or she would have received had the deceased died without spouse or civil partner. It is likely that a deceased civil partner may not have many children, and many only have one or two. In the case of an only child, the additional provision could amount to the entire estate.[50]

[1.91] As the 2010 Act is still in its infancy there is no jurisprudence yet on how a court may approach such an application. It is likely, however, that the criteria applied to s 117 claims as summarised by Kearns J and set out above would be considered relevant or at least provide a starting point. Much will depend on how the deceased civil partner had provided for his or her child during his or her (the parent's life) and of course the needs of the child.

[1.92] It has been previously pointed out that the inability to alter the rights of spouse and children on intestacy could work an injustice. Arguably, this is compounded by the 2010 Act. The 2010 Act now gives rise to an anomaly where children of a deceased parent who was in a civil partnership can have intestacy entitlements altered, whereas children whose parent is married (and maybe not to the child's parent) cannot. Depending on your point of view, this may discriminate against surviving civil partners on the one hand and/or children whose deceased parent is married on the other. This may have ramifications for the constitutionality of the provisions in the 2010 Act unless the 1965 Act were amended so as to provide a similar right to children of married persons. Such amendment could contain a provision that would maintain the position where the surviving spouse was the parent of the children on the basis that that parent in

---

49.   See s 67A (3) of the 1965 Act as inserted by the 2010 Act.

50.   Section 67A(4)(b) of the 1965 Act as inserted by the 2010 Act.

his or her turn will have a moral duty to provide for his or her children in due course. A step-parent, however, has no such moral duty.

Children of a civil partner under s 117

[1.93] While s 117(3) provides in the case of a spouse who is the parent of a child that the child cannot interfere with the legal right share of the spouse or any benefit passing to him or her under a will of the deceased parent, a similar protection is not afforded to civil partners.

As noted, only one party to the civil partnership will be the biological parent of a child being brought up by the civil partners. Section 117 does not extend to persons to whom a testator may have stood *in loco parentis*.

The legal right share of the surviving civil partner or benefits under a will are not fully protected from a s 117 claim. Instead, under s 117(3A) the court will have regard to the testator's 'financial circumstances', the 'obligations' of the deceased civil partner to the surviving civil partner. Having had regard to those criteria (and all the other criteria applicable to a s 117 case) the court will then consider whether it is just to make an order under s 117 in favour of a claiming child. The fluidity of s 117 had always made it difficult to advise a testator who is a parent but s 117(3A) increases the difficulty exponentially.

'Financial circumstances' could be broader or narrower than 'the testator's means'; that awaits judicial interpretations.

The 'obligations' of the deceased civil partner to the surviving civil partner will also have to be judicially interpreted and presumably will vary from case to case.

Then there are the criteria for deciding whether it is just in all the circumstances to make an order under s 117.

I hesitate to say it, but it is something of a mess.

Where a person in a civil partnership who has children of whom he or she is the biological parent comes to make a will, he or she must be made aware of s 117(3A) and try to arrange his or her affairs to avoid a potential action under s 117.

It would be imperative that the person taking instructions for the will take very full instructions in cases such as this where there may be potential for an action under s 117 and the applicability of s 117(3A) may arise.

Additional considerations for testators who are cohabiting with another person

[1.94] The 2010 Act, in introducing the changes concerning civil partners relating to matters of succession and wills, largely harmonises the provisions relating to civil partners to those which previously related to spouses only. They will, therefore, be more easily borne in mind and to a large extent the same rights that repose in a spouse will fall to be considered in relation to a civil partner.

There are some exceptions to these general statements and these have been referred to in the preceding section.

The changes wrought by the 2010 Act in relation to cohabitants largely stand alone and are contained in Pt 15 of the 2010 Act.

It will usually be obvious that a testator is married or in a civil partnership; cohabitation may be more concealed or, as it is said, 'under the radar'.

Prior to the 2010 Act persons who were cohabiting had no rights in relation to the estate of a deceased cohabitant.

Part 15 of the 2010 Act confers certain limited rights on cohabitants on the termination of the relationship and one of the occasions of termination is the death of one cohabitant. It is only the context of the death of a cohabitant that is of relevance to this text.

[1.95] A cohabitant is defined by s 172 as follows:

'Cohabitant and qualified cohabitant

(1) For the purposes of this Part, a cohabitant is one of 2 adults (whether of the same or the opposite sex) who live together as a couple in an intimate and committed relationship and who are not related to each other within the prohibited degrees of relationship or married to each other or civil partners of each other.

(2) In determining whether or not 2 adults are cohabitants, the court shall take into account all the circumstances of the relationship and in particular shall have regard to the following:

(a)   the duration of the relationship;

(b)   the basis on which the couple live together;

(c)   the degree of financial dependence of either adult on the other and any agreements in respect of their finances;

(d)   the degree and nature of any financial arrangements between the adults including any joint purchase of an estate or interest in land or joint acquisition of personal property;

(e)   whether there are one or more dependent children;

(f)   whether one of the adults cares for and supports the children of the other; and

(g)   the degree to which the adults present themselves to others as a couple.

(3) For the avoidance of doubt a relationship does not cease to be an intimate relationship for the purpose of this section merely because it is no longer sexual in nature.

(4) For the purposes of this section, 2 adults are within a prohibited degree of relationship if—

(a)   they would be prohibited from marrying each other in the State, or

(b)   they are in a relationship referred to in the Third Schedule to the Civil Registration Act 2004 inserted by section 26 of this Act.

(5) For the purposes of this Part, a qualified cohabitant means an adult who was in a relationship of cohabitation with another adult and who, immediately before the time that that relationship ended, whether through death or otherwise, was living with the other adult as a couple for a period—

(a)   of 2 years or more, in the case where they are the parents of one or more dependent children, and

(b)   of 5 years or more, in any other case.

(6) Notwithstanding subsection (5), an adult who would otherwise be a qualified cohabitant is not a qualified cohabitant if—

(a)   one or both of the adults is or was, at any time during the relationship concerned, an adult who was married to someone else, and

(b)   at the time the relationship concerned ends, each adult who is or was married has not lived apart from his or her spouse for a period or periods of at least 4 years during the previous 5 years.'

[1.96] If taking instructions for a testator, who the practitioner knows is unmarried, widowed or not in a civil partnership, the testator should be asked if they might be cohabiting. If the check list is in printed form, the question on the possibility of cohabitation should be included. An assumption that the person is not cohabiting should not be made.

While, thus far, married persons are always of the opposite sex and civil partners are of the same sex, persons cohabiting may be of the opposite sex or of the same sex.

It should be note that in order to be cohabiting, the relationship must at some stage have been '*intimate and committed*'. The persons cannot be within the prohibited degrees of relationship. At s 172 the Act lays down the matters to which the court can have regard in deciding if the persons are cohabiting.

[1.97] The Act at s 194 permits a 'qualified cohabitant' to apply to court for provision, in the context of drawing a will, from the deceased cohabitant's estate. Section 194 provides as follows:

'**Application for provision from estate of deceased cohabitant**

(1) A qualified cohabitant may, after the death of his or her cohabitant but not more than 6 months after representation is first granted under the Succession Act 1965 in respect of that cohabitant's estate, apply for an order under this section for provision out of the net estate.

(2) Notwithstanding subsection (1), a qualified cohabitant shall not apply for an order under this section where the relationship concerned ended 2 years or more before the death of the deceased, unless the applicant—

(a)   was in receipt of periodical payments from the deceased, whether under an order made under section 175 or pursuant to a cohabitants' agreement or otherwise,

(b)   had, not later than 2 years after that relationship ended, made an application for an order under section 174, 175 or 187 and either—

    (i)   the proceedings were pending at the time of the death, or

    (ii)   any such order made by the court had not yet been executed,

    or

(c)   had, not later than 2 years after the relationship ended, made an application for an order under section 174, 175 or 187, the order was made, an application under section 173(6) was subsequently made in respect of that order and either—

    (i)   the proceedings in respect of that application were pending at the time of the death, or

(ii)   any such order made by the court under section 173(6) in favour of the qualified cohabitant who is the applicant under this section had not yet been executed.

(3) The court may by order make the provision for the applicant that the court considers appropriate having regard to the rights of any other person having an interest in the matter, if the court is satisfied that proper provision in the circumstances was not made for the applicant during the lifetime of the deceased for any reason other than conduct by the applicant that, in the opinion of the court, it would in all the circumstances be unjust to disregard.

(4) In considering whether to make an order under this section, the court shall have regard to all the circumstances of the case, including—

(a)   an order made under section 173(6), 174, 175 or 187 in favour of the applicant,

(b)   a devise or bequest made by the deceased in favour of the applicant,

(c)   the interests of the beneficiaries of the estate, and

(d)   the factors set out in section 173(3).

(5) The court shall not make an order under this section where the relationship concerned ended before the death of the deceased and—

(a)   the court is not satisfied that the applicant is financially dependent on the deceased within the meaning of section 173(2), or

(b)   the applicant has married or registered in a civil partnership, or in a legal relationship of a class that is the subject of an order under section 5.

(6) The applicant shall give notice of an application under this section to the personal representative of the deceased, any spouse or civil partner of the deceased and to any other persons that the court may direct and, in deciding whether to make the order and in determining the provisions of the order, the court shall have regard to any representations made by any of those persons.

(7) The total value for the applicant of the provision made by an order referred to in subsection (4)(a) on the date on which that order was made and an order made under this section shall not exceed any share of the applicant in the estate of the deceased qualified cohabitant to which the applicant would have been entitled if the qualified cohabitants had been spouses or civil partners of each other.

(8) If the qualified cohabitant does not notify the personal representative as required by subsection (6), the personal representative may distribute the assets of the deceased qualified cohabitant or any part of them amongst the persons entitled to them and is not liable to the qualified cohabitant for that distribution.

(9) Nothing in this section prejudices the rights of the qualified cohabitant to follow assets into the hands of a person who has received them.

(10) An order under this section shall not affect the legal right of a surviving spouse.

(11) For the purposes of this section, "net estate", with respect to the estate of a person, means the estate that remains after provision for the satisfaction of—

(a)   other liabilities of the estate having priority over the rights referred to in paragraphs (b) and (c),

(b)   any rights, under the Succession Act 1965, of any surviving spouse of the person, and

(c)   any rights, under the Succession Act 1965, of any surviving civil partner of the person.'

The section maintains the six-month time limit for bringing an application from the date upon which representation is first raised to the estate of the relevant deceased person.

[1.98] It should be noted, however, that under s 195 'save in exceptional circumstances' an application cannot be maintained two years after the end of the relationship by the death of the deceased cohabitant. This is an additional cut-off point to the six-month period. It remains to be seen how the court will interpret 'exceptional circumstances', eg, if the persons entitled to raise representation could be shown to have deliberately waited for two years to extract the grant in an effort to bar the claim of the cohabitant. Each case will be judged on its own facts as to whether 'exceptional circumstances' arise.

This additional outer limit is not applied to claims by spouses, civil partners or children.

There is no onus under the section for the personal representative to notify the cohabitant of the right to bring the application. The cohabitant must be proactive.

Further, an application will not lie, subject to certain exceptions set out in the section, where the relationship has ended two years or more prior to the death of the deceased former cohabitant.

[1.99] The rights of the cohabitant to seek provision is from the net estate and the rights to a large extent rank behind other rights, eg, the rights of a spouse or civil partner under the Act of 1965. It should be noted that under s 194(11) these rights are not restricted to the 'legal right share' under the Act of 1965 (as amended). If, therefore, the deceased cohabitant dies intestate, childless, there is a subsisting marriage or civil partnership and the spouse or civil partner is not unworthy to succeed, the spouse or civil partner would be entitled to the entire estate.

In certain circumstances it may be better for a cohabitant not to make a will if he or she wishes to exclude a surviving cohabitant and instead wishes to benefit to the maximum a spouse or civil partner.

It is curious, however, that s 194(10) only makes reference to the legal right share of the spouse, it makes no reference to the legal right share of a civil partner, which under the Act of 1965 appears to have equal status. One wonders if that is a drafting error in s 194(10). It must, however, stand as enacted until amended.

Section 194(11) defines the net estate, from which provision for the cohabitant is to be made, if at all, as the estate after, *inter alia*, rights of a surviving spouse or civil partner are provided for. As noted on intestacy where there are no children of the deceased, this could be the entire estate.

[1.100] Section 173(3) sets out the matters the court may take into account in considering whether to make an order in favour of the applicant under s 194. These are directly relevant to a person drafting a will for a person who is cohabiting. They should be borne in mind and considered. They are as follows:

'**Application for redress in respect of economically dependent qualified cohabitant**

...

(3) In determining whether or not it is just and equitable to make an order in all the circumstances, the court shall have regard to—

(a) the financial circumstances, needs and obligations of each qualified cohabitant existing as at the date of the application or which are likely to arise in the future,

(b) subject to subsection (5), the rights and entitlements of any spouse or former spouse,

(c) the rights and entitlements of any civil partner or former civil partner,

(d) the rights and entitlements of any dependent child or of any child of a previous relationship of either cohabitant,

(e) the duration of the parties' relationship, the basis on which the parties entered into the relationship and the degree of commitment of the parties to one another,

(f) the contributions that each of the cohabitants made or is likely to make in the foreseeable future to the welfare of the cohabitants or either of them including any contribution made by each of them to the income, earning capacity or property and financial resources of the other,

(g) any contributions made by either of them in looking after the home,

(h) the effect on the earning capacity of each of the cohabitants of the responsibilities assumed by each of them during the period they lived together as a couple and the degree to which the future earning capacity of a qualified cohabitant is impaired by reason of that qualified cohabitant having relinquished or foregone the opportunity of remunerative activity in order to look after the home,

(i) any physical or mental disability of the qualified cohabitant, and

(j) the conduct of each of the cohabitants, if the conduct is such that, in the opinion of the court, it would be unjust to disregard it.'

Cohabitation agreements

[1.101] Also relevant to the consideration of the person drafting a will for a person who is or has been cohabiting is the existence of any cohabitation agreement. Under s 202 of the 2010 Act cohabitants may enter into an agreement to provide for 'financial matters ... when the relationship ends ... through death ...' It would be important to enquire as to the existence of such an agreement. Obtain a copy and scrutinise it in the context of drawing the will or codicil.

[1.102] For the agreement to be valid:

• The agreement must have been made on the basis of independent legal advice; or

• If the parties to the agreement were advised together they must waive *in writing* their entitlement to have such advice.

- The agreement, *itself*, must be in writing and signed by both parties; and

- The general law of contract must be complied with.

Under s 194(3), the agreement can provide that *'neither'* cohabitant apply for relief under s 194. It does not seem to allow for a situation where one person could apply for relief and the other could not. It appears that there must be a mutual agreement not to apply for relief under s 194 in relation to either estate.

The court has power to vary or set aside a cohabitants' agreement in 'exceptional *circumstances*, where its enforceability would cause a *serious* injustice' (author's emphasis).

Additional considerations for testators who have property outside of Ireland

[1.103] While many countries are signatories to the Hague Convention in relation to the recognition of foreign testamentary dispositions, an Irish practitioner should not assume that a will drawn up and executed in accordance with Irish law will be competent to deal with foreign property.

Where a country is a signatory to the Hague Convention, a testamentary disposition will be regarded as valid in signatory countries with regard to form, where it complies with the internal law of:

(a)   the place where the testator made the testamentary disposition;

(b)   a nationality possessed by the testator, either at the time when he or she made the disposition or at the time of his or her death;

(c)   a place in which the testator had his or her domicile, either at the time when he or she made the disposition or at the time of his or her death;

(d)   a place in which the testator had his or her habitual residence, either at the time when he or she made the disposition or at the time of his or her death;

(e)   insofar as immovables are concerned, the place where they are situated.

These criteria are given effect in Irish law in s 102 of the Succession Act 1965.

[1.104] Articles 1 and 2 of the Hague Convention provide for a broad recognition of foreign testamentary dispositions in signatory countries. Nevertheless, where a testator has, in particular, immovable property, in a foreign country, it would be prudent for a will to be made in the country where the property is situate.

If the testator is adopting that course, he or she should be advised to indicate this to his or her advisers in the foreign jurisdiction to ensure that the will made in the foreign jurisdiction does not revoke his or her Irish will or any other will dealing with property elsewhere. In other words, any revocation clause contained in the will dealing with the foreign property should restrict itself to revoking wills and other testamentary dispositions dealing with the foreign property only.

Similarly, if a testator has already made a will dealing with property in another jurisdiction, which will he or she wishes to stand, the Irish will should take care not to revoke the testamentary disposition dealing with the foreign property, and the revocation clause should state that it is revoking only previous wills and other testamentary dispositions dealing with Irish property.

As a general rule of thumb, under the rules of private international law or conflicts of laws, a will dealing with movable property will be construed according to the laws of the domicile of the person making it, whereas a will dealing with immovable property will be construed according to the laws of the place where the property is situate. Legal terms dealing with Irish property may not be understood or may not have a counterpart in the foreign jurisdiction and therefore it is preferable that a will dealing with immovable property in another jurisdiction be drawn up by a lawyer in that jurisdiction.

If all else fails, the Irish practitioner should draw up a will dealing with the foreign property as best he or she can, but the testator should be advised of difficulties that might ensue and the giving of such advice should be carefully recorded in an attendance drawn up at the time the will is made.

Tax considerations

[1.105] Regard may have to be had to the existence or non-existence of double taxation agreements.

Attendances

[1.106] Attendances in relation to the drawing up and execution of wills are of particular importance. If the will is challenged or a question arises as to the construction of a will, a full attendance upon the testator will be of vital importance. The attendance should record:

(a)   the examination, where necessary, to ascertain that the testator had testamentary capacity; the tests laid down in *Banks v Goodfellow* should be borne in mind;

(b)   the instructions taken from the testator in relation to the nature and extent of his or her estate, the dispositive provisions in his or her will and the reasons therefor;

(c)   advices, if necessary, in relation to provision for a spouse/civil partner and/or children, with reference to their entitlements under Pt IX of the Succession Act 1965;

(d)   information in relation to any desertion;

(e)   information and advices re any cohabitation;

(f)   information in relation to any child or children not being provided for or relevant to any claim under s 117;

(g)   reference to any advices given concerning the validity of foreign divorces, the provisions of separation agreements, or unworthiness to succeed where applicable;

(h)   if the client has attended upon the practitioner for the first time for the purposes of making a will, whether the testator had any previous will made; the reason for altering the previous will, if any; where the testator had a previous practitioner advising him or her, why this practitioner is not being used on this occasion; where contact with the practitioner drafting the will is made by a third party who may or may not be a beneficiary under the will, the practitioner should indicate that he or she has ascertained that the testator is acting freely and voluntarily, that instructions for the will were taken with the testator while the testator was alone and that enquiries were made to ensure that the testator was not in any sense acting under duress or undue influence;

(i)   any tax advice given;

(j)   any advice given concerning wills in other jurisdictions;

(k)   any other matter that may be peculiar to the particular case and the particular testator.

The attendance or further attendance should indicate how, when and where the will was executed. If there is any unusual feature concerning the due execution of the will, such as the testator's signature being feeble or the testator making a signature by mark, or someone else signing the will on behalf of the testator (in his or her presence and at his or her direction), then the attendance should deal with that.

Note: where there is an unusual feature concerning due execution, the Probate Office will always require evidence of due execution, even if the will would appear to be properly executed on its face and the attestation clause deals with the necessary prerequisites. In circumstances where there is an unusual feature in relation to the execution of the will, an affidavit of both attesting witnesses might be prepared and sworn after the execution of the will and left with the will in case there should be any difficulty in tracing a witness after the testator's death or in case a witness should predecease a testator. Precedent affidavits appear in **Appendix 3**.

PART II: CHECK LIST FOR CONTENTS OF A SIMPLE WILL

[1.107]

(a)   Name and address of testator and date of will;

(b)   Revocation clause;

(c)   Appointment of executor(s) (and trustees);

(d)   Appointment of trustees if different from executors;

(e)   Appointment of testamentary guardian if required;

(f)   List of general pecuniary legacies;

(g)   List of specific bequests;

(h)   List of demonstrative legacies, if any;

(i)   Residuary bequests;

(j)   If trust created in respect of residue, powers of trustees;

(k)   If trust arises, indemnity to trustees;

(l)   Charging clause, if required;

(m)   Signature of testator;

(n)   Date of will, if not given in introductory clause;

(o)   Attestation clause;

(p)   Signatures and addresses of witnesses.

PART III: CHECK LIST FOR DUE EXECUTION OF A WILL

(a) Standard execution

[1.108]

(i)   *Signature of testator*. The testator must sign in the presence of two witnesses, both present at the same time, who then sign in the presence of the testator. It is not necessary that the witnesses sign in each other's presence.

(ii)   *Acknowledgement of signature*. The testator must acknowledge that the signature on the will is his or hers in the presence of two witnesses, both present at the same time, who then sign their names as witnesses, in the presence of the testator. It is not necessary that the witnesses sign in the presence of each other.

(b) Signature by mark

[1.109] The testator may sign by mark if he or she is unable to write due to illiteracy or physical infirmity. The will must be read over to the testator prior to execution or alternatively he or she must read it to him or herself and be satisfied with its contents. The reading over of the will should be carried out in the presence of both witnesses. The attestation clause should make a reference to the will being read over to the testator prior to execution or to his or her reading over it and that he or she is of sound disposing mind. The attestation clause should also state the reason for signature by mark.[51] The witnesses will have to be satisfied that the testator was of sound disposing mind and that he or she understood the will. This should be covered by the practitioner's attendance and as a precaution both witnesses might swear affidavits to be left with the will stating that all of the above was complied with.[52] The will should then be signed by the testator making his or her mark in the presence of both witnesses, both present at the same time, and they should then sign their names as witnesses in the presence of the testator. It is not necessary that the witnesses sign in the presence of each other.

(c) Enfeebled signature

[1.110] If the testator is likely to make an enfeebled signature, then the same procedure as for signature by mark should be adopted.

(d) Blind testator

[1.111] In the case of a blind testator, the law requires that the witnesses sign their names to the will in such a position that had the testator had his or her sight, he or she would have been able to see them sign. This is because the requirement of 'presence' of the witnesses when the testator signs or when the witnesses sign has generally been held to mean visual presence. The blind testator should sign the will in the ordinary way in the presence of two witnesses, both present at the same time, and the two witnesses should then sign their names in the presence of the testator, but it is not necessary that

---

51.   See precedent attestation clauses in **Ch 14**.
52.   See precedent affidavits in **Appendix 3**.

they sign the will in each other's presence. An affidavit should be left with the will stating that the will was signed by the witnesses in such a manner that had the testator had sight, he or she would have been able to see them so sign.[53]

(e) Signature by third party on behalf of the testator

[1.112] A third party may sign the will on behalf of the testator and he or she may sign either the testator's name or his or her own name. He or she must make the signature at the direction of the testator *and* in the presence of the testator, and both witnesses must witness the fact that the signature was made at the direction of the testator and in his presence. The signature therefore is made by the third party at the express direction of the testator, in his or her presence and in the presence of the two witnesses, both present at the same time, and they then sign the will as witnesses in the presence of the testator, but not necessarily of each other.[54]

(f) Amendments, alterations, interlineations or obliterations

[1.113] If there is any alteration to the will prior to its execution, the amendment should be covered in the attestation clause and the attestation clause should state that the particular amendment, by giving details of it, was made prior to execution. Alternatively or in addition, the amendment may be initialled by the testator and by the two witnesses in exactly the same manner as for the execution of the will, that is to say by the testator appending his or her initial to the amendment in the presence of the two witnesses, both present at the same time, and by the witnesses appending their initials to the amendment in the presence of the testator, but not necessarily of each other. It is worthwhile leaving an affidavit with the will stating that the amendments were made prior to execution.[55]

(g) Will on separate sheets of paper

[1.114] Where a will is drawn up on separate sheets of paper, it is imperative that all the sheets of papers be in the same room at the time of execution, and an affidavit of attesting witness will be required by the Probate Office to confirm that all sheets of paper were in the same room at the time of execution. If a practitioner has to draw up a will therefore by using separate sheets of paper in a situation perhaps where the will is being drawn up as a matter of urgency, then it would be prudent to also draft an affidavit confirming that all sheets of paper were in the same room at the time when the will was executed. If the sheets of paper are separate sheets of paper not joined together at the time of execution, it is best to leave them in that condition rather than join them by a clip, pin or staple later, as this may give rise to a query as to whether anything additional of a testamentary nature was attached to the will. The will should be executed in the normal way depending on the circumstances.[56]

---

53. See precedent affidavits in **Appendix 3**.
54. See precedent attestation clauses in **Ch 14** and precedent affidavits in **Appendix 3**.
55. See precedent attestation clauses in **Ch 14** and precedent affidavits in **Appendix 3**.
56. See precedent affidavits in **Appendix 3**.

(h) Incorporating a list or map into the will

[1.115] The requirements for incorporation of a document into the will are dealt with in **Ch 6**. It is necessary that the document be in existence at the time the will is executed and the document be clearly identified in the will. As a further precaution, it would be worthwhile to have the testator and the witnesses sign the document concerned and again to leave an affidavit with the will, sworn by the testator, stating that the document was in existence when the will was executed and verifying the identification of the document in the will.[57]

(i) Double signatures

[1.116] If the testator should inadvertently sign the will twice, perhaps by signing the will in the wrong place and then signing again in the correct place, it will be necessary for an affidavit of attesting witness to be supplied confirming that both signatures were made in one continuous act of execution. It would therefore be prudent in the event that this arises to leave an affidavit with the will confirming that this is the position.[58]

(j) Signature in the wrong position

[1.117] If the testator appends his signature to the will in the wrong position, either below the attestation clause or in some other incorrect place, an affidavit of attesting witness will be required to confirm that the signature was intended to give effect to the will and that the execution was otherwise regular. It would again be worthwhile to leave an affidavit with the will confirming that the will was validly executed.[59]

---

57.   See precedent affidavits in **Appendix 3**.
58.   See precedent affidavits in **Appendix 3**.
59.   See precedent affidavits in **Appendix 3**.

Chapter 2

PRINCIPLES OF DRAFTING AND CONSTRUCTION

[2.01] This book is not intended to be a substantive text in relation to the principles applicable to construction of wills, but the principles applicable to construction of wills should be borne in mind when drafting a will to avoid unintended results in a court of construction.

This chapter might be read repeatedly by practitioners who draft wills so that the principles and pitfalls are engrained.

Any person who drafts wills would see their life pass in front of their eyes if they heard, about a will that they had drafted, what was said in the case of *In Re Kenny Deceased; Roberts and others v Roberts*.[1] Geoghegan J in a High Court decision (at p 34 of the report) expressed the frustration that may often confront a court of construction:

> 'Let me state at the outset that in my view the will is well nigh impossible to construe with any degree of certainty and it seems to me almost inconceivable that the testatrix, no matter how well advised she was by her solicitor, could possibly have understood its implications ... I must therefore do the best I can in construing it.
>
> The will was drafted for the testatrix by her solicitor. I cannot imagine any solicitor would have drawn up such a will ...'

It is best, as a person drafting a will, not to find oneself on the receiving end of such an unvarnished observation.

[2.02] In terms of case law, previously decided cases are only a guide and should be approached with an element of caution. As Lowry LCJ, in the Northern Ireland case of *Heron v Ulster Bank Limited*, said:

> '... Finally, and I suggest not until the disputed passage has been exhaustively studied, one may get help from the opinion of other courts and judges on similar words, rarely as binding precedents since it has been well said that "no will has a twin brother" (*per* Warner J in the *Matter of King*),[2] but more often as examples (sometimes of the highest authority) of how judicial minds nurtured in the same discipline have interpreted words in similar contexts.'[3]

[2.03] It should be borne in mind also that extrinsic evidence will only be admissible if there is a contradiction or ambiguity on the face of the will. (*Rowe v Law*[4]; *In re Collins – O'Connell and Another v Governor and Company of the Bank of Ireland and Another*.[5]) This view was recently re-stated by Laffoy J in *Hickey v O'Dwyer and*

---

1.   *In Re Kenny Deceased; Roberts and others v Roberts* [2000] I IR 33.
2.   *Matter of King* 200 NY 189 192 (1910).
3.   *Heron v Ulster Bank Limited* [1974] NI 44.
4.   *Rowe v Law* [1978] IR 55.
5.   *In re Collins – O'Connell and Another v Governor and Company of the Bank of Ireland and Another* [1998] 2 IR 596.

others.[6] Laffoy J found that the will was clear on its face. However, the judge did have regard to evidence, such as it was, to ascertain whether the testator intended a beneficiary to receive both the benefit contained in a will and under a related trust. But no extrinsic evidence was admissible to construe the will itself because it was clear on its face.

If a will drafted by a legal practitioner gives rise to a constructional difficulty, then unless it can be shown that the testator was fully advised and went against that advice, there may be a difficulty in negligence. The practitioner, who drafted the will, should give thought as to whether he or she can act in the matter as there exists a strong potential for a conflict of interest. It must be remembered that the duty of care is not only owed to the testator but also to the beneficiaries.

[2.04] Generally speaking, the task of a court of construction, where a difficulty arises, is to seek to ascertain the intention of the testator (see *Curtin v O'Mahony*[7]). However, the court ascertains this intention by reference to a number of well-settled principles:

(a)   Generally speaking, legal or technical terms will be given their legal or technical meaning.

(b)   Popular or colloquial words will be given their popular or colloquial meaning. But a cautionary note should be sounded based on the result in the case of *Crawford and another v Lawless and others*[8] (see below).

(c)   Where there is an ambiguity on the face of the will rendering the intent of the testator difficult to ascertain, then extrinsic evidence will be admissible to assist in ascertaining the intention of the testator (see s 90 of the Succession Act 1965 and the Supreme Court decision in *Rowe v Law*[9]). Generally speaking, where the will is clear on its face, even if it does not reflect the intention of the testator, extrinsic evidence will not be admissible to ascertain the intention of the testator. There must first be an ambiguity on the face of the will, either latent or patent, before extrinsic evidence becomes admissible (see also *In re Collins – O'Connell and Another v Governor and Company of the Bank of Ireland and Another*[10]).

It is useful when drafting a will to have regard to the principles or method the court will apply if a constructional difficulty arises. It will assist the practitioner drafting the will to see if the intention of the testator is clearly reflected in the text. If in doubt it is worthwhile to have a colleague read the will and objectively assess whether there is potential for ambiguity or contradiction that could give rise to expensive proceedings to have the will construed.

---

6.   *Hickey v O'Dwyer and others* [2005] IEHC 365.

7.   *Curtin v O'Mahony* [1991] 2 IR 562.

8.   *Crawford and another v Lawless and others* [2002] IR 416.

9.   *Rowe v Law* [1978] IR 55.

10.   *In re Collins – O'Connell and Another v Governor and Company of the Bank of Ireland and Another* [1998] 2 IR 596.

On the construction of wills generally, a statement by Lowry LCJ in Northern Ireland has been approved in Ireland by Carroll J in *Howell v Howell*.[11] In *Heron v Ulster Bank Ltd*,[12] Lowry LCJ stated:

'I consider that, having first read the whole will, one may with advantage adopt the following procedure:

1. Read the immediately relevant portion of the will as a piece of English and decide, if possible, what it means.

2. Look at the other material parts of the will and see whether they tend to confirm the apparently plain meaning of the immediately relevant portion or whether they suggest the need for modification in order to make harmonious sense of the whole, or alternatively, whether an ambiguity in the immediate relevant portion can be resolved.

3. If the ambiguity persists, have regard to the scheme of the will and consider what the testator was trying to do.

4. One may at this stage have resort to rules of construction, where applicable, and aids, such as the presumption of early vesting and the presumptions against intestacy and in favour of equality.

5. Then see whether any rule of law prevents a particular interpretation being adopted.

6. Finally, and I suggest not until the disputed passage has been exhaustively studied, one may get help from the opinion of other courts and judges on similar words, rarely as binding precedents since it has been well said that 'no will has a twin brother' (per Warner J in the *Matter of King*,[13] but more often as examples (sometimes of the highest authority) of how judicial minds nurtured in the same discipline have interpreted words in similar contexts.'

These principles have been applied in a number of cases in this jurisdiction since. (*The Governor and Company of the Bank of Ireland v Gaynor and others*;[14] *Crawford and another v Lawless and others*;[15] *Butler v Butler and Others*;[16] *Corrigan v Corrigan and another*;[17] and *McGuinness v Sherry and others*.[18])

[2.05] In *Crawford and another v Lawless and others*,[19] the testator described a beneficiary in his will as his 'daughter'. She was not his daughter, but in fact was the daughter of his former spouse born after her marriage to the testator had been dissolved. The testator knew the woman concerned was not his daughter. The solicitor drawing the will also knew that the woman in question was not the testator's daughter. The testator,

---

11. *Howell v Howell* [1992] 1 IR 290.
12. *Heron v Ulster Bank Ltd* [1974] NI 44.
13. *Matter of King* 200 NY 189 192 (1910).
14. *The Governor and Company of the Bank of Ireland v Gaynor and Others* (29 June 1999, unreported) HC.
15. *Crawford and another v Lawless and others* [2002] IR 416.
16. *Butler v Butler and Others* [2006] IEHC 104.
17. *Corrigan v Corrigan and another* [2007] IEHC 367.
18. *McGuinness v Sherry and Others* [2008] IEHC 134.
19. *Crawford and another v Lawless and Others* [2002] IR 416.

however, said that he wanted to obtain the benefit of a tax threshold available to a child. He was advised that that would not be possible, but he insisted that she be so described in connection with a substantial pecuniary bequest, which would have exceeded her tax threshold as a stranger-in-blood. Later in his will the testator created a discretionary trust the objects of which included his children. He left a letter of wishes, which stated that his intended object of that trust was his only biological daughter. It transpired after his death that he also had some other biological children, but he had not been married to their mothers. Clearly all these biological children were within the objects of the discretionary trust created by the will. The person who was named in the will as a 'daughter' claimed that she should also be considered an object of the discretionary trust. The executors brought an application for directions. The court held that the testator in his will had created his own 'lexicon' and that as the testator had chosen in one part of his will to describe this person as his daughter then, in the absence of anything to the contrary, she should also be regarded as a child for the purpose of the discretionary trust.

Clearly, in the *Crawford* case the testator had been fully advised but insisted on going against the advice given.

The approach in *Crawford* is echoed in the case of *In Re Doran Deceased*.[20] In that case, a sister in religion appointed two alternative office holders as executors. A question arose as to whether the appointment was void for uncertainty. The court held that it was not void, as what the testator intended to do was to appoint substitutional executors the second only to act if the first was not available or was unwilling to act. Herbert J had regard to the words 'adopted' by the testatrix herself in construing the will. While Herbert J did not himself seem to feel it was necessary for the first appointed executor to renounce to allow the substituted executor to act, he felt that he should not depart from long-established practice and required the non-proving executor to renounce.

While the *Doran* case had a happy outcome, perhaps due to the judicial ingenuity of Herbert J, it is still better to avoid such conundra as inevitably they will incur significant cost, delay and uncertainty for the estate.

[2.06] A cautious approach should be adopted and testators fully advised so they can avoid what might be unforeseen consequences.

A person drafting a will, therefore, should try to state as clearly and as simply as possible what the testator intends. Generally speaking, clear, simple English is better than 'legalese', and persons drafting a will should avoid a mixture of legal terminology and colloquial terminology which might lead to confusion.

A person drafting a will should also have regard to rules which may result in a particular provision in a will being held void. A bequest can be void for uncertainty. Uncertainty can arise from a lack of clarity as to the beneficiary, subject matter or some condition attaching to a bequest. In the case of a condition, it may be possible to sever it from the bequest or if it is held to be a condition subsequent and void then the bequest takes effect freed from the condition (see further below).

---

20.   *In Re Doran Deceased* [2000] 4 IR 551.

[2.07] In *Thornton v Timlin*,[21] there was a pecuniary legacy to 'Mayo County Council (Ballina area) Workers' but no such designation existed within the County Council. Laffoy J held that the admission of extrinsic evidence was permissible to try to ascertain the intention of the testator under limb 2 of the rule. This was because a will speaks from death (s 89 of the 1965 Act) and it was not clear at that time whom the deceased intended to benefit. The extrinsic evidence did not assist in ascertaining what the testator intended. Laffoy J reluctantly found that the bequest must fail for uncertainty.

[2.08] In relation to 'property', s 16 the 2009 Act has abolished the rules relating to further interests such as the rule against perpetuities. 'Property' is defined in s 3 of the 2009 Act as including 'real and personal' property.

[2.09] Where a condition is to be attached to a particular bequest, care should be taken to ensure that the bequest or condition attaching to it does not:

(a)   become void as being contrary to public policy, where, for example, the condition amounts to a restraint on alienation or a restraint on marriage;

(b)   become void for uncertainty, eg, imposes conditions as to residence.

Where conditions are imposed upon gifts, the distinction between a condition precedent and a condition subsequent should be understood. A condition precedent is a condition which will prevent the gift vesting until such time as the condition is satisfied. By contrast, a condition subsequent is a condition which will result in the subject matter of the bequest divesting should the condition not be fulfilled.

In the event that a *condition precedent* is held void for uncertainty or some other reason, then *the entire bequest will fail* and the subject matter of the bequest will fall into the residue of the estate, or, in the case of a residuary bequest, it will give rise to a partial intestacy.

On the other hand, if a *condition subsequent* is held void, then the bequest *will take effect freed from the condition* so that the beneficiary takes the subject matter of the bequest absolutely; this may appear to flout the testator's intention and may give rise to difficulty.

Generally speaking, one cannot give a beneficiary an absolute interest in a portion of property and then seek to attach conditions which restrict the enjoyment of that absolute interest. The testator should instead give the beneficiary some form of limited interest in the property and provide for a gift over when that limited interest ceases.

[2.10] Generally speaking, because the courts favour early vesting of interests in property, they will be inclined to treat conditions attaching to bequests as *prima facie* conditions subsequent unless there is no option but to hold that the particular condition is a condition precedent (see *Mackessy v Fitzgibbon*[22]). This approach was described by Laffoy J as well-settled in the more recent case of *McGowan v Kelly*.[23] The executrix, who had sought to challenge the validity of the entire bequest notwithstanding the well-settled law, was not entitled to her costs out of the estate and had to bear her own costs.

---

21.   *Thornton v Timlin* [2012] IEHC 239.
22.   *Mackessy v Fitzgibbon* [1993] 1 IR 520.
23.   *McGowan v Kelly* [2007] IEHC 228.

The case shows that it is a fallacy to think that in all cases of construction the estate will bear all the costs of the proceedings.

Where a particular point is well-settled, the person persisting with construction proceedings is at risk on costs.

Both cases involved a condition attached to a bequest of land that the beneficiary reside on and/or farm the land. In both instances, the condition was treated as a condition subsequent and was found void for uncertainty so that the beneficiary took the bequest freed from the condition.

As a condition precedent will prevent the subject matter of the gift vesting, it may offend against the rule against perpetuities, and the person drafting the will should direct his or her mind to that possibility. If the rule against perpetuities is offended against, the entire bequest will fail.

It is not always possible to achieve, even by the most skilful draftsmanship, what the testator might require. Some testators wish to dictate the fate of their property for generations to come, but the more complicated the will, the greater the likelihood that bequests will require construction, which will result in expensive litigation.

The court has no special power to vary the terms of a will to validate an inoperative provision.[24] In *Re Malpass (decd)*,[25] however, Sir Robert Megarry VC held that where a will had granted a testamentary option, but the machinery for ascertaining the price to be paid was ineffective, the court could and should make good the deficiency by providing alternative machinery for determining the price.[26]

Duty of care owed to beneficiaries

[2.11] It has long been established now that a practitioner drafting a will owes a duty of care not only to the testator but also, in certain circumstances, to a beneficiary (*Wall v Hegarty and Anor*[27]). The standard of care is that which would be exercised by a 'reasonably careful solicitor' (*Roche v Peilow*[28]).

In the recent case of *Darby v Shanley and Another*,[29] Irvine J held that the principles of the duty of care should not be over-extended. A duty of care to beneficiaries arose, say, where a solicitor took instructions to have a will drafted and executed but failed to do so and also where the provision of a will was incorrectly drafted so that the intention of the testator was frustrated and a beneficiary did not received a benefit intended for him or her.

In the *Darby* case, the plaintiff beneficiary suffered loss because the husband of the testatrix elected to take his legal right share to one-half of the estate. As a result, the benefit intended for the beneficiary was reduced. However Irvine J held that that leg of the plaintiff's claim failed because it did not come within the forseeability test. The court, however, accepted the evidence of the solicitor that the testatrix had been advised

24. See *Re Koeppler's Will Trusts* [1984] 2 All ER 111.
25. *Re Malpass (decd)* [1984] 2 All ER 313.
26. See also *Talbot v Talbot* [1967] 2 All ER 920. However, see *Curtin v O'Mahony* [1991] 2 IR 562 and *Mulhern v Brennan* [1999] 3 IR 528.
27. *Wall v Hegarty and Anor* [1980] ILRM 124.
28. *Roche v Peilow* [1985] IR 252.
29. *Darby v Shanley and Another* [2009] IEHC 459.

that her husband could elect to take his legal right share and nevertheless instructed the solicitor to draft the will in the form in which he did. The decision might have been different had the solicitor been found not to have adverted to that possibility.

On the duty of care owed, Irvine J stated at para 5.13 of the judgment as follows:

> 'On the basis of the case law referred to earlier, the Court must conclude that the Defendants in the present circumstances did owe a duty of care not only to the testatrix but also to the intended beneficiaries named in her Will. They were obliged to act prudently to ensure that her wishes expressed in her will were not frustrated. To the forefront of those obligations, having regard to the circumstances in which they were asked to prepare Bridie Bird's will, was a requirement that they would seek to satisfy themselves that her instructions had been given independently of any influence that might have been exerted upon her by those who were to be the beneficiaries of her intended will.'

The *Darby* decision is also interesting because it was alleged that the plaintiff's claim was statute barred, in that if negligence arose, it arose when the will was made and the limitation period of six years had elapsed. But the court found that the cause of action did not accrue in the plaintiff until proceedings brought by the surviving husband had been settled and the time for bringing the claim did not run until then.

Chapter 3

INTRODUCTORY CLAUSES

PART I: COMMENTARY

Identifying the testator

[3.01] Generally speaking, it will be sufficient to commence wills by stating that it is the last will and testament of the testator, identifying him or her by his or her name and address. However, there will be cases where a testator may have been known by other names, eg, where he or she used an alias or where he or she changed his or her name, and property is held in different names.

In some instances, a person may be known by a particular forename, but his or her birth certificate may show him or her with a different forename, or a person may use a second forename habitually while having a different first forename on his or her birth certificate.

Married women now with greater regularity continue to use their pre-marriage name, but they may also wish to include a reference to their married name in the will to avoid any confusion. Paradoxically, sometimes women who are not married to the person they are cohabiting with adopt that person's surname to give an outward appearance of regularity to their relationship, but when making a will, they may wish it to include their own name.

So far as I am aware, civil partners do not usually change their surnames on entry into a civil partnership but, in individual cases it would be worth enquiring as to the position.

Divorced women may revert to a pre-marriage surname. On remarriage, a woman may wish to adopt the name of her new spouse but still make reference to her former married name or perhaps her pre-marriage name, by which name she might still be widely known.

Generally speaking, if the will does not make reference to another name, the grant of representation will normally issue in the name that the testator used in his or her will. This could cause a difficulty with banks or other financial institutions if an alias is used in respect of accounts in these institutions. The bank or financial institution may not be willing to act on foot of a grant of representation which gives the testator's name as Mary Smith if the account they are operating is in the name of Lucy O'Brien.

PART II: PRECEDENT CLAUSES

Normal introductory clause of testator

[3.02]

THIS IS THE LAST WILL AND TESTAMENT OF *(insert full name)*, of *(full residential address)*, made by me on the *(date)* day of *(month)*, *(year)*.

Introductory clause where testator uses an alias

[3.03]

THIS IS THE LAST WILL AND TESTAMENT OF *(insert full usual name)*, otherwise known as *(alias)*, of *(full residential address)*, made by me on the *(date)* day of *(month)*, *(year)*.

Introductory clause where testator has altered his or her name by marriage, deed poll or otherwise

[3.04]

THIS IS THE LAST WILL AND TESTAMENT OF *(insert current name)*, formerly known as *(former name)*, of *(full residential address)*, made by me on the *(date)* day of *(month)*, *(year)*.

Introductory clause where testator's name is different to that which appears on his or her birth certificate

[3.05]

THIS IS THE LAST WILL AND TESTAMENT OF *(insert name usually used)*, described on my birth certificate as *(name appearing on birth certificate)*, of *(full residential address)*, made by me on the *(date)* day of *(month)*, *(year)*.

Introductory clause where testator has used the name on his or her birth certificate on formal occasions but is known by another name colloquially or informally

[3.06]

THIS IS THE LAST WILL AND TESTAMENT OF *(insert name appearing on birth certificate)*, otherwise and usually known as *(informal or colloquial name)*, made by me on the *(date)* day of *(month)*, *(year)*.

Introductory clause where testator has more than one address

[3.07]

THIS IS THE LAST WILL AND TESTAMENT OF *(insert name of testator)*, of *(first residential address)*, and also of *(second residential address)*, made by me on the *(date)* day of *(month)*, *(year)*.

Introductory clause where testatrix is married but uses her unmarried name and wishes reference to be made to her married name to avoid any confusion of identity

[3.08]

> THIS IS THE LAST WILL AND TESTAMENT OF *(insert unmarried name)*, now sometimes known as *(married name)*, of *(full residential address)*, made by me on the *(date)* day of *(month)*, *(year)*.

Introductory clause where testatrix has been married, divorced and remarried and wishes to make reference to her unmarried name, previous married name and new married name

[3.09]

> THIS IS THE LAST WILL AND TESTAMENT OF *(insert unmarried name)*, now known as *(new married name)* and formerly known as *(previous married name)*, of *(full residential address)*, made by me on the *(date)* day of *(month)*, *(year)*.

Chapter 4

REVOCATION OF WILLS

PART I: COMMENTARY

Revocation of wills

[4.01] Section 85 of the Succession Act 1965 governs the revocation of wills and provides that a will is revoked in the following circumstances:

(a) By a subsequent marriage or entry into civil partnership, except a will made in contemplation of that particular marriage or entry in to a civil partnership. (It is unnecessary that the will states on its face that the will is made in contemplation of marriage or entry into a civil partnership. I consider, however, that it is desirable that the will would state that it was made in contemplation of marriage or entry into a civil partnership. The contemplation of marriage or entry into a civil partnership, if not stated in the will, can be proved by extrinsic evidence.)

Note: the dissolution of the marriage or civil partnership does not effect a revocation of the will and if acting for someone who is divorcing or dissolving a civil partnership it is imperative that a new will be made even in advance of the actual dissolution.

(b) By a will or codicil properly executed, containing a revocation clause.

(c) By some *writing* declaring an intention to revoke the will and executed in the manner in which the will is required to be executed.

(d) By the burning, tearing or destruction of the will by the testator, *with the intention of revoking it.*

(e) By the burning, tearing or destruction of the will by some person (a) *in the presence of the testator* and (b) *by his or her direction,* with the intention of revoking it.

These are the finite ways in which a will can be revoked. Section 85 provides that a will cannot be revoked in any other way.

Automatic revocation

[4.02] The only way in which a will is automatically revoked under Irish law is by marriage or entry into a civil partnership. *All testators* should be advised that if they marry, remarry or enter into a civil partnership, their will will be automatically revoked and it is imperative that they make a new will in its stead. The exception to this is where a will is made in contemplation of the *particular* marriage, remarriage or entry into a civil partnership. A general intention to marry, remarry or enter into a civil partnership will not suffice.

Capacity

[4.03] In common with making a will, the testator must have capacity to revoke the will. In the case of automatic revocation, the testator must have the capacity to contract a valid marriage or civil partnership. In relation to the other methods of revocation, discussed below, the testator must have the capacity to understand that he or she is revoking a will and the consequences of such revocation. If a will, codicil or 'paper-writing' revokes a will, then the testator must have the mental capacity to execute the instrument. Similarly a marriage, civil partnership or other form of revocation procured by duress or undue influence would not effect a revocation because the mode of revocation would be tainted by invalidity.

Failure to include revocation clause

[4.04] A new will or codicil will only expressly revoke an earlier will if it contains an explicit revocation clause. If the will or codicil does not contain an explicit revocation clause, it will only revoke the earlier will (or will and codicils) in so far as the later will is inconsistent with the earlier will. In such circumstances, the earlier will (and codicils, if any) and the later will (and codicils, if any) would all be proved together as constituting the last will and testament, and the administration of the estate would proceed on the basis that the provisions in the later will would prevail insofar as they were inconsistent with provisions in the earlier will. This would necessitate a court application to the Probate Judge in the High Court (non-contentious probate side) to have all documents admitted as together constituting the last will of the testator. Constructional difficulties may arise in relation to the terms of the various documents and how they affect one another, which might necessitate a construction summons unless the persons affected can agree as to how the documents are to be interpreted.

In order to avoid difficulty, therefore, it is better that a full revocation clause be contained in all new wills. It is unusual for a will to be revoked by a codicil and the practice should not be encouraged.

Foreign element

[4.05] It is important to reiterate in this context that if the testator has property outside the jurisdiction and has made a will dealing with that property, which he or she wishes to remain in force, the revocation clause should make explicit reference to the will dealing with the property in the other jurisdiction(s) and should explicitly state that it is only revoking previous wills dealing with the testator's property in Ireland, or as the case may be. Similarly, such person should be advised that if he or she makes a will in another jurisdiction but wishes his or her Irish will to remain in force that the foreign will should explicitly state that any revocation by the foreign will does not revoke any will made in Ireland. If acting for someone who has property abroad it would be important to ask if a will has been made abroad and ideally to see the foreign will to ensure that the wills do not give rise to any inconsistency. It would be useful to liaise with the foreign lawyer in relation to the wills made in both (or various) jurisdictions to ensure that all wills are consistent each with the other.

One needs to tread delicately; lawyers in other jurisdictions (and perhaps in this one) can be touchy about any perceived interference with them doing their job. Tact is important.

Revocation by paper writing duly executed

[4.06] The formality of a will or codicil is not necessary to revoke a previous will. Section 85 makes provision for the revocation of a will and/or codicil by a simple paper writing, eg, a letter expressing an intention to revoke the will/codicil. The document must, however, be executed in the same manner as is a valid will, ie, the signature of the testator must be made or acknowledged by the testator (or by some other person in his or her presence and at his or her direction) in the presence of two witnesses, both present at the same time, and they must then sign their names in the presence of the testator. It is not necessary that they sign their names in each other's presence. Such a document is likely to be informal and could give rise to difficulty. If possible, testators should be encouraged to effect any revocation of a will through their legal adviser.

Destruction by testator

[4.07] As can be seen, a will can also be revoked by the physical destruction of it, by tearing, burning or otherwise destroying it. There must be *both* the *animus* (the intention) and the *actus* (the act) of revocation, ie, destruction. Destruction on its own does not revoke the will. It must be destroyed with the intention of revoking it. Therefore, if a testator, *per incuriam* or through inadvertence, destroys his or her will, the will is not revoked. If a copy of it is extant at the testator's death or the will can be reconstructed, it may be proved in terms of a copy. Similarly, if the testator destroyed the will but did not have the capacity to form the intention to revoke the will, the will is not revoked. If there is a copy of it extant at the testator's death or a copy of it can be reconstructed, the will can be proved in terms of a copy. This would, of course, necessitate an application to court to the Probate Judge on notice to all persons who would be prejudiced by the proof of the will.

Destruction by third party

[4.08] Where the will is destroyed not by the testator but by some other person at his or her direction, the testator having formed the intention of revoking it, it is *imperative* that the testator be present when the will is destroyed by the third party. If the will is destroyed by the third party without the testator being present, then the will will not be revoked.

In such a circumstance, if the testator was not present when the will was destroyed and the person who destroyed the will is a professional person, who ought to know that the testator must be present in order to give effect to a proper revocation, there would be a cause of action arising against the person who destroyed the will without having the testator present. In such an instance, if the testator intended to die intestate, the next-of-kin could sue the person who destroyed the will on the basis that the revocation was not properly effected.

For example, a testator telephones or writes to his solicitor instructing the solicitor to destroy the will, which is in the solicitor's custody. The letter is not executed in the manner required for a will. The solicitor destroys the will, which left everything to a stranger-in-blood. The testator intends that his next-of-kin would benefit instead. The testator dies without making any new will, but the stranger-in-blood attends upon the solicitor, being aware of the existence of the will in his or her favour, and requires that it be proved. The will has not been properly revoked and the stranger-in-blood would be entitled to the estate of the testator. A cause of action would arise against the solicitor at the suit of the next-of-kin.

Presumed revocation

[4.09] Where an original will is traceable to a testator's custody and cannot be found after his or her death, it will be presumed that the will was destroyed with the intention of revoking it (see *In Re Coster*[1]).

Rebutting the presumption

[4.10] The presumption of revocation could be rebutted by showing that the destruction of the will may have happened *per incuriam,* or alternatively, by showing that while the testator had custody of the will, he or she did not have the capacity to revoke the will during the period that it was in his or her custody. Generally speaking, however, the presumption of revocation in such circumstances is quite difficult to overcome. This is because the circumstances surrounding the destruction will probably not be known or the actual date of destruction may not be known, rendering it difficult to ascertain the capacity or intention of the testator, at the material time.

Safe custody of will

[4.11] Therefore, where a practitioner is giving the original will to a testator after execution for safe-keeping, instead of retaining it in his or her office, or if the testator insists upon taking the original will away, it should be recorded that the original will has been handed over to the testator, though a copy should be carefully kept in the practitioner's office in case an application to prove the will in terms of a copy is capable of being brought.

The testator should be instructed to keep the will safely and to inform his or her executors as to where the will might be found and, if possible, perhaps to lodge it in a bank or some other place of safe custody. It should be impressed upon the testator that some person should know of the whereabouts of the will. The testator should be advised that in the event that the original will is lost or is not forthcoming after his or her death, it will be presumed to have been revoked by destruction and this may result in him or her dying intestate.

Note: the revocation of a later will does not revive an earlier will. If an earlier will is to be revived it must be re-executed.

Dependent relative revocation

[4.12] Except for revocation on marriage or entry into a civil partnership, revocation requires the testator to form the intention of revoking his or her will. A testator, however, may not intend to revoke his or her will unless a certain condition is satisfied or a certain state of affairs exists. For example, a testator may believe that a particular beneficiary under his or her will is dead and decide to revoke the gift to him or her. If the revocation

---

1.   *In Re Coster* (19 January 1979, unreported) SC.

is based upon a particular fact – which transpires to be false – then it may be implied that the revocation was conditional upon the fact upon which the revocation was based being true. In *Campbell v French*,[2] a testator revoked legacies by a codicil, believing all the beneficiaries of the revoked bequests were dead. It transpired in fact that they were alive and the revocation of the legacies therefore was held to be ineffective.

The doctrine of dependent relative revocation most usually arises where the testator revokes his or her will with the intention of making a new one and fails to carry that intention into effect, or alternatively carries the intention into effect, but the later will is for some reason invalid. In this circumstance, the revocation may be ineffective (see *In the Goods of Hogan*[3]). It must be shown, however, that there was a connection between the act of revocation and the intention to make a substitutional testamentary disposition.

In *In Re Coster*, Mrs Coster attended upon her solicitor and took up from him her original will. When she died, the original will could not be found among her papers, although there was a copy of her will among her papers. Also found among her papers was a blank will form that had been purchased in a large newsagents. The will form was not completed in any way. It was argued that the existence of the will form indicated an intention on the part of Mrs Coster to make a new will. Therefore, if she destroyed her earlier will with the intention of revoking it, as had to be presumed given that the original was in her custody, then the revocation was imperfect as she had not drawn up her new will in substitution for the will presumed to be revoked.

Kenny J could find no connection between the purchase of the will form and the taking up of the original will from the solicitor's office. While Mrs Coster may have intended to make a new will at some time in the future, this did not mean that the revocation was conditional and, therefore, he did not apply the doctrine of dependent relative revocation. It would appear, therefore, that the doctrine of dependent relative revocation will only be applied in certain limited circumstances where there is a very clear link between the revocation of the existing will and a demonstrable intention to make a new will in substitution for it.

---

2.   *Campbell v French* (1797) 3 Ves 32.
3.   *In the Goods of Hogan* (18 February 1980, unreported) HC.

PART II: PRECEDENT CLAUSES

Usual general revocation clause

[4.13]

> **I HEREBY REVOKE** all wills and other testamentary dispositions previously made by me.

Shorter form of general revocation clause

[4.14]

> **I HEREBY REVOKE** all previous testamentary dispositions.

Revocation clause where there is a will dealing with property in another jurisdiction which the testator wishes to remain in force

[4.15]

> **I HEREBY REVOKE** all wills and other testamentary dispositions previously made by me dealing with my estate in the Republic of Ireland only. This revocation does not affect any will or other testamentary disposition I may previously have made dealing with my property in any other jurisdiction.
>
> (*Note*: it is imperative that if the testator intends to make a will in another jurisdiction in the future, the practitioner in the other jurisdiction be advised that the new will should not revoke the will dealing with Irish property, unless that is what the testator intends. Where the Probate Office is aware that there is another will dealing with property in another jurisdiction, sight of a plain copy of that other will will be required to ensure that the foreign will does not revoke the Irish will.)

Alternative means of commencing a will where there is a will in another jurisdiction

[4.16]

> **THIS IS THE LAST WILL AND TESTAMENT OF** (*insert name of testator*), of (*full residential address*), made by me on the (*date*) day of (*month*), (*year*).
>
> This will is intended to deal with my property in the Republic of Ireland only and all provisions in this my will relate only to my property in the Republic of Ireland.
>
> **I HEREBY REVOKE** all wills and other testamentary dispositions previously made by me.

Paper writing revoking a will without the same being a will or codicil

[4.17]

> **TO WHOM IT MAY CONCERN, I,** (*insert name of testator*), of (*full residential address*), **HEREBY REVOKE** my will dated the (*date*) day of

(month), *(year)* [and the codicil(s) thereto dated the *(date)* day of *(month)*, *(year)* and the *(date)* day of *(month)*, *(year)]*.

Dated the *(date)* day of *(month)*, *(year)*.

SIGNATURE OF TESTATOR:

SIGNED BY *(TESTATOR'S FULL NAME)* IN THE PRESENCE OF US, BOTH PRESENT AT THE SAME TIME, AND BY US IN THE PRESENCE OF *(TESTATOR'S FULL NAME)*.

Witness 1:

Address:

Witness 2:

Address:

Statement where a will is made in contemplation of marriage or civil partnership

[4.18]

(Note: the 1965 Act expressly provides at s 85 (as amended by the 2010 Act) that the will does not have to be expressly made in contemplation of marriage or entry into a civil partnership, but to avoid doubt it is better that a declaration to that effect be made. It is important that the testator be contemplating a particular marriage and not just marriage in general.)

THIS IS THE LAST WILL AND TESTAMENT OF *(insert name of testator)*, of *(full residential address)*, made by me on the *(date)* day of *(month)*, *(year)*.

I HEREBY REVOKE all former wills and other testamentary dispositions previously made by me.

I DECLARE that this will is made by me in contemplation of my marriage to **OR** entry into a civil partnership with *(name of intended spouse/civil partner)*, of *(full residential address)*.

Clause where the testator intends that the will shall only take effect if the marriage/civil partnership in contemplation proceeds

[4.19]

THIS IS THE LAST WILL AND TESTAMENT OF *(insert name of testator)*, of *(full residential address)*, made by me on the *(date)* day of *(month)*, *(year)*.

I make this will in contemplation of my marriage to **OR** entry into civil partnership with *(name of intended spouse/civil partner)*, of *(full residential address)*. It is my intention that this will shall only take effect in the event of my marriage to **OR** entry into a civil partnership with the said *(name of intended spouse/civil partner)* proceeding and, in the event that the marriage/civil partnership does not take place prior to my death, I intend that my existing will dated the (*date*) day of (*month*), (*year*), would constitute my last will and testament. This document will only constitute my last will and testament in the event that my marriage to **OR** entry into a civil partnership with the said (*name of intended spouse/ civil partner*) proceeds.

Chapter 5

APPOINTMENT OF EXECUTORS, TRUSTEES AND GUARDIANS

PART I: COMMENTARY

Appointment of executors

[5.01] In order for a document to constitute a will, it must do one of two things:

(a)   appoint an executor; or

(b)   dispose of some property.

A document that does neither of these things is not regarded as being of a testamentary nature, even though it might be executed in the same manner as a will is executed.

[5.02] Aside from dispositive provisions – including a residuary clause, and the revocation of previous testamentary documents so as to create a clean sheet to work from – the most important part of a will is the appointment of executors. This is for a number of reasons:

(a)   It allows the testator to select the person or persons who will administer his or her estate and carry his or her wishes into effect. The court will not lightly interfere with this choice should there be an effort to oust the executor(s) appointed (but see the section below on the removal of executors). There has been some development of the jurisprudence since this book was first published and it is set out below.

(b)   The executor of a deceased person's estate is in fact the person who is entitled to custody of the body after death and to arrange the funeral of the deceased. If the testator has particular requirements in that regard, it is useful to appoint perhaps a trusted friend or relative as executor so that those requirements will be respected.

(c)   In the absence of expressly appointed trustees, if trustees of the estate or any part thereof are required, the executors will act as trustees. This will be particularly important where a 'trust of land', within the meaning of the Land and Conveyancing Law Reform Act 2009 ('the 2009 Act'), is created by the will, either expressly or by implication, or perhaps where the will sets up a discretionary trust. Once the will is proved or any grant of representation is extracted, the personal representatives are statutory trustees of the estate for the persons entitle thereto (see s 10 of the 1965 Act) and have a fiduciary duty in relation to the administration of the estate.

(d)   Executors have wide powers in relation to the testator's estate conferred on them by statute and these can be amplified by the will. If, on the other hand, the executor is relying on the statutory powers, while they are quite comprehensive, there may be a shortfall in a power which might otherwise be conferred, eg, the power to run a business. Under the 2009 Act, trustees of a trust of land have all the powers of a beneficial owner so their powers are very wide.

(e)   The extraction of a grant of representation is generally more straightforward where there is an executor appointed. Where a person other than an executor is extracting a grant of representation, it is normally necessary to furnish an administration bond. Since the last edition of this book, the President of the High Court has removed the need for sureties, though the Probate Officer or the court has a residual power to require a surety in an appropriate case. An administration bond is still necessary.

(f)   If the executors appointed are trusted relatives and friends, they will generally know what the testator's intentions in relation to the estate would be, although they are not formally expressed in a will. If, for example, decisions are to be taken in relation to the estate, eg, the sale of assets in order to administer the estate or the provision for beneficiaries who are minors, they may be able to make more informed decisions in line with what the testator would have wanted. The executors are, of course, bound to administer the estate in accordance with the terms of the will and the law.

(g)   In the case of very large and complicated estates, it is possible, for example, to appoint a trust corporation such as a bank to act as trustees and while high fees may be incurred by such appointment, with very complex investments and/or requiring a lot of management, this may often be worthwhile. It is imperative to ensure that the trust corporation is empowered to act in Ireland in that behalf. Further, it would be important to obtain a schedule of such charges as may arise and advise the testator accordingly. Of course, the trust corporation will always reserve the right to alter its fees, and they could become prohibitive. The trust corporation might decline to act when the time comes especially if the estate has dropped in value. For that reason it is always advisable to have an alternative executor available in the event that the corporation decides not to act when the will comes to be proved.

[5.03] Where a number of persons are appointed as executors, the chances are that one or more of them will survive the deceased and therefore be able to act. Furthermore, if, for any reason, an executor is unable or unwilling act, there should still be someone available to act as executor.

[5.04] In the case where the executor is choosing executors personally known to him, it would be wise to suggest that the testator tell the persons he or she proposes to appoint and obtain their agreement to act as such, all other things being equal, when the time comes. The testator should also be advised to tell the executors where the will is so they are in position to access it soon after the death.

[5.05] The testator should be advised that an executor appointed by a will may decide:

•   to act;

•   to renounce his or her rights to act; or

•   to reserve his or her rights to act.

Renunciation by an executor

[5.06] If an executor renounces his or her rights, then his or her rights to act in respect of the administration of the estate are generally speaking lost for all time, save and except that the renunciation may be withdrawn up to the time the grant of probate issues. Alternatively, in certain circumstances, the executor may be permitted to act in the future with leave of the court, notwithstanding the earlier renunciation.

An executor must renounce his or her rights to act prior to accepting his or her office and must not intermeddle in the estate in any way prior to renunciation. Where the executor has intermeddled in the estate and then wishes to renounce his or her rights, he or her must apply to the court in order to renounce. Applications to the court in this connection are made to the Probate Judge exercising the non-contentious probate jurisdiction of the High Court. The application will incur costs and the errant executor may be fixed with the costs. In a case in which I acted, an executor had gone as far as extracting the grant. Later she injured herself while visiting a property comprised in the estate and wanted to sue the estate for damages. An application to allow her to renounce her rights and have the grant revoked was necessary so that she could sue the estate. The court granted the application to allow her renounce but ordered her to pay the costs of the application, the revocation of the grant and the extraction of the new grant.

If there is any possibility of an executor having a claim against or dispute with the estate he or she should not act. A child of the testator who is appointed as executor, who wants to bring an application under s 117, should not intermeddle with the estate in any way. Neither should the solicitor with carriage of the estate give any advice to him or her in that regard, but should immediately refer the child for independent legal advice.

If an executor wishes to challenge a will in respect of its formal or essential validity, he or she should immediately renounce and be directed to take independent legal advice.

Real conflicts of interest that may repose in an executor should be identified early; the person with such conflict should not be allowed to intermeddle and should be directed to take independent legal advice. (See next section.)

Removal of an executor by the court

[5.07] Because an executor is specifically chosen by the testator to administer his or her estate, the courts are very reluctant to intervene to remove an executor. It will only do so in 'serious special circumstances' (Supreme Court in *Dunne v Heffernan*[1]) where the case for removal is made out.

[5.08] Three cases are instructive.

In *Dunne v Heffernan*,[2] the plaintiff sought to remove his sister as executrix of his father's estate. The plaintiff alleged that there was a series of conflicts of interest on the part of his sister. The executrix was director of a number of companies within the large family business and was trustee of family trusts. He argued that these roles were not compatible with her acting as executrix. No actual conflict or misconduct was alleged. The Supreme Court held that an executor can only be removed in 'serious special circumstances' and that in this type of case it would not be unusual for a family member

---

1.   *Dunne v Heffernan* [1997] 3 IR 431.
2.   *Dunne v Heffernan* [1997] 3 IR 431.

to have a number of different roles but this did not of itself amount to a conflict of interest. The Supreme Court declined to remove the executrix.

By contrast, in the case of *In Re Flood*[3] an executor was removed because there was a dispute about money received by the executor from the deceased. The beneficiaries alleged it was a loan and repayable by the executor to the estate. The executor countered that it was a gift and not repayable. Macken J held that such defence was incompatible with the role of executor and removed the executor on the basis of a conflict of interest. Macken J had regard to the principles for removal laid down by the Supreme Court in *Dunne*.

In the recent case of *Scally v Rhatigan (No 2),*[4] Laffoy J removed a solicitor executor because she believed there was a clear conflict interest, which the executor would not be able to overcome. Two executors had been appointed in the will. One of them survived the deceased, but died before the will was proved. That left a sole surviving executor who was the testator's solicitor.

We have seen in **Ch 1** that in *Scally v Rhatigan (No 1),*[5] Laffoy J found the testator did have capacity to execute his will, notwithstanding that some medical personnel were at least doubtful and further despite a lapse of time between taking instructions and the execution of the will. The testator's health had been deteriorating over the time between when initial instructions were taken and the will was executed.

In *Scally v Rhatigan (No 2)*, objections, by way of counterclaim, to the solicitor, who drafted the will, acting as executor were upheld. The twin decisions demonstrate how an estate can become enmeshed in expensive litigation. The court dealt with the proceedings in two modules. The first related to the challenge to the essential validity of the will. The second concerned the defendant's counterclaim, which, *inter alia,* sought to remove the plaintiff as the sole surviving executor. Clearly there was a case to answer in relation to testamentary capacity, even though the will was found valid. The second limb of the litigation demonstrates how it is important to recognise the potential for a conflict of interest, and when it emerges for a professional executor to step aside.

[5.09] Laffoy J, having had regard to the principles as stated in the previous two cases and in particular the Supreme Court decision (at para 2.3 *et seq*), stated the reason for the removal of the executrix at para 7.3 of the judgment as follows:

> 'It is her past professional involvement as solicitor for the Testator and for the multiplicity of corporate vehicles in which the assets of Golden Promise Trust were vested, which gives rise to the professional conflict, coupled with the justified opposition of the Defendant, as a major beneficiary of the estate assets, which in my view, precludes the Plaintiff from acting as executor of the will. That involvement goes way beyond the three examples, I have addressed in detail in this judgment. While one can understand that the Plaintiff would like to fulfil the task which the Testator reposed in her, I am of the view that it would be impossible for her to steer a non-conflicted passage, between the beneficiaries of the estate assets, on the one hand, and the interest of the beneficiaries of the non-estate assets, on the other hand, so as to take all of the steps in the administration,

---

3.   *In Re Flood – Flood v Flood* [1999] 2 IR 234.
4.   *Scally v Rhatigan (No 2)* [2012] IEHC 140.
5.   *Scally v Rhatigan (No 1)* [2010] IEHC 475.

including the protection of assets, of the estate of the testator and of the trusts created by the will that require to be taken by the personal representative.'

[5.10] At para 7.4, Laffoy J adverted to the trustee status of a personal representative created by s 10 of the 1965 Act and the fiduciary duty imposed thereby. The executor, Laffoy J found, would be faced with a 'myriad of issues' which would involve a choice between the interests of the beneficiaries of the estate and non-estate beneficiaries having an interest in the same assets. Laffoy J found there was an actual conflict of interest as opposed to a perceived one. The solicitor who had been appointed as an executor in a will she had drafted would have to make a full disclosure to the beneficiaries of the estate, which would be a breach of the duty of the confidentiality to persons for whom she had previously acted as a solicitor.

Laffoy J stated baldly at the end of para 7.4:

'The court cannot allow that situation to arise.'

Laffoy J concluded at para 7.5 that the case came within the 'serious special circumstances' stated by the Supreme Court in *Dunne v Heffernan* to justify the removal of an executor. Further, the judge found that the protection of the beneficiaries warranted the removal.

The twin decisions in *Scally v Rhatigan* are a salutary tale.

[5.11] It can arise that beneficiaries are not happy with the manner in which an estate is being administered due to delay or may have suspicion as to the propriety or honesty of the executor's *modus operandi*. An application to remove an executor should not be lightly brought. The executor should be given every opportunity to explain him or herself. If the estate is not being properly administered or there is delay, an administration suit should be considered but as part of the relief in that action the removal of the executor might be sought. If a clear case for removal emerges at an interlocutory stage, a motion might be considered to have the executor removed. Clear malfeasance or a conflict of interest on the part of the executor should be present.

Reservation of rights to act

[5.12] As an alternative, an executor's rights may be reserved. This will arise where he or she is unwilling to act at a particular time, but wishes to retain the possibility of acting in the future. This is particularly useful, for example, where an executor is outside the jurisdiction and the administration of the estate might become cumbersome if he or she was to act. The executor, however, may intend to return to the jurisdiction at a later time and may then wish to act. Alternatively, he or she may wish to act in the event that the acting executor dies without completing the administration of the estate. In the former case, a grant of double probate would have to be applied for and, in the latter case, it would be a grant of unadministered probate.

While it is normally prudent to obtain some form of letter or acknowledgement from the executor whose rights are being reserved, the Probate Office does not seek any evidence of the willingness of an executor to have his or her rights reserved. In a case of urgency, where a grant is needed expeditiously and an executor cannot be contacted or is untraceable, it would be possible for the other executor(s) to extract the grant, reserving the rights of the absent executor.

Trust corporations

[5.13] Where a corporation is appointed executor, it must be a trust corporation within the meaning of s 30(4) of the 1965 Act, otherwise the trust corporation will not be able to extract a grant of representation to the estate of the deceased in the Republic of Ireland. In the case of a bank being appointed, it must also be a bank within the jurisdiction under the Central Bank Act 1942.

[5.14] Section 30(4)(c) makes provision for a corporation being deemed a trust corporation by the President of the High Court. The section provides as follows:

> 'A corporation which satisfies the President of the High Court that it undertakes the administration of any charitable, ecclesiastical or public trust without remuneration or that by its constitution it is required to apply the whole of its net income for charitable, ecclesiastical or public purposes and is prohibited from distributing directly or indirectly any part thereof by way of profit, and is authorised by the President of the High Court to act in relation to such trusts as a trust corporation [will be a trust corporation within the meaning of the Act].'

A number of charitable institutions have been deemed to be trust corporations under this section by the President of the High Court; the Probate Office maintains a list of such organisations. Once the President of the High Court has deemed a particular organisation to be a trust corporation, it is unnecessary for a further application to be made and such a corporation can then act as an executor in respect of wills of its members.

[5.15] The current list of trust corporations, correct at the time of going to print is:

Association for Relief of Distressed Protestants;

Mercer's Hospital;

St Flannan's Diocesan Trust;

St Patrick's Missionary Society, Kiltegan;

Representative Church Body of Ireland;

The Irish Cancer Society Limited;

The Maynooth Mission to China;

Ex Service Mental Welfare Society;

Gorta;

St Brendan's Trust;

Dublin Society for the Prevention of Cruelty to Animals;

Royal College of Surgeons;

St Peter Claver (African Mission) Association;

The Frederick Oznam Trust (Incorp) (St Vincent de Paul);

The Scripture Gift Mission;

Our Lady's Hospital, Crumlin;

The Provost and Fellows of Trinity College;

Order of Discalced Friars of the Blessed Virgin Mary of Mount Carmel (orse Discalced Carmelites (Clarendon St));

The Pontifical Society for the Propagation of the Faith;

The Salvation Army of Ireland;

The Sacred Heart Missionary Education Trust;

Concern;

St John of God Trust (Ireland);

Bank of Ireland Finance Ltd (s 30(4)(b));

St Vincent Pallotti Trust (Ireland) Ltd (orse Pallotine Fathers orse Society of the Catholic Apostolate);

The Sisters of Mercy (Tuam Diocese) Co Ltd;

Alzheimer Society of Ireland;

FMA Trustees;

Trócaire;

Aileach Centres Ireland;

St Francis Hospice.

Applications were refused in respect of the Mother Teresa Calcutta Fund, and the Bon Secours trustees were refused.

[5.16] Any of the approved societies could now be appointed an executor in a will and act as such. This might be useful if, for example, a testator wished to leave his or estate to the Society of St Vincent De Paul, which society's proper name is The Frederick Oznam Trust Incorporated.

[5.17] An application to the President of the High Court to deem an organisation of this type a trust corporation normally arises where the organisation is left the residue of a person's estate and there is no executor available to act or the executor who was acting died leaving part of the estate unadministered. In order for the charitable organisation to make such an application it must be an incorporated entity under the Companies Acts 1963–2012.

[5.18] The application need only be made once and, if granted, the corporation can act in any other case that may arise. A copy of the relevant order approving the entity to act will be available in the Probate Office and might be lodged with the papers applying for the grant.[6]

[5.19] Section 30(1)(b) of the 1965 Act provides that the grant of representation may be granted either to the trust corporation on its own or jointly with another person.

Section 30(2) provides that representation shall not be granted to any person on behalf of a trust corporation, so it is not possible for a trust corporation to appoint an attorney to act on its behalf.

Section 30(3) provides that any authorised officer can act on behalf of the trust corporation in relation to the swearing and execution of documents and doing any other act relevant to the extraction of a grant of representation, and any acts done by that authorised officer are binding upon the trust corporation.

---

6.   The Probate Office maintains a list of the estates in which the initial order was made and see *Spierin, The Succession Act 1965 and Related Legislation, a Commentary* (4th edn, Bloomsbury Professional, 2011) para 184.

[5.20] Except where a professional person is being appointed an executor (eg, the testator's solicitor or accountant) or a trust corporation is being appointed, it is usually preferable that the executor have some interest in the estate of the testator. Many wills appoint the same person executor and universal legatee and devisee. While this can be attractive in its simplicity, if the sole beneficiary is the spouse/civil partner of the testator, then the chances are that the spouse/civil partner of the testator may be advanced in years at the time the will comes to be proved. It would be preferable that some other person be appointed to act with the spouse/civil partner in case the spouse/civil partner is old and infirm and perhaps not competent or feels able to administer the estate. There might also be a concern that if the administration is complex or may involve litigation, an older executor may not see the administration through to completion or may not wish to become involved in contentious litigation.

Appointment of a professional person as executor

[5.21] The testator may wish to appoint his or her solicitor or a firm of solicitors to act as his or her executor, and in this regard a number of points should be noted.

In the light of *Scally v Rhatigan (No 2)*, a solicitor who has acted for the deceased must examine his or her conscience and consider whether a conflict of interest might arise in administering the estate. The *Scally* case turned on its own facts. It points to questions that a solicitor proposing to be appointed executor by a testator should ask him or herself, before he or she decides to agree to be appointed. The question posed in the *Scally* case by Laffoy J is whether the executor will be able to 'steer a non-conflicted passage' in due course of the administration of the estate?

[5.22] In considering this question, the professional person, which might include, say, the testator's accountant, should have regard to professional duties owed to other parties for whom the professional person acted in the past. In the *Scally* case, the testator's affairs were somewhat labyrinthine and the solicitor executor had been involved in his affairs at various different levels. The solicitor executor also had duties, including a duty of confidentiality to other persons connected commercially to the testator or his companies for whom she had acted.

[5.23] The *Scally* case does not mean a solicitor or other professional adviser should not be appointed as executor or, if appointed, should not act. It does call such an executor to circumspection. If there is any possibility of a conflict, the solicitor or other professional person might be best not to act.

[5.24] In the absence of any provision to the contrary, where a firm of solicitors is appointed, the persons entitled to extract a grant of representation to the estate of the testator are the partners in the firm for the time being *at the date the will is made*.

[5.25] This is an exception to the general rule that a will speaks from the date of death. If a testator requires that the persons entitled to prove his or her will shall be the partners in the firm at the date of his or her death, then the will shall have to expressly provide for this. It would be generally preferable for a person or a number of persons in the firm to be named as executors and then to provide as a substitutional provision that in the event that these persons predecease the testator, any partner in the firm at the date of death be appointed in their stead. This gives the testator the benefit of appointing named persons in the firm whom he or she knows and trusts, with a fall-back position in the event that they should predecease the testator. The same position would apply to a firm of accountants.

[5.26] As firms of solicitors can change their names or amalgamate with other firms, it is usually advisable that the clause appointing the firm of solicitors would contain a provision to the effect that in the event that the firm amalgamates with another firm or becomes incorporated into another firm, that firm shall then be entitled to act in lieu of the named firm.

[5.27] It would be advisable to appoint a person who is outside the firm to act in addition to members of the firm so that in the event that there is any acrimony between the members of the firm at the time the will comes to be proved, the rights of the members of the firm can be reserved and the other person can proceed until members of the firm are in a position to act.

[5.28] Similarly, it may be that when the date of death arrives, members of the firm may not wish to become involved in the administration of the estate of the testator. Where additional executors are appointed, then they can take on the duties of executors with the members of the firm renouncing their rights or alternatively reserving their rights.

[5.29] It sometimes occurs that the testator will give a direction that a particular firm of solicitors be retained in respect of the administration of his or her estate. This direction is not binding upon the executors as it has been held to be an interference with the executors' discretion to employ such advisers and agents as they may think fit.

[5.30] As the purpose of appointing executors is to ensure that persons whom the testator chooses will administer the estate, it is important that the persons appointed are likely to survive the testator and be available to administer the estate after the testator dies. Thought should be given, therefore, to the age of the persons appointed as executors and to their ability and competence to administer the estate of the testator, particularly if the administration may be somewhat protracted or complex.

[5.31] In order to extract a grant of representation, a person must be of the age of majority (18 years of age) and, while it is not invalid to appoint a minor as an executor, that person could only act through his or her guardian until he or she attained the age of 18 years, in which case the grant of representation would have to be a grant of administration with the will annexed and would require an administration bond. If, therefore, a minor is being appointed, it would be important to appoint an adult with the minor. If the person, who is a minor at the date the will is made, has not attained his or her majority by the time the will comes to be proved, there will be an adult able to act. The rights of the minor can be reserved and he or she can then extract a grant of double probate in due course when he or she attains his or her majority.

[5.32] It would be important also that the person being appointed as an executor would not have a conflict of interest in relation to the estate of the testator. This might arise where there is a discretionary trust in respect of which the executor is a potential beneficiary or where there is a contingent bequest and the executor might have control over whether the contingency might be fulfilled, or not, as the case may be. (And see *In re Flood; Flood v Flood*[7] and *Scally v Rhatigan (No 2)*.[8])

[5.33] Generally speaking, where there is a settlement created by the will, now a trust of land under the 2009 Act, it would be preferable that either the life tenant or a remainder person not be appointed executor as this could give rise to a conflict of interest. It would be preferable that independent persons be appointed. These persons should also be appointed trustees of the trust of land within the meaning of the 2009 Act.

[5.34] Provided an executor is not a beneficiary under the will (and in this context a benefit would include the ability to charge professional fees under a charging clause – see below), the executor can act as a witness to the will, as can a spouse of an executor.

[5.35] If the executor is receiving some benefit from the will (including the ability to charge fees under a charging clause – see below), the executor or his or her spouse (or, where a firm of solicitors or accountants is appointed executors with the power to charge professional fees, a partner in the firm) *cannot* act as a witness.[9]

Death or insanity of an executor

[5.36] A testator should be advised that in the event that an appointed executor dies or becomes insane (eg due to dementia), a new executor should be appointed in his or her stead by codicil or indeed by a new will. It is a circumstance that should be addressed with urgency unless a number of executors appointed by the will are still living and sane.

Appointment of trustees

[5.37] Section 10(3) of the 1965 Act provides:

> 'The personal representatives shall be the representatives of the deceased in regard to his real and personal estate and shall hold the estate as trustees for the persons by law entitled thereto.'

The term 'personal representative' is wider than the term executor and it includes, in addition to executors, persons who would be administering the estate of the testator on the basis of either whole or partial intestacy on foot of a grant of administration intestate or a grant of administration with the will annexed. Executors who act in respect of the administration of the estate of the testator will become his or her legal personal representatives and, therefore, would be statutory trustees in accordance with the provisions of s 10(3) of the 1965 Act. Executors should be made aware of the duties and trust obligations they are undertaking, and this would particularly important where they derive no benefit from the estate.

---

7.   *In Re Flood – Flood v Flood* [1999] 2 IR 234

8.   *Scally v Rhatigan (No 2)* [2012] IEHC 140.

9.   See s 82 of the 1965 Act and, further, *Spierin, The Succession Act 1965 and Related Legislation, a Commentary* (4th edn, Bloomsbury Professional, 2011) para 569 *et seq.*

[5.38] As Laffoy J noted in *Scally v Rhatigan (No 2)*[10] and Finnegan P (as he then was) noted in *Messitt v Henry,*[11] the statutory trusteeship of personal representatives gives rise to a fiduciary duty. The personal representatives must be careful not to secure any advantage for themselves in the administration of the estate or place themselves in a position of conflict.

Any need to appoint trustees?

[5.39] Unless a will actually creates a trust, or a trust of land within the meaning of the 2009 Act arises, there is in fact no need to appoint a trustee. Frequently I have seen wills that unnecessarily create a trust or refer to trustees where no trust arises or would arise under the 2009 Act. Normally this will just be superfluity but a good draftsperson will not make unnecessary reference to trusts and trustees where none exists. Keeping matters simple is a great virtue.

Expressly appointed trustees and trustees of land under the 2009 Act

[5.40] What is being considered here, however, is the appointment of trustees in relation to trusts that are expressly created in the will or that will now come into being by statute under the provisions of the 2009 Act. In most instances, the persons who are appointed executors will also be appointed trustees by the deceased, but there is no reason why different persons may not be appointed.

[5.41] The provisions of Pt 4 of 2009 Act only apply to trusts of land and do not apply to trusts of assets other than land. This is particularly pertinent in relation to the powers of trustees to deal with assets other than land. Because of this limitation of the 2009 Act, practitioners drafting wills should bear in mind the distinction between trusts of land under the 2009 Act and trusts relating to other assets.

It is, of course, possible to give trustees appointed by a will the same powers as those accorded to them in the language of the 2009 Act.

[5.42] A trust of land arises under Pt 4 of the 2009 Act in the circumstances set out in s 18 of that Act:

PART 4
Trusts of Land

Trusts of land

(1) Subject to this Part, where land is—

[SLA 1882, ss 2, 59, 60]

(a)   for the time being limited by an instrument, whenever executed, to persons by way of succession without the interposition of a trust (in this Part referred to as a 'strict settlement'), or

(b)   held, either with or without other property, on a trust whenever it arises and of whatever kind, or

---

10.   *Scally v Rhatigan (No 2)* [2012] IEHC 140.
11.   *Messitt v Henry* [2001] 3 IR 313.

(c)   vested, whether before or after the commencement of this Part, in a minor,

there is a trust of land for the purposes of this Part.

(2) For the purposes of—

(a)   subsection (1)(a), a strict settlement exists where an estate or interest in reversion or remainder is not disposed of and reverts to the settlor or the testator's successors in title, but does not exist where a person owns a fee simple in possession,

(b)   subsection (1)(b), a trust includes an express, implied, resulting, constructive and bare trust and a trust for sale.

(3) Subject to this Part, a trust of land is governed by the general law of trusts.

(4) Conversion of a life estate into an equitable interest only does not affect a life owner's liability for waste.

[LEA 1695]

(5) Where, by reason of absence from the State or otherwise, it remains uncertain for a period of at least 7 years as to whether a person upon whose life an estate or interest depends is alive, it shall continue to be presumed that the person is dead.

(6) If such presumption is applied to a person but subsequently rebutted by proof to the contrary, that person may bring an action for damages or another remedy for any loss suffered.

(7) In dealing with an action under subsection (6), the court may make such order as appears to it to be just and equitable in the circumstances of the case.

(8) Any party to a conveyance shall, unless the contrary is proved, be presumed to have attained full age at the date of the conveyance.

(9) This Part does not apply to land held directly for a charitable purpose and not by way of a remainder.

[5.43] An 'instrument' under s 18 includes a will (s 3 of the 2009 Act).

A 'trust of land' is very widely defined and covers circumstances where the land is held on a bare trust, an express trust, an implied trust, a trust for sale, a constructive trust or a resulting trust.

[5.44] In the case of trusts of land under the Pt 4 of the 2009 Act, s 19(1) provides which persons are deemed to be trustees of the trust of land. The persons deemed to be trustees of such a trust are set out in s 19 of the 2009 Act.

[5.45] Where a trust of land is created by will, I consider that it is important that the will itself appoint trustees of the trust of land.

19 Trustees of land

[SLA 1882, ss 38, 39]

(1) The following persons are the trustees of a trust of land—

(a)   in the case of a strict settlement, where it—

     (i)   exists at the commencement of this Part, the tenant for life within the meaning of the Settled Land Act 1882 together with any trustees of the settlement for the purposes of that Act,

(ii)   is purported to be created after the commencement of this Part, the persons who would fall within paragraph (b) if the instrument creating it were deemed to be an instrument creating a trust of land,

(b)   in the case of a trust of land created expressly—

    (i)   any trustee nominated by the trust instrument, but, if there is no such person, then,

    (ii)   any person on whom the trust instrument confers a present or future power of sale of the land, or power of consent to or approval of the exercise of such a power of sale, but, if there is no such person, then,

    (iii)   any person who, under either the trust instrument or the general law of trusts, has power to appoint a trustee of the land, but, if there is no such person, then,

    (iv)   the settlor or, in the case of a trust created by will, the testator's personal representative or representatives,

(c)   in the case of land vested in a minor before the commencement of this Part or purporting so to vest after such commencement, the persons who would fall within paragraph (b) if the instrument vesting the land were deemed to be an instrument creating a trust of land,

(d)   in the case of land the subject of an implied, resulting, constructive or bare trust, the person in whom the legal title to the land is vested.

(2) For the purposes of—

(a)   subsection (1)(a)(ii) and (1)(c), the references in subsection (1)(b) to 'trustee' and 'trustee of the land' include a trustee of the settlement,

(b)   subsection (1)(b)(iii) a power to appoint a trustee includes a power to appoint where no previous appointment has been made.

(3) Nothing in this section affects the right of any person to obtain an order of the court appointing a trustee of land or vesting land in a person as trustee.

Henceforth, a will that creates any trust of land should appoint the executors or some other persons as trustees for the purposes of the 2009 Act.

The entire of Pt 4 of the 2009 Act is reproduced in **Appendix 12, Pt 1**.

[5.46] It must be borne in mind that the persons who are appointed both executors and trustees or who are trustees by reason of the 2009 Act are endowed with two separate capacities. The capacity of executor is quite separate and distinct from the capacity of trustee. Where persons are appointed executors and trustees, it will be necessary for them to vest in themselves the legal estate in their capacity as trustees in order for them to exercise the various trust powers that may have been conferred upon them in the will or by statute.

[5.47] Many wills use the terms 'executors' and 'trustees' interchangeably and while this is perfectly in order where the same persons are appointed to both capacities, it is preferable for the person drafting the will to keep the two capacities separate in his or her mind.

Where it arises, the testator should give consideration as to whether he or she wishes the same persons to act as executors and trustees.

[5.48] The 1965 Act confers a wide number of powers on personal representatives (including executors). These powers would not be capable of exercise by trustees. The trustees will have the powers available to them under the Trustee Act 1893, which are quite limited, eg, a trustee does not have a power of sale unless the power of sale is expressly conferred upon him or her. By contrast, a personal representative has a power of sale by virtue of s 50 of the Succession Act 1965.

[5.49] By virtue of s 20 of the 2009 Act, a trustee of a trust of land within the meaning of that Act 'has full power of an owner to convey *or otherwise deal with it* ... subject to the duties of a trustee, any restrictions imposed by any statute or court order relating to the land' (author's emphasis). This gives wide powers to such a trustee to deal with the land the subject of the trust, which will be in addition to any powers of the personal representative that may arise under the 1965 Act or given in the instrument creating the trust of land, in this context a will or codicil.

[5.50] I reiterate that the powers conferred by the 2009 Act only apply to trusts of land and do not apply to trusts of assets other than land. Because of this limitation of the 2009 Act, practitioners drafting wills should bear in mind the distinction between trusts of land under the 2009 Act and trusts relating to other assets.

[5.51] Where the trust powers given to trustees in the will are not, therefore, particularly extensive or the trustees are relying solely on their limited statutory powers, save in the case of a trust of land under the 2009 Act, it may be better for the property to remain vested in the executors in their capacity as such, so that the powers available to the executors by statute, in respect of the administration of the estate, remain available and are capable of being exercised, when necessary. This is something that must be judged in the light of the terms of the will and as the administration of the estate proceeds.

[5.52] If trustees are being appointed, where there is an express trust, it is important that as many powers as possible or as are advisable be conferred upon the trustees to enable them to administer the trust in accordance with the intention of the testator.

[5.53] Where the trust being set up by the will is a bare trust to hold property upon trust for named persons, until perhaps they attain a particular age, then it is probably preferable that the same persons be appointed executors and trustees.

[5.54] Where, however, a discretionary trust is being created, or a trust with a special power of appointment, it may be preferable that the trustees be persons with a personal knowledge of or link to the testator so that they can exercise a discretion in respect of the exercise of the power of appointment or distribution under the discretionary trust in the manner in which the testator may himself or herself have exercised it.

Trustees under the Settled Land Acts 1882–90 and trustees of trusts for land under the 2009 Act

[5.55] The differentiation between trustees of a trust and trustees of a settlement under the Settled Land Acts 1882–90 will, for many practitioners, often remained a mystery. Happily, since the 2009 Act matters have been simplified.

[5.56] Trustees under the Settled Land Acts 1882–90 did not need to have any estate or interest in the property the subject matter of the settlement. Their function was an entirely supervisory one, in that they supervised the tenant for life in the exercise of his or her powers under the Settled Land Acts 1882–90 and also received capital moneys on the sale of settled property and part of the income from the property where it is required by the Settled Land Acts 1882–90 to be held as capital moneys.

Where a settlement, therefore, was created by a will, it was important that trustees of the settlement would be appointed.

[5.57] Section 50(3) of the Succession Act 1965 provides as follows:

'Where land is settled by will and there are no trustees of the settlement, the personal representatives *proving the will*, shall for all purposes be deemed to be trustees of the settlement until trustees of the settlement are appointed, but a sole personal representative shall not be deemed to be a trustee for the purposes of the Settled Land Acts 1882–90 until at least one other trustee is appointed.' (*Author's emphasis.*)

The 1965 Act, therefore, contains a provision whereby two or more personal representatives shall be deemed to be trustees of the settlement created by a will if no trustees are expressly appointed. In order for the persons to be deemed to be trustees of the settlement, they had firstly to prove the will. Therefore, if there were two executors appointed in the will and one proved and the other, for whatever reason, did not, then the person proving the will was not deemed to be a trustee of the settlement. Furthermore, where there was only one executor appointed or one executor available to act, that person was not deemed to be a trustee of the settlement.

[5.58] The combined provisions of the Trustee Act 1893 and the Settled Land Acts 1882–90 provide that an existing trustee of the settlement or a legal personal representative of the last surviving trustee of the settlement may appoint a new trustee of the settlement, but in the absence of a trustee of the settlement, where, for example, there is only one executor acting or available to act, an application to court would be necessary in order to have a new trustee of the settlement appointed, with consequential expense.

[5.59] Where a trust or settlement of land is being created by will, it will now give rise to a trust of land under the 2009 Act and the will should appoint a trustee or trustees for that purpose. In the absence of such appointment, the provision of s 19 of the 2009 Act will operate to supply a trustee of the trust of land within the meaning of the 2009 Act (see above and **Appendix 12, Pt 1**). In the case of an older will, which has not been revised in line with the 2009 Act, the provisions of s 19 should be examined to see who might be the trustee(s) of the trust of land within the meaning of the 2009 Act.

[5.60] A settlement will be created by the will wherever there are successive interests in the land, eg, where property is left to one person for life, with the remainder over to another or others on the death of the life tenant. Even if there is no express provision for a remainder in the will, the remainder interest would pass to the persons entitled to the residue, so that there would still be a settlement created, and it would be necessary to have trustees of the settlement appointed.

Any will being revised from now on should take the provisions of Pt 4 of the Act into account.

[5.61] Prior to the 2009 Act, if land was left to a person who was a minor (under the age of 18 years), a settlement arose because the Settled Land Acts 1882–90 provide that property to which a minor is entitled is automatically deemed to be settled property within the meaning of the Settled Land Acts 1882–90.

[5.62] Section 18 of the 2009 Act now provides that land vested in a minor whether before or after the commencement of Pt 4 of the 2009 Act is deemed to be a trust of land and the provisions of Pt 4 of the Act apply accordingly.

Trustees under s 57 of the Succession Act 1965

[5.63] Section 57 of the 1965 Act provides as follows:

'(1) Where an infant is entitled to any share in the estate of a deceased person and there are no trustees of such share able and willing to act, the personal representatives of the deceased may appoint a trust corporation or any two or more persons (who may include the personal representatives or any of them or a trust corporation) to be trustees of such share for the infant and may execute such assurance or take such other action as may be necessary for vesting the share in the trustee so appointed. In default of appointment, the personal representatives shall be trustees for the purposes of this Section.

(2) On such appointment, the personal representatives, as such, shall be discharged from all further liability in respect of the property vested in the trustees so appointed.'

The section speaks for itself. It is useful where a person who is a minor (under the age of 18 years) becomes entitled to property in the will, to appoint the executors as trustees for the purposes of s 57. Such appointment under the will would not prevent them from appointing new or additional trustees under the section if they so desire.

This section operates independently of the provisions of Pt 4 of the 2009 Act and is broader in its application. The provisions of the 2009 Act only apply to land, s 57 of the 1965 Act applies to any kind of property both real and personal.

Trustee for the purposes of the Conveyancing Acts 1881–92

[5.64] Section 43 of the Conveyancing Act 1881 empowers trustees to use trust income towards the maintenance, education or benefit of beneficiaries under a trust, who are minors, in certain circumstances. Where the power is exercisable, the trustees may pay the maintenance to the parent of the minor or to his or her legal or testamentary guardian. Section 43 can be availed of where the property is held upon trust for the beneficiary, who is a minor, for life or for any greater interest, whether absolutely or contingently upon the minor attaining the age of 18 years or on the happening of any event before attaining that age, eg, marriage. If, on the other hand, the vesting of the interest is contingent upon the beneficiary reaching an age greater than 18 or on the happening of some event that cannot occur until he or she is over 18, the statutory power cannot be availed of by the trustees.

[5.65] In many instances, testators will feel that 18 is too young an age for a beneficiary to become entitled absolutely to trust property and, therefore, the will should confer a power to apply income for the maintenance, education and benefit of a beneficiary and to pay such maintenance to the beneficiary's legal or testamentary guardians. Where, however, the circumstances allowing the trustees to avail of the power in s 43 pertain, then the executors should be appointed trustees for the purposes of the Conveyancing Acts 1881–92.

Charging clause

[5.66] Where a trust corporation or a professional person is appointed as an executor, it is usual and indeed advisable that a charging clause be included in the will. A charging clause is a clause that will allow the professional person or trust corporation to charge fees for work done in connection with the administration of the estate. It is normal to provide that the executor or trustee may charge for work done, whether it is of a professional nature or not.

[5.67] Banks and other trust corporations will not act unless there is a clause allowing for their remuneration. The reason behind the clause is that an executor or trustee is not permitted to profit from his or her office as such and therefore in order for a professional person or trust corporation to charge fees for work done, it is necessary that the will make provision for this.

[5.68] One difficulty that arises in relation to charging clauses is that in England and Wales it has been held that they amount to a legacy and therefore if the person entitled to benefit under the charging clause or a spouse of that person acts as a witness to the will, then the charging clause shall be invalidated unless confirmed in a later codicil in respect of which the person benefiting under the charging clause or his or her spouse does not act as a witness. (See *In Re Pooley*[12] and *In Re Barker*[13] and s 82 of the Succession Act 1965.)

[5.69] Another consequence of the charging clause being treated as a legacy is that it will abate with other legacies if there are insufficient funds in the estate to pay all of the legacies. If there is a doubt, therefore, that the estate will be able to meet all of the legacies and the charging clause, a provision should be inserted in the charging clause to the effect that it is to have priority over other legacies and devises.

This state of affairs has been amended by statute in England and Wales and it is a reform that would be worth considering here.

Testamentary guardians

[5.70] Where the other parent in respect of the child of a testator is still living, that parent will be the legal guardian of the child in most instances. In the case of a non-marital child, it is necessary under the provisions of the Status of Children Act 1987 for

---

12.   *In Re Pooley* (1888) 40 Ch 1.
13.   *In Re Barker* (1886) 31 Ch D 665.

a father to apply to court to be appointed a guardian. The natural mother automatically has guardianship rights.

[5.71] Where, therefore, the other parent of the child belonging to the testator is dead or may not survive the testator or dies in a common calamity with the testator, or where the testator wishes there to be another person acting with the legal guardian, it is necessary to appoint a testamentary guardian. Under the provisions of the Guardianship of Infants Act 1964, such a person will act with the legal guardian (if any) in respect of the guardianship of the infant concerned.

[5.72] Section 7 of the Guardianship of Infants Act 1964 provides as follows:

'(1) The father of an infant may by deed or will appoint a person or persons to be guardian or guardians of the infant after his death.

(2) The mother of an infant may by deed or will appoint a person or persons to be guardian or guardians of the infant after her death.

(3) A testamentary guardian shall act jointly with the surviving parent of the infant, so long as the surviving parent remains alive, unless the surviving parent objects to his so acting.

(4) If the surviving parent so objects or if a testamentary guardian considers the surviving parent unfit to have custody of the infant, the testamentary guardian may apply to the court for an order under this section.

(5) The court may—

(a)   refuse to make an order (in which case the surviving parent shall remain sole guardian), or

(b)   make an order that the guardian shall act jointly with the surviving parent, or

(c)   make an order that he shall act as guardian of the infant to the exclusion, so far as the court thinks proper, of the surviving parent.

(6) In the case mentioned at paragraph (c) of sub-section (5), the court may make such order regarding the custody of the infant and the right of access to the infant of the surviving parent as the court thinks proper and the court may further order that the surviving parent shall pay the guardian or guardians, or any of them, towards the maintenance of the infant, such weekly or other periodical sum as, having regard to the means of the surviving parent, the court considers reasonable.

(7) A person under the age of [18 years] shall be entitled to appoint guardians by will, notwithstanding s 7 of the Wills Act, 1837.

(8) An appointment of a guardian by deed may be revoked by a subsequent deed or by will.'

If there is a dispute as between the legal guardian and the testamentary guardian, then the dispute shall be resolved by the court and, as in all guardianship matters, the primary concern of the court will be the welfare and well-being of the child.

[5.73] The executors and trustees may be appointed testamentary guardians or alternatively another person may be appointed testamentary guardian. Much will depend on the specific circumstances of the case. Where the executors and trustees are administering the estate for the benefit of the child of the testator during his or her minority, it is perhaps preferable that such person would also be testamentary guardian, rather than introduce an additional person into the equation. It may, however, be that the child has a particular affinity towards a relative, or the testator reposes greater trust in respect of a particular person concerning guardianship matters. That person may not wish to be an executor or trustee or may not have the acumen to act as such. In which circumstances an additional person might be appointed as a testamentary guardian.

Certainty

[5.74] Where the testator is appointing persons as executors or trustees or testamentary guardians, it is important that the provision appointing such persons be clear and certain and not be voided for uncertainty, eg, a provision in a will that appoints 'any one of my sons or daughters as my executor' would be void for uncertainty as it is not clear which person was intended by the deceased to act as executor (see *In Re Baylis Deceased;*[14] *In the Goods of Blackwell Deceased*[15]). If the testator wishes to appoint a person as an executor with an alternative appointment in certain events, then the events giving rise to such alternative appointment should be clearly stated in the will.

[5.75] However, in the case of *In Re Doran Deceased*[16] Herbert J upheld an appointment of two alternative office holders in a religious order as executors. A question arose as to whether the appointment was void for uncertainty. Herbert J upheld the appointment on the basis that the testatrix, a sister in religion, intended to appointed substitutional executors, one to act in the event that the other was not available or was unwilling to act. Herbert J, with characteristic linguistic erudition, had regard to the intention of the testatrix and the duty of the court to give effect to it.

It is, however, best to void any lack of clarity because it may give rise to litigation with attendant cost, delay and uncertainty.

---

14.   *In Re Baylis Deceased* (1862) 2 Swabey and Tristram 263.
15.   *In the Goods of Blackwell Deceased* (1877) 2 PD 72.
16.   *In Re Doran Deceased* [2000] 4 IR 551.

PART II: PRECEDENT CLAUSES

Appointment of sole executor

[5.76]

> I HEREBY APPOINT [my (insert relationship to testator, if any)] (name of executor), of (address) as sole executor of this my will.

Appointment of two or more persons as executors simpliciter

[5.77]

> I HEREBY APPOINT [my *(insert relationship to testator, if any)*] *(name of executor)*, of *(address)* and [my *(relationship to testator, if any)*] *(name of executor)*, of *(address)*, as executors of this my will.

Appointment of two or more persons as executors with additional provisions appointing them trustees under various statutes

[5.78]

> I HEREBY APPOINT [my *(insert relationship to testator, if any)*] *(name of executor)*, of *(address)* and [my *(relationship to testator, if any)*] *(name of executor)*, of *(address)*, as executors of this my will [and I APPOINT them as trustees for the purposes of Section 57 of the Succession Act 1965, the Conveyancing Acts 1881–92 and the Land and Conveyancing Law Reform Act 2009*].

> (*This appointment should only be included if there is a trust of land within the meaning of the 2009 Act arising under the will.)

Appointment of sole executor with a proviso that he or she survive the testator for a particular period, with an alternative appointment in certain circumstances

[5.79]

> I HEREBY APPOINT [my *(insert relationship to testator, if any)] (name of executor), of (address)* as sole executor of this my will, but if he/she does not survive me for a period of thirty days or dies without proving my will or renounces his/her rights to prove my will or is unable to act as my executor, then in those events, or any of them, I APPOINT [my *(relationship to testator, if any)] (name of executor), of (address)* as sole executor of this my will.

Appointment of two or more persons as executors and trustees, while also appointing them as trustees under various statutes

[5.80]

> I HEREBY APPOINT [my *(insert relationship to testator, if any)*] *(name of executor)*, of *(address)* and [my *(relationship to testator, if any)*] (name of executor), of *(address)*, as executors and trustees of this my will [and I

APPOINT them as trustees for the purposes of Section 57 of the Succession Act 1965, the Conveyancing Acts 1881–92 and the Land and Conveyancing Law Reform Act 2009*].

(*This appointment should only be included if there is a trust of land within the meaning of the 2009 Act arising under the will.)

Appointment of two or more persons as executors with two or more different persons being appointed as trustees

[5.81]

I HEREBY APPOINT [my (*insert relationship to testator, if any*)] (*name of executor*), of (*address*) and [my (*relationship to testator, if any*] (*name of executor*), of (*address*), as executors of this my will.

I HEREBY APPOINT [my (*relationship to testator, if any*)] (*name of trustee*), of (*address*) and [my (*relationship to testator, if any*)] (*name of trustee*), of (*address*), as trustees of the trust created by this my will and I HEREBY APPOINT [my (*relationship to testator, if any*)] (*name of trustee*), of (*address*) and [my (*relationship to testator, if any*)] (*name of trustee*), of (*address*), as trustees for the purposes of Section 57 of the Succession Act 1965, the Conveyancing Acts 1881–92 and the Land and Conveyancing Law Reform Act 2009*].

(*This appointment should only be included if there is a trust of land within the meaning of the 2009 Act arising under the will.)

Appointment of professional persons as executors and trustees with a charging clause

[5.82]

I HEREBY APPOINT my solicitor (*insert name*), of (*address*) and my accountant (*name*), of (*address*), as executors and trustees of the trust created by this my will [and I APPOINT them as trustees for the purposes of Section 57 of the Succession Act 1965, the Conveyancing Acts 1881–92 and the Land and Conveyancing Law Reform Act 2009*].

(*This appointment should only be included if there is a trust of land within the meaning of the 2009 Act arising under the will.)

Any of my executors or trustees who is engaged in a profession may charge fees for work done by him or her and/or his or her firm, whether or not the work is of a professional nature, on the same basis as if he or she were not one of my executors or trustees but employed to carry out work on behalf of my executors and trustees *and the fees so charged shall be paid in priority to all other bequests contained in this my will.**

(*Delete italicised section if not required.)

Appointment of a firm of solicitors as executors simpliciter (which will mean the partners for the time being at the time of the making of the will are the persons appointed)

[5.83]

> **I HEREBY APPOINT** the firm of solicitors practising under the style and title of *(insert name of firm),* of *(business address),* as executors and trustees of this my will [and **I APPOINT** the said firm as trustees for the purposes of Section 57 of the Succession Act 1965, the Conveyancing Acts 1881–92 and the Land and Conveyancing Law Reform Act 2009*].
>
> (*This appointment should only be included if there is a trust of land within the meaning of the 2009 Act arising under the will.)
>
> The said firm of solicitors shall be entitled to charge professional fees for work done by it or its members in connection with my estate, whether or not the work is of a professional nature, on the same basis as if the said firm were not my executors and trustees but employed to carry out work on their behalf *and the fees so charged shall be paid in priority to all other bequests under this my will.* *
>
> (*Delete italicised section if not required.)

Appointment of a firm of solicitors with a proviso that the persons entitled to prove the will are the partners of the said firm at the date of death of the testator

[5.84]

> **I HEREBY APPOINT** the firm of solicitors practising under the style and title of *(insert name of firm),* of *(business address),* as executors and trustees of this my will, provided always that it shall be the partners of the said firm at the date of my death who shall be entitled to prove the said will [and **I APPOINT** the said firm as trustees for the purposes of Section 57 of the Succession Act 1965, the Conveyancing Acts 1881–92 and the Land and Conveyancing Law Reform Act 2009*].
>
> (*This appointment should only be included if there is a trust of land within the meaning of the 2009 Act arising under the will.)
>
> The said firm of solicitors shall be entitled to charge professional fees for work done by it or its members in connection with my estate, whether or not the work is of a professional nature, on the same basis as if the said firm were not my executors and trustees but employed to carry out work on their behalf *and the fees so charged shall be paid in priority to all other bequests under this my will.* *
>
> (*Delete italicised section if not required.)

Appointment of a firm of solicitors with a proviso that the appointment shall include the partners of any firm which amalgamates with the firm appointed or any firm incorporating the firm appointed

[5.85]

I HEREBY APPOINT the firm of solicitors practising under the style and title of *(insert name of firm)*, of *(business address)*, as executors and trustees of this my will, provided always that it shall be the partners of the said firm at the date of my death who shall be entitled to prove the said will and in the event that the said firm shall amalgamate with another firm under its own or a new name, or the said firm shall be incorporated into another firm of solicitors, the amalgamated firm of solicitors or the firm of solicitors into which the said firm shall be incorporated, shall be deemed to be executors and trustees of this my will. [**I APPOINT** the said firm as trustees for the purposes of Section 57 of the Succession Act 1965, the Conveyancing Acts 1881–92 and the Land and Conveyancing Law Reform Act 2009*].

(*This appointment should only be included if there is a trust of land within the meaning of the 2009 Act arising under the will.)

The said firm of solicitors shall be entitled to charge professional fees for work done by it or its members in connection with my estate, whether or not the work is of a professional nature, on the same basis as if the said firm were not my executors and trustees but employed to carry out work on their behalf *and the fees so charged shall be paid in priority to all other bequests under this my will.*

(*Delete italicised section if not required.)

Appointment of named partners in a firm as executors

[5.86]

I HEREBY APPOINT *(insert name)* and *(name)* and *(name)*, partners in the firm of solicitors practising under the style and title of *(name of firm)*, of *(business address)*, as executors and trustees of this my will [and **I APPOINT** the said partners as trustees for the purposes of Section 57 of the Succession Act 1965, the Conveyancing Acts 1881–92 and the Land and Conveyancing Law Reform Act 2009*] provided always that if any of the said persons is no longer a partner of the said firm of solicitors at the date of my death, then the appointment of executors under this my will shall be construed as if that person was omitted from the executors appointed of this my will.

(*This appointment should only be included if there is a trust of land within the meaning of the 2009 Act arising under the will.)

Any of my executors who acts in relation to my will shall be entitled to charge professional fees for work done by them in connection with my estate, whether or not the work is of a professional nature, on the same basis as if the said partners were not my executors and trustees but employed to carry out work on their behalf *and the fees so charged shall be paid in priority to all other bequests under this my will.* *

(*Delete italicised section if not required.)

Appointment of a trust corporation as executor

[5.87] Where a trust corporation is being appointed, it will normally be a bank or some other such entity. Trust corporations who are willing to act as executors will usually have published their conditions of appointment and charges; before appointing a trust corporation as an executor, it is worthwhile obtaining details of its conditions of appointment and its charges and advising the testator of these. It would also be prudent to submit a draft of the will to the trust corporation for its perusal and also to give the trust corporation some details of the likely estate of the testator, so that the trust corporation can indicate whether or not it wishes to become involved. This is to avoid the possibility of the trust corporation being appointed and then being unwilling to act when the testator dies, with the result that perhaps there is no executor appointed in the will.

> **I HEREBY APPOINT** (*insert name of trust corporation – be sure to name it by its correct corporate name, eg, Bank of Ireland is 'the Governor and Company of the Bank of Ireland'*) having its (*head*) registered office at (*address*), as executor and trustee of this my will.
>
> The conditions upon which *(name of trust corporation)* acts as executor and trustee last published before the date of this will shall apply to its appointment and the said trust corporation shall be remunerated in accordance with the scale for such remuneration current at the date of my death and as may be varied from time to time in accordance with the aforesaid conditions during the course of the administration of my estate and any trust arising under this my will.

Appointment of a trust corporation as executor with one other person where there is a settlement created by the will and an additional trustee is required for the purposes of the Settled Land Acts 1882–90 by virtue of the provisions of s 50(3) of the Succession Act 1965 or in case the trust corporation declines to act

[5.88]

> **I HEREBY APPOINT** (*insert name of trust corporation*) having its (*head*) registered office at (*address*) and (*name of additional executor, which may be a corporation associated with the trust corporation but not a trust corporation itself*), of [or, having its (*head*) registered office at] (*address*) as executors and trustees of this my will [and **I APPOINT** them as trustees for the purposes of Section 57 of the Succession Act 1965, the Conveyancing Acts 1881–92 and the Land and Conveyancing Law Reform Act 2009*].
>
> (*This appointment should only be included if there is a trust of land within the meaning of the 2009 Act arising under the will.)
>
> The conditions upon which *(name of trust corporation)* acts as executor and trustee last published before the date of this will shall apply to its appointment

and the said trust corporation shall be remunerated in accordance with the scale for such remuneration current at the date of my death and as may be varied from time to time in accordance with the aforesaid conditions during the course of the administration of my estate and any trust arising under this my will.

Appointment of two persons as executors, one of whom is a minor

[5.89]

I HEREBY APPOINT [my (*insert relationship to testator, if any*)] (*name of executor*), of (*address*) and [my (*relationship to testator, if any*)] (*name of executor*), of (*address*), as executors and trustees of this my will provided always that the said (*name of minor*) should only act when he/she attains the age of eighteen years and in the meantime the said (*name of adult executor*) shall be entitled to act as sole executor of this my will.

Appointment of a testamentary guardian

[5.90]

I HEREBY APPOINT *(insert name), of (address)* as testamentary guardian of any of my children who are under the age of eighteen at the date of my death.

Appointment of testamentary guardians

[5.91]

I HEREBY APPOINT *(insert name), of (address)* and *(name), of (address)* as testamentary guardians of any of my children who are under the age of eighteen at the date of my death.

Appointment of testamentary guardians to take effect only where the other parent of the testator's children predeceases the testator

[5.92]

In the event that the mother/father of my children who are under the age of eighteen years has predeceased me or has died in common calamity with me, **I APPOINT** *(insert name), of (address)* and *(name), of (address)* as guardians of my children who are under the age of eighteen years at the date of my death.

Power to appoint additional testamentary guardians

[5.93]

The father/mother of my children under the age of eighteen years at the date of my death shall have power to appoint new or additional testamentary guardians of my said children and on the death of the parent of my children who are under the age of eighteen years, the testamentary guardian appointed by this my will shall have the power to appoint new or additional testamentary guardians in respect of my children who are under the age of eighteen years at the date of my death.

Chapter 6

LEGACIES

PART I: COMMENTARY

[6.01] I have decided to deal with bequests of personal property and real property in separate chapters so as to assist a practitioner in distinguishing between the two types of property. Since the passing of the Succession Act 1965, real and personal estate vest on death, in the case of a will, in the executors and in the case of intestacy, or where there is a will with no executor appointed or where the executors appointed have died, in the President of the High Court.

[6.02] The Succession Act 1965 abolished the distinctions between the devolution of real and personal estate, and abolished the canons of descent and the concept of the heir-at-law and escheat in relation to real property. Notwithstanding this, I think that it is useful for the person drafting a will to distinguish in his or her mind the difference between real and personal property, to consider the dispositive provisions in respect of each type of property and to take instructions from the testator accordingly. This will avoid difficulties concerning, for example, the bequest of the dwelling house of the testator and the contents of the dwelling house. In many instances, the testator may wish the same beneficiary or beneficiaries to have both, but in other cases the testator may wish to leave specific items to specific persons, or may wish to leave the house to one person while leaving the contents to a different beneficiary or series of beneficiaries. It is important that the person drafting the will does his or her best to take full and complete instructions in relation to all of the testator's estate so that the will can be as comprehensive as possible and achieve the intentions of the testator. That, after all, is the ultimate goal and one that has been repeatedly stated by courts of construction; if possible the achievement of what the testator intended is the paramount consideration.

Types of legacy

[6.03] There are three types of legacy of personal property: general, specific and demonstrative legacies.

(a) General legacy

[6.04] A general legacy normally takes the form of a pecuniary legacy which is payable out of the testator's general estate. No particular fund is earmarked for the legacy. A fund must be retained out of the residue of the estate of the testator to meet the pecuniary legacies. If the estate is insufficient to meet the pecuniary legacies, then they will abate on a *pro rata* basis or entirely, as the case may be.

A general legacy may also take the form of an item of personal property which is not specified, eg, a legacy of a painting without specifying which painting from the testator's collection.

(b) Specific legacy

[6.05] A specific legacy constitutes a legacy of a specific item of personal property. It may be the proceeds of a specified bank account, shares in a particular company, securities held by the deceased, particular items of furniture, jewellery, works of art and so on. Care should be taken to describe the subject matter of the specific legacy as precisely as possible.

A specific legacy will only abate after the residue and the general legacies have abated in full, and once again, if the specific legacies are abating, they will abate on a *pro rata* basis, so that the various items would have to be independently valued and they would then abate *pro rata*.

Specific legacies are liable to adeem. This is a fate that cannot befall a general legacy: either there will be funds to meet a general legacy or there will not. If, however, there is a specific legacy of a particular item and that item is not available at the death of the testator, then the legacy will be adeemed. Generally speaking, it will not matter that the particular item was replaced with a similar item; the legatee will lose the benefit of the specific legacy. In order to avoid ademption in the case of bequest of moneys or investments, therefore, it is sometimes better to try to avoid specific pecuniary legacies and instead to utilise general or demonstrative legacies in the case of bequests of money.

(c) Demonstrative legacy

[6.06] A demonstrative legacy is where there is a particular fund designated for the payment of the legacy concerned, eg '1,000.00 euro from my account with the Governor and Company of the Bank of Ireland'. This type of legacy is a hybrid of the specific and general legacies. For the purposes of abatement, it is treated as a specific legacy and will not abate with the general pecuniary legacies. On the other hand, for the purposes of ademption, it is treated as a general legacy and will still be payable out of the testator's general estate, even though the particular fund designated for its payment does not exist at the date of death of the testator.

The doctrine of lapse

[6.07] The doctrine of lapse applies to both legacies and devises and it arises (subject to exceptions) where a beneficiary predeceases the testator or where the beneficiary dies in circumstances rendering it impossible to decide whether the testator or the beneficiary survived each other, eg, where the testator and the beneficiary both die in a road traffic accident or other calamity.

[6.08] Section 5 of the Succession Act 1965 deals with *commorientes* under Irish law. Under the section, where two or more persons have died in circumstances rendering it uncertain which of them survived the other or others, then for the purpose of distribution of the estate of any of them, they shall all be deemed to have died simultaneously. In the case of *In the estates of Timothy Kennedy and Teresa Kennedy Deceased,*[1] Kearns J (as he then was) decided that 'uncertainty' can only be displaced with 'certainty'. The

---

1.   *In the estates of Timothy Kennedy and Teresa Kennedy Deceased* [2000] 2 IR 571.

evidence adduced to displace the presumption in s 5 must yield certainty that one person survived the other.

|6.09| In recent years, since the publication of the first edition, there has been a distressing number of cases where persons die in suicide pacts. In such a case, it may not be possible to say which of the persons survived. Additionally, there have been cases where spouses or a family are killed by one member of the marriage or family. In such cases, the perpetrator, who may have killed him or herself, in the overall tragedy, may demonstrably be the survivor for the purpose of s 5. In such a case, if the perpetrator can be shown to have been guilty of the murder or manslaughter of his or her victims, he or she will be unworthy to succeed. In such cases, there will be no criminal trial if the perpetrator is deceased and the civil court may have to decide if the word 'guilty' in s 120 of the 1965 Act connotes a criminal conviction or whether the perpetrator could be found 'guilty' on the civil standard of the balance of probability so that his or her estate does not profit from his or her crime.

The effect of a simultaneous death is that the beneficiary under the testator's will shall be treated as if he or she had predeceased the testator.

Exceptions to the doctrine of lapse

|6.10| Exceptions to the doctrine include:

*   Section 98 of the Succession Act 1965;

*   Bequest in discharge of legal or moral obligation;

*   Bequest to person on trust for another;

*   Alternative dispositions.

Section 98 of the Succession Act 1965

|6.11| There is one statutory exception to the doctrine of lapse, which is often misunderstood. That exception is provided by s 98 of the Succession Act 1965. The section provides:

> 'Where a person, being a child *or other issue* of the testator to whom any property is given (whether by devise or bequest or by the exercise by will of any power of appointment, and whether as a gift to that person as an individual or as a member of a class) for any estate or interest not determinable at or before the death of that person, dies in the lifetime of the testator *leaving issue*, and any such issue of that person is living at the time of death of the testator, the gift shall not lapse, but *shall take effect as if the death of that person had happened immediately after the death of the testator*, unless a contrary intention appears from the will.' (*Author's emphasis*.)

This section deserves specific analysis in order to be understood:

(a)   the gift in the will must be to a child or other issue of the testator, that is to say to a child, grandchild or other descendant;

(b)   the section applies to all gifts under the will, whether it be a legacy, a devise or a class gift;

(c)   the trigger for the operation of s 98 is that the child, grandchild or other descendant of the testator predeceases the testator leaving issue, that is to say a child, grandchild or other descendant.

[6.12] It is important to note, however, that the gift given by the testator to the beneficiary under the will who predeceases him or her does not pass to his or her child, grandchild or other descendant, as would be the case where the child predeceases the deceased in the case of an intestacy. Instead, the bequest takes effect as if the beneficiary had survived the testator and died immediately after him or her.

[6.13] This means that the benefit conferred on the original beneficiary, who is a child, grandchild or other descendant of the testator, forms part of his or her estate and is distributed according to his or her will or intestacy as the case may be.

[6.14] If, therefore, the original beneficiary makes a will leaving everything to his or her spouse, then the benefit in the testator's will shall pass to the spouse. The issue will have no interest in the benefit. Similarly, if the original beneficiary dies intestate leaving a spouse and children, the benefit will pass two-thirds to the spouse and one-third to the children.

[6.15] The section yields to a contrary intention expressed in the will of the testator and, therefore, the operation of the section can be avoided. If, therefore, a testator wishes to leave property to a son or daughter and to provide that in the event that the son or daughter predeceases him or her, the property is to pass to the son's or daughter's children, then this should be specifically stated in the will so as to show a contrary intention to avoid the operation of s 98.

Other exceptions to the doctrine of lapse

[6.16]

(1)   Where the legacy is left in discharge of some legal or moral obligation on the part of the testator, then the subject matter of the legacy will still be payable to the estate of the beneficiary who predeceases him or her.

(2)   Further, where the legacy is left to a particular person, but on trust for the benefit of another, and the trustee dies prior to the testator, the bequest will not lapse but will pass to the person intended to take the benefit, provided of course that he or she survives the testator.

(3)   Inclusion in the will of an alternative disposition in the event that the particular beneficiary predeceases the testator.

Care should be taken, therefore, in drafting a will to ascertain from the testator what his or her intentions would be in the event of a particular beneficiary predeceasing the testator.

Class gifts

[6.17] The operation of the doctrine of lapse to class gifts also falls to be considered. As can be seen from s 98, its provisions will apply to the lapse of a class gift, except where the gift is to a class of persons as joint tenants, in which case where a beneficiary predeceases the testator, other members of the class will take the benefit of the gift as joint tenants.

[6.18] Where, however a gift is left to a class in equal or unequal shares so that they take as tenants in common, then unless there is a contrary intention expressed in the will, where any member of the class is issue of the testator, then the provisions of s 98 will apply to the share of that member of the class who predeceases the testator, but in all other instances where a class gift is left to persons as tenants in common and one of their number predeceases the testator, then the share of that person will lapse and fall into the residue (see s 91 of the Succession Act 1965), and in the event that the class gift is a residuary gift, it will give rise to a partial intestacy.

Mortgages and charges affecting property bequeathed

[6.19] Section 47 of the Succession Act 1965 provides as follows:

'(1) Where a person dies possessed of, or entitled to, or, under a general power of appointment, by his will disposes of, an interest in property, which at the time of his death is charged with the payment of money, whether by way of legal or equitable mortgage or charge or otherwise (including a lien for unpaid purchase money), and the deceased person has not by will, deed or other document signified a contrary or other intention, the interest so charged shall, as between different persons claiming through the deceased person, be primarily liable for the payment of the charge; and every part of the said interest, according to its value, shall bear a proportionate part of the charge on the whole thereof.

(2) Such contrary or other intention shall *not* be deemed to be signified—

(a)   By a general direction for the payment of debts or of all the debts of the testator out of his estate or any part thereof, or

(b)   By a charge of debts upon any such estate,

unless such intention is further signified by words expressly or by necessary implication referring to all or some part of the charge.

(3) Nothing in this Section affects the right of a person entitled to the charge to obtain payment or satisfaction thereof either out of the other assets of the deceased or otherwise.' (*Author's emphasis.*)

[6.20] Where, therefore, a testator is disposing of property, which is the subject of a charge or mortgage of any type, including a lien for unpaid purchase money, then unless the will otherwise provides, the property bequeathed will bear the charge or mortgage.

[6.21] As most wills contain a general direction to the executors for the payment of debts out of the testator's estate, such a statement in a will shall not nullify the provisions of s 47 and be deemed to be a contrary intention. Therefore, where a testator wishes a charge on property to be borne out of the residue of his or her estate or out of some other property, the will must specifically and clearly state this.

[6.22] In the context of personal property, regard should be had as to whether the testator owns the personal property being bequeathed outright, or whether the property is subject to perhaps a hire purchase agreement or other consumer credit arrangement. If the property is held subject to such an arrangement, regard should be had to the hire purchase or consumer credit agreement under which the property has been purchased and provisions relating to the position under the agreement on the death of the testator should be ascertained.

[6.23] In many instances, the legal personal representative will be able to take over the responsibilities of the testator on death and will be able to discharge the outstanding balance and pass the subject property to the beneficiary, but where a property is subject to such agreement, it is perhaps advisable that the bequest specify that the property passing to the beneficiary is subject to the terms of the hire purchase or credit sale agreement on the basis that whatever the strict legal interpretation of the agreement is, the person financing the purchase of the property will be happy to transfer ownership of the property to the beneficiary, once payment for the goods has been made.

Discretionary trusts

[6.24] While it is perhaps more usual for a testator to create a discretionary trust with regard to his or her residuary estate, it is possible for a testator to create a residuary trust over a fund and to direct the executors and trustees to distribute the fund as they in their absolute discretion shall think fit. This may assist, for example, where a testator wishes to make provision for grandchildren, perhaps for their education, or for his or her own children where the children are of a very young age when the will is being drawn up. The bequest can state the purpose for which the fund is being set up or it can be left to the trustees in a general way to be distributed amongst the testator's children. But where the bequest is left in a general way and the testator has views as to how the fund might be utilised, it would be useful for the testator to leave with his or her will a letter of wishes, which, while not binding upon the executors and trustees, will give them guidance as to how the testator intends that the property would be utilised.

[6.25] Care should be taken in the definition of the class of persons to benefit from the trust, and we saw in **Ch 2** that where a testator described a person to whom he was giving a pecuniary legacy as his 'daughter', though she was not his daughter, she was held entitled to be considered as a beneficiary of a discretionary trust the beneficiaries of which were, *inter alia,* his children. The court held that the testator having chosen his own 'lexicon' for his will could not describe the person in one part of the will as his daughter and then by implication exclude her from the class of his 'children'. He would have had to do so explicitly. (See *Crawford and anor v Lawless and Others.*[2])

Gifts to charity

[6.26] It is quite common for Irish testators to decide to leave either pecuniary legacies or gifts of specific items of personal property (and indeed realty) to charity. A number of difficulties in this regard should be borne in mind.

At the time of writing the provisions of the Charities Act 2009, have not yet been brought into force but nevertheless with an eye to the future persons drafting wills

---

2.   *Crawford and anor v Lawless and Others* [2002] IR 416.

should have regard to its provisions.The Relevant portions of the Act are set out in **Appendix 13**.

[6.27] The person drafting the will should take great care to describe the charity properly so that the property passes to the intended beneficiary. Care should be taken in so far as possible to obtain the correct name of the charitable institution concerned and to describe it by reference to its address. In certain instances, particular charities may have branches in different localities and if the testator intends a branch in a particular locality to benefit, then the person drafting the will should take care to ensure that the particular local branch is referred to. For example the Society of St Vincent de Paul has branches, known as conferences, all over Ireland. It may well be that the testator intends that the society generally would benefit, but if he or she intends a particular conference close to his or her locality to benefit, then care should be taken to ensure that the will explicitly states this. Similarly, the Samaritans organisation has a number of branches throughout the country. If the testator intends that, say, the Limerick branch of the Samaritans should benefit, rather than the Samaritan organisation nationally throughout Ireland, care should be taken to ensure that the will explicitly states this.

[6.28] Many charitable organisations will not be incorporated and therefore a gift to the charity is in fact a gift to all the members of the charity. To obviate the difficulty concerning receipts, it is important that the bequest would contain a statement to the effect that the receipt of the treasurer or some other proper officer of the charity would be sufficient discharge to the executors in respect of the payment of the legacy.

[6.29] In Ireland, gifts for the celebration of Masses for the repose of the soul of the testator or his or her family are quite common. It used to be the case that the testator would leave a sum of money to perhaps a particular religious order or priest for the saying of Masses and the testator would specify the honorarium for each Mass. This practice should now be discouraged and instead the sum of money should be left to the particular religious order or priest for the saying of Masses generally for the repose of the soul of the testator or other persons as the testator may designate, without specifying an *honorarium* in respect of the Masses.

[6.30] Where the testator requires Masses to be said for the repose of his or her soul or other named persons, it is perhaps better that the bequest be to a religious order or parish of priests so that there will be some degree of continuity. If the bequest is to a particular priest for the purpose of saying Masses and the priest predeceases the testator, administrative difficulties could ensue concerning the bequest and it may be necessary to try to obtain a substitute priest to celebrate the Masses. Generally speaking, a charitable legacy will not be subject to the doctrine of lapse.

Where there is a gift to a clergy person, the gift should specify whether it is of a charitable nature or whether the gift is to the clergy person personally.

[6.31] Where the gift is of the nature whereby a fund is to be applied for a particular purpose, care should be taken in the following:

1. Ensure that the purpose referred to is within the legal definition of a charitable purpose. This will be changed in due course by s 3 of the Charities Act 2009, though the Act largely codifies what case law laid down over the years. While

the law remains as it is until the Charities Act 2009 becomes operative by Ministerial Order, nevertheless, practitioners should have regard to its provisions to ensure that any will drafted now will not contravene the 2009 Act. In Keane, *Equity and Trusts in the Republic of Ireland* (2nd edn, Bloomsbury Professional, 2011), the learned author notes at para [11.02]:

'The Act, however, while it gives statutory effect to many of the principles laid down by the Courts for the purpose of determining what constitutes a charity in law, does not itself provide a comprehensive definition of a legal charity.'

As matters stand in Ireland, under the Statute of Charles I (10 Chas 1 Sess 3 c 1) by reference to *Commissioners for Special Purposes of Income Tax v Pemsel* (*Pemsel's* case),[3] a charitable purpose is one that is for:

(i)   the advancement of religion;

(ii)   the relief of poverty;

(iii)   the advancement of education;

(iv)   the advancement of other purposes beneficial to the community at large.

The Charities Act 2009, retains these classifications but it has provisions which refine the law in relation to gifts for the advancement of religion (s 3(5), (6) and (10)) and what constitutes a public benefit (s 3(2), (3) and (4) and it gives examples of cases where gifts would be deemed of benefit to the community at large (s 3(11)).

Under the law as it stands (and probably after the coming into operation of The Charities Act 2009) a gift therefore for the education of the testator's children and grandchildren would not be charitable because the class of persons entitled to benefit has a direct connection with the testator and is not sufficiently wide to confer a benefit on the community at large. A gift however for the education of necessitous persons in a particular parish or district where the testator resides would be charitable because the class of persons would be sufficiently wide and those persons have no direct connection with the testator and, as well as the advancement of education, there is also an intention to relieve poverty.

The importance of this is that should the purpose for which the gift is intended fail, be fulfilled, or be rendered impracticable, it may be necessary to apply for the approval of a cy pres scheme to the Commissioners of Charitable Donations and Bequests in Ireland. It is a necessary prerequisite that the gift be a charitable one before the *cy pres* jurisdiction can be invoked. The Commissioners now have unlimited jurisdiction in such matters though with a discretion to refer any matter to the court. (see s 16 in Pt 2 of the Social Welfare (Miscellaneous Provisions) Act 2002 and the Second Schedule of the Act).

2.   In formulating the purpose for which the fund is to be applied, care should also be taken to ensure that a general charitable intention is expressed by the testator, so that if necessary the cy pres jurisdiction of the Commissioners of Charitable Donations and Bequests in Ireland can be invoked and applied. *Marren v*

---

3.   *Commissioners for Special Purposes of Income Tax v Pemsel* [1891] AC 531.

Masonic Havens Limited[4] the testatrix left the residue of her estate to the 'Committee for the time being of the Haven Blackrock for the charitable purposes of that body'. While the court had difficulty identifying the actual beneficiary because there was no charity know as The Haven, Blackrock, the Court nevertheless found that a general charitable intent was found to exist.

3.   If possible, and if time permits, where the charitable legacy is to be given to a particular office holder such as a bishop or to an organisation to be applied for a *particular* purpose, as specified by the testator, the views of the recipient might be sought as to the practicality of the purpose being suggested by the testator and in case the purpose or objective being specified by the testator would be outside the scope of the particular charitable organisation concerned.

4.   Care should also be taken to ensure that the charitable organisation intended to be benefited exists. A gift to the Cats and Dogs Home in Dublin, for example, would no longer be of practical effect because the Cats and Dogs Home no longer exists. Constructional difficulties could therefore arise as to whether the gift was intended to go to the ISPCA or the DSPCA, or whether the gift should fail altogether.

[6.32] Care should also be taken to try to avoid the result in the case of In *Re Julian*.[5] In that case, the testatrix was of the Protestant faith and she wished to confer a benefit on the Protestant Mission for Seamen. The Roman Catholic institution for seamen and the Protestant institution for seamen bore similar names, but they carried on their business at different addresses. The person drafting the will, while correctly describing the name of the Protestant institution, inserted the address of the Catholic institution. When the will came to be construed, the court refused to admit extrinsic evidence to show that the testatrix would have intended to benefit the Protestant institution rather than the Catholic institution, because the will was clear on its face.

The case predated the enactment of s 90 of the Succession Act 1965, which widened the circumstances in which extrinsic evidence is admissible. To avoid any lack of certainty, care should be taken in the first instance to properly describe the institution intended to receive the benefit by the testator. By virtue of s 90 and the decisions in *Rowe v Law*[6] and *O'Connell and Another v Governor and Company of the Bank of Ireland and Another*,[7] the case of *In Re Julian* would be decided differently today.

[6.33] In the case of *Marren v Masonic Havens Limited*[8] the Court found a general charitable intent on the part of the testatrix in a relation to her residuary bequest but found an ambiguity in relation to the identity of the beneficiary. The court admitted extrinsic evidence under s 90 to ascertain the intention of the testatrix and resolve the ambiguity. The husband of the testatrix was involved with Masonic Havens Limited,

---

4.   *Marren v Masonic Havens Limited* [2011] IEHC 525.

5.   *Re Julian* [1950] IR 57.

6.   *Rowe v Law* [1978] IR 55.

7.   *O'Connell and Another v Governor and Company of the Bank of Ireland and Another* (April 1998, unreported) SC.

8.   *Marren v Masonic Havens Limited* [2011] IEHC 525.

which provided accommodation for the elderly and raised funds from friends of the Masonic Order.

Identification of beneficiaries

[6.34] Care should be taken to properly identify any beneficiary in a will. This may seem to state the obvious but difficulties have arisen and the identity of witnesses called into question.

In certain families in Ireland, it is common to find a number of generations bearing the same name. Patrick Murphy may have a son called Patrick Murphy who in turn may have a son called Patrick Murphy. It would be quite possible for a testator to have two nephews or nieces bearing the same name. Where possible, therefore, reference should be made to the precise relationship between the testator and the beneficiary, and the beneficiary might also be identified by reference to his or her address, eg 'my niece Mary Murphy of *(address)*, daughter of my sister Breda Murphy'.

In *Thornton v Timlin*,[9] Laffoy J was faced with a situation where the beneficiaries were inadequately described and the bequest failed for uncertainty. There was a bequest to 'Mayo County Council (Ballina Area) Workers'. Evidence from colleagues of the deceased as to his intention was ruled inadmissible under s 90 of the 1965 Act, because it did not 'show what the intention was in the particular context'. The evidence merely 'reflected the opinion and belief of the witnesses'. To construe the will on the basis of the evidence tendered would have been to 're-write' the will, which the court was not permitted to do. Reluctantly, the court had to hold that the bequest was void for uncertainty.

Identifying specific chattels

[6.35] Some testators may have a large number of specific chattels, which they may wish to leave to particular beneficiaries. Any item not specifically disposed of in the will will form part of the residuary estate, unless, for example, the dwelling house of the testator is left with all contents therein to particular persons, in which case many of the personal items of the testator would probably pass under the bequest of household contents.

Where the testator requires to leave individual items specifically to named beneficiaries, great care should be taken to describe the items concerned as precisely as possible.

Further, insofar as is possible, an effort should be made to maintain the integrity of the will as a complete document by including in the will all of the specific bequests that the testator wishes to make. It is possible to bequeath personal items by reference to a list or inventory drawn up by the testator, but in such an instance, in order for the list to be incorporated into the will, it must:

(a)   be specifically identified in the will; and

(b)   be in existence at the time the will is executed.

---

9.   *Thornton v Timlin* [2012] IEHC 239.

It is not competent for a testator to make his or her will by reference to a list that is subsequently prepared by him or her.

[6.36] It is always preferable that one document should deal with all of the dispositive provisions intended by the testator. The difficulty with a list that is to be incorporated in the will is that if the list contains any alterations or amendments, the question might arise as to whether the alteration or amendment was made prior to the will being executed, and as attesting witnesses may not have seen the list, they may not be in a position to state whether or not the amendments to the list were made prior to or after execution of the will. Where a list is being used, it is preferable that an affidavit be sworn by the witnesses or testator identifying the list and stating that the list was in existence at the time the will was executed.

Co-ownership and words of severance

[6.37] The importance of this topic will be more apparent when dealing with bequests of real property and therefore it is dealt with in greater detail in **Ch 7**.

If money or a specific chattel is left to a number of beneficiaries without the inclusion of words of severance, they will take the property as joint tenants and the right of survivorship will, therefore, apply. If, on the other hand, words of severance, eg, 'amongst', 'between', 'equally', 'in equal shares', 'share and share alike', are included or the words attaching to the bequest indicate that the beneficiaries are to take in unequal shares, then the bequest will fall to the beneficiaries as tenants in common. The significance of the difference should be explained to testators.

Vested and contingent bequests

[6.38] See **Ch 7** under vested and contingent devises, where the same considerations apply. It is less likely, however, that the testator will wish to attach conditions to legacies.

PART II: PRECEDENT CLAUSES

Pecuniary legacies

Simple general pecuniary legacy

[6.39]

> **I GIVE** the sum of € (*insert amount in figures and words*), to [my (*relationship to testator, if any*)] (*name*), of (*address*).

Simple pecuniary legacy with alternative provision in the event that the beneficiary predeceases the testator

[6.40]

> **I GIVE** the sum of € (*insert amount in figures and words*), to [my *(relationship to testator, if any)*] *(name)*, of *(address)*. In the event that the said *(name)* predeceases me, **I GIVE** the said sum to *(name)*, of *(address)* **or** to such of his/her children as may be living at the date of my death.

Simple pecuniary legacy to a child of the testator

[6.41]

> **I GIVE** the sum of € (*insert amount in figures and words*), to my daughter (*name*), of (*address*).

> (*Note*: if this beneficiary were to predecease the testator *leaving issue*, then the provisions of s 98 of the Succession Act 1965 would apply and the bequest would form part of the beneficiary's estate to be distributed in accordance with her will or intestacy, as the case may be.)

Simple pecuniary legacy to a child of the testator with provision that the gift shall pass to the children of the original beneficiary, should the original beneficiary predecease the testator

[6.42]

> **I GIVE** the sum of € *(insert amount in figures and words)*, to my son *(name)*, of *(address)*, but in the event that he shall predecease me, **I DIRECT** that the said sum shall be payable to his children, as are living at the date of my death in equal shares.

Pecuniary legacy – specific

[6.43]

> **I GIVE** to [my *(insert relationship to testator, if any)*] *(name)*, of *(address)* all my money on deposit with the EBS Building Society at the date of my death.

> (*Note*: this bequest would be subject to the doctrine of ademption if the testator does not have an account with the EBS Building Society at the date of his or her death. It is advisable that pecuniary legacies be left in a general way.)

Pecuniary legacy – demonstrative

[6.44]

> I GIVE the sum of € *(insert amount in figures and words)*, to [my *(relationship to testator, if any)*] *(name)*, of *(address)*, which said sum is to be paid out of my account, number *(account number)*, with the Governor and Company of the Bank of Ireland, at its branch at *(address of branch)*.

> *(Note:* this legacy will not be subject to the doctrine of ademption should the testator not have an account with the Governor and Company of the Bank of Ireland at the specified branch at the date of his or her death; the legacy will still be payable out of the testator's general estate. Further it will be treated as a specific legacy in the case of an abatement of general pecuniary legacies.)

Joint general pecuniary legacy

[6.45]

> I GIVE the sum of € *(insert amount in figures and words)*, to *(name)*, of *(address)* and *(name)*, of *(address)*, jointly.

> *(Note:* in the event that one of the beneficiaries predeceases the deceased, then the other beneficiary will take the entire amount.)

Pecuniary legacy – alternative form with provision for accruer

[6.46]

> I GIVE the sum of €2,000.00 (Two Thousand euro) to each of *(insert name)*, of *(address)* and *(name)*, of *(address)*, but if either of them dies before me, I GIVE the sum of €4,000.00 (Four Thousand euro) to the survivor of them.

Legacy to two or more persons as tenants in common

[6.47]

> I GIVE the sum of € (insert amount in figures and words) to *(name)*, of *(address)* and *(name)*, of *(address)* and *(name)*, of *(address)* in equal shares.

> *(Note:* in this bequest, if any of the beneficiaries were to predecease the testator, the bequest would lapse and fall into the residue of the estate of the testator — see s 91 of the Succession Act 1965 – except where the beneficiary was a child of the testator and died leaving issue, in which case s 98 of the Succession Act 1965 would apply and the share of that beneficiary would fall into his or her estate to be distributed in accordance with his or her will or on intestacy as the case may be. If the testator requires, the share of any of these beneficiaries would be disposed of in a different way or would not lapse, provided an alternative provision is included – see clause [6.46] above.)

Legacy to a minor with provision for payment to a guardian, either legal or testamentary

[6.48]

I **GIVE** the sum of € *(insert amount in figures and words)* to [my *(relationship to testator, if any)*] *(name)*, of *(address)*. If the said *(name)* is under the age of eighteen years at the date of my death, then the said sum may be paid to the legal or testamentary guardian of the said *(name)* and the receipt of such legal or testamentary guardian to my executors shall be sufficient discharge of the legacy.

Legacy to grandchildren of the testator where they are to take the benefit per capita *according to their number*

[6.49]

I **GIVE** the sum of € *(insert amount in figures and words)* to be divided in equal shares amongst my grandchildren living at the date of my death.

Legacy to grandchildren of the testator where they are to take per stirpes

[6.50]

I **GIVE** the sum of € *(insert amount in figures and words)* as to one-third share thereof amongst the children of my daughter *(name)* living at the date of my death, and as to one-third share thereof to the children of my daughter *(name)* living at the date of my death and as to the remaining one-third thereof to the children of my son *(name)* living at the date of my death.

Alternative method:

(a)   I **GIVE** the sum of € *(insert amount in figures and words)* to be divided equally amongst the children of my son *(name)*, who are living at the date of my death.

(b)   I **GIVE** the sum of € *(amount in figures and words)* to be divided equally amongst the children of my daughter *(name)*, who are living at the date of my death.

(c)   I **GIVE** the sum of € *(amount in figures and words)* to be divided equally amongst the children of my daughter *(name)*, who are living at the date of my death.

Legacy of a specified amount to be applied at the discretion of the executors for the benefit of the maintenance, welfare and education of the children of the testator, with provision that any surplus over after the last of the children has attained the age of 21 years or has completed full time education is to be divided amongst the children then living

[6.51]

I **GIVE** the sum of € *(insert amount in figures and words)* to my executors and trustees to be applied by them for the maintenance, welfare and education of such of my children as are living at the date of my death, as they in their absolute discretion shall think fit. In the event that there is a surplus remaining when the last of my children has attained the age of twenty-one years or has completed full time education, whichever event shall happen first, then any surplus remaining in the hands of my executors is to be distributed among my children living at that time in equal shares.

My executors and trustees shall exercise their discretionary powers hereunder in such manner and at such time as they shall think fit and shall not be under any obligation to make payments to or for the benefit of all of my children, nor shall they be obliged to ensure equality of provision amongst those to whom provision is made.

My executors and trustees can make any payment under this clause to the surviving parent or legal or testamentary guardian of any of my children until any of my said children attains the age of eighteen years and thereafter to the child him or herself and the receipt of the surviving parent or legal or testamentary guardian or child shall be sufficient discharge to my executors and trustees.

(*Note 1*: a discretionary trust for the benefit of minors or persons under 21 years of age and in full time education will be exempt from discretionary trust tax.)

(*Note 2*: the power to the executors to make payments to the surviving parent or legal or testamentary guardian or child is necessitated by the provisions of s 43 of the Conveyancing Act 1881.)

Legacy in favour of grandchildren to be held on a discretionary trust

[6.52]

I GIVE to my executors and trustees the sum of € *(insert amount in figures and words)* (hereinafter called 'the Fund') on the following discretionary trust, that is to say:

(i)   To invest the Fund as if they were beneficially entitled thereto without liability for any loss.

(ii)   To apply the income and/or capital of the Fund for the benefit of any of my grandchildren, living at the date of my death, who are under the age of eighteen years, as my executors and trustees may think fit.

(iii)   To accumulate any undistributed income and to add the same to the capital of the Fund.

(iv)   When all of my grandchildren have attained the age of eighteen years or died under that age, to end the trust by distributing the Fund amongst one or more of my grandchildren, as my executors and trustees may in their absolute discretion think fit.

(v)   My executors and trustees may exercise the discretionary powers hereby conferred upon them at such time and in such manner as they in their absolute discretion shall think fit and they shall not be under any obligation to make payments to or for the benefit of all of my grandchildren nor to ensure equality of provision amongst those for whom provision is made.

(vi)   In making provision for my grandchildren under this clause, my executors and trustees may pay such provision to the legal or testamentary guardian of any of my grandchildren and the receipt of such legal or testamentary guardian shall be sufficient discharge to my executors and trustees in respect of such payment.

[(vii)   **Optional**

Reference to grandchildren in this clause shall only include grandchildren born within lawful wedlock and any child adopted by any child of mine.*]

(*Note*: under the Status of Children Act 1987, in any will drawn up after 14 June 1988 where there is a reference in the will to the relationship between the testator and any beneficiary the relationship is to be construed without regard to any marital relationship in the chain of relationship. This, however, yields to a contrary intention and it is competent for a testator to specify that only persons born within lawful wedlock are to benefit under a particular clause in a will. It is necessary for a testator to expressly state that this is so.)

Conditional legacy to executors, provided they act as such

[6.53]

I GIVE the sum of € *(insert amount in figures and words)* to each of my executors, provided they act as my executors and take upon themselves the burden of the administration of my estate.

Legacy to executors whether or not they take on the office of executor

[6.54]

I GIVE the sum of € *(insert amount in figures and words)* to each of my executors and this legacy is payable whether or not my executors or any of them accept the office of executor and act in the administration of my estate. ·

Legacy to spouse/civil partner expressed to be in addition to his or her legal right share

[6.55]

I GIVE the sum of € *(insert amount in figures and words)* to my husband/wife/ civil partner *(name)*, of *(address)*, which said sum is to be in addition to the legal right share to which my said husband/wife/civil partner is entitled by reason of the provisions of Part IX of the Succession Act 1965 as amended by the Civil Partnership and Certian Obligations of Co-habitants Act 2010.

Legacy to spouse/civil partner expressed to be taken in whole or part satisfaction of his or her legal right share

[6.56]

I GIVE AND BEQUEATH unto my husband/wife/civil partner *(insert name)*, of *(address)*, the sum of € *(amount in figures and words)*, which said bequest is to be taken in whole or partial satisfaction of the legal right share of my said husband/wife/civil partner in my estate, if he/she elects to take such share.

Legacy to spouse/civil partner notwithstanding renunciation of his or her legal right share

[6.57]

Whereas my husband/wife/civil partner *(insert name)*, of *(address)*, renounced his/her legal right share to my estate in an Ante-Nuptial/Civil Partnership Agreement dated the *(date)* day of *(month)*, *(year)*, [*or*, in a Separation Agreement dated the *(date)* day of *(month)*, *(year)*, *or*, by Deed of Renunciation dated the *(date)* day of *(month)*, *(year)*, *or*, as part of the terms of an order made in proceedings entitled *(full title of proceedings, including the relevant court, the circuit and county if in the Circuit Court, the record number and the parties)*], notwithstanding such renunciation, **I GIVE AND BEQUEATH** unto my said husband/wife/civil partner *(name)*, of *(address)*, the sum of € *(amount in figures and words)*, but this bequest is not to be taken as in any way reviving the rights renounced by my husband/wife/civil partner as aforesaid.

Statement in will that spouse/civil partner has been in desertion of the testator and therefore not entitled to benefit under the will of the testator as an explanation for no provision being made for the spouse

[6.58]

My husband/wife/civil partner *(insert name, and address (if known))* has been in desertion of me for a period of *(number)* years and in such circumstances is unworthy to succeed to my estate. I am therefore making no provision in this my will for my husband/wife/civil partner.

(*Note*: while this statement in the will may be of assistance in showing that the spouse was in desertion at the date the will was made, under s 120 of the Succession Act 1965, in order for the spouse to be unworthy to succeed, the desertion must continue up until the date of death – see further **Appendix 8**.)

Statement in will that a decree of divorce a mensa et thoro or judicial separation was obtained against the spouse and that no provision is being made for the spouse

[6.59]

By an order of the High/Circuit Court on the *(date)* day of *(month)*, *(year)*, I was granted a decree of divorce *a mensa et thoro* against my husband/wife *(name)*, of *(address)* [*or*, a decree of judicial separation under the Family Law (Judicial Separation) Act 1989 was made]. In consequence thereof, my said husband/wife is not entitled to benefit from my estate. For this reason I am making no provision for my husband/wife in this my will.

(*Note*: if a marriage or civil partnership has been dissolved the relationship on which the marriage or civil partnership was founded no longer exists.)

Pecuniary legacy in favour of a child of the testator with an assertion by the testator that he or she has made adequate provision for the child and fulfilled any moral duty pursuant to s 117 of the Succession Act 1965

[6.60]

> **I GIVE** the sum of € *(insert amount in figures and words)* to my son/daughter *(name)*, of *(address)* and **I DECLARE** that I have made proper provision for my said son/daughter in accordance with my means during the course of my life and I make this pecuniary legacy in final fulfillment of any moral duty I may be deemed to owe to my said son/daughter pursuant to the provisions of Section 117 of the Succession Act 1965.

> *(Note*: while the view of the testator in respect of proper provision being made for the child is by no means conclusive of the question before a court, should a child wish to bring an application pursuant to s 117, it will be useful to show that the testator had at least directed his or her mind to the question of proper provision and deemed himself or herself to have fulfilled any such moral duty.)

Legacy to executors and trustees for the benefit of a particular child who is not capable of managing his or her affairs to be applied for the benefit of the child in such manner as the executors and trustees may think fit, with provision for a gift over of the surplus of the fund to a charitable institution at the death of the child of the testator

[6.61]

> **I GIVE** to my executors and trustees the sum of € *(insert amount in figures and words)* (hereinafter called 'the Fund') to be applied by them for the benefit of my daughter *(name)* currently resident at *(address)* who is incapable of managing her own affairs. In relation to the Fund, my executors and trustees shall have the following powers:

> (i)   To invest the Fund as if they were beneficially entitled thereto, without any responsibility for loss.

> (ii)   To apply the income and the capital of the Fund for the sole benefit of my said daughter *(name)* for as long as she shall live, with the power to accumulate any undistributed income with the capital of the Fund, but with the intention that in so far as possible, the entire of the Fund and the income shall be applied for the benefit of my said daughter.

> In the event of there being any surplus of the Fund remaining at the date of my said daughter's death, **I GIVE** the said surplus to *(name precisely charitable institution)* of *(address)* to be applied by them for the welfare and benefit of persons in their care in such manner as the said *(name charitable institution)* may think fit and the receipt of the treasurer or other proper officer of the said charitable organisation shall be sufficient discharge to my executors and trustees in respect of the payment of any such surplus to the said *(name charitable institution)*.

> If at the date of death of my said daughter the said *(name charitable institution)* has ceased to exist or has amalgamated or been incorporated into another

charitable institution, or has changed its name, then the said surplus shall not fail, but my executors and trustees shall pay the said surplus to a charitable institution which they consider most nearly fulfils the purposes that I intend to benefit by this bequest.

(*Note*: provision for a child who is incapable of managing his or her affairs might also be made by the setting up of a fully-secret or half-secret trust – see **Ch 9**.)

Legacy to person in the employ of the testator at the time of the testator's death

[6.62]

I **GIVE** the sum of € *(insert amount in figures and words)* to *(name)*, of *(address)*, provided that he/she is employed by me at the date of my death and is not under any notice of termination of such employment.

Legacy to parish priest for Masses for the repose of the soul of the testator

[6.63]

I **GIVE** the sum of € *(insert amount in figures and words)* to the parish priest for the time being at the date of my death of the parish of *(name and location of parish)* for Masses to be said for the repose of my soul (and those of my deceased relatives).

Legacy to a religious order of priests for Masses for the repose of the soul of the testator

[6.64]

I **GIVE** the sum of € *(insert amount in figures and words)* to the provincial/ bursar of the order of Roman Catholic priests known as *(name precisely the religious order)*, of *(address)*, for Masses to be said by the members of the said *(name religious order)* for the repose of my soul (and those of my deceased relatives).

Pecuniary legacy to a charity without imposing any obligation as to how the legacy may be applied

[6.65]

I **GIVE** the sum of € *(insert amount in figures and words)* to *(name charity precisely, eg, the Galway branch of the Samaritans)*, at *(address)*, for the general purposes of the said charity.

The receipt of the treasurer or other proper officer of the said charity shall be sufficient discharge to my executors in the payment of this legacy.

If at the date of my death, the said charity has ceased to exist or has amalgamated or become incorporated with another charity or has changed its name, then this legacy shall not fail, but my executors shall pay the legacy to such charitable organisation as they consider most nearly fulfils the objects of that which I intended to benefit.

Gift to a charity with a purpose specified but without creating a binding obligation

[6.66]

> **I GIVE** the sum of € (*insert amount in figures and words*) to the conference of
> the Society of St Vincent de Paul at Arran Quay in the City of Dublin and it is my
> wish, without creating any binding obligation on the said conference of the said
> society, that this gift be used solely for the relief of poverty within the Parish of
> St Paul's, Arran Quay, in the City of Dublin, but in the event that it shall not be
> practicable or possible to expend the said legacy in this way, then the said legacy
> shall be applied by the said conference of the Society of St Vincent de Paul in
> such manner as the conference may in its absolute discretion think fit.

> The receipt of the treasurer or other proper officer of the said conference of the
> Society of St Vincent de Paul shall be sufficient discharge to my executors in the
> payment of this legacy.

Ensuring that legacies keep pace with inflation

[6.67]

> Where the testator intends that the sum of money being left to a particular legatee
> should keep pace with inflation, the following formula might be inserted after the
> reference to the amount being left in figures and words. The formula leaves it to
> the executors to assess what sum should be paid so as to compensate for
> inflationary trends as the indices that may be applicable from time to time alter
> and change their names and if at the date of death of the testator there were no
> such indices referred to in the will, then the provision might not operate. For this
> reason, it is better to leave a general discretion open to the executors.

> **I GIVE** to my son (*insert name*), of (*address*), the sum of € (*amount in figures
> and words*), *or such larger sums as my executors calculate to have the same
> value at the date of my death as ... euro (amount in figures and words) had at the
> date of this my will.*

> (*Note*: the formula italicised can be incorporated into any of the other legacies set
> out in the preceding precedents.)

Bequests of general and specific items of personal property

Bequest of specific items

[6.68]

> **I MAKE** the following bequest of items from my personal property.

> (a)   To my son (*insert name*), of (*address*), my painting entitled (*title of
>   painting*) by (*name of artist*).

> (b)   To my nephew (*name*), son of my brother/sister (*name*), of (*address*), my
>   silver Georgian tea service.

(c)   To my granddaughter (*name*), daughter of my son/daughter (*name*), of (*address*), my circular mahogany dining table with six Hepplewhite dining chairs.

Bequest of specific items of personal property with reference to a list to be incorporated into the will

[6.69]

I GIVE the items of my personal property as set out in a list, prepared by me, prior to the execution of this my will, and handed to my solicitor in a manila envelope marked 'List', which list is typed on two A4 pages of paper, to the persons named in the said list.

(*Note*: this list must be in existence at the time the will is executed and the Probate Office will require evidence to that effect before incorporating the list into the will.)

Bequest of household chattels as defined by s 56 of the Succession Act 1965

[6.70]

I GIVE my household chattels as defined by Section 56 of the Succession Act 1965 to [my *(insert relationship to testator, if any)*] *(name)*, of *(address)* for his/her own use absolutely.

General bequest of household contents

[6.71]

I GIVE the contents of my dwelling house at (*insert address of dwelling house*) to [my (*relationship to testator, if any*)] (*name*), of (*address*).

General bequest of jewellery and personal effects

[6.72]

I GIVE all my clothing, jewellery and articles of personal use and adornment to [my *(insert relationship to testator, if any)*] *(name)*, of *(address)*.

Bequest of any motor car owned by the testator at the date of his or her death

[6.73]

I GIVE any motor car that I may own at the date of my death to [my *(insert relationship to testator, if any)*] *(name)*, of *(address)*.

General bequest of personal chattels to certain named persons with power of selection from the personal chattels to those persons, with a gift over of remaining chattels to the residue of the estate of the testator

[6.74]

> **I GIVE** all of my personal chattels that comprise in articles of personal use or adornment or articles of household use or ornament to my executors upon trust:
>
> (i)   To permit my friends *(insert name)*, of *(address)*, and *(name)*, of *(address)*, and *(name)*, of *(address)* and *(name)*, of *(address)* to select as mementoes up to three items from my said personal chattels to which this trust relates.
>
> (ii)   Any personal chattels not selected as aforesaid shall form part of the residue of my estate.

Bequest of a particular item of property in the possession of the testator on foot of a hire purchase agreement

[6.75]

> **I GIVE** the yacht known as *(insert name of yacht)* to *(name)*, of *(address)* and **I DIRECT** that if the said yacht is in my possession at the date of my death under the terms of a hire purchase agreement, my executors shall take such steps as are practical to vest the ownership of the said yacht in the said *(name)* at the expense of my residuary estate.

Bequest of a chattel in the possession of the testator on foot of a leasing, lease purchase or other agreement, but not owned by the testator

[6.76]

> **I GIVE** any motor car in my possession at the date of my death to *(insert name)*, of *(address)* and **I DIRECT** that if the said motor car is in my possession at the date of my death under the terms of a leasing agreement or a lease purchase agreement, or other similar agreement, my executors shall take such steps as are practical to vest the ownership of the said motor car in the said *(name)* at the expense of my residuary estate.
>
> (*Note*: a will speaks from the date of death and is ambulatory in nature. The fact that a testator has disposed of a specific item of property in his or her will does not prevent him or her from disposing of that property during the course of his or her life. If the testator does dispose of the property during the course of his or her life and it is not available as part of his or her estate at the date of his or her death, then the legacy will be adeemed.)

Specific legacy to spouse/civil partner expressed to be in addition to his or her legal right share

[6.77]

> **I GIVE AND BEQUEATH** unto my husband/wife/civil partner *(insert name)*, of *(address)*, my motor car, registration number *(registration number)*, which

said bequest is in addition to my husband/wife/civil partner's legal right share in my estate, if he/she elects to take such share.

Specific legacy to spouse/civil partner expressed to be taken in whole or part satisfaction of his or her legal right share

[6.78]

I GIVE AND BEQUEATH unto my husband/wife/civil partner *(insert name)*, of *(address)*, my painting entitled *(title of painting)*, by *(name of artist)*, which said bequest is to be taken in whole or part satisfaction of my husband/wife/civil partner's legal right share in my estate, if he/she elects to take such share.

Chapter 7

DEVISES

PART I: COMMENTARY

Types of devise

[7.01] There are two types of devise: a general devise and a specific devise. A *general devise* is a devise of an unspecified portion of the testator's real estate. A *specific devise* is a devise of an identified portion of the testator's real property. It would be more usual for devises to be specific rather than general.

[7.02] Many of the remarks made in the commentary to **Ch 6** on legacies are also applicable to devises of land. A general devise will abate with general legacies and a specific devise will only abate when all general legacies and devises have abated.

[7.03] A specific devise will be subject to the doctrine of ademption. Precision should be used in relation to devises because in many instances, the testator's real property will be his or her most valuable asset. In my experience ademption usually arises through inadvertence and can have very serious consequences. People are inclined to sell houses or farms in later life to 'trade down' or 'down size'; if they have left the house or farm by way of specific devise but have disposed of it during their lifetime the devisee will obtain nothing. It should be remembered that even the entry into a binding contract for sale constitutes a disposal and even if the contract is not complete by the date of death ademption would still arise.

[7.04] As with the commentary on legacies, I re-enter the caveat that if a testator disposes of a specific item of real property his or her will should be reviewed to see what impact that may have on the disposition of property and, if necessary, the will revised to take account of it.

[7.05] It may be that the testator is quite happy that the devisee of the property disposed of receives nothing but it would be important to ascertain that, and record it so that the disappointed devisee does not seek to sue.

[7.06] It will also be common for testators to create limited interests in real property such as life estates or rights of residence, maintenance and support. Previously this could give rise to the operation of the Settled Land Acts 1882–1890 and now will activate the provisions of Pt 4 of the 2009 Act. The circumstances under which a trust of land arises and the provisions relating to the appointment of trustees are set out in **Ch 5**. Part 4 of the 2009 Act is set out in full in **Appendix 4**.

[7.07] Testators may often wish to attach a condition to a devise of land and where this arises, great care has to be exercised. Care should be taken to ensure that the condition attaching to the devise is one that is capable of enforcement and is not void as being contrary to public policy, for uncertainty or for offending against the rules that pertain to future interests and class gifts. (See **Ch 2**.)

'Words of limitation' not generally required for a devise are no longer required in a conveyance either

[7.08] 'Words of Limitation' and 'words of purchase', so long the bane of the life of every student of real property, are now passing into history with the passing of the 2009 Act. This is in line with the scheme of the 2009 Act to simplify conveyancing and abolish feudal tenures and the estates that sprung from them. The wonders of the fee tail, barring the entail, leases for lives renewable for ever, base fees and fee farm grants will not trouble the real property student from here on out. When one thinks of the energy expended down the years in teaching all these concepts to mystified minds one could weep. The various forms of tenure will no doubt be the subject of learned historical theses in the future.

[7.09] Under the provisions of the 1965 Act, it is not necessary to include in a will 'words of limitation' in order to pass to a devisee a freehold estate, and the bequest will be deemed to pass to the beneficiary the greatest estate held by the testator unless the contrary intention appears.

[7.10] Section 94 of the 1965 Act provides as follows:

'Where real estate is devised to a person (including a trustee or executor) without any words of limitation, the devise shall be construed to pass the whole estate or interest which the testator had power to dispose of by will in the real estate, unless a contrary intention appears from the will.'

[7.11] Section 4(a) of the 1965 Act defines real estate as follows:

'"Real estate" includes chattels real, and land in possession, remainder, or reversion, and every estate or interest in or over land (including real estate held by way of mortgage or security, but not including money to arise under a trust for sale of land, or money secured or charged on land).'

[7.12] The provisions of s 94 are now echoed in s 67 of the 2009 Act, which abolishes the need for words of limitation in deeds of conveyance and applies the section with certain savers to conveyances executed before the 2009 Act came into operation. Section 67 of the 2009 Act provides as follows:

'**Words of limitation**

[CA 1881, s 51]

(1) A conveyance of unregistered land with or without words of limitation, or any equivalent expression, passes the fee simple or the other entire estate or interest which the grantor had power to create or convey, unless a contrary intention appears in the conveyance.

(2) A conveyance of unregistered land to a corporation sole by that person's corporate designation without the word "successors" passes to the corporation the fee simple or the other entire estate or interest which the grantor had power to create or convey, unless a contrary intention appears in the conveyance.

(3) Where an interest in land is expressed to be given to—

(a)   the heir or heirs, or

(b)   any particular heir, or

(c)   any class of heirs, or

(d)   issue,

of any person in words which, under the rule known as the Rule in *Shelley's Case*, would have operated to give that person a fee simple, those words operate as words of purchase and not of limitation and take effect in equity accordingly.

(4) Subject to section 68, subsections (1) to (3) apply to conveyances executed before the commencement of this Chapter, but without prejudice to any act or thing done or any interest disposed of or acquired before that commencement in consequence of the failure to use words of limitation in such a conveyance or the application of the Rule in *Shelley's Case*.'

The creation of a fee tail by will

[7.13] There was one exception to the lack of requirement for words of limitation in relation to a devise by will contained in the 1965 Act and that related to the creation of a fee tail estate by will. Section 95 of the 1965 Act provides as follows:

'(1) An estate tail (whether general, in tail male, in tail female or in tail special) in real estate may be created by will only by the use of the same words of limitation as those by which a similar estate tail may be created by deed.

(2) Words of limitation contained in a will in respect of real estate which have not the effect of creating an estate in fee simple or an estate tail shall have the same effect, as near as may be, as similar words used in a deed in respect of personal property.'

By virtue of this section, it was only possible to create an estate tail by will by using the words of limitation required by statute and common law. I have omitted from the precedent clauses below, clauses showing how to create fee tail estates by will. This is because the 2009 Act abolishes the fee tail estate and prohibits their creation by any instrument, which would include a will. (Viewers of *Downton Abbey* take note.) Section 13 of the 2009 Act makes no mention of s 95 of the 1965 Act but by implication it has ceased to be operative.

An 'instrument' is defined by s 3 of the 2009 Act as including a will. I have never come across a will in modern times that attempted the creation a fee tail.

[7.14] Section 13 of the 2009 Act provides as follows:

'**Abolition of the fee tail**

(1) The creation of a fee tail of any kind at law or in equity is prohibited.

(2) Any instrument executed after the commencement of this Part purporting to create a fee tail in favour of any person vests in that person a legal fee simple or, as the case may be, an equitable fee simple and any contract for such a creation entered into before or after such commencement operates as a contract for such vesting.

(3) Where—

(a)   immediately before the commencement of this Part, a person was entitled to a fee tail at law or in equity, or

(b)   after such commencement, a person becomes entitled to such a fee tail,

a legal or, as the case may be, an equitable fee simple vests in that person on such commencement or on that person becoming so entitled provided any protectorship has ended.

(4) In subsection (3) "fee tail" includes—

(a)   a base fee provided the protectorship has ended,

(b)   a base fee created by failure to enrol the disentailing deed,

but does not include the estate of a tenant in tail after possibility of issue extinct.

(5) A fee simple which vests under subsection (2) or subsection (3) is—

(a)   not subject to any estates or interests limited by the instrument creating the fee tail to take effect after the termination of the fee tail,

(b)   subject to any estates or interests limited to take effect in defeasance of the fee tail which would be valid if limited to take effect in defeasance of a fee simple.'

The Settled Land Acts 1882–90 and the Land and Conveyancing Law Reform Act 2009

[7.15] Any devise which creates a settlement within the meaning of the Settled Land Acts 1882–90 will now constitute a trust of land within the meaning of Pt 4 of the 2009 Act. The operation of the 2009 Act simplifies some of the pitfalls that arose under the Settled Land Acts 1882–1890.

Part 4 of the 2009 Act is reproduced in full in **Appendix 12, Pt 1**.

In general terms, a settlement and now a trust of land will arise, *inter alia*, where successive interests are created or where land is left to an infant.

Any will already executed, but which makes no mention of the 2009 Act, will in my view have the provisions of the 2009 Act applied to it, because the instrument, in this case the will or codicil, will only become operative when the testator dies. Practitioners might, however, give thought to the revision of wills in the light of the 2009 Act and consider whether wills should be up-dated.

Testators in any event should review their wills certainly on the happening of any significant event, which may have a bearing on the testator's intentions, eg, the death of an executor, a beneficiary or disposal of a significant portion of their estate. Practitioners should, in my view, encourage a testator to review their will, say, every two years to guard against provisions becoming obsolete or no longer appropriate.

The doctrine of lapse

[7.16] The doctrine of lapse applies to both legacies and devises; see **Ch 6** for a discussion of the doctrine and the exceptions to it.

Once again the failure or lapse of a devise of a significant item of real property might have more far-reaching effects than that of a legacy, so great care should be taken.

Mortgages and charges affecting land bequeathed

[7.17] See **Ch 6** for a discussion of this topic.

Co-ownership: form of co-ownership under which the testator may hold his or her estate

[7.18] Where the testator at law and in equity holds his or her property as a joint tenant with another or others, there is nothing to devise as the testator's interest in the property will cease on death. A testator may, of course, wish to provide for the possibility of his or her surviving his or her fellow joint tenants, in which case he or she could make a devise contingent on that eventuality.

[7.19] To this must be added the rider that if a joint tenant is guilty of the murder of his or her fellow joint tenant, the surviving joint tenant will take the property by right of survivorship at law but hold it on a constructive trust as to the extent of the beneficial ownership in equity. In the case of *In re Cawley – Cawley and others v Lillis*,[1] the defendant was convicted of the manslaughter of his wife. They held a variety of assets jointly. The defendant claimed, up to the morning of the trial of an application for directions by the executors, that he was entitled to the entirety of the joint property by right of survivorship. Laffoy J held that the property passed by right of survivorship at law but that the defendant held the property on a constructive trust on the facts of the case as to 50 per cent for himself and 50 per cent for the estate of the wife whose death he had caused.

[7.20] Where the testator is the owner of a share in the subject matter of the bequest, then he or she will only have disposing power over that share. Care should be taken to ascertain the precise interest of the testator in any property. Persons will often state that they own property 'jointly' with someone else when, in fact, they hold it as tenants in common. Or persons may believe they own a half share in something when, in fact, they own it jointly. The practitioner drawing the will should precisely ascertain the correct position and advise accordingly. In the English case of *Carr-Glynn v Frearsons*,[2] a solicitor relied on her client's view that the property was held as tenants in common when in fact it was held under a joint tenancy. A bequest in the will drawn on foot of the erroneous assumption was inoperative and the solicitor was found liable in negligence because she had not checked the true position. In England and Wales it was possible to sever the joint tenancy unilaterally so that the joint tenancy could have been easily severed and effect given to the testatrix's wishes.

[7.21] In Ireland, by virtue of Pt 7 and s 30 the 2009 Act, it is now possible, with the consent of the joint tenants, to sever a joint tenancy, and the court has power in an appropriate case to dispense with the consent (s 31(2)(e)).

[7.22] The exceptions where 'equity leans against' a joint tenancy should be noted:

(a)   where the property concerned is partnership property or is held as part of some commercial venture;

(b)   where the purchase moneys have been contributed in unequal shares;

---

1.   *Cawley and others v Lillis* [2011] IEHC 515.
2.   *Carr-Glynn v Frearsons* [1997] 2 All ER 614.

(c)   where the property is mortgaged to two persons or institutions, the mortgagees will hold the property as tenants in common.

The jurisdiction of the court to find a severance at equity is retained intact by virtue of s 30(4) of the 2009 Act.

[7.23] Where the property is held by the testator with co-owners jointly, regard should be had as to whether there has been any event giving rise to a severance of the joint tenancy:

(a)   The alienation by one joint tenant of his or her interest either voluntarily or involuntarily – it is now provided under the 2009 Act that any such alienation will be void unless the consent of the other joint tenant(s) in writing is first obtained (s 30(1)(a) and (2)) though the consent can de dispensed with by the court (s 31(2)(e)). Further, the Act provides that the registration of a judgment mortgage against the interest of a joint tenant does not sever the joint tenancy and the judgment mortgage will be extinguished on the death of the judgment debtor (s 30(3)).

(b)   The acquisition by one joint tenant of an additional interest in the property after the creation of the joint tenancy – under the 2009 Act any acquisition is avoided unless the consent in writing of the other joint tenant(s) is obtained (s 30(1)(b)).

(c)   The voluntary severance of the joint tenancy by the parties to the joint tenancy (but see Pt 7 of the 2009 Act).

It is imperative, therefore, when drafting a will, to examine any title document to the property being devised and further to make all relevant enquiries as to any circumstance that would have altered the title to the property or the form of co-ownership, if any.

Form of co-ownership created by the devise

[7.24] Generally speaking, the two forms of co-ownership that concern the person drafting a will are:

(a)   joint tenancy; and

(b)   tenancy in common.

The difference between the two types of co-ownership should be explained to the testator.

[7.25] Under a devise by way of a joint tenancy, the beneficiaries will own the entire property jointly and as each beneficiary dies his or her interest will pass to those remaining until only one person remains, provided there has been no severance of the joint tenancy in the meantime (see Pt 7 of the 2009 Act).

[7.26] Where the property is left to the beneficiaries as tenants in common, they will each hold an undivided share in the property, either equal or unequal, and when each beneficiary dies, his or her share will form part of his or her estate. The parties may also partition the property, if that is practicable, so that each person holds a portion commensurate with his or her share in the property, or where partition is not practicable a sale of the property in lieu of partition may be made (this now governed by Pt 7 of the 2009 Act).

Words of severance

[7.27] The form of co-ownership, created by the will, will depend on whether or not words of severance are present in the devise. Great care should be taken in the drafting so that that there is no confusion, eg, 'I leave my property at ... to X, Y and Z jointly as tenants in common'.

[7.28] Where the property is left to a number of beneficiaries without the inclusion of words of severance, they will take the property as joint tenants and the right of survivorship will therefore apply.

[7.29] On the other hand, where words of severance are used, eg, 'amongst', 'between', 'equally', 'in equal shares', 'share and share alike' or the words attaching to the bequest indicate that they are to take in unequal shares, then the bequest will fall to the beneficiaries as tenants in common.

[7.30] It is, of course, a matter of construction as to what form of co-ownership arises but the creation of one form or another by inadvertence should be avoided. Great care should be taken. It should be remembered that if the will is clear on its face, extrinsic evidence will not be admissible even if the intention of the testator is not carried into effect (s 90 of the 1965 Act, *Rowe v Law*[3] and *In re Collins*[4]). In such an instance, the practitioner may be sued in negligence.

Vested and contingent devises

[7.31] Thought should be given as to whether the devise is to be a vested one or a contingent one. By virtue of s 15 of the 2009 Act, all future interests in land, whether vested or contingent, 'exist in equity only'.

Vested

[7.32] The devise may be vested in possession or vested in interest. Property is said to be vested in possession where the person is entitled to enjoy immediate possession of the property. In this context, if the property is vested absolutely in the beneficiary, subject to the executor or legal personal representative passing legal title to him or her, the interest will be vested in possession as of the date of death.

[7.33] If, on the other hand, the interest of the beneficiary is postponed by some prior estate, such as life estate, then the interest will still be vested, but vested in interest. In

---

3.   *Rowe v Law* [1978] IR 55.
4.   *In re Collins – O'Connell and another v Governor and Company of the Bank of Ireland* [1998] 2 IR 596.

this instance, interests in succession in respect of the subject matter of the devise arise and a trust of land within the meaning of Pt 4 of the 2009 Act arises.

Example 1

I GIVE, DEVISE AND BEQUEATH my dwelling house at *(insert location of house)* to my son Christopher.

Christopher has an interest in the dwelling house vested in possession as of the date of death, subject to the legal estate being vested in him by the executors or legal personal representatives.

Example 2

I GIVE, DEVISE AND BEQUEATH any dwelling house I may own at the date of my death to my wife for her life and on her death to my son Christopher absolutely.

Assuming that the wife of the testator survives him, then she will have an interest in the dwelling house vested in possession for her life, but Christopher's interest will be vested in interest. The provisions of Part 4 of the 2009 Act in relation to trusts for land are applicable.

Contingent

[7.34] A contingent interest in a devise will arise where the vesting is postponed for some reason. This may happen in two ways:

(a)   where the beneficiary has to fulfil some condition before the devise vests in him or her, eg, attain the age of 18 years;

(b)   where there is a class bequest and the class has not closed. In order for an interest to be vested, the person in whom it is vested must be known and the precise extent of the interest must be known. In the case of a class bequest, where the class is not closed, it may not be possible to state that the interest is vested until the class closes.

Example

I GIVE, DEVISE AND BEQUEATH my farm comprised in folio *(insert number of folio and county in which the lands are situate)* to such of my children as attain the age of twenty-one years in equal shares.

Until the last child of the testator attains the age of twenty-one years, it will not be known how many persons comprise the class and until such time as the class closes, the interest will remain a contingent one.

[7.35] Where conditions are placed upon bequests in an attempt to prevent the vesting of the bequest, the validity of the contingency should be considered. Uncertain conditions or conditions void as being against public policy will be void, and if they are construed as a condition subsequent the beneficiary will take freed from the condition. On the other hand, if the condition is construed as a condition precedent and is void for uncertainty or as being void for public policy reasons then the entire bequest will fail. In the latter case, the disappointed beneficiary may have a cause of action in negligence against the practitioner who drafted the will if he or she cannot show that the testator was advised of the potential or actual invalidity of the bequest but decided to proceed.

[7.36] Where a testator decides to act against advice, he or she should be required to indicate in writing that he or she has been fully advised and has decided to proceed against that advice.

Abolition of the rule against perpetuities and other rules relating to future interests

[7.37] Many an evil real property examiner must be vexed or turning in his or her grave by the abolition of the arcane and impenetrable rules relating to future interests.

[7.38] Section 13(1) of the 2009 Act provides that future interests in relation to land operate in equity only, though s 13(2) excepts:

(a)   a possibility of reverter; or

(b)   a right of entry or of re-entry attached to a legal estate.

The two exemptions are not likely to concern a person drafting a will.

[7.39] Subject to s 17 of the 2009 Act, s 16 abolishes the following rules:

(a)   the rules known as the common law contingent remainder rules;

(b)   the rule known as the 'Rule in *Purefoy v Rogers*';

(c)   the rule known as the 'Rule in *Whitby v Mitchell*' (also known as the old rule against perpetuities and the rule against double possibilities);

(d)   the rule against perpetuities;

(e)   the rule against accumulations.

Section 17 is transitional and provides that the abolition applies to any interest in property whenever created but does apply where in belief on an interest being invalid (by reason of offending against one of the abolished rules):

(a)   the property has been distributed or otherwise dealt with; or

(b)   any person has done or omitted to do any thing which renders the position of that or any person materially altered to that person's detriment after the commencement of Pt 3 of the 2009 Act.

By s 3 of the 2009 Act, 'property' is defined as meaning *any real or personal property or any part or combination of such property.* So the abolition of rules relating to future interests applies to devises and legacies.

[7.40] The necessity for the other provisions in s 17 is born of the fact that where a devise or limitation was found to offend against the rules relating to future interest, the devise or limitation was void *ab initio* and there was no 'wait and see' approach. The effect, therefore, was draconian and there was little if any room for manoeuvre. As time passes, however, reliance on s 17 will become less necessary, although one could foresee a court having to rule on whether s 17 is applicable to the facts of any particular case.

[7.41] From the point of view of drafting a will in relation to devises of land, the concerns that arose relating to avoidance for offending against the various rules abolished has been defused.

PART II: PRECEDENT CLAUSES

Devises of real property

Devise of dwelling house (simple)

[7.42]

> **I GIVE, DEVISE AND BEQUEATH** my dwelling house situate at (*insert address of dwelling house*) to [my (*relationship to testator, if any*)] (*name*), of (*address*).
>
> (*Note 1*: this will pass the greatest estate held by the testator, so if the testator holds a leasehold estate, it will pass the leasehold estate and if the testator holds a freehold estate, it will pass a freehold estate.)
>
> (*Note 2*: where the dwelling house is subject to any charge or mortgage at the date of death of the deceased, the beneficiary will take subject to the charge – s 47 of the Succession Act 1965.)
>
> (*Note 3*: where the testator is married or has entered into a civil partnership, the right of appropriation reposing in the spouse or civil partner under s 56 of the 1965 Act as amended by the 2010 Act must be considered.)

Devise of dwelling house to create fee tail estate

[7.43]

> The creation of a fee tail, by will or any other instrument, is now prohibited by the 2009 Act and, therefore, these precedent clauses have been omitted from this edition.

Devise of dwelling house where any mortgage or charge is to be discharged out of the residuary estate of the testator, thus avoiding the provisions of s 47 of the Succession Act 1965

[7.44]

> **I GIVE, DEVISE AND BEQUEATH** my dwelling house situate at *(insert address of dwelling house)* to [my *(relationship to testator, if any)*] *(name)*, of *(address)* and **I DIRECT** that any mortgage or charge to which my house is subject at the date of my death shall be paid out of the residue of my estate.

Devise of dwelling house to two or more beneficiaries (simple) where beneficiaries will take as joint tenants

[7.45]

> **I GIVE, DEVISE AND BEQUEATH** my dwelling house situate at (*insert address of dwelling house*) to [my (*relationship to testator, if any*)] (*name*), of (address) and [my (relationship to testator, if any)] (*name*), of (*address*) and [my (*relationship to testator, if any*)] (*name*), of (*address*) as joint tenants.
>
> (*Note*: Under this bequest, if there are no words of severance or the words 'as joint tenants' or 'jointly' are used, the beneficiaries will take as joint tenants and the right of survivorship will thus apply. If any of the beneficiaries predeceases

the testator, then the remaining beneficiaries will take as joint tenants. If there is only one beneficiary remaining at the date of death, that beneficiary will take absolutely. The beneficiaries can sever the joint tenancy by consent by virtue of Pt 7 of the 2009 Act.)

Devise of dwelling house to two or more beneficiaries (simple), where beneficiaries will take as tenants in common, with no gift over in respect of any of the shares should a beneficiary predecease the testator

[7.46]

(i) **I GIVE, DEVISE AND BEQUEATH** my dwelling house situate at (*insert address of dwelling house*) <u>between</u> [my (*relationship to testator, if any*)] (*name*), of (*address*) and [my (relationship *to testator, if any*)] (*name*), of (*address*) and [my (*relationship to testator, if any*)], (*name*), of (*address*).

(ii) **I GIVE, DEVISE AND BEQUEATH** my dwelling house situate at (*insert address of dwelling house*) to [my (*relationship to testator, if any*)] (*name*), of (*address*) and [my (*relationship to testator, if any*)], (*name*), of (*address*) and [my (*relationship to testator, if any*)] (*name*), of (*address*) <u>equally</u>.

(iii) **I GIVE, DEVISE AND BEQUEATH** my dwelling house situate at (*insert address of dwelling house*) <u>amongst</u> [my (*relationship to testator, if any*)] (*name*), of (*address*) and [my (*relationship to testator, if any*)] (*name*), of (*address*) and [my (*relationship to testator, if any*)] (*name*), of (*address*).

(iv) **I GIVE, DEVISE AND BEQUEATH** my dwelling house situate at (*insert address of dwelling house*) to [my (*relationship to testator, if any*)] (*name*), of (*address*) and [my (*relationship to testator, if any*)] (*name*), of (*address*) and [my (*relationship to testator, if any*)] (*name*), of (*address*) <u>in equal shares</u>.

(v) **I GIVE, DEVISE AND BEQUEATH** my dwelling house situate at (*insert address of dwelling house*) to [my (*relationship to testator, if any*)] (*name*), of (*address*) and [my (*relationship to testator, if any*)] (*name*), of (*address*) and [my (*relationship to testator, if any*)] (*name*), of (*address*) <u>share and share alike</u>.

(vi) **I GIVE, DEVISE AND BEQUEATH** my dwelling house situate at (*insert address of dwelling house*) to [my (*relationship to testator, if any*)] (*name*), of (*address*) as to one half share thereof and as to the remaining half share thereof, <u>between</u> [my (*relationship to testator, if any*)] (*name*), of (*address*) and [my (*relationship to testator, if any*)] (*name*), of (*address*).

(*Note 1*: the question of whether a particular devise creates a joint tenancy or tenancy in common is a question of construction in each particular case, based upon the intention of the testator. Generally speaking, the words underlined in clauses (i)–(vi) above have been taken to create a tenancy in common because they are deemed to be 'words of severance', indicating that the beneficiaries are to take the property in undivided but equal shares. The beneficiaries will similarly take as tenants in common where the property is left to them in unequal shares, as in clause (vi) above.)

(*Note 2*: where any of the beneficiaries who take under the above devises predeceases the testator, the share of that beneficiary, except in situations where s 98 of the Succession Act 1965 applies (see below), would fall into the residue of the estate of the testator – see s 91 of the Succession Act 1965.)

(*Note 3*: Section 98 of the Succession Act 1965 will apply where any one of the beneficiaries is issue of the testator and dies leaving issue. Under s 98, if those circumstances pertain, the bequest to that beneficiary will not lapse but will take effect as if the beneficiary survived the testator and died immediately after him or her and so will form part of that deceased beneficiary's estate to be distributed in accordance with his or her will or intestacy as the case may be.

If the testator does not wish these results to obtain, then the bequest should make an alternative provision in the event that one of the beneficiaries predeceases the testator.)

Devise of dwelling house to two or more beneficiaries where the beneficiaries take as tenants in common, where one of the beneficiaries is a child of the testator and where the testator wishes to provide that the share of that child would pass to the issue of that child, should the child predecease the testator

[7.47]

    I GIVE, DEVISE AND BEQUEATH my dwelling house situate at *(insert address of dwelling house)* to my daughter *(name)*, of *(address)* and *(name)*, of *(address)* and *(name)*, of *(address)* as tenants in common provided always that in the event that my daughter predeceases me, **I DIRECT** that the share that she would have been entitled to shall pass to her children living at the date of my death and, if more than one, in equal shares. In the event of either *(name of second beneficiary)* or *(name of third beneficiary)* predeceasing me, the share of either of them shall pass to my said daughter and the survivor of them in equal shares, or if both the said *(name of second beneficiary)* and the said *(name of third beneficiary)* predecease me, then their respective shares shall pass to my daughter so that she shall be entitled to my dwelling house absolutely, or if she should be deceased also at the date of my death, the dwelling house shall pass to the children of my daughter living at the date of my death and if more than one in equal shares.

Devise of land to two or more beneficiaries as tenants in common, with gift over to the children of any beneficiary that predeceases the testator

[7.48]

    I GIVE, DEVISE AND BEQUEATH my dwelling house situate at *(address of dwelling house)* to *(name)*, of *(address)* and *(name)*, of *(address)* and *(name)*, of *(address)* in equal shares provided always that in the event that any of my beneficiaries shall predecease me, then the share of that beneficiary shall pass to any children of the beneficiary living at the date of my death and if more than one in equal shares.

Devise of any dwelling house owned by the testator at the date of his or her death

[7.49]

I GIVE, DEVISE AND BEQUEATH any dwelling house which I may own at the date of my death to [my *(insert relationship to testator, if any)*] *(name)*, of *(address)*.

(*Note*: a bequest in this form will avoid ademption should a specific dwelling house be sold and another purchased. Of course, if the dwelling house was sold and no new dwelling house purchased, eg, if an elderly person was going into residential care, the bequest would be adeemed. The proceeds of sale would fall into the residue of the estate. In such a situation the will should be revised as soon as a binding contract for sale comes into being.)

Devise of dwelling house where the testator owns only a share in the dwelling house

[7.50]

I GIVE, DEVISE AND BEQUEATH my interest or share in the dwelling house at *(insert address of dwelling house)* to [my *(relationship to testator, if any)*] *(name)*, of *(address)*.

(*Note 1*: the testator is only able to leave a share in the dwelling house if he or she holds the dwelling house as tenant in common with other persons. If the testator holds under a joint tenancy, the testator's interest will cease on death – see s 4 of the Succession Act 1965. Before there could be a bequest in this form, the joint tenancy would have to be severed on consent as provided for in Pt 7 of the 2009 Act. In the absence of consent, the consent can be dispensed by the court if the court considers it just to do so.)

(*Note 2*: if the testator's interest in the property is on the basis of a fee tail estate, then the interest of the tenants in tail in possession is not devisable by will – see s 4 of the Succession Act 1965. By virtue of s 13 of the 2009 Act, any existing fee tail is converted, subject to certain provisos, into a fee simple.)

Devise of dwelling house subject to an exclusive general right of residence (maintenance and support)

[7.51]

I CONFER upon [my *(insert relationship to testator, if any)*] *(name)*, of *(address)*, an exclusive general right of residence in my dwelling house at *(address of dwelling house)*, together with a right of maintenance and support, out of my residuary estate, for his/her life or for so long as he/she remains unmarried, and subject thereto **I GIVE, DEVISE AND BEQUEATH** my dwelling house to *(name)*, of *(address)*.

(*Note*: it has been suggested in *National Bank v Keegan*[5] that an exclusive general right of residence is tantamount to creating a life estate. A question of construction might arise and the testator's intention would have to be ascertained. Where the person is given an exclusive general right of residence, he or she would be entitled to exclude other persons from the dwelling house so that the person entitled to the dwelling house under the devise would really have no right to enter into the dwelling house until such time as the person entitled to the right of residence has died.

In general terms, the type of interest created by rights of residence under Irish law is unclear and there is no doubt that they are an encumbrance on the property over which they have been created. With regard to registered land, the Registration of Title Act 1964 provides that rights of residence are in the nature of a lien for money or money's worth and therefore they can be discharged by being capitalised and moneys being paid into court, but the position in relation to unregistered land is less clear.

Normally, rights of residence are created to provide for an elderly person, such as the testator's spouse or parent, or perhaps for an unmarried member of the family. While their creation is preferable to imposing conditions on a bequest as to residence, it would be generally preferable to give the person entitled to the right of residence an actual life estate in the property, so that the position concerning the property is beyond doubt.

If *National Bank v Keegan* is correct and a life estate is created by the creation of an exclusive right of residence, then a trust of land under Pt 4 of the 2009 Act arises and regard should be had to the provisions of that part. Part 4 of the 2009 Act is set out at **Appendix 12, Pt 1**.)

Devise of dwelling house with a right of residence limited to particular rooms in the dwelling house

[7.52]

I **CONFER** upon [my *(insert relationship to testator, if any)*] *(name)*, of *(address)*, a right of residence in my dwelling house at *(address of dwelling house)*, for his/her life or for so long as he/she remains unmarried, limited to the use of the larger of the two bedrooms in the front of the house, together with the use of all of the other rooms in the house in common with other persons as may occupy the said dwelling house from time to time. Subject to the said right of residence, **I GIVE, DEVISE AND BEQUEATH** my dwelling house to *(name)*, of *(address)*.

(*Note 1*: where creating a right of residence, it is important to be as explicit as possible as to the type of right of residence intended by the testator to avoid constructional difficulties at a later stage.)

(*Note 2*: while the nature of a right of residence may be uncertain in Irish law, it is nevertheless a valuable interest in land and will be more valuable depending

---

5.   *National Bank v Keegan* [1931] IR 344, 66 ILTR 101 (SC).

on the age of the person upon whom it is conferred. A right of residence for life conferred upon a relatively young beneficiary could be tantamount to the value of the entire property when capitalised.)

Specific devise of unregistered land

[7.53]

> **I GIVE, DEVISE AND BEQUEATH** my lands at (*insert precise description of location of lands*) comprising in (*state approximate acreage*) to [my (*relationship to testator, if any*)] (*name*), of (*address*).

Specific devise of registered land

[7.54]

> **I GIVE, DEVISE AND BEQUEATH** all my lands comprised in Folio (*insert folio number*) of the Register County of (*county*) to [my (*relationship to testator, if any*)] (*name*), of (*address*).

Specific devise of a site on the lands of the testator (registered or unregistered) to a particular beneficiary

[7.55]

> **I GIVE, DEVISE AND BEQUEATH** a site as shown on the map intended to be incorporated into this my will, which map I have marked with the letter 'A' to which I have appended my signature, to which said map the witnesses to my will have also appended their signature, on which said map the site is shown outlined in red, to [my (*insert relationship to testator, if any*)] (*name*), of (*address*). The lands upon which the site is shown are part of my lands situate at (*precise description of location of lands*) [*or,* comprised in Folio (*folio number*) of the Register County of (*county*)]. **I DIRECT** that any charge or mortgage upon my said lands shall be charged upon the remaining lands and the said (*name*) shall be entitled to the said site freed and discharged from any such charge or mortgage [*or,* any charge or mortgage over the said lands shall be discharged out of the residue of my estate].

> (*Note 1*: the map will be incorporated by reference into the will and shall be proved with the will. Therefore, the map must be clearly identified in the will in the manner shown above or by some other method and also the map must be *in existence at the time the will is executed* – see precedent affidavit of attesting witness in **Appendix 3**.)

> (*Note 2*: where the testator is leaving a site to a beneficiary, he or she may particularly wish that the site would be freed from any charge or mortgage affecting the lands. It may or may not be possible, depending on the terms of the charge or mortgage, to provide that the remaining lands shall be liable to the charge or mortgage and the site freed from the charge or mortgage. This would normally require the consent of the charge holder or mortgagee and much would depend upon the value of the lands and whether there is sufficient security in the remaining of the lands to service the charge or mortgage. If there is a doubt,

therefore, it might be better to provide that the charge would be paid out of the residue of the estate of the deceased, provided, of course, that there is sufficient residue to discharge the charge or mortgage.)

Devise of lands of testator (registered or unregistered) with a general exclusive right of residence in the dwelling house on the lands

[7.56]

I GIVE, DEVISE AND BEQUEATH my lands at (*insert precise description of location of lands*) comprising (*state approximate acreage*) [or, comprised in Folio (*folio number*) of the Register County of (*county*)] to [my (*relationship to testator, if any*)] (*name*), of (*address*), subject to an exclusive general right of residence in the dwelling house standing on the said lands to my husband/wife (*name*) for his/her life or until he/she shall remarry.

(*Note 1*: where creating a right of residence, it is important to be as explicit as possible as to the type of right of residence intended by the testator to avoid constructional difficulties at a later stage.)

(*Note 2*: while the nature of a right of residence may be uncertain in Irish law, it is nevertheless a valuable interest in land and will be more valuable depending on the age of the person upon whom it is conferred. A right of residence for life conferred upon a relatively young beneficiary could be tantamount to the value of the entire property when capitalised.)

Devise creating a life estate

[7.57]

Any devise that creates a life estate will create a trust of land under Part 4 of the 2009 Act and the provisions of that part will apply. Part 4 of the 2009 Act is set out in **Appendix 12, Pt 1**.

A devise creating a life estate should provide for a gift over in remainder. If the devise creating the life estate fails to do so, then the remainder interest will pass to the persons entitled to the residue of the testator's estate.

(i) Specific devise of dwelling house to spouse with gift over in remainder to children of testator

[7.58]

I GIVE, DEVISE AND BEQUEATH my dwelling house at (*insert address of dwelling house*) to my husband/wife/civil partner (*name*) for life, with remainder over after his/her death to my children living at the date of his/her death in equal shares.

Or

I GIVE, DEVISE AND BEQUEATH my dwelling house at (insert *address of dwelling house*) to my executors and trustees upon a trust of land within the meaning of the Land and Conveyancing Law Reform Act 2009 to hold same for the benefit of my spouse/civil partner *(name)* with remainder over after his/her death to my children at the date of his/her death in equal shares.

(ii) Specific devise of land to eldest daughter for her life, with gift over in remainder to the other children of the testator as joint tenants or tenants in common

[7.59]

I GIVE, DEVISE AND BEQUEATH my lands at *(insert precise description of location of lands)* comprising *(state approximate acreage)* [*or,* my lands comprised in Folio *(folio number)* of the Register County of *(county)*] to my eldest daughter *(name)* for her life, and from and after her death to such of my children as shall be living at the date of death of my said daughter (jointly or as joint tenants *or* in equal shares).

Or

I GIVE, DEVISE AND BEQUEATH my lands at *(insert precise description of location of lands)* comprising *(state approximate acreage)* [*or,* my lands comprised in Folio *(folio number)* of the Register County of *(county)*] to my executors and trustees upon a trust of land with the meaning of the Land and Conveyancing Law Reform Act, 2009 to hold same for my eldest daughter *(name)* for her life, and from and after her death to such of my children as shall be living at the date of death of my said daughter (jointly or as joint tenants *or* in equal shares).

Specific devise to spouse or civil partner expressed to be in addition to his or her legal right share

[7.60]

I GIVE, DEVISE AND BEQUEATH unto my husband/wife/civil partner *(insert name)*, of *(address)*, my lands comprised in Folio *(folio number)*, of the Register County of *(county)* which said devise is in addition to my husband's/wife's/civil partner's legal right share in my estate, if he/she elects to take such share.

Specific devise to spouse or civil partner expressed to be taken in whole or part satisfaction of his or her legal right share

[7.61]

I GIVE, DEVISE AND BEQUEATH unto my husband/wife/civil partner *(insert name)*, of *(address)*, my business premises at *(address)* [together with the goodwill of my business of *(describe business)* carried on at the said premises] which said devise is to be taken in whole or partial satisfaction of the legal right share of my said husband/wife/civil partner in my estate, if he/she elects to take such share.

General devise to spouse or civil partner notwithstanding renunciation of his or her legal right share

[7.62]

Whereas my husband/wife/civil partner, *(insert name)*, of *(address)*, renounced his/her legal right share to my estate in an Ante-Nuptial Agreement *or* Agreement Prior to the registration of our Civil Partnership dated the *(date)* day of *(month)*, *(year)* [*or*, in a Separation Agreement dated the *(date)* day of *(month)*, *(year)*, *or*, by Deed of Renunciation dated the *(date)* day of *(month)*, *(year)*, *or*, as part of the terms of an order made in proceedings entitled *(full title of proceedings, including the relevant court, the circuit and county if in the Circuit Court, the record number and the parties)*], notwithstanding such renunciation, **I GIVE, DEVISE AND BEQUEATH** unto my said husband/wife *(name)*, of *(address)*, an apartment of his/her choosing from the apartments comprised in my estate, but this devise is not to be taken as in any way reviving the rights renounced by my husband/wife as aforesaid.

Bequests of other types of special property

Bequest of business premises and goodwill of business

[7.63]

I GIVE, DEVISE AND BEQUEATH my business premises comprising the lock-up shop and offices situate at *(insert precise address of business premises)* together with the goodwill of my business of *(describe business)* carried on at the said premises to [my *(relationship to testator, if any)*] *(name)*, of *(address)* absolutely.

Pending the vesting of the business premises and the goodwill of the business in the beneficiary under this bequest **I DIRECT** that my executors shall be empowered to carry on my said business at the said premises and to employ the said beneficiary in the running of the said business and to pay him/her such remuneration as to my executors in their absolute discretion shall seem proper.

Bequest of an interest in a partnership where no formal partnership agreement exists

[7.64]

I GIVE, DEVISE AND BEQUEATH all my share and interest in my partnership with *(insert name of partner)* to [my *(relationship to testator, if any)*] *(name)*, of *(address)* and this bequest shall be deemed to include my share of all of the assets of the business, including the business premises at *(address)*. This bequest shall be subject to any debts or liabilities that I may have accrued in the course of my partnership arrangement with *(name of partner)* and the said *(name of beneficiary)* shall take the benefit of the said bequest subject to his/her indemnifying my residuary estate in respect of all such debts and liabilities.

(Note 1: where property is held under a partnership arrangement, even where there is no partnership agreement, at equity all property of the partners shall be

held as tenants in common, even if in law they hold the property as joint tenants. The interest of one of the partners, therefore, is capable of being the subject matter of a bequest in his or her will.)

(*Note 2*: if the business is incorporated, then the share holding in the company should additionally be left to the beneficiary.)

(*Note 3*: if the business premises is owned by the company, then it is inappropriate to include a devise of a business premises.)

Bequest of shareholding in a company

[7.65]

I GIVE AND BEQUEATH my shareholding in the company known as *(insert name of company)* having its registered office at *(registered office of company)* to [my *(relationship to testator, if any)*] *(name), of (address)* absolutely.

(*Note*: cases can arise where there is a bequest of a specific asset to a beneficiary, but the testator did not own the asset in question. The asset was owned by a limited company in which the testator may have been the principal share holder. In such circumstances, it is appropriate that the share holding of the company be left to the beneficiary, not the asset in question.)

Gift of shareholding with a provision for amalgamation, reconstruction or take-over of the company in which the shares are held

[7.66]

I GIVE AND BEQUEATH my shareholding in the company known as *(insert name of company)* having its registered office at *(registered office of company)* to *(name), of (address)* and if any of the shares comprised in this gift are as a result of a take-over, amalgamation or reconstruction represented by a different share holding, this bequest shall take effect as if it were a gift of that share holding.

(*Note*: The proviso in this bequest will prevent, to a certain extent, ademption or disputes as to whether property is adeemed.)

Chapter 8

ADEMPTION, SATISFACTION, ADVANCEMENT AND THE RELEASE OF DEBTS

PART I: COMMENTARY

Ademption

[8.01] So far, mention of ademption has been made with regard to specific bequests. Where a testator leaves a specific item of property, either real or personal, to a beneficiary and at the time of the testator's death the specific item of property is no longer part of the testator's estate, the bequest will be said to be adeemed. The beneficiary will receive nothing.

We have seen that in precedent clauses it is possible to try to avoid this result by, for example, bequeathing to a beneficiary 'any dwelling house which I might own at the date of my death' or 'any motor car that I might own at the date of my death' rather than naming a specific dwelling house or a specific motor vehicle. This is only of assistance, of course, if the testator is likely to die leaving only one dwelling house or one motor car. If the testator owns a number of properties, then unless he or she wishes to leave all of his or her properties to one specific person, they will have to be dealt with by way of specific bequest. The doctrine of ademption would apply if any of the properties had been disposed of by the testator prior to his or her death.

Ademption and satisfaction

[8.02] There is another context in which ademption arises and in this context the doctrine of ademption is similar to the doctrine of satisfaction. Ademption in this context arises from the operation of the twin equitable maxims, *equity imputes an intention to fulfil an obligation* and *equity leans against double portions.*

Ademption of legacies by portions and portions by legacies

[8.03] A 'portion' is a financial provision of a significant kind, such as would be needed to make permanent provision for a child, eg, on the child's marriage, or setting him or her up in business or in a profession. Where a parent of a child or a person *in loco parentis* undertakes or covenants to make provision for a child in such a manner, the undertaking or covenant gives rise to a portion debt, whereby the person who undertakes or covenants to make the provision is indebted to the child.

[8.04] If the person, who has covenanted or undertaken to make the provision, dies before making the provision, but leaving a legacy to the child in his or her will, the child will be unable to claim both the portion debt and the legacy. The legacy will be deemed to have been given in satisfaction of the obligation to provide a portion unless the will

131

states otherwise. On the other hand, if the portion has been paid prior to the *execution* of the will, then no question of an ademption can arise.

[8.05] Because 'equity leans against double portions', ademption of a legacy by a portion can also arise. Where a parent or a person *in loco parentis* leaves a legacy to a child and subsequent to the execution of the will gives a portion to that child, the legacy will be adeemed by the portion, unless the will otherwise specifies.

[8.06] The application of these equitable doctrines may be rebutted and, in general terms, it is easier to rebut the presumption of ademption of portion debts by legacies than it is to rebut the presumption of ademption of a legacy by a portion.

[8.07] Generally speaking, the presumptions can be rebutted where there is a difference in character between the nature of the portion to be provided and the nature of the legacy contained in the will. So if a parent were to covenant to give a child an advancement of money in cash and then there is a legacy to the child in the will of shares or stock in a company, it would be easier to rebut the presumption of ademption. The presumption can also be rebutted by extrinsic evidence to show that the testator intended the child to take both the legacy and the portion.

[8.08] In the case of *In Re Hickey; Hickey v Dwyer and others,*[1] nearly all the principles as stated above came into illustrative focus and were applied by Laffoy J. In that case, the deceased by will made a bequest in favour of his only child and daughter in the sum of IR£100,000. He later took out a bond in respect of which he had a power of appointment amongst a class of beneficiaries. In default of the exercise of the power by him, the proceeds were to pass to his daughter. He did not exercise the power so the default provision applied. The bond yielded a sum in excess of €280,000. A number of questions arose and were posed for the court's determination.

[8.09] Had the testator by his will exercised the power of appointment? The answer was 'no'. Though the will spoke from death, the instrument creating the power of appointment only came into being after the will so the testator could not have intended to exercise the power of appointment when he included the legacy in his will.

[8.10] Was the daughter entitled to both the legacy and the proceeds of the bond? The answer was 'no'. The court considered the presumption that arose against the plaintiff taking both benefits because of the maxim 'equity leans against double portions'. Extrinsic evidence was not admissible in relation to the bequest in the will because the will was clear on its face. Without explicitly saying so, the court appears to have accepted the submission that extrinsic evidence was admissible on the satisfaction issue. The evidence was not particularly determinate of the issue. As it did not rebut the presumption, the court held that the daughter was not entitled to the legacy and the portion and she would have to elect between the two benefits. The court, in making its decision, regarded the two benefits of a similar character both being a provision by the testator to provide for his daughter by way of a sum of money, even though the bond yield was higher than the legacy. The court, in coming to its conclusion, also noticed that

---

1.   *Re Hickey; Hickey v Dwyer and others* [2005] IEHC 365.

this species of the doctrine was usually applicable as between parent and child and persons who stood *in loco parentis* to a child.

[8.11] For the reasons set out, in drafting a will where provision is being made for children either by way of specific bequest or alternatively by way of residuary bequest, instructions should be taken to ascertain whether the testator has entered into any obligation to make provision for the child or might intend to do so in the future. Where such obligation arises, the will should make clear the testator's intention as to whether the legacy or portion will be considered to be adeemed or not by the provision contained in the will.

Satisfaction of debts by legacies

[8.12] If a testator is indebted to a person and leaves that person a benefit in the will, a question can arise as to whether the beneficiary/creditor is entitled to claim both the legacy and the debt.

In certain circumstances, the legacy may be deemed to be left in satisfaction of the debt, but generally speaking the courts have a dislike for the doctrine of satisfaction of debts by legacies. Unless the will makes clear that the legacy is intended to be in satisfaction of the debt and does in fact discharge the debt, the doctrine of satisfaction may not apply.

There are a number of exceptions to the doctrine of satisfaction of debts by legacies:

(a)   If the debt was not incurred until after the execution of the will, then the doctrine of satisfaction will not apply and the beneficiary/creditor will be entitled to both the legacy and the debt. This is because the testator could not have intended the legacy to be in satisfaction of a debt that did exist at the time the will was made. It is something of an exception to a will speaking from death.

(b)   If the legacy is less than the amount of the debt, then the beneficiary will be entitled to claim both the debt and the legacy.

(c)   If the legacy is different in character to the character of the debt, eg, if the debt is for a particular amount of money and the testator leaves the beneficiary the proceeds of government stock, then the beneficiary/creditor will be entitled to claim both the debt and the legacy.

Advancement

[8.13] The question of advancement more usually applies in relation to residuary gifts, but it could equally apply where a fund or a specific piece of property is left as a class gift amongst the children of the testator. Under the doctrine of advancement, a child who has received an advancement from a testator during the course of the testator's life will be required to bring that advancement into account when the shares of the children under the testator's will are being ascertained. This is to try to do equity as between the children and to prevent a double provision being made for some children over others.

[8.14] Section 63 of the 1965 Act deals with the doctrine of advancement. It is possible to exclude the operation of s 63 from a will. In an appropriate case, a testator's instructions should be taken where provision is being made for his or her children as to whether he or she wishes the doctrine of advancement to apply or not.

The doctrine applies where the person making the advancement and making provision in his or her will is a parent of the child or the person who stands *in loco parentis*.

[8.15] Section 63 of the Succession Act 1965 provides as follows:

'(1) Any advancement made to the child of a deceased person during his lifetime shall, *subject to any contrary intention expressed or appearing from the circumstances of the case*, be taken as being so made in or towards satisfaction of the share of such child in the estate of the deceased or the share which such child would have taken if living at the death of the deceased, and as between the children shall be brought into account in distributing the estate.

(2) The advancement shall, for the purposes of this Section only, be reckoned as part of the estate of the deceased and its value shall be reckoned *as at the date of the advancement*.

(3) If the advancement is equal to or greater than the share which the child is entitled to receive under the will or on intestacy, the child or the issue of the child shall be excluded from any such share in the estate.

(4) If the advancement is less than such share, the child or the issue of the child shall be entitled to receive in satisfaction of such share so much only of the estate as, when added to the advancement, is sufficient, as nearly as can be estimated, to make up the full amount of that share.

(5) The onus of proving that a child has been made an advancement shall be upon the person so asserting, unless the advancement has been expressed in writing by the deceased.

(6) For the purposes of this Section, "advancement" means a gift intended to make permanent provision for a child and includes advancement by way of portion or settlement, including any life or lesser interest and including property covenanted to be paid or settled. It also includes an advance or portion for the purpose of establishing a child in a profession, vocation, trade or business, a marriage portion and payments made for the education of a child to a standard higher than that provided by the deceased for any other or others of his children.

(7) For the purposes of this Section, personal representatives may employ a duly qualified valuer.

(8) Nothing in this Section shall prevent a child retaining the advancement and abandoning his right to a share under the will or on intestacy.

(9) Nothing in this Section shall affect any rule of law as to the satisfaction of portion debts by legacies.

(10) In this Section 'child' includes a person to whom the deceased was in loco parentis.' (Author's emphasis.)

I have quoted the section in full so that the ramifications of the section will be apparent to persons who draft wills and so that the testator's intention can be clearly ascertained and, in turn, expressed in the will.

[8.16] The constitutionality of the section was raised recently in the case of *In Re Hickey Deceased Hickey v Dwyer and others*,[2] but as the constitutional point had not been pleaded, and as it would have necessitated the joinder of the Attorney General, Laffoy J refused to comment on the arguments raised.

[8.17] It is to be noted that the doctrine of advancement applies not merely to benefits arising under a will, but also to benefits arising on intestacy. However, in the context of this book, the concern is to ensure that a person drafting a will shall be aware of the ramifications of the doctrine of advancement and be able to take the testator's instructions in relation to it.

[8.18] It is to be noted that the operation of the section can be excluded by 'any contrary intention expressed or appearing from the circumstances of the case'. On this basis, the contrary intention does not have to appear in the will of the testator. It would be possible to prove the contrary intention from evidence outside the will. This, however, might be difficult of proof. For this reason, I would consider it advisable that the contrary intention would be expressed in the will of the testator.

[8.19] It should also be noted that the value of the advancement is to be 'as at the date of the advancement' and not the date of death of the testator. In times of fluctuating property values, this, of course, could have a significant bearing on the distribution, particularly where the advancement was made many years before the death of the testator. At the time of writing, an advancement by way of a gift of real property in 2006 would have a significantly greater value, say, where the testator dies in 2012. I hope that by the time of the next edition the situation will have reversed itself once more.

[8.20] It should also be noted that where the value of the advancement is greater than the benefit that would accrue to the child under the will, or intestacy as the case may be, the child will take nothing. This highlights the necessity for a testator to clearly state in his or her will whether the section is to apply or not.

Attention is also drawn to the broad definition of 'advancement' in s 63.

---

2.   *In Re Hickey Deceased; Hickey v Dwyer and Others* [2005] IEHC 365.

PART II: PRECEDENT CLAUSES

Bequest to child where the portion debt is expressed not to have been adeemed by the bequest

[8.21]

> **I GIVE AND BEQUEATH** to my son/daughter *(insert name)*, of *(address)*, [*or, to (name), of (address)*, to whom I stand *in loco parentis*,*], the sum of € *(amount in figures and words)* which sum is to be taken by my said son/daughter [*or, (name)*, to whom I stand *in loco parentis*] in addition to any moneys which I may have covenanted to pay to my said son/daughter [*or, (name)*, to whom I stand *in loco parentis*] by way of portion.

Bequest to child which will be considered adeemed in the event of a portion debt being paid

[8.22]

> I have covenanted to pay to my son/daughter *(insert name)*, of *(address)*, [*or, to (name), of (address)*, to whom I stand *in loco parentis*,*], the sum of € *(amount in figures and words)* on his/her marriage. **I GIVE AND BEQUEATH** the sum of € *(amount in figures and words)* to my said son/daughter [*or, (name)*, to whom I stand *in loco parentis*] provided always that if the sum I have covenanted to be paid has been paid by me upon the marriage of my said son/daughter [*or, (name)*, to whom I stand *in loco parentis*], this legacy will be considered adeemed and satisfied.

Exclusion of the ademption of a legacy by the payment of a portion

[8.23]

> **I GIVE AND BEQUEATH** the sum of € *(insert amount in figures and words)* to my son/daughter *(name)*, of *(address)*, [*or, to (name), of (address)*, to whom I stand *in loco parentis*,*] and the said legacy is to be paid even if I have made provision for my said son/daughter [*or, (name)*, to whom I stand *in loco parentis*] by way of portion during the course of my life.

Bequest to child which will be adeemed if portion is paid to child during the lifetime of the testator

[8.24]

> **I GIVE AND BEQUEATH** the sum of € *(insert amount in figures and words)* to my son/daughter *(name)*, of *(address)*, [*or, to (name), of (address)*, to whom I stand *in loco parentis*,*] provided always that if I have made provision for my said son/daughter [*or, (name)*, to whom I stand *in loco parentis*] during the course of my lifetime, the said legacy shall be considered adeemed and satisfied.

Bequest to creditor, which is expressed to be in satisfaction of the debt owed to the creditor by the testator at the date of the testator's death, with provision for priority

[8.25]

> **WHEREAS** at the date of execution of this, my will, I am indebted to *(insert name), of (address),* in the sum of € *(amount in figures and words)* without provision for interest. If the said indebtedness is not discharged by me during the course of my lifetime, then **I GIVE AND BEQUEATH** the sum of € *(amount in figures and words)* to the said *(name)* which is to be deemed to be in satisfaction of my indebtedness to him/her. *(Optional:* This bequest is to be paid in priority to all other bequests in this my will.)

Bequest to creditor in satisfaction of a debt to allow for the payment of interest, with provision for priority

[8.26]

> **WHEREAS** at the date of execution of this, my will, I am indebted to *(insert name), of (address),* in the sum of € *(amount in figures and words)* with interest accruing thereon at the rate of *(rate)* per centime per annum. Unless the said indebtedness has been discharged by me during the course of my lifetime, **I GIVE AND BEQUEATH** unto the said *(name)* such sum from my estate as will discharge the said indebtedness with accrued interest thereon up to the date of payment of the said indebtedness. *(Optional:* This bequest is to be paid in priority to all other bequests in this my will.)

Bequest to creditor, which is expressed to be in addition to any indebtedness due to the creditor at the date of death of the testator

[8.27]

> **WHEREAS** at the date of execution of this, my will, I am indebted to *(insert name), of (address),* in the sum of € *(amount in figures and words).* Whether or not the said indebtedness has been discharged by me during the course of my lifetime, **I GIVE AND BEQUEATH** the sum of € *(amount in figures and words)* to the said *(name)* and this sum is to be paid to the said *(name)* without prejudice to the right of the said to prove for the payment of the debt in the course of the administration of my estate.

Class gift to children of the testator or person to whom he or she stands in loco parentis with an express exclusion of the doctrine of advancement

[8.28]

> **I GIVE AND BEQUEATH** the sum of € *(insert amount in figures and words)* to my children living at the date of my death, [*or,* to my children living at the date of my death, including *(name), of (address),* to whom I stand *in loco parentis,*] in equal shares and in calculating the shares of my children [*or,* my children and the said *(name),* to whom I stand *in loco parentis*], the provisions of Section 63 of the Succession Act 1965 shall not apply and the shares of my children shall be calculated without regard to any advancement that may have

been made to any of my children [*or,* my children and the said *(name),* to whom I stand *in loco parentis*].

General exclusion of the operation of s 63 of the Succession Act 1965

[8.29]

In calculating the share of any child or person to whom I stand *in loco parentis* under this my will, or arising on any partial intestacy, the provisions of Section 63 of the Succession Act 1965 shall not be taken into account and the operation of Section 63 shall be excluded from this my will and any share arising on foot of any partial intestacy.

Release of debts by the testator

[8.30]

A testator may wish to release a debtor from the payment of a debt after his or her death, whether the debt be secured subject to interest or be unsecured. If so, the following clauses may be inserted in the will of the testator.

(i)   Release of debt, without provision for interest, not repaid by the debtor at the date of the testator's death

WHEREAS there is a sum of € *(insert amount in figures and words),* without provision for interest, due and owing to me from *(name),* of *(address).* If the amount due on foot of the said debt has not been repaid to me by the said *(name)* at the date of my death, **I HEREBY RELEASE** the said *(name)* [and his/her estate in the event that he/she predeceases me] from the payment of the debt of the said sum of € *(amount).*

(ii)   Release of debt, where there is provision for interest, not repaid by the debtor at the date of the testator's death

WHEREAS there is a sum of € *(insert amount in figures and words)* due and owing to me from *(name),* of *(address)* together with interest thereon at the rate of *(rate)* per centum per annum. If the amount due on foot of the said debt has not been repaid to me by the said *(name)* at the date of my death, **I HEREBY RELEASE** the said *(name)* [and his/her estate in the event that he/she predeceases me] from the payment of the debt and all interest due and owing to me on foot of the said indebtedness.

(iii)   Release of secured debt with expenses of release to be borne by residue

WHEREAS there is a sum of € *(insert amount in figures and words)* due and owing to me from *(name),* of *(address)* together with interest thereon at the rate of *(rate)* per centum per annum, the payment of which said debt is secured by way of mortgage/charge on lands belonging to the said *(name),* at *(insert address, or otherwise describe security).* If the amount due on foot of the said debt has not been repaid to me by the said *(name)* at the date of my death, **I HEREBY RELEASE** the said *(name)* [and his/ her estate in the event that he/she predeceases me] from the payment of the said debt and interest due and owing on foot of the said debt and **I DIRECT** my executors to take all necessary steps to release the said charge/mortgage, the costs of such release to be borne by the residue of my estate.

Chapter 9

FULLY-SECRET AND HALF-SECRET TRUSTS

PART I: COMMENTARY

[9.01] Sections 77 and 78 of the 1965 Act lay down the requirements for a valid will, but a general maxim of equity is that *equity will not allow a statute to be used as an instrument of fraud.* By reason of this maxim, the law has recognised the creation of fully-secret or half-secret trusts by wills.

In the case of a fully-secret trust, the existence of the trust is not revealed on the face of the will and ostensibly the person named as the beneficiary in the will is entitled to the benefit conferred upon him or her. In the case of a half-secret trust, the existence of the trust will be revealed on the face of the will, but the object or objects of the trust will be kept secret.

Example

> I GIVE AND BEQUEATH the sum of €5,000.00 (five thousand euro) to my son
> Peter, upon trust.

It is clear that Peter is not the beneficial owner of the €5,000, but the identity of the true beneficiary is kept secret.

In order for a fully-secret or half-secret trust to be enforceable against the person named as beneficiary, it must be communicated to the beneficiary that he or she is not entitled to the benefit of the bequest but is holding the subject matter of the bequest on trust for some person.

Further, the beneficiary named in the will must acquiesce in this arrangement. Further, it appears that where a benefit is conferred on a number of persons as joint tenants, the true nature of the bequest need only be communicated to one of the beneficiaries, whereas it appears that where the benefit is left to a number of persons as tenants in common, the true nature of the bequest must be communicated to each of them. There appears to be no logical explanation for the distinction.

[9.02] To avoid difficulties arising at a later time, it is best when creating a fully-secret or half-secret trust in a will to draw up a document, which is to be signed by all the persons who might appear to be the beneficiaries, which acknowledges that the true nature of the bequest has been communicated to them and that they will fulfil the testator's wishes with regard to the bequest.

The device of a fully-secret or half-secret trust might be used where, for some reason or another, the testator does not wish the true beneficiary's identity to be revealed. It must be remembered that when wills are proved, they become public documents and are open to inspection by the public. By using correctly the device of the fully-secret or half-secret trust, the testator can keep his or her true intentions secret, because the fully-secret or half-secret trust is said to operate *de hors* (or outside) the will. The document acknowledging the true nature of the fully-secret or half-secret trust, the true nature of the bequest and the acquiescence of the ostensible beneficiary in the arrangement is not a testamentary document and, therefore, will not be proved as part of the will.

The bequest creating the fully-secret or half-secret trust will not differ from any other bequest in the will. It may be a general pecuniary bequest, a general bequest, a demonstrative legacy, a specific legacy or devise, or a residuary bequest. As pointed out, the difference between the fully-secret and half-secret trust is that the latter reveals the existence of the trust.

Authorities are not particularly settled as to when communication must be made to the ostensible beneficiary, but it is better that communication be made either before the will is executed or at least at the same time as the will is being executed.

It should be noted that a fully-secret or half-secret trust is still a trust and general trust law will be applicable to it. The trustee will have the usual trust and fiduciary duties to the beneficiary. If the subject matter of the fully-secret or half-secret trust involves land, then the provision of the 2009 Act in relation to trusts for land will be applicable.

PART II: PRECEDENT

Precedent for document that might be signed by the ostensible beneficiary or beneficiaries acknowledging the true nature of the bequest and their acquiescence in holding the property on foot of the fully-secret or half-secret trust

[9.03]

This acknowledgement made the (*insert date*) day of (*month*), (*year*), to (*name of testator*), of (*address*), (hereinafter called 'the Testator'), by (*name of ostensible beneficiary/trustee*), of (*address*) [if there is more than one ostensible beneficiary or trustee, insert all of their names and addresses], (hereinafter called 'the Trustee[s]').

WHEREAS:

1. The Testator has made and duly executed his/her last will and testament on the same day as the date of this acknowledgement.

2. In the said will, the Testator has included the following bequest.

   I GIVE, DEVISE AND BEQUEATH the sum of € (*insert amount in figures and words*) to [my (*relationship to testator, if any*)] (*name of ostensible beneficiary/trustee*), of (*address*).

   [*Fully-secret trust*]

or **I GIVE, DEVISE AND BEQUEATH** my dwelling house at (*insert address of dwelling house*) to [my (*relationship to testator, if any*)] (*name of ostensible beneficiary/trustee*), of (*address*) in trust.

   [*Half-secret trust*]

or **I GIVE, DEVISE AND BEQUEATH** all the rest, residue and remainder of my property of every nature and kind and wheresoever situate unto [my (*insert relationship to testator, if any*)] (*name of first ostensible beneficiary/trustee*), of (*address*) and [my (*relationship to testator, if any*)] (*name of second ostensible beneficiary/trustee*), of (*address*) and (*name of third ostensible beneficiary/trustee*), of (*address*) jointly.

   [*Fully-secret trust – joint tenants*]

or **I GIVE, DEVISE AND BEQUEATH** all my estate of every nature and description and kind wheresoever situate to [my (*insert relationship to testator, if any*)] (*name of first ostensible beneficiary/trustee*), of (*address*) and [my (*relationship to testator, if any*)] (*name of second ostensible beneficiary/trustee*), of (*address*) and (*name of third ostensible beneficiary/trustee*), of (*address*) in trust.

   [*Universal bequest – half-secret trust – tenants in common*]

   It has been communicated to me/us that the bequest contained in the said will is for the benefit of (*name of true beneficiary/ beneficiaries*) of (*address of true beneficiary/beneficiaries*) and that I am/we are to hold the subject matter of the bequest upon trust for *(name of true beneficiary/ beneficiaries)*.

NOW I/WE, the Trustee[s], **HEREBY ACKNOWLEDGE AND CONFIRM** that the true nature of the bequest contained in the will of the Testator has been communicated and explained to me/us and **I/WE HEREBY UNDERTAKE** to apply the subject matter of the bequest contained in the will of the Testator for the benefit of *(name of true beneficiary/beneficiaries)*, of *(address of true beneficiary/beneficiaries)*.

DATED THE *(DATE)* DAY OF *(MONTH)*, *(YEAR)*.

SIGNED BY

(NAME OF TESTATOR)

IN THE PRESENCE OF:

SIGNED BY

(NAME OF TRUSTEE)

IN THE PRESENCE OF:

(If more than one trustee, have an execution clause for each.)

Chapter 10

RESIDUARY BEQUESTS

PART I: COMMENTARY

Importance of residuary bequest

[10.01] Even where the will, by means of specific and other bequests, appears to dispose of the entirety of the estate, it is always presumed that there is a residuary estate. Therefore, it is an essential provision of a well-drafted will that there be a bequest of the residue of the testator's estate.

[10.02] It is possible that even the most meticulously prepared testator may neglect to dispose of certain assets, particularly items of personal effect. Pecuniary legacies may not exhaust the entire of the amount of funds at the testator's disposal when the will comes into operation. It is equally possible that the testator may come into an inheritance shortly before he or she dies, which was unexpected, or he or she could win the National Lottery, in which case his or her residuary legatees and devisees could do very well indeed!

[10.03] Any legacy that fails or lapses will, as a general rule, fall into the residuary estate (s 91 of the Succession Act 1965). The testator may have a view as to whom he or she wishes to benefit in that event.

[10.04] The evaluation of the residue of the estate at the time the will is drawn up is most important. It enables the testator to consider what property he or she has disposed of by way of general, pecuniary or specific bequests and what property will pass under the residuary bequest. It is possible, when this evaluation is made, that a testator may decide to dispose of assets that would otherwise form part of the residue in a specific or general way.

[10.05] It would be important, therefore, for a practitioner, after a list of general and specific legacies has been made, to explain to the testator what the residue of his or her estate comprises in before the testator goes on to give instructions as to the disposition of the residue. It would also be important to explain to a testator that if he or she has any large acquisition of property after the date of making his or her will and that property is not specifically mentioned in the will because of its late acquisition, the property would pass under the residuary clause. Therefore, he or she should keep his or her will under review, particularly after any major (in relative terms) acquisition or, indeed, disposal of an asset.

In the context of the failure of a legacy or bequest, I would reiterate that if a residuary bequest fails or lapses, this will give rise to a partial intestacy.

[10.06] The destination of the residue of a person's estate is important for another reason. Generally speaking, where there is no executor able to act in relation to the administration of the estate of a deceased person, either because the executor has predeceased the deceased, there is no executor appointed, or the executors appointed

145

have renounced their rights, the next person or persons entitled to administer the estate of the deceased will be his or her residuary legatees and devisees. If there is no clear disposition of the residue of the estate of the deceased, then the persons who will usually be entitled to administer the estate of the deceased and raise representation to his or her estate will be the persons entitled to his or her estate under the intestacy rules (s 74 of the 1965 Act).

[10.07] The residue of the estate can be left to persons in trust for other persons, in which case the will shall create:

(a)   residuary legatees and devisees in trust;

(b)   beneficial residuary legatees and devisees, either for life, in remainder or absolute.

[10.08] Generally speaking, the order of entitlement to raise representation in respect of the estate of a deceased person, where there is no executor available to act, shall be as follows:

(a)   the residuary legatee and devisee in trust;

(b)   if there is no residuary legatee and devisee in trust, or that person has predeceased the deceased, the residuary legatee and devisee for life;

(c)   if there is no residuary legatee and devisee in trust or for life, then the ultimate residuary legatee and devisee or the residuary legatee and devisee in remainder.

Whether a trust should be created and trusts of land where residue will comprise land

[10.09] There is no necessity to create a trust in respect of the residue of the estate of the testator. A trust should only really be created where the persons entitled to the residue would not be able or would not wish to manage the property themselves, either due to incapacity as a result of minority or mental capacity, or perhaps through old age.

[10.10] Where, however, the residue is left to a person or persons for life, with remainder over to another person or persons, then that will create a settlement, and if the residue comprises land, the provisions of the 2009 Act in relation to trusts of land will apply. Further, if the residue may pass to minors and includes land, this will also create a trust of land under the 2009 Act. The executors, for the sake of clarity, might additionally be appointed trustees of any trust arising under the 2009 Act; if not, the provisions of the Act will be relied upon to identify the trustees. Part 4 of the 2009 Act is set out in full at **Appendix 12, Pt 1**.

Variation of trusts

[10.11] See **Ch 13** in relation to the variation by court of 'relevant trusts', for the benefit of a 'relevant person' by way of 'arrangement' under the provisions of Pt 5 of the 2009 Act.

Considerations in relation to residuary trusts – bare trust, discretionary trust, trust for sale

[10.12] If a trust is to be created in respect of the residue, consideration should be given to the following:

(a)   Whether the trust is to be simply a bare trust, whereby the trustees are to hold the residue of the estate upon trust for named beneficiaries, with the shares to which the beneficiaries are to be entitled being defined by the testator. Even where a bare trust is to be created, it is important that certain basic powers be given to the trustees, such as powers of investment, power to run a business and powers of sale in respect of the residuary estate.

(b)   Whether the residue should be the subject matter of a discretionary trust or perhaps a special power of appointment among certain beneficiaries as defined in the will. A discretionary trust arises where the property is given to trustees with discretion to them to apply the property for the benefit of the beneficiaries in such manner as the trustees in their discretion shall think fit. A special power of appointment arises where a property is left to a person (usually for life) with a power to appoint the property amongst a class of persons excluding the donee of the power, eg, the testator's spouse/civil partner, children or a more broadly defined class. Care should be take to properly define the class so the persons exercising the power of appointment or discretion under the discretionary trust can easily identify in whose favour they are to exercise the power or discretion (See *Crawford and another v Lawless*;[1] see also *O'Byrne v Davoren*.[2])

(c)   Regard should be had to the tax provisions in relation to the type of trust the will will create. While these may change from time to time and be different at the time the will comes into operation, the tendency is to increase the level of such taxation rather than decrease it. The testator should be encouraged to review the terms of his or her will in line with changes in taxation.

(d)   Where a discretionary trust is being set up for the benefit of some person who is not capable of managing his or her affairs, or a child of the testator under the age of 18, or under the age of 21 and in full-time education, this will attract an exemption from the discretionary trust tax. It is useful to state on the face of the will the purpose for which the discretionary trust is being set up, so that the exemption may be more easily availed of.

(e)   In the case of a discretionary trust, regard should also be given to the trust powers that may be given to the trustees. These powers should be as extensive as possible, having regard to the assets that will likely comprise the estate of the testator. Where land forms part of the trust, consideration must be given to Pt 4 of the 2009 Act, which is set out at **Appendix 4** and dealt with more fully in **Ch 5**.

(f)   Consideration should also be given as to whether a trust for sale might be created. This will most usually arise in relation to land, though it is not unusual

---

1.   *Crawford and another v Lawless* [2002] IR 416.
2.   *O'Byrne v Davoren* [1994] 3 IR 373.

for the entire residue to be left on trust for sale. The residue may often include more than land. A trust for the sale of land is a trust of land within the meaning of Pt 4 of the 2009 Act. There will be no need to create a trust for sale where the persons who will become entitled to the residue are likely to be all of full age, not suffering from any incapacity, and absolutely entitled to the property. In such a case, the executors will simply vest the assets comprising the residue in the residuary legatees and devisees and they can deal with the property as they think fit. Alternatively, the residuary legatees and devisees can give their directions to the executors to deal with the property as they may require.

(g)   The advantage of a trust for sale is that it removes any doubt in respect of the trustees' power of sale, as they are in fact under an imperative obligation to sell the property, although, of course, wills should provide that the obligation to sell under the trust for sale may be postponed at the discretion of the trustees. A trust for sale of land now gives rise to trust of land under the 2009 Act and its provisions shall apply. Part 4 of the 2009 Act is set out at **Appendix 12, Pt 1**.

Powers of trustees

[10.13] Where a trust is to be created in respect of the residue, the testator needs to decide whether he or she wishes to appoint trustees separate from his or her executors to deal with the residue or whether he or she will constitute his or her executors his or her trustees also. In the course of the administration of the estate, it should be remembered that the capacity of executor is different to the capacity of trustees, and before a personal representative takes the step of vesting the property in the trustees, regard should be had to the power of the trustees to deal with the property as given by the will as against the power of the executor to deal with the property in his or her capacity as such, eg, an executor, by being a personal representative, has a power of sale under s 50 of the Succession Act 1965. For so long as the property remains in him or her in his or her capacity as executor, he or she can, therefore, sell the property under his or her statutory power.

Where, however, the executors are also trustees (or other persons are trustees and the property is vested in them in their capacity as such) and the will does not confer a power of sale on the trustees, the trustees, in that capacity, will not be able to sell the property except with the leave of all of the beneficiaries who are *sui juris* or, alternatively, with the leave of the court.

In any case, therefore, where trustees are being appointed, they should be given sufficient powers to enable them to deal flexibly with the property of the testator as might comprise his or her estate at the date of his or her death.

In relation to trusts of land, regard should be had to the provisions of Pt 4 of the 2009 Act, which is set out in full at **Appendix 12, Pt 1**.

See further **Ch 12** on executor and trustee powers.

Vested and contingent residuary bequests

[10.14] Thought should be given as to whether the residuary bequest is to be a vested one or a contingent one.

The residuary bequest may be vested in possession or vested in interest. Property is said to be vested in possession where the person is entitled to enjoy immediate possession of the property. In this context, if the property is vested absolutely in the beneficiary, subject to the executor or legal personal representative passing legal title to him or her, the interest will be vested in possession as of the date of death.

If, on the other hand, the interest of the beneficiary is postponed by some prior estate, such as a life estate, then the interest will still be vested, but vested in interest.

A person with a vested or contingent interest may constitute a 'relevant person' in relation to a 'relevant trust', which may be varied by 'arrangement' approved by the court. See **Ch 13**.

Example 1:

'**I GIVE, DEVISE AND BEQUEATH** all the rest, residue and remainder of my property to my son Christopher.'

Christopher has an interest in the residue vested in possession as of the date of death, subject to the legal estate being vested in him by the executors or legal personal representatives.

Example 2:

'**I GIVE, DEVISE AND BEQUEATH** all the rest, residue and remainder of my estate to my wife for her life and on her death to my son Christopher absolutely.'

Assuming that the wife of the testator survived him, then she will have an interest in the residue vested in possession, but Christopher's interest will be vested in interest.

[10.15] A contingent interest in the residue will arise where the vesting is postponed for some reason. This may happen in two ways:

(a)   where the beneficiary has to fulfil some condition before the residue vests in him or her, eg, attain the age of 18 years;

(b)   where there is a class bequest and the class has not closed. In order for an interest to be vested, the person in whom it is vested must be known and the precise extent of the interest must be known. In the case of a class bequest, where the class is not closed, it may not be possible to state that the interest is vested until the class closes.

Example

'**I GIVE, DEVISE AND BEQUEATH** all the rest, residue and remainder of my property to such of my children as attain the age of twenty-one years in equal shares.'

Until the last child of the testator attains the age of 21 years, it will not be known how many persons comprise the class and until such time as the class closes, the interest will remain a contingent one.

[10.16] Section 16 of the 2009 Act abolishes:

  (a) the common law contingent remainder rules;

  (b) the rule in *Purefoy v Rogers*;

  (c) the rule in *Whitby v Mitchell*;

  (d) the rule against perpetuities;

  (e) the rule against accumulations.

Section 17 of the 2009 Act provides that the abolition applies to 'any interest in property'. Section 3 of the 2009 Act defines property as 'any real or personal property or any part or combination of such property'.

So those 'rules' do not concern the drafter of a will from here on out; however, regard should be had to drafting any condition with clarity and to ensuring that the same is not void for uncertainty or leads to an ambiguity that can only be resolved by recourse to court with attendant costs.

Universal bequest

[10.17] Where all of the estate of a testator is left to one beneficiary or to a number of beneficiaries, they are generally known as the universal legatees and devisees. This is still a residuary bequest because it must be borne in mind that the death, funeral and testamentary expenses of the testator have to be paid prior to a distribution of the estate. Therefore, the universal legatees and devisees will take the residue left when the death, funeral and testamentary expenses have been paid.

Generally speaking, however, where all of the estate is left to one particular person or a number of persons, they will be characterised as *universal legatees and devisees* when extracting a grant of representation to the estate of the testator in the event that there is no executor available to act.

PART II: PRECEDENT CLAUSES

Bequest of entire estate of the testator

[10.18]

> After payment of all my just debts, funeral and testamentary expenses, **I GIVE, DEVISE AND BEQUEATH** all my estate of every nature and description and kind, wheresoever situate, to [my *(insert relationship to testator, if any)*] *(name)*, of *(address)* absolutely.

Bequest of entire estate to two or more persons where they are to take as joint tenants

[10.19]

> After payment of all my just debts, funeral and testamentary expenses, **I GIVE, DEVISE AND BEQUEATH** all my estate of every nature and description and kind, wheresoever situate, to [my *(insert relationship to testator, if any)*] *(name)*, of *(address)* and [my *(relationship to testator, if any)*] *(name)*, of *(address)* [jointly *or* as joint tenants].

> (*Note*: it is not necessary to include the words 'jointly' or 'as joint tenants'. Where there are no words of severance the persons taking under the bequest will take jointly. If one of the beneficiaries predeceases the testator, the survivors will take that person's share; this will also be the case even if the beneficiary who predeceases the testator is issue of the testator and dies leaving issue. Section 98 of the Succession Act 1965 provides that the bequest will take effect in such circumstances as if the beneficiary survived the testator and died immediately after him or her. Where property is left to persons as joint tenants and a person survives the testator and later dies, then the property passes to the other beneficiaries by right of survivorship.)

Bequest of entire estate to two or more persons where they are to take as tenants in common

[10.20]

> After payment of all my just debts, funeral and testamentary expenses, **I GIVE, DEVISE AND BEQUEATH** all my estate of every nature and description and kind, wheresoever situate, [amongst, between, to be divided between] [my *(insert relationship to testator, if any)*] *(name)*, of *(address)* and [my *(relationship to testator, if any)*] *(name)*, of *(address)* and [my *(relationship to testator, if any)*] *(name)*, of *(address)* [equally, in equal shares, share and share alike, as tenants in common].

> (*Note*: where any of the words underlined are used, these will constitute words of severance and the bequest will be taken by the named persons as tenants in common. If any of the beneficiaries predeceases the testator, then unless the exception in s 98 of the Succession Act 1965 applies, the bequest to the

particular beneficiary will lapse and give rise to a partial intestacy, and the share of that person will pass to the next-of-kin of the testator living at the date of his or her death. Where s 98 does apply, ie, where one of the beneficiaries, being issue of the testator, predeceases him or her, leaving issue, then the share of that beneficiary will form part of his or her estate to be distributed in accordance with his or her will or intestacy as the case may be.)

Bequest of entire estate where the beneficiaries are to take as tenants in common with an alternative provision in the event of any of the universal legatees and devisees predeceasing the testator

[10.21]

After payment of all my just debts, funeral and testamentary expenses, **I GIVE, DEVISE AND BEQUEATH** all my estate of every nature and description and kind, wheresoever situate, [amongst, between, to be divided between] [my *(insert relationship to testator, if any)*] *(name), of (address)* and [my *(relationship to testator, if any)*] *(name), of (address)* and [my *(relationship to testator, if any)*] *(name), of (address)* [equally, in equal shares, share and share alike, as tenants in common]. In the event of any of the said *(name)* or *(name)* or *(name)* predeceasing me, then **I GIVE, DEVISE AND BEQUEATH** the share of that beneficiary to the children of that beneficiary living at the date of my death, and if more than one in equal shares. In the event that one of the said beneficiaries predeceases me without leaving issue, then **I DIRECT** that the share of that beneficiary shall pass to the remaining beneficiaries in equal shares, and if only one beneficiary should survive me, then the entire of my estate shall pass to that beneficiary.

(*Note 1*: the underlined words constitute words of severance.)

(*Note 2*: see **Ch 11** re alternative gifts over.)

Bequest of legal right share to spouse/civil partner with residue of the estate to the children of the testator, with provision for the spouse/civil partner of the testator predeceasing him or her or dying simultaneously with him or her, and with further provision that the share of any of the children shall pass to the children of that child in the event that any of the children predeceases the testator

[10.22]

After payment of all my just debts, funeral and testamentary expenses, **I GIVE, DEVISE AND BEQUEATH** one-third of my entire estate of every nature and description and kind, wheresoever situate, to my husband/wife/civil partner, *(insert name), of (address, if different from testator)* in satisfaction of his/her legal right share in my estate. All the rest, residue and remainder of my estate, **I GIVE, DEVISE AND BEQUEATH** to my children in equal shares.

In the event that my husband/wife/civil partner predeceases me or dies in common calamity with me, then **I GIVE, DEVISE AND BEQUEATH** the one-third share bequeathed to my husband/wife to my said children in equal shares.

In the event of any of my children predeceasing me, then **I DIRECT** that the share of that child shall pass to any children of that child in equal shares and in the event that any of my children predeceases me without leaving children, then the share of that child shall pass to my children living at the date of my death.

(*Note 1*: it would be futile to put in a provision making the bequest of the legal right share subject to the spouse surviving the testator by a period of a particular number of days, because in the case of *O'Dwyer and Another v Keegan and Others*,[3] the Supreme Court held that the legal right share vests in the spouse on death, where there is no other provision made for the spouse in the will.)

(*Note 2*: see **Ch 11** re alternative gifts over.)

Bequest of legal right share to spouse/civil partner where there are no children, with provision for the residue of the estate to be bequeathed to other persons and with provision dealing with the legal right share in the event that the spouse predeceases the testator or dies simultaneously with him or her

[10.23]

After payment of all my just debts, funeral and testamentary expenses, **I GIVE, DEVISE AND BEQUEATH** one-half of my entire estate of every nature and description and kind, wheresoever situate, to my husband/wife/civil partner, *(insert name)*, of *(address, if different from testator)*, in satisfaction of his/her legal right share in my estate.

All the rest, residue and remainder of my property **I GIVE, DEVISE AND BEQUEATH** to [my *(relationship to testator, if any)*] *(name)*, of *(address)* and [my *(relationship to testator, if any)*] *(name)*, of *(address)* and [my *(relationship to testator, if any)*] *(name)*, of *(address)* in equal shares.

In the event that my husband/wife/civil partner predeceases me or dies simultaneously with me, then **I DIRECT** that the one-half share of the estate bequeathed to him/her shall be bequeathed to the Samaritans (Dublin Branch) of 112 Marlborough Street, in the City of Dublin.

In the event of any of the said *(name)* or *(name)* or *(name)* predeceasing me, then **I DIRECT** that the share of that beneficiary shall pass to any children of him/her living at the date of my death in equal shares, or in the event that the said beneficiary predeceases me without leaving children, the said share to which that beneficiary would have been entitled shall pass to the remaining beneficiaries

---

3.   *O'Dwyer and Another v Keegan and Others* [1997] 2 IR 585.

and if only one of the said beneficiaries shall survive me, to that beneficiary absolutely.

(*Note*: see **Ch 11** re alternative gifts over.)

Bequest of residue of the estate of the testator to a single beneficiary

[10.24]

I GIVE, DEVISE AND BEQUEATH all the rest, residue and remainder of my estate of every nature and description and kind, wheresoever situate, to [my *(insert relationship to testator, if any)*] *(name)*, of *(address)* absolutely.

Bequest of residue to two or more persons, where they are to take as joint tenants

[10.25]

I GIVE, DEVISE AND BEQUEATH all the rest, residue and remainder of my estate of every nature and description and kind, wheresoever situate, to [my *(insert relationship to testator, if any)*] *(name)*, of *(address)* and [my *(relationship to testator, if any)*] *(name)*, of *(address)* [jointly *or* as joint tenants].

(*Note*: it is not necessary to include the words 'jointly' or 'as joint tenants'. Where the bequest does not contain words of severance the persons taking under the bequest will take jointly. If one of the beneficiaries predeceases the testator, the survivors will take that person's share. That will be the case even if the beneficiary who predeceases the testator is issue of the testator and dies leaving issue. Section 98 of the Succession Act 1965 provides that the bequest will take effect in such circumstances as if the beneficiary survived the testator and died immediately after him or her. Where property is left to persons as joint tenants and a person survives the testator and later dies, then the property passes to the other beneficiaries by right of survivorship.)

Bequest of residue to two or more persons where they are to take as tenants in common

[10.26]

I GIVE, DEVISE AND BEQUEATH all the rest, residue and remainder of my estate of every nature and description and kind, wheresoever situate, [amongst, between, to be divided between] [my *(insert relationship to testator, if any)*] *(name)*, of *(address)* and [my *(relationship to testator, if any)*] *(name)*, of *(address)* and [my *(relationship to testator, if any)*] *(name)*, of *(address)* [equally, in equal shares, share and share alike, as tenants in common].

(*Note*: if any of the underlined words are used, these will constitute words of severance and the bequest will be taken by the named persons as tenants in common. Where any of the beneficiaries predeceases the testator, then unless the exception in s 98 of the Succession Act 1965 applies, the bequest to the particular beneficiary will lapse and give rise to a partial intestacy, and the share of that person will pass to the next-of-kin of the testator living at the date of his or her death. Where s 98 does apply, ie, where one of the beneficiaries, being issue of the testator, predeceases him or her, leaving issue, then the share of that beneficiary will form part of his or her estate to be distributed in accordance with his or her will or intestacy as the case may be.)

Bequest of residue where the beneficiaries are to take as tenants in common with an alternative provision in the event of any of the universal legatees and devisees predeceasing the testator

[10.27]

I GIVE, DEVISE AND BEQUEATH all the rest, residue and remainder of my estate of every nature and description and kind, wheresoever situate, [amongst, between, to be divided between] [my *(insert relationship to testator, if any)*] *(name),* of *(address)* and [my *(relationship to testator, if any)*] *(name),* of *(address)* and [my *(relationship to testator, if any)*] *(name),* of *(address)* [equally, in equal shares, share and share alike, as tenants in common]. In the event of any of the said *(name)* or *(name)* or *(name)* predeceasing me, then I GIVE, DEVISE AND BEQUEATH the share of that beneficiary to the children of that beneficiary living at the date of my death, and if more than one in equal shares. In the event that one of the said beneficiaries predeceases me without leaving issue, then I DIRECT that the share of that beneficiary shall pass to the remaining beneficiaries in equal shares, and if only one beneficiary should survive me, then the entire of my estate shall pass to that beneficiary.

(*Note 1*: the words underlined constitute words of severance.)

(*Note 2*: see **Ch 11** re alternative gifts over.)

Bequest of residue to spouse/civil partner for life with provision for gift over of remainder

[10.28]

I GIVE, DEVISE AND BEQUEATH all the rest, residue and remainder of my estate of every nature and description and kind, wheresoever situate, to my husband/wife/civil partner, *(insert name),* of *(address, if different from testator)*, for life, with remainder over to my children in equal shares and in the event that any of my children predeceases me, then I DIRECT that the share of that child shall pass to the children of such child and in the event that any of my children predeceases me without leaving issue, then the share of that child shall pass to my remaining children.

(*Note 1*: where there is a bequest of this nature, the spouse/civil partner would have to be put to his or her election under the provisions of s 115 of the Succession Act 1965 (as amended by the 2010 Act) and the spouse/civil partner would have to choose between the value of his or her legal right share and the value of the life estate in the residuary estate. In instances where the spouse/civil

155

partner is quite young, the value of the life estate might outweigh the value of the legal right share. Even in cases where the spouse/civil partner is quite elderly, the benefit of income from the residue of the estate of the testator might be better than one-third or one-half share in the estate absolutely.)

(*Note 2*: the creation of a life estate may also create a trust of land if the residue comprises real estate, and in that event trustees of the trusts of land should be appointed. Part 4 of the 2009 Act is set out in **Appendix 12, Pt 1**.)

(*Note 3*: see **Ch 11** re alternative gifts over.)

Bequest of residue to the executors upon trust for the spouse/civil partner of the testator during his or her life or until he or she shall remarry or enter into a civil partnership, with remainder over to the children of the testator living at the date of death of the spouse or the date of his or her remarriage

[10.29]

> **I GIVE, DEVISE AND BEQUEATH** all the rest, residue and remainder of my estate of every nature and description and kind, wheresoever situate, to my executors and trustees upon the following trusts.
>
> (a)   For my husband/wife/civil partner *(insert name)*, of *(address, if different from testator)* for his/her life or until he/she might remarry or enter into a civil partnership.
>
> (b)   Upon the death of my husband/wife or upon his/her remarriage or entry into a civil partnership, upon trust for my children, living at date of the remarriage or death of my husband/wife, and if more than one, in equal shares.

(*Note 1*: it should not be assumed that because the surviving spouse was in a heterosexual relationship that he or she might not at some time enter into a civil partnership. If the contingency is limited to marriage only and the surviving spouse were to enter into a civil partnership, the estate of the spouse would not divest.)

(*Note 2*: in this instance, the spouse or civil partner would have to be put to his or her election.)

(*Note 3*: in this instance, as the executors and trustees are being appointed the residuary legatees and devisees in trust, it would be necessary to appoint the executors and trustees as trustees for the purposes of any trust of land that arises under the provisions of Pt 4 of the 2009 Act.)

(*Note 4*: where the residue of the estate is left upon trust, consideration should be given to the powers that might be given to the trustees, and unless the residue is left upon a trust for sale, consideration should be given as to whether the trustees are to have a power of sale – see **Ch 12** dealing with powers of trustees.)

Bequest of residue to trustees to hold the property on trust for the spouse/ civil partner of the testator for his or her life, or for so long as he or she shall not remarry or enter into a civil partnership, with remainder over to the brothers and sisters of the testator (assuming he or she has no issue), where the trustees are different to the executors appointed in the will

[10.30]

> **I GIVE, DEVISE AND BEQUEATH** all the rest, residue and remainder of my estate of every nature and description and kind, wheresoever situate, unto *(insert name), of (address)* and *(name), of (address)* (hereinafter called 'my trustees') to hold the same upon the following trust, that is to say:
>
> (a) Upon trust for my husband/wife/civil partner *(name), of (address, if different from testator)* for his/her life, or until his/her remarriage or entry into a civil partnership.
>
> (b) To hold the same in remainder for the benefit of my brothers and sisters as are living at the date of death or remarriage or civil partnership of my said husband/wife/civil partner in equal shares.
>
> I appoint my trustees, trustees for the purposes of the Land and Conveyancing Law Reform Act 2009.
>
> *(Note 1:* it should not be assumed that because the surviving spouse was in a heterosexual relationship that he or she might not at some time enter into a civil partnership. If the contingency is limited to marriage only and the surviving spouse were to enter into a civil partnership, the estate of the spouse would not divest.)
>
> *(Note 2:* in this instance, the spouse or civil partner would have to be put to his or her election.)
>
> *(Note 3:* in this instance, as the executors and trustees are being appointed the residuary legatees and devisees in trust, it would be necessary to appoint the executors and trustees as trustees for the purposes of any trust of land that arises under the provisions of Pt 4 of the 2009 Act.)
>
> *(Note 4:* where the residue of the estate is left upon trust, consideration should be given to the powers that might be given to the trustees, and unless the residue is left upon a trust for sale, consideration should be given as to whether the trustees are to have a power of sale – see **Ch 12** dealing with powers of trustees.)

Absolute bequest of residue to the children of the testator, with alternative provision to the spouse/civil partner of any child who predeceases the testator, and in the event that a child dies without spouse/civil partner, to the children of that child of the testator

[10.31]

I GIVE, DEVISE AND BEQUEATH all the rest, residue and remainder of my estate of every nature and description and kind, wheresoever situate, to my children in equal shares.

In the event that any child predeceases me leaving a spouse or civil partner, then **I DIRECT** that the share of that child shall pass to his/her spouse or civil partner.

In the event that any of my children predeceases me without leaving a spouse/ civil partner (or leaving a spouse/civil partner from whom he/she is judicially separated or separated by agreement, or who is in desertion of him/her at the date of my death, however long that desertion may have been at the date of my death, or who would be otherwise unworthy to succeed to the estate of my child by virtue of the provisions of Section 120 of the Succession Act 1965), but leaving children, then **I GIVE** the share of that child to his/her children, and if more than one, in equal shares.

And in the event that any of my children dies leaving no spouse/civil partner (or leaving a spouse/civil partner from whom he/she is judicially separated or separated by agreement, or who is in desertion of him/her at the date of my death, however long that desertion may have been at the date of my death, or who would be otherwise unworthy to succeed to the estate of my child by virtue of the provisions of Section 120 of the Succession Act 1965), and no children, then the share of that child shall pass to my children living at the date of my death in equal shares.

(*Note*: see **Ch 11** re alternative gifts over.)

Bare trust of residue for the benefit of the children of the testator who attain the age of 18 years

[10.32]

I GIVE, DEVISE AND BEQUEATH all the rest, residue and remainder of my estate of every nature and description and kind, wheresoever situate, unto my executors and trustees, upon trust to divide the same amongst my children living at the date of my death and who attain the age of eighteen years, and if more than one, in equal shares. But if any of my said children dies before attaining the age of eighteen years leaving a spouse, civil partner or children, then the share of that child shall pass to his/her spouse, civil partner and children in equal shares.

(*Note*: as there is a potential for infants to become entitled to a share in the estate of the testator, this could create a trust of land under Pt 4 of the 2009 Act and, therefore, the executors and trustees should be appointed trustees for the purposes of that Act and for the purposes of s 57 of the Succession Act 1965 – see precedents in **Ch 5** dealing with appointment of executors. Consideration should also be given as to the powers that may be given to the trustees pending the vesting of the bequests in the children of the testator – see **Ch 12** on powers of trustees.)

Bequest of residue to spouse/civil partner for life with a special power of appointment amongst the children of the testator as the spouse/civil partner may in his or her discretion by deed or will appoint

[10.33]

I GIVE, DEVISE AND BEQUEATH all the rest, residue and remainder of my estate of every nature and description and kind, wheresoever situate, unto my husband/wife/civil partner *(insert name)*, of *(address, if different from testator)* for his/her life and thereafter such one or more of my children and in such shares or proportions as he/she may by deed or will appoint and in default of my said husband/wife/civil partner exercising the said special power of appointment hereby created, to my children in equal shares.

(Note 1: once again, this will potentially create a trust of land, so it would be important to have trustees appointed for the purpose of the 2009 Act.)

(Note 2: attention is drawn to the underlined words in the bequest. If these words are omitted, then it would mean that the power of appointment could only be effectively exercised by the spouse of the testator appointing the property to one child. A special power of appointment must be exercised strictly in accordance with its terms and any defective exercise will be void. Great care should be taken in drafting the specific terms within which the power of appointment is to be exercised. In this bequest, as drafted, the special power may be exercised by deed *or* will. It would be possible to provide that the power be exercised by deed only or by will only. Where this is done, the power can only be validly exercised in that way and any other method of exercise would be void. It is advisable to give maximum flexibility in the exercise of the power.)

(Note 3: note also the provision that allows for the remainder interest to pass to the children in equal shares in default of the exercise of power by the spouse/civil partner. If the testator requires that the remainder would pass to perhaps his or her eldest child or specifically one of his or her children in default of the exercise of the power, then this, of course, should be clearly stated. This might arise, for example, where the residue of the estate included a farm of land and where one particular child was involved in the farming business. Instead of the testator leaving the farm to the child in remainder, he or she may wish to leave the option open to his or her spouse/civil partner to leave it to another child or amongst the other children in the event that the child involved in running the farm later becomes disaffected from farming, or to provide for some other similar event.)

(Note 4: the spouse/civil partner would have to be put to his or her election pursuant to the provisions of s 115 of the Succession Act 1965 as between his or her legal right share and the life interest in the residue of the estate. Further, if

any of the children felt that they would not be adequately provided for by the terms of the will, they could apply under s 117 of the Succession Act 1965 to have provision made for them. The spouse/civil partner or children should be independently legally advised in such event.)

Bequest of residue in terms of a discretionary trust for the benefit of the testator's children

[10.34]

I GIVE, DEVISE AND BEQUEATH all the rest, residue and remainder of my estate of every nature and description and kind, wheresoever situate, unto my executors and trustees, upon the following trusts:

(i)   To apply the capital and income thereof for the benefit of my children in such shares and in such proportions as my executors and trustees in their absolute discretion shall think fit.

(ii)   For as long as any of my children remains under the age of eighteen years or under the age of twenty-one years and in full time education, to apply the income from my residuary estate for the benefit of my children in such shares and in such manner as they in their absolute discretion shall think fit, with power to accumulate the income.

(iii)   Upon all of my children having attained the age of twenty-one years, to terminate the said trust by dividing my residuary estate amongst my children in such shares and in such manner as they in their absolute discretion shall think fit.

(iv)   If any of my children predeceases me and dies before all of my children have attained the age of twenty-one years, leaving children, then those children shall be included amongst the beneficiaries in whose favour my executors and trustees may exercise their discretion under this trust.

(v)   My executors and trustees may exercise their discretionary powers under this trust in such manner as they in their absolute discretion shall think fit and shall not be under any obligation to make any payment to or for the benefit of any person in whose favour they can exercise their discretion, nor are they obliged to ensure equality of distribution amongst the persons who are benefited.

(*Note 1*: any bequest, to a child who is a minor, that includes land will create a trust of land within the meaning of Pt 4 of the 2009 Act and regard should be had to the provisions of that Act.)

(*Note 2*: see **Ch 11** re alternative gifts over.)

(*Note 3*: consideration should be given to what powers the executors and trustees may need in addition to the bare setting up of the discretionary trust – see **Ch 12** on the powers of trustees.)

(*Note 4*: this type of discretionary trust is most likely to be used where the children of the testator may be under the age of 18 years at the death of the testator and where the testator is concerned to ensure that the residue of his or her estate is used to the best effect.)

(*Note 5*: the testator should give thought to the persons who might be appointed as executors and trustees and he or she should appoint persons who might use the residue of his or her estate in as close a manner to the way he or she might use it him or herself.)

(*Note 6*: thought should also be given to appointing testamentary guardians and as to whether the executors and trustees should act in that role or whether there should be additional persons appointed in that role.)

(*Note 7*: thought should also be given as to whether the trustees should be the same persons as the executors or different persons.)

(*Note 8*: the testator should be advised in relation to the discretionary trust tax provisions, but the trust is drafted in such a way so as to ensure exemption from the tax. Where, however, the trust is to continue beyond the age of 18, or 21 if a person is in full-time education, the testator should be advised as to the tax that might arise.)

(*Note 9*: it might also be useful for the executors and trustees to have a letter of wishes from the testator indicating the manner in which he or she would like the residuary estate applied. A letter of wishes shall not be binding upon the executors and trustees, but will give them useful guidance in relation to the application of the fund.)

Bequest of residue in terms of a general discretionary trust where the word 'beneficiaries' is defined in the will

[10.35]

I GIVE, DEVISE AND BEQUEATH all the rest, residue and remainder of my estate of every nature and description and kind, wheresoever situate, unto my executors and trustees, upon trust:

(i)   To apply the said residue, both as to income and as to capital, for the benefit of the beneficiaries hereinafter defined.

(ii)   In the application of the income of my residuary estate, my executors and trustees may apply the income for the benefit of any one or more of the beneficiaries, as they in their absolute discretion shall think fit, or may accumulate the said income and add same to the capital of my residuary estate, as they in their absolute discretion shall think fit.

(iii)   This trust must be brought to an end within twenty-one years of the date of death of my last surviving child. My executors and trustees may exercise their discretionary powers as they in their absolute discretion shall think fit and shall not be under any obligation to make payments to and for the benefit of all of those in whose favour they can exercise their discretion, nor to ensure equality amongst those whom they do decide to benefit.

'Beneficiaries'

In this my will, 'beneficiaries' shall include my spouse/civil partner and my children and if any of my children predeceases me, the spouse/civil partner of such child and the children of such child as might predecease me living at the date of my death.

(*Note 1*: consideration should be given as to what powers the executors and trustees might have in addition to their general discretion for the distribution of the estate – see **Ch 12** dealing with powers of trustees.)

(*Note 2*: the definition of beneficiaries can be as wide as the testator would require but it should be clear as to whether any given person would be within the class. With the abolition of the various rules under s 16 of the 2009 Act (see above) there is less concern about class gifts. But clarity must be a by-word.)

(*Note 3*: if the residuary estate includes land then a trust of land within the meaning of Pt 4 of the 2009 Act arises and trustees for the purposes of that Act might be appointed.)

Bequest of residue to parents of the testator with substitutional bequest in the event that parents predecease him or her

[10.36]

I GIVE, DEVISE AND BEQUEATH all the rest, residue and remainder of my estate of every nature and description and kind, wheresoever situate, to my parents *(insert names),* of *(address)* jointly or to such one of my parents as survives me at the date of my death.

In the event that my parents predecease me, then **I GIVE, DEVISE AND BEQUEATH** all the rest, residue and remainder of my property of every nature and kind and description, wheresoever situate, to such of my brothers and sisters as are living at the date of my death in equal shares.

(*Note*: see **Ch 11** re alternative gifts over.)

Bequest of residue to brothers and sisters of the testator with substitutional bequest in the event that any of the brothers and sisters predeceases the testator

[10.37]

I GIVE, DEVISE AND BEQUEATH all the rest, residue and remainder of my estate of every nature and description and kind, wheresoever situate, to my brothers and sisters in equal shares and in the event that any of my brothers and sisters predeceases me, then **I DIRECT** that the share of that brother or sister shall pass to the children of that brother or sister in equal shares, or if any of my brothers or sisters predeceases me leaving no issue, then the share to which that brother or sister would have been entitled shall pass to my remaining brothers and sisters.

(*Note 1*: in the case of a class bequest to persons other than issue, in equal shares, if any of the members of the class predeceases the testator, the residuary bequest will lapse and give rise to a partial intestacy. The provisions of s 98 of the Succession Act 1965 only apply to bequests to issue who predecease the testator leaving issue. With class bequests, therefore, of this kind, it is important that the testator would give thought to a substitutional gift in the event that any one of his or her brothers or sisters might predecease him or her. The usual course would be to leave the share of that brother or sister to his or her children or perhaps to his or her spouse, though equally the share could be left to charity.)

(*Note 2*: see **Ch 11** re alternative gifts over.)

Bequest of residue to brothers and sisters in unequal shares

[10.38]

> **I GIVE, DEVISE AND BEQUEATH** all the rest, residue and remainder of my estate of every nature and description and kind, wheresoever situate, as follows:
>
> (i)   As to one-half share thereof to my brother/sister *(insert name),* of *(address)*.
>
> (ii)   As to one-quarter share thereof to my brother/sister *(name),* of *(address)*.
>
> (iii)   As to one-eighth share thereof to my brother/sister *(name),* of *(address)*.
>
> (iv)   As to one-eighth share thereof to my brother/sister *(name),* of *(address)*.
>
> In the event that any of my said brothers and sisters predeceases me, then the share to which that brother or sister would have been entitled shall pass to his/her spouse, or in the event that he/she dies without spouse, shall pass to his/her children in equal shares, and in the event that he/she dies without spouse and without children, shall pass to my remaining brothers and sisters in equal shares [*or,* proportionately to their shares in the residue set out in this my will].
>
> (*Note*: when dividing the residue into differing shares, ensure that all of the shares add up to one unit, as otherwise constructional difficulties may arise or there may be a partial intestacy.)

Bequest of residue to named charities

[10.39]

> **I GIVE, DEVISE AND BEQUEATH** all the rest, residue and remainder of my estate of every nature and description and kind, wheresoever situate, unto my executors and trustees, upon trust to divide the same equally amongst the following charities:

(In separate numbered paragraphs, specify the names of the charities. Be careful in the description of the charities to specify each by its correct name and address to avoid any constructional difficulties later on and if the particular charity is broken down into constituent branches, ensure that the correct branch is mentioned, eg:

(i)   *The Society of St Vincent de Paul, Law Library Conference.*

(ii)   *The Samaritans (Dublin Branch), 112 Marlborough Street, in the City of Dublin.)*

If at the date of my death any of the above charities has ceased to exist, or has become amalgamated with another charity, or has been incorporated into another charity, or has changed its name, the gift to that charity shall not fail, but my executors and trustees shall apply all of the residue to which the said charitable organisation would have been entitled to the charitable organisation which they consider most nearly fulfils the objects of the charity I intended to benefit.

The receipt of the treasurer or other proper officer of the various charities to my executors and trustees shall be sufficient discharge in relation to the payment of the bequest hereunder.

Bequest of residue to a number of charitable institutions, with discretion being given to the executors and trustees to apply the residue to the various charitable institutions in such manner as they may think fit

[10.40]

I GIVE, DEVISE AND BEQUEATH all the rest, residue and remainder of my estate of every nature and description and kind, wheresoever situate, unto my executors and trustees, upon trust to apply the same to the following charities in such shares and in such manner as they in their absolute discretion shall think fit.

(In separate numbered paragraphs, specify the names of the charities. Be careful in the description of the charities to specify each by its correct name and address to avoid any constructional difficulties later on and if the particular charity is broken down into constituent branches, ensure that the correct branch is mentioned, eg:

(i)   *The Society of St Vincent de Paul, Law Library Conference.*

(ii)   *The Samaritans (Dublin Branch), 112 Marlborough Street, in the City of Dublin.)*

If at the date of my death any of the above charities has ceased to exist, or has become amalgamated with another charity, or has been incorporated into another charity, or has changed its name, the gift to that charity shall not fail, but my executors and trustees may apply the residue of my estate to the charitable organisation which they consider most nearly fulfils the objects of the charity I intended my executors and trustees to consider when exercising their discretion.

The receipt of the treasurer or other proper officer of the various charities to my executors and trustees shall be sufficient discharge in relation to appointment hereunder.

General bequest of residue to achieve specified charitable purposes, with discretion to be given to the executors and trustees as to how those purposes might be achieved

[10.41]

I GIVE, DEVISE AND BEQUEATH all the rest, residue and remainder of my estate of every nature and description and kind, wheresoever situate, unto my executors and trustees, upon trust to apply the same to charities who have for their objects the following purposes:

(Set out the objects and purposes which the testator intends to benefit, eg:

(i)   *The education of necessitous children.*

(ii)   *Cancer research.*

(iii) *Care of persons with AIDS.)*

The receipt of the treasurer or other proper officer of a charity which my executors and trustees believe fulfils any of the objects hereinbefore specified, shall be sufficient discharge in relation to the payment of any bequest hereunder.

Bequest of residue for such general charitable purposes as the executors and trustees may think fit

[10.42]

I GIVE, DEVISE AND BEQUEATH all the rest, residue and remainder of my estate of every nature and description and kind, wheresoever situate, unto my executors and trustees, upon trust to apply for such general charitable purposes as my executors and trustees in their absolute discretion shall think fit.

Bequest of residue to a large number of beneficiaries in equal parts

[10.43]

I GIVE, DEVISE AND BEQUEATH all the rest, residue and remainder of my estate of every nature and description and kind, wheresoever situate, unto my executors and trustees, upon trust to divide the same into *(insert number, eg, thirty)* equal parts as follows:

(Set out in separate numbered paragraphs the various beneficiaries who are to take a share. If some beneficiaries are to take more than a one-thirtieth part, state the number of parts that this beneficiary is to take, eg:

(i)   One-thirtieth share thereof to the children of my brother (name), of (address), who survive me, and if more than one, in equal shares.)

If for any reason any of the above bequests fails to take effect, then **I DIRECT** that the subject matter of the failed bequest shall be divided pro rata amongst the other beneficiaries.

(*Note*: when dividing the residue amongst a large number of beneficiaries, ensure that all the parts so allocated add up to the number of parts specified, in this example 30.)

Bequest of residue upon trust for sale with no power to postpone sale, where the estate is to be divided amongst a large number of beneficiaries and where they are to take percentage shares

[10.44]

I GIVE, DEVISE AND BEQUEATH all the rest, residue and remainder of my estate of every nature and description and kind, wheresoever situate, unto my executors and trustees, upon trust to sell same and to divide the proceeds of sale as follows:

(i)   Twenty per cent thereof amongst my brothers and sisters living at the date of my death, and if more than one, in equal shares.

(ii)   Five per cent to my nephew *(insert name)*, of *(address)*, and in the event that he predeceases me, leaving a spouse and issue, **I DIRECT** that the said five per cent of my estate pass to his spouse and issue in equal shares. In the event that my nephew dies leaving neither spouse nor issue, **I DIRECT** that the said five per cent share shall pass to the Society of St Vincent de Paul (Ballymun Conference) and the receipt of the treasurer or other proper officer of the said conference of the said society to my executors and trustees shall be sufficient discharge in relation to the payment of this bequest.

(iii)   (*Continue bequests as required by the testator.*)

If any of the bequests hereinbefore set out fails for any reason, the proceeds of the bequest which fails shall be paid to the *(name of religious order of priests)*, of *(address)*, to be used for the saying of Masses for the repose of my soul and those of my deceased relatives and the receipt of the provincial or bursar of the said *(name of order)* shall be sufficient discharge to my executors and trustees in the payment of this bequest.

(*Note 1*: where the residue is to be divided in percentages, ensure that all of the bequests add up to only 100 per cent. In the case of *Curtin v O'Mahony*,[4] the residue of the estate was divided into percentages, but when all the percentages were added up, they came to 100.5 per cent.)

(*Note 2*: the residue here is held upon a trust for sale and no power to postpone the sale has been given, so that the executors are under an imperative to sell the property forming part of the estate as soon as may be practicable – see precedent

---

4.   *Curtin v O'Mahony* [1991] 2 IR 562.

clause at **[10.56]** for bequest of the residue on trust for sale with power to postpone sale.)

(*Note 3*: if the residue comprises land, then a trust of sale creates a trust of land and appointment of trustees should be considered, having regard to the 2009 Act and its provisions in relation to a trust of land.)

Bequest of residue upon trust for sale with power to postpone sale, with the proceeds of sale to be held upon a discretionary trust

[10.45]

I GIVE, DEVISE AND BEQUEATH all the rest, residue and remainder of my estate of every nature and description and kind, wheresoever situate, unto my executors and trustees, upon trust to sell the same, with power in their absolute discretion to postpone the said sale and to hold the proceeds of such sale, or my residuary estate for so long as the same remains unsold, upon trust for the benefit of my children until they attain the age of twenty-one years, and when the last of my children attains twenty-one years, to bring the trust to an end and to divide my residuary estate amongst such one or more of my children and in such shares or proportions as my executors and trustees in their absolute discretion shall think fit.

(i) Pending the termination of the said trust in the manner as hereinbefore provided, my executors and trustees shall have power to apply the income from my residuary estate for the benefit of my children in such manner and in such shares as they in their absolute discretion shall think fit, or to accumulate the said income with the capital.

(ii) It is my wish however, without creating any binding obligation upon my executors and trustees, that they would apply the income from my residuary estate and the capital if necessary towards the maintenance, welfare and education of my children until the last one of my children attains the age of twenty-one years.

(iii) My executors and trustees may exercise their discretionary powers under this trust in such manner as they in their absolute discretion shall think fit and shall not be under any obligation to make payment to or for the benefit of all those in whose favour they can exercise their discretion, nor to ensure equality of distribution amongst those who are benefiting.

(iv) If any of my said children dies before me, or before the said trust is terminated in accordance with the terms of this my will, leaving children, then the children of such child shall be included amongst those in whose favour my executors and trustees may exercise their discretion under this my will.

(*Note*: if the residue comprises land, then a trust for sale gives rise to a trust of land and appointment of trustees should be considered, having regard to the 2009 Act and its provisions in relation to a trust of land.)

Universal bequest where the property being dealt with by the will is restricted to property situate within the Republic of Ireland or to which Irish law applies

[10.46]

> **I GIVE, DEVISE AND BEQUEATH** all my estate of every nature and description and kind situated within the Republic of Ireland or to which Irish law applies at the date of my death to [my *(insert relationship to testator, if any)*] *(name),* of *(address).*

> (*Note*: movable property is generally governed by *lex domicilii,* or the law of the domicile of the testator, and if that is an Irish domicile, then the movable property wheresoever situate would be governed by Irish law. Immovable property is governed by *lex situs,* or the law of where the property is situated, and, therefore, immovable property in Ireland would be governed by Irish law.)

Residuary bequest restricted to property situate within the Republic of Ireland or to which Irish law applies

[10.47]

> **I GIVE, DEVISE AND BEQUEATH** all the rest, residue and remainder my estate of every nature and description and kind situated within the Republic of Ireland or to which Irish law applies at the date of my death to [my *(insert relationship to testator, if any)*] *(name),* of *(address).*

Chapter 11

ALTERNATIVE DISPOSITION OR ACCRUER OVER IN THE EVENT THAT A BEQUEST FAILS

PART I: COMMENTARY

[11.01] The inclusion of an alternative disposition or an accruer clause is particularly beneficial in the case of class bequests where the testator does not know if members of the class will survive him or her. It can also be used in a general way in a will where there are a number of beneficiaries in the will and the testator wants to provide that in the event of any of the beneficiaries predeceasing him or her, the bequest to that beneficiary shall pass to the remaining beneficiaries. It can avoid a partial intestacy, particularly in the case where there is a lapse of a residuary benefit, and it can also avoid the operation of s 98 of the 1965 Act if the operation of that section is not required.

[11.02] It should be noted that in the precedent clauses in **Pt II**, the alternative provision or accruer only arises if the initial beneficiary *predeceases* the deceased. The clauses are clear and unambiguous, which is what every person drafting a will should strive for.

[11.03] A difficulty arose in an unreported decision of the High Court where the gift over was to apply in the event that the initial beneficiary was to '*die without issue*'. The question arose as to whether it was intended by the testator that the initial beneficiary would die in the life of the testator or die at any time. In other words, was the gift to the initial beneficiary contingent and defeasible in the event that he or she would die at any time in the future without issue? The court held that it was.

[11.04] The case was *In re O'Donoghoe Deceased – Mulhern v Brennan*.[1] McCracken J was faced with a residuary bequest that the left the residue to four named sons of the deceased as tenants in common. The clause then contained the following provision:

> '... in the event of any of my children dying without issue the surviving brothers
> or brother shall take his share original and accruing but in the event of him leaving
> such issue, such issue shall be entitled to their parent's share.'

The court noted that at the time the will was made probably only one of the sons was of age. By the time the clause came to be construed all four sons, having survived their father, had died without issue.

[11.05] McCracken J referred to the rule of construction that where a benefit in a will is subject to a contingency that the beneficiary was not to die that such a condition related only to the beneficiary dying in the lifetime of the testator as otherwise it was not a contingency but a certainty (*In Re Hall*[2]). But in the clause McCracken J was considering, there was a dual facet to the contingency, the son was not only to die to lose his benefit but he had to die without issue.

---

1.   *In re O'Donoghoe Deceased – Mulhern v Brennan* (26 May 1998, unreported) HC.
2.   *In re Hall* [1944] IR 54.

[11.06] The simple rule of construction as referred to above may only apply *ex necessitate*, ie, to bring certainty to an uncertain event, that is to say, death. It is certain to happen but it is not certain when. But it should not be applied where necessity does not dictate (*Woodroofe v Woodroofe[3]*). The clause in the *Woodroofe* case was very similar to that being considered by McCracken J.

[11.07] McCracken J held, therefore, that the shares of the four sons were defeasible at any time were they to die without issue. So that as each son died without issue his share passed to his other brother until the last son remained and took absolutely. McCracken J noted that the testator had not provided for what was to happen if the contingency applied to all his sons. In the event, that is what happened. It was arguable, the judge observed, that it give rise to intestacy. But the court noted that where someone dies testate it is presumed that he or she does not intend to die intestate with regard to any part of his or her estate. This being so, he held that the last remaining son took the residue and it passed to his estate. In effect, it was as if the residue had been left to the four sons as joint tenants.

[11.08] The approach of McCracken J is similar to the approach adopted by the Supreme Court in *Curtin v O'Mahony[4]* where a partial intestacy was prevented. The Supreme Court held that the meticulous testator could not have intended to die intestate. McCracken J instead cited the colourful *dictum* of Esher MR in *In Re Harrison:[5]*

> 'There is one rule of construction which is to my mind a golden rule viz., that when a testator has executed a Will in solemn form that you must assume that he did not intend to create a solemn farce – that he did not intend to die intestate having gone through the form of making a will. You ought, if possible, to read the will as to lead to a testacy, not an intestacy. This is a golden rule.'

Had the court in the *Mulhern* case found an intestacy, then, assuming the testator was a widower and had no other children or issue of a predeceased child, the residue would have passed to the four sons equally but that would have set at nought the contingency in the will, and presumably the testator intended to import some effect to that by including it in his will.

PART II: PRECEDENT CLAUSES

Provision for alternative disposition or accruer where the lapsed benefit is to pass to other beneficiaries in equal shares

[11.09]

> If any of the beneficiaries named in this bequest predeceases me, then the benefit that this beneficiary would have taken, had he/she survived me, shall pass in equal shares amongst the surviving beneficiaries under the bequest.

3.　　*Woodroofe v Woodroofe* (1894) 1 Ch 299.
4.　　*Curtin v O'Mahony* [1991] 2 IR 562.
5.　　*In re Harrison* (1885) 30 Ch D.

Provision for alternative disposition or accruer where the beneficiaries are taking in unequal shares and the lapsed benefit therefore should pass to them pro rata

[11.10]

If any of the beneficiaries named in this bequest predeceases me, then the benefit that this beneficiary would have taken, had he/she survived me, shall be added pro rata to the shares of the surviving beneficiaries under the bequest.

Chapter 12

EXECUTOR AND TRUSTEE POWERS

PART I: COMMENTARY

[12.01] It is useful to remember that the executors under the will may have different powers by virtue of the will itself and statute. The executors' powers under the Succession Act 1965 are far wider than the powers that trustees would have under the Trustee Act 1893.

Where a trust of land, as defined in Pt 4 of the 2009 Act, arises or may arise under the terms of the will, regard should be had to the provisions of Pt 4 of the 2009 Act, which are set out in full at **Appendix 12, Pt 1**.

Where the testator appoints persons as both executors and trustees, whether they are the same or different persons, it is important to bear in mind that the capacity of executor and trustee is different and if the property passes out of the hands of the executors in their capacity as such and into their own hands in their capacity as trustees, and the powers given to the trustees are inadequate, this may hinder dealing with the estate of the deceased.

There is, however, no necessity to give a wide variety of powers to either executors or trustees in the will, except perhaps if it is envisaged that the bulk of the estate will be held by the executors or trustees for a long period of time to be administered for the benefit of beneficiaries who are minors or perhaps a person who is of unsound mind. In such a case, the executors and trustees should be given wide powers to deal with the estate and their statutory powers should be augmented in the will.

The powers to be given to executors or trustees should be judged by the terms of the will itself. The will should make sense as a harmonious whole.

A. Powers of executors (and legal personal representatives) pursuant to the provisions of the Succession Act 1965

[12.02] An executor appointed by will has greater power to deal with the estate of the deceased prior to a grant of probate being extracted than the person entitled to be administrator where there is no executor appointed by the will or where there is an intestacy.

In the case of an intestacy or where there is a will but there is no executor appointed or available to act, the powers of the legal personal representative will only arise from the date of the extraction of the grant. Up until that time, the estate of the deceased is vested in the President of the High Court.

An executor, however, derives his or her title under the will and so has power to deal with the estate even before a grant is extracted. In many transactions, however, such as the sale of property, the person dealing with the executor will require sight of a grant of representation before completing the transaction, but there is nothing to stop the executor entering into a transaction, which will be binding prior to the extraction of the grant.

Generally speaking, where a number of executors prove the will, they are required to act jointly in respect of the administration of the estate of the deceased. However, if some of the executors do not prove the will of the deceased, their concurrence in the exercise of any power by an executor or other executors who have proved the will is not required.

Section 20(1) of the 1965 Act provides that where probate is granted to some of two or more persons named as executors (whether or not the rights of the other executors to prove the will are reserved), all powers conferred by the Act on the executors may be exercised by the proving executors or the survivor of them and shall be as effectual as if all persons named as executors had concurred therein.

(*Note*: this section applies whether the deceased died before or after the commencement date of the 1965 Act, ie 1 January 1967.)

Section 21 of the 1965 Act provides that if administration has been granted in respect of the estate of a deceased person, no person can act as an executor until the grant of administration has been recalled or has been revoked or has expired.

Section 22(1) of the 1965 Act provides that where a person makes any payment or accepts a disposition in good faith under a grant of representation, the act done shall not be invalidated by any defect affecting the validity of the representation. Further, s 22(2) provides that where a grant of representation is revoked, all payments and dispositions made in good faith to the personal representative for revocation shall be valid.

Section 25 of the Act provides that all conveyances of any estate or interest of a deceased person made to a purchaser (being a *bona fide* purchaser for value) will be valid notwithstanding any subsequent revocation of the grant of representation.

(*Note*: this section applies whether the deceased died before or after the commencement of the 1965 Act.)

Administration of estate

[12.03] The executors and legal personal representatives have a power to administer the estate of the deceased, and the duty of the executors and personal representatives is to administer the estate:

(i)   properly, in accordance with law;

(ii)   in accordance with the provisions of the will;

(iii)   in accordance with the provisions of the 1965 Act; and

(iv)   with regard to whether the estate is solvent or insolvent. For the application of assets where the estate is solvent or insolvent – see ss 45 and 46 of the 1965 Act and Pt I and Pt II of the First Schedule to the 1965 Act.

Appointment of trustees

[12.04] By virtue of s 57 of the 1965 Act, the executors or legal personal representatives may appoint a trust corporation or any two or more persons (who may include the executors and personal representatives or any of them) to be trustees of the share of any infant (a person under the age of 18 years) in the estate of a deceased person and may execute such assurance or take such other action as may be necessary for the vesting of the share of the infant in the trustee or trustees so appointed. In default of such appointment, the executors or personal representatives shall be trustees for the purposes of s 57 of the 1965 Act. On such appointment, the personal representatives in their capacity as such shall be discharged from all further liability in respect of property vested in the trustees so appointed. Note also: that under the 2009 Act land held for the benefit of a minor constitutes a trust of land within the meaning of Pt 4 of the 2009 Act and regard should be had to its provisions.

Appropriation – ss 55 and 56 of the 1965 Act

[12.05] The executors and legal personal representatives have the power to appropriate any part of the estate of the deceased in its actual condition or state of investment (at the time of appropriation) in or towards satisfaction of any share in the estate (whether settled or not) according to the rights of persons interested in the estate (see s 55 of the 1965 Act).

In order to exercise this power, the executors and personal representatives are required to give requisite notices by s 55 and also to obtain certain consents referred to in s 55. If the power of appropriation of the executors and personal representatives is to be broadened in the will to allow for appropriation without giving the requisite notices or obtaining the requisite consents, the will would need to include a provision to that effect. The executors/personal representatives in exercising the power of appropriation must act as trustees. Because whether or not they expressly appointed trustees, they are statutory trustees by virtue of s 10 of the 1965 Act (see *Messitt v Henry*[1]).

The spouse/civil partnership has a right under s 56 of the 1965 Act to require appropriation of a dwelling in which he or she was ordinarily resident at the date of death of the deceased, which dwelling forms part of the estate of the deceased. The executor(s)/legal personal representative(s) is/are under a mandatory duty to notify the spouse/civil partner of this right – see **Appendix 6** and **Ch 1**.

Assents

[12.06] By virtue of s 52 of the 1965 Act, the executors and legal personal representatives have power to execute an assent vesting any real property of the estate of the deceased in the person entitled thereto. By virtue of s 52(5), the assent is required to be in writing.

In relation to unregistered land, s 53(3) of the 1965 Act provides that an assent or conveyance of unregistered land by a personal representative shall, in favour of a purchaser (being a *bona fide* purchaser for value), be conclusive evidence that the person in whose favour the assent or conveyance is given or made is the person who is entitled to have the estate or interest vested in him or her (see *Mohan v Roche*[2]).

Collect in assets

[12.07] The primary duty of the executors and legal personal representatives is to collect in the assets of the deceased, and with this duty comes the power to collect in assets and

---

1. *Messitt v Henry* [2001] 2 IR 313.
2. *Mohan v Roche* [1990] 1 IR 560.

to seek information in relation to the assets. The administrator of an intestate or under a grant of administration with the will annexed or under a grant of administration intestate shall only have this power from the date of the grant, but the executor or personal representative has the power from the date of death. Many financial institutions will, however, require a grant of probate for access to funds or transfer of funds.

Completion of transactions

[12.08] The executors and legal personal representatives have the power to complete any transaction which the deceased commenced prior to his or her death but which was not completed at the date of death, and nothing in s 60 is to prejudice that right (see s 60(4) of the 1965 Act).

Compromise

[12.09] Section 60 of the 1965 Act contains a number of powers which the executors and legal personal representatives may exercise. Under s 60(8)(e), the executors and personal representatives have power to compromise, compound, abandon, submit to arbitration or otherwise settle any debt, account, dispute, claim or other matter relating to the estate of the deceased.

In *In Re MK Deceased A, B and C v TD and others*,[3] Laffoy J held that this did not extend to the compromise of a s 117 claim because the finding of a failure in the moral duty and the provision to be made in the event of such failure was solely a matter for the court. A beneficiary under a will was objecting to a proposed settlement between three s 117 claimants. The executors sought to have the court rule that the settlement could proceed under s 60(8)(e). The court held that the executors could not compromise the claim in such circumstances. In the absence of agreement by all persons affected by the settlement, only the court could adjudicate on the matter. This is because under s 117, the court has to find that there was a failure in the moral duty towards the claimant(s) on the part of the parent, and further, the discretion as to what provision may be made for the claimant(s) reposes only in the court.

Creditors

[12.10] By virtue of s 46(2) of the 1965 Act, the executors and legal personal representatives have power to prefer creditors and to pay one creditor in preference to other creditors who have debts of equal priority. This right of preferment of creditors continues even where the estate is insolvent.

Debts due to the deceased

[12.11] By virtue of s 60(8) of the 1965 Act, legal personal representatives may accept any property before the time at which it is transferable or payable (s 60(8)(a)); pay or allow any debt or claim on any evidence that they may reasonably deem sufficient (s 60(8)(b)); accept any composition or security for any debt or property claimed (s 60(8)(c)); allow time for the payment of any debt (s 60(8)(d)); compromise, compound, abandon, submit to arbitration, or otherwise settle any debt (s 60(8)(e)).

---

3.   *In Re MK Deceased A, B and C v TD and others* (16 April 2010, unreported) HC.

Distress

[12.12] By virtue of s 60(5) of the 1965 Act, the executors and legal personal representatives of the deceased may distrain upon land for arrears of rent due or accruing to the deceased, in the same way as the deceased might have done had he or she been living.

Section 60(6) provides that arrears of rent may be distrained for after the termination of the lease or tenancy as if the term had not determined, provided the distress is made:

(a)   within six months after the termination of the tenancy;

(b)   during the continuance of possession of the lessee or tenant from whom the arrears were due.

Section 60(6) also provides that enactments relating to distress for rent apply to any distress made pursuant to s 60(6).

Section 60(7) provides that the executors and personal representatives may distrain for arrears of a *rent charge* due or accruing to the deceased in his or her lifetime on land affected or charged therewith, for so long as the land remains in possession of the person liable to pay the rent charge or of persons deriving title under him or her.

Leasing

[12.13] By virtue of s 60(1)(a) of the 1965 Act, the executors and legal personal representatives have a power to make such leases of land as may be reasonably necessary for the due administration of the estate of the deceased owner. Further, by virtue of s 60(1)(b), with the consent of the beneficiaries or with the approval of the court, the executors and legal personal representatives may make leases of land for such term and on such conditions as the personal representatives may think proper.

By virtue of s 60(1)(c), as amended by the Second Schedule of the 2009 Act, the legal personal representatives may create a sub-lease thereof with a nominal reversion and where this amounts in substance to a sale. The executors and personal representatives will have to satisfy themselves that this is the most appropriate method of disposing of the land in due course of the administration of the estate. The ability to create a fee farm grant or sub-fee farm grant is no longer possible following the 2009 Act.

Coupled with these powers, s 60(2) gives the executors and personal representatives the right to recover possession of any premises demised by them in accordance with the provisions of s 60(1)(a).

Mortgage and charge

[12.14] By virtue of s 60(3) of the 1965 Act, the executors and legal personal representatives may raise money by way of mortgage or charge for the payment of:

(a)   expenses;

(b)   debts and liabilities;

(c)   any legal right share;

(d)   the erection, repair and improvement or completion of buildings or improvement of land forming part of the estate of the deceased, with the approval (but not otherwise) of all the beneficiaries who are *sui juris* (of full age and of sound mind, memory and understanding).

If this power of mortgage is to be augmented, then the will would need to contain express provision to that effect.

Proof of will

[12.15] An executor has an absolute right to prove the will of the deceased and that power will not easily be set aside. However, by virtue of s 16 of the 1965 Act, the High Court has the power to summon any person named as an executor in a will to prove or to renounce probate. This is done by way of citation through the Probate Office.

Section 17 provides that the executor's right to prove will cease in the following circumstances:

(a)   where the executor survives the testator but dies without having taken out probate;

(b)   where the executor is cited to take out probate, but does not appear to the citation;

(c)   where the executor renounces his or her right to probate.

In these circumstances, the right of the executor to prove the will shall cease and the right to administer the estate of the deceased shall pass to the next person in the order of priority, as if the executor had not been appointed.

Note that the renunciation of an executor does not become final until it is lodged in the Probate Office and recorded in the issued grant of probate (see *In the Goods of Morant*[4]).

[12.16] While a renunciation may be withdrawn at any stage prior to the issue of the grant, without leave of the court, if, notwithstanding a renunciation and the issue of a grant, an executor later wishes to prove the will, he or she must seek leave of the court to do so (s 18 of the 1965 Act).

Where an executor or personal representative reserves his or her rights to act, he or she can later apply for a grant of representation either while the primary grant is still in force, by extracting a grant of double probate, or alternatively after the death of the acting executor, by extracting a grant of unadministered probate.

Remuneration of trust corporation

[12.17] By virtue of s 60(8)(f) of the 1965 Act, the executors and legal personal representatives have a power to fix reasonable terms of remuneration of any trust corporation appointed by the executors and personal representatives under s 57 of the 1965 Act to act as a trustee in respect of property in which an infant has an interest, and

---

4.   *In the Goods of Morant* (1874) LR 3 PD 151.

further to authorise the trust corporation to charge and retain such remuneration out of the property held by the trust corporation under its appointment under s 57.

Sale

[12.18] By virtue of s 50(1) of the 1965 Act, the executors and legal personal representatives may sell the whole or any part of the estate of a deceased person for the purpose of not only paying the debts of the deceased, but also distributing the estate amongst the persons entitled thereto.

The executors and personal representatives are required by s 50(1) to have regard, as far as practicable, to the wishes of the persons of full age entitled to the property intended to be sold, or, in the case of a dispute, to the wishes of the majority of the persons who are entitled (according to the value of their combined interest).

However, a purchaser from an executor or personal representative is absolutely protected and is not concerned to see that the wishes of the beneficiaries are regarded or complied with. It is also not necessary for any of the beneficiaries to concur in a sale by the executor or personal representative.

Section 50(2) provides that it shall not be lawful for some or any one of several executors or personal representatives, without leave of the court, to exercise the power of sale or any of the powers conferred upon an executor or personal representative in s 60, to dispose of land.

[12.19] Section 51 provides a protection for purchasers, in that a purchaser from an executor or personal representative is entitled to hold the property sold, freed and discharged from any debts or liabilities of the deceased, except such debts or liabilities as are charged otherwise than by the will of the deceased and from the claim of all persons entitled to any share in the estate of the deceased and shall not be concerned as to the application of purchase moneys.

The executor or legal personal representative may sell by private treaty or by public auction, but must sell to the best advantage and for the best price.

(*Note*: the provisions of s 51 apply whether the deceased died before or after the commencement of the 1965 Act.)

[12.20] Trustees of a trust of land created by will would have the very wide power of dealing with the property accorded to them by Pt 4 of the 2009 Act (s 20). The trustees have the 'full power of an owner' to deal with land, subject to the duties of a trustee and 'any restriction imposed by any statutory provision ... or the general law of trusts or by any instrument or court order relating to the land'.

[12.21] So it still may be preferable to sell in the capacity of personal representative because the protection given to purchasers from a personal representative should be sufficient for any purchaser for value from the personal representative (see definition of 'purchaser' in s 3 of the 1965 Act).

Transfer of land to persons entitled

[12.22] By virtue of s 52(2) of the Succession Act 1965, the executors and legal personal representatives have power to transfer an interest in land to the person entitled thereto. This may be done by way of an assent or by way of a deed of conveyance or assignment.

By virtue of s 52(4), if, after the expiration of one year from the death of the deceased, the executors and personal representatives have failed, on the request of the person entitled, to transfer by assent or otherwise the land to which the person is entitled, the court may, on application of the person entitled, direct the executors and personal representatives to make such transfer. If the executors and personal representatives make default in making such a transfer within a reasonable time, then the court may make an order vesting the land in the person entitled.

B. Trustee powers and duties

[12.23] Readers are referred to works on trusts and trustees for greater detail on the powers and duties of trustees. The following, however, are the principal powers and duties of a trustee, arising by statute and general law.

Further powers may be conferred by the will, and where the trustees will hold the assets over a reasonably long period it is advisable that the powers be added to and/or extended in the will.

Once a trustee has taken upon himself or herself the office of trustee, he or she should acquaint himself or herself with the nature of the trust. Regard should be had to the trust instrument and to the property forming part of the trust. The trustee should also ascertain the current state of investment of the trust fund.

The trustee is under a duty to ensure that all of the trust property is brought under his or her control. When the assets of the trust are collected in, the trustee should make an inventory of the trust and inform any institutions that are holding investments on behalf of the trust of the existence of the trust and his or her appointment as trustee. It may be necessary for the trustee to institute proceedings to recover any property on behalf of the trust and in that regard, the Statute of Limitations should be considered.

Power of investment

[12.24] The trustees have a power of investment, but generally speaking the trustees can only invest in authorised investments, although modern trusts will very often extend the powers of trustees to invest the assets forming part of the trusts as if they were beneficially entitled to them.

The statutory power of investment by trustees is to be found in s 1 of the Trustee Act 1893 and s 1 of the Trustee (Authorised Investments) Act 1958. The investments in which a trustee can invest are as follows:

(a) Irish government securities;

(b) securities guaranteed as to capital and interest by the Minister for Finance;

(c) British government securities;

(d) real securities in Ireland;

(e) securities or mortgages of certain local authorities and similar bodies, eg, the Harbour Commissioners;

(f) Bank of Ireland stocks;

(g) certain loan stock of the Governor and Company of the Bank of Ireland and Allied Irish Banks plc;

(h) securities of the Electricity Supply Board, the Agricultural Credit Corporation plc and Bord na Móna;

(i) debentures or debenture stock of publicly quoted industrial and commercial companies registered in Ireland, provided that the total of such debentures and stock does not exceed the paid up share capital and that a dividend of at least five per cent has been paid on the ordinary shares in each of the preceding five years;

(j) interest bearing deposit accounts in specified banks and credit institutions, including the Agricultural Credit Corporation plc, the Industrial Credit Corporation plc and major building societies.

The trustees are required to exercise ordinary prudence in relation to investment.

The trustees also have a limited power to mortgage lands, but this power can be extended by the instrument creating the trust.

Power of sale

[12.25] No power of sale was conferred upon trustees by statute or general law; the trust instrument had to empower the trustees to sell any assets comprised in the trust. This would still be true of trusts of personalty.

Where a trust of land is created, then under the provisions of s 20 of the 2009 Act the trustees have wide powers of dealing with the land.

Where, however, the trustees hold the trust property upon trust for sale, they are under a duty to sell and s 13 of the Trustee Act 1893 empowers them to sell by public auction or private treaty. A trust for sale of land now comes within the definition of a trust of land under the 2009 Act and the provisions of Pt 4 of that Act will apply to it. Part 4 of the 2009 Act is fully set out at **Appendix 4**.

Where trustees are empowered to sell or hold under a trust for sale they must sell for the best price and the best advantage; an executor exercising his or her power of sale is under the same duty. This is still the position following the enactment of the 2009 Act because the power to deal with the land is subject to the restrictions of general trust law and the duties of trustees.

By virtue of s 20 of the Trustee Act 1893, where trustees are empowered to sell, their receipt for the purchase moneys is sufficient discharge to a purchaser.

Power to maintain

[12.26] Power to maintain will arise where trust property is held for the benefit of minors, and the will should make express provision in this regard. Under s 43 of the Conveyancing Act 1881, trustees may apply income from the trust towards the maintenance, education or welfare of a minor, who is a beneficiary of the trust. The maintenance may be paid to the parent or guardian of the minor.

The power may be exercised where the trust property is held for the minor for life, or some greater interest, whether absolutely or contingently upon the minor attaining 18 years. If it is held contingently upon the minor attaining a greater age than 18, the power does not arise and an express power would be required in the will.

There is no power to make an advancement from capital except with leave of the court under s 11 of the Guardianship of Infants Act 1964.

Power to compound with creditors

[12.27] Section 21 of the Trustee Act 1893 empowers trustees to compromise, compound, abandon, submit to arbitration or otherwise settle any debt or claim without responsibility for any loss, provided the trustees act in good faith. A similar power is conferred upon a legal personal representative by s 60 of the 1965 Act.

Insurance of trust assets

[12.28] By s 18 of the Trustee Act 1893, trustees may insure trust property against loss or damage by fire only for an amount not exceeding three-quarters of the value of the property. This is clearly not a sufficient insuring power so the will should confer a full power to insure assets and to pay the premia out of the trust property.

Inadequacy of trust power

[12.29] As can be seen from the above very brief résumé of trust powers available to trustees, they will often be inadequate to administer trust property. It is important that wills, therefore, give trustees such powers as will assist them in dealing with the trust property having regard to the assets to be comprised in the trust.

No delegation of powers

[12.30] As a general rule, trustees are precluded from delegating their powers to third parties because the person who appointed them will have reposed particular trust and confidence in them. This, however, does not preclude a trustee from employing an agent where an ordinary prudent person of business would do so.

PART II: PRECEDENT CLAUSES

Introductory clause where executors and trustees are the same persons

[12.31]

In addition to the powers conferred upon them by statute and by general law, I confer the following powers upon my executors and trustees:

Introductory clause where the trustees are different persons to the executors

[12.32]

In addition to the powers conferred upon my trustees by statute and by general law, I confer upon them the following additional powers:

Power to appoint new trustees

[12.33]

The power to appoint new trustees under this my will shall be vested in my spouse *(insert name)* [*or*, my brother *(name)*, *or* my sister *(name)*, *or* my (executors and) trustees, or the survivor of them], and in exercising the power to appoint new trustees, my spouse *(name)* [*or*, my brother *(name)*, *or* my sister *(name)*, *or* my (executors and) trustees] shall have the power to appoint a professional trustee or a trust corporation upon such terms as to remuneration and otherwise as he/she/they in his/her/their absolute discretion shall think fit.

Power of sale

[12.34]

To sell, realise or dispose of any asset forming part of the residue of my estate and to hold the proceeds of sale upon the same trust as the residue of my estate is held.

(*Note*: while the executors themselves will have a power of sale conferred by s 50 of the Succession Act 1965, if they vest the property in themselves as trustees, then they will be required to have a power of sale in that capacity. Additionally, if different persons to the executors are appointed trustees, then when the estate is vested in them, they will require a power of sale. Where the property is left upon trust for sale, it will be unnecessary to include a power of sale.)

Power to acquire property

[12.35]

The power on the realisation of any asset forming part of my (residuary) estate, or with any moneys forming part of my (residuary) estate, to acquire real property (leasehold and freehold) and to hold the said property upon the same trusts as my estate is held by them.

Power to use capital or income of estate

[12.36]

To use the capital or income of my (residuary) estate in the maintenance and/or improvement of any real property (whether freehold or leasehold) comprised in my estate or acquired by my (executors and) trustees after my death under the powers contained in this my will.

Power of investment

[12.37]

To invest any asset forming part of my (residuary) estate or the proceeds of sale thereof as if they were beneficially entitled to the said asset and this power, without liability for loss, includes the following rights:

(i)   To invest in unsecured interest free loans to any beneficiary.

(ii)   To invest in other non-income producing assets, including life assurance policies, with power to pay the premiums out of the income or capital of my estate.

(iii)   To invest in the acquisition of a property or premises for the occupation of any beneficiary of this my will.

(iv)   To hold investments in the name of any person or body as they think fit.

Power to insure assets forming part of the estate

[12.38]

To insure any asset forming part of my (residuary) estate (or acquired by my trustees under the power conferred in this my will) upon such terms and upon such conditions as they in their absolute discretion shall think fit, and:

(i)   To pay the premiums out of the income or capital of my (residuary) estate, and

(ii)   To use any moneys paid on foot of such insurance policy to restore the asset insured, or if this is not possible or not deemed expedient by my trustees as they in their absolute discretion shall think fit, to apply the moneys received on foot of such insurance policy as if it were proceeds of the asset's sale and hold the same upon the same trust as they hold my (residuary) estate.

Power to carry on any business of the testator

[12.39]

To carry on and continue any business I am engaged in at the date of my death for so long as my (executors and) trustees think fit and without prejudice to the generality of this power:

(i)   To use in the running of the said business any assets comprised in my (residuary) estate.

(ii)   To become employed in the said business and to retain out of the profits of the said business reasonable remuneration.

(iii)   To incorporate the said business or to form a company for the purposes of carrying on the said business.

(iv)   To become a director of any company formed and to retain from the profits of the said business any reasonable remuneration for themselves.

(v)   To be indemnified for any loss incurred in the running of the said business out of my (residuary) estate.

(*Note*: in the absence of an express power to continue running a business, the executors' duty in respect of a business which forms part of the estate of the deceased is to run it only for so long as is necessary to sell the business as a going concern. This may be too restrictive and, therefore, even if the business is of a type which is very personal to the testator and which may not necessarily have a goodwill without the testator's involvement, it is still better to include this express power to give the option to the executors and trustees to run the business in case they consider it necessary.)

Power to borrow money

[12.40]

To borrow from such person, institution or corporation, upon such terms and upon such conditions as they in their absolute discretion may think fit and to use the money borrowed for any purpose for which the assets comprised in my estate may be used and to furnish security for any money borrowed.

(*Note*: the Trustee Act 1893 only gives trustees limited power to borrow money. This provision will give a wider power to borrow money which can be useful in the course of the administration of the estate.)

Power of trustees to purchase assets forming part of the estate

[12.41]

To sell any asset comprised in my (residuary) estate at its full open market value to any one or more of my trustees (*or, if a particular trustee is to be named as the only person who can purchase an asset, name of that trustee*). Before selling any asset under this provision, my trustees shall obtain two independent valuations from reputable firms of valuers and shall sell the asset for the higher of the two valuations.

(*Note*: as a general rule a trustee cannot profit from his or her office. As part of this general rule it is also generally the case that a trustee cannot deal with trust property. This admits of an exception where the instrument creating the trust (in this context a will) permits the trustee to purchase an asset forming part of the trust. Where no such power exists the trustee could only purchase an asset with leave of the court or where all the beneficiaries being *sui juris* agree that the trustee can purchase the asset.

The reasons for the restrictions on a trustee are obvious. 'Self dealing', as it has been called, could lead to a conflict of interest which may be best avoided. If such a provision is to be included in a will, the reasons for and against its inclusion should be discussed with the testator.)

Power to advance capital to any beneficiary who is primarily only entitled to a life estate

[12.42]

To apply the whole or any part of the capital of my (residuary) estate for the benefit of *(insert name of beneficiary)* as they in their absolute discretion shall think fit.

(*Note*: this power may be useful where the testator wishes to confer a life estate on perhaps a spouse or a child who is incapable of managing his or her own affairs, but the spouse, of course, will have a right to elect to take his or her legal right share (if he or she considers the life estate inadequate).)

Power to accumulate or apply income

[12.43]

My (executors and) trustees may in their absolute discretion accumulate the income derived from my (residuary) estate or apply the said income for the benefit of any beneficiary under the trust hereby created.

Power to make payment to a guardian in respect of a beneficiary who is under the age of 18 years

[12.44]

Where any beneficiary under the trust hereby created is under the age of eighteen years, my (executors and) trustees may pay any money from the income or capital of my (residuary) estate to his or her parent and/or other legal or testamentary guardian for the benefit of the said beneficiary who is a minor and the receipt of the parent or legal or testamentary guardian shall be sufficient discharge to my (executors and) trustees in respect of such payment.

Power to allow any beneficiary to use a chattel where the beneficiary's entitlement to the chattel is contingent upon the beneficiary reaching a certain age

[12.45]

> While any of the beneficiaries under this trust are under the age of *(insert age specified in contingency),* my (executors and) trustees may allow the said beneficiary to have the use of any personal chattel forming part of my estate to which he or she may become entitled.

Power to advance capital to a beneficiary who is a minor

[12.46]

> My (executors and) trustees may advance, for the benefit of any beneficiary under the trust hereby created, who is a minor, the whole or any part of the capital to which the beneficiary is entitled or may become entitled by paying the said income or capital to the parent or legal or testamentary guardian of the said beneficiary and the receipt of the parent or legal or testamentary guardian of the beneficiary shall be sufficient discharge to my (executors and) trustees.

Power to appropriate without the service of notices or obtaining of consents as required by s 55 of the Succession Act 1965

[12.47]

> My (executors and) trustees shall have power to appropriate any asset forming part of my estate in accordance with the provisions of s 55 of the Succession Act 1965 without the service of the notices required by that section or the obtaining of the consents where required by that section.

Chapter 13

VARIATION OF 'RELEVANT TRUSTS' (UNDER PART 5 OF THE LAND AND CONVEYANCING REFORM ACT 2009)

COMMENTARY

General

[13.01] By virtue of Pt 5 of the 2009 Act, an 'appropriate person' can apply to court for the variation by an approved 'arrangement' of a 'relevant trust' for the benefit of a 'relevant person'. The definition of 'relevant person' below limits the general application of Pt 5. It is further limited by the fact that the court cannot approve an arrangement if the Revenue Commissioners satisfy the court that it is motivated substantially to avoid or reduce the incident of tax. Nevertheless, the provisions of Pt 5 represent a change in the law of which testators should be made aware when they are creating a trust by will.

At the time of going to print, there is one written judgment on such an application in the case of *W v M (APUM).*[1] In the text that follows, I have woven in the various findings and rulings of Laffoy J.

Definitions

[13.02] Section 23 contains the definitions applicable. I have re-ordered them, for the purpose of this text, into an order that I feel is more logical, but Pt 5 of the Act is set out in full in **Appendix 12, Pt 1**.

[13.03] A 'relevant person' means:

(a)   A person who has a vested or contingent interest under the trust but who is incapable of assenting to an arrangement by reason of lack of capacity (whether by reason of minority or absence of mental capacity). In *W v M (APUM),*[2] the 'relevant person' was both a person of unsound mind not so found by inquisition and a minor. It was not necessary that the 'relevant person' be in wardship for the application to proceed.

(b)   An unborn person.

(c)   A person whose identity, existence or whereabouts cannot be established by taking reasonable measures.

(d)   A person who has a contingent interest under a trust but who does not fall within paragraph (a).

---

1.   *W v M (APUM)* [2011] IEHC 217.
2.   *W v M (APUM)* [2011] IEHC 217.

The Act does not spell out what 'reasonable measures' might be undertaken to establish the identity, existence or whereabouts of a 'relevant person'. It would normally involve searches and advertising in appropriate national newspapers in the jurisdiction or abroad. This can be expensive, so it would be wise to seek the directions of the court and have the form of advertisement settled to ensure the court would be happy with the form and breadth of the advertising. This will ultimately save on costs. Much will turn on the circumstances of the individual case.

[13.04] A 'relevant trust' '...means a trust arising, whether before or after the commencement of this section, under a will settlement or other disposition'.

Note that despite the thrust of the 2009 Act, a 'relevant trust' is not restricted to a trust of land. In *W v M (APUM)*,[3] the trust concerned was not a trust of land.

Part (b) of the definition provides that a 'relevant trust' does not include:

–   a trust created for charitable purposes within the meaning of the Charities Acts 1961 and 1973 and the Charities Act 2009;

–   an occupational pension scheme within the meaning of the Pensions Act 1990 established under a trust;

–   a trust created by a British statute;

–   a trust created by a Saorstat Éireann statute;

–   a trust created by an Act of the Oireachtas, whether passed before or after the commencement of this section.

[13.05] An 'appropriate person' means:

(a)   a trustee of, or a beneficiary under, the trust; or

(b)   any other person that the court to which the application is made under s 24 considers appropriate.

In *W v M (APUM)*,[4] the court was satisfied that the applicant was an 'appropriate person'.

[13.06] An 'arrangement' means:

An arrangement:

(a)   varying, revoking or resettling the trust, or

(b)   varying, enlarging, adding to or restricting the powers of the trustees under the trust to manage or administer the property the subject of the trust.

[13.07] Under s 24 of the 2009 Act, an 'appropriate person' may make an application to court in respect of a 'relevant trust' to approve an 'arrangement' specified in the application for the benefit of a 'relevant person' specified in the application provided the arrangement has been assented to *in writing* by each other person (if any) who:

(a)   is not a 'relevant person';

(b)   is beneficially interested in the trust; and

(c)   is capable of assenting to the arrangement.

---

3.   *W v M (APUM)* [2011] IEHC 217.

4.   *W v M (APUM)* [2011] IEHC 217.

The 2009 Act does not confer on the court any express power to dispense with the assent in writing of the persons specified. Nor does it confer on the court any power to assent on behalf of a person who does not have capacity to assent. In the case of a minor or person of unsound mind, therefore, whose consent is required, it maybe necessary to have them taken into wardship and have the President of the High Court or Committee assent on their behalf.

Notice and jurisdiction of the court

[13.08] Section 24(2) provides that a court has no jurisdiction to hear the application at all unless notice is given to:

(a)   the Revenue Commissioners, and

(b)   to such persons as be may be prescribed by rules of court (see Ords 15 and 72A of the Rules of the Superior Courts),

at least two weeks before the hearing of the application.

It is important to note that the terms of s 24(2) prohibit the court from hearing the application unless the appropriate persons are given notice.

In *W v M (APUM)*,[5] the Revenue Commissioners were a notice party to the proceedings as opposed to a full party. Counsel appeared and indicated that the Revenue was not opposing the application and was relieved from appearing further but the Revenue indicated that it would be applying for its costs as a statutory notice party to the application.

Hearing may be '*in camera*'

[13.09] Section 23(4) permits the court to hear the application otherwise than in public, if it considers it appropriate. An application for a hearing otherwise than in public should be made to the trial judge at the commencement of the trial and might be mentioned to the court when a date is being fixed for hearing.

In *W v M (APUM)*,[6] Laffoy J held that because the application before her involved a person of unsound mind not so found by inquisition and a minor, it was appropriate that the proceedings be heard *in camera.*

Form of proceedings

A. The High Court

[13.10] Order 72A of the Rules of the Superior Courts provides that applications under s 24 to approve an arrangement shall be by way of special summons. As is usual with the special summons procedure, the contents of the summons will be verified by a

---

5.   *W v M (APUM)* [2011] IEHC 217.
6.   *W v M (APUM)* [2011] IEHC 217.

comprehensive affidavit setting out the matter in full. At a minimum, the affidavit would need to:

(a)   Establish that the trust concerned is a 'relevant' trust as defined by s 23, exhibiting the instrument creating the trust.

(b)   Demonstrate how the applicant(s) is/are an 'appropriate person(s)' as defined by s 23.

(c)   Identify the specified 'relevant person' for whose benefit the application is brought. In *W v M (APUM)*,[7] the relevant person was the defendant/respondent in the application though a person of unsound mind not so found by inquisition. The defendant/respondent was, therefore, not a ward of court. Laffoy J was satisfied that under the terms of the 2009 Act, she had jurisdiction to hear the matter, even though the defendant/respondent was not in wardship. However, the proceedings had been procedurally incorrect in that no guardian *ad litem* had been sued but a guardian consented to be joined and had undertaken to lodge an appearance.

(d)   Identify any other 'relevant persons'. In *W v M (APUM)*,[8] Laffoy J decided, on considering the facts, that there was no person other than 'M' who was a relevant person. She further stated that even if certain persons were 'relevant persons', the arrangement was for their benefit also and, therefore, they were not required to be given notice.

(e)   Identify the persons who need to consent under s 24 and exhibit the written consent(s) to the arrangement.

(f)   Identify any other person required to be given notice pursuant to the Rules of Court (see Ord 72A of the Rules of the Superior Courts).

(g)   Refer to the proposed arrangement, setting out its terms and exhibiting the draft arrangement that requires the court's approval.

(h)   Demonstrate how the arrangement is beneficial in accordance with the terms of s 24 and show how it may or may not affect any other person with an interest in the 'relevant trust'.

(i)   State that the arrangement is not 'substantially motivated' by the avoidance or reduction in the incidence of tax. In *W v M (APUM)*,[9] the Revenue Commissioners did not oppose the application so the court had only to consider if the arrangement was for the benefit of the 'relevant person'.

(j)   Include any other background information that will be of assistance of the court, eg, the value of the trust's assets; the circumstances in which the testator/settlor set up the trust.

(k)   Seek the approval of the court.

---

7.   *W v M (APUM)* [2011] IEHC 217.
8.   *W v M (APUM)* [2011] IEHC 217.
9.   *W v M (APUM)* [2011] IEHC 217.

In *W v M (APUM)*,[10] it is evident from the judgment that a number of affidavits were filed including that of a financial adviser, presumably as to the beneficial effects of the arrangement. So, the persons advising on the application should consider what other evidence may be necessary to achieve a successful outcome. The applicant should give as much assistance to the court as is possible.

The application must be served in the ordinary way as required by court and will be given a return date for the Master's Court. When the matter is ready, it will be referred to the Judge's List, being the Monday Chancery Motions List. A decision will have to be taken as to whether it will be possible to have the arrangement approved in that list or to refer the case to a list to fix dates. That will largely depend on whether the application is being opposed by one of the notice parties or the Revenue Commissioners. In *W v M (APUM)*,[11] Laffoy J had given her preliminary views on the application and then, when her views had been taken on board, she ruled upon the application and applied the criteria as laid down by the 2009 Act.

B. The Circuit Court

[13.11] Order 46A of the Rules of the Circuit Court provides that an action under s 24 shall be commenced by equity civil bill. It would need to set out in pleading form the matters listed above as being contained in the affidavit verifying the special summons. It will be necessary, however, to prove the necessary matters, facts and documents by *vive voce* evidence.

Relevant considerations for the court

[13.12] The court may approve the arrangement if it is satisfied the carrying out of the arrangement would be for the benefit of the relevant person specified in the application and any other relevant person.

It will not approve the arrangement if not so satisfied or if the Revenue Commissioners satisfy the court that the application is substantially motivated by the avoidance of or to reduce the incidence of tax. Note that the avoidance of tax is regarded as legal *per se,* but the court cannot approve an arrangement that is substantially motivated by that purpose (s 24(4)).

In determining whether an arrangement would be for the benefit of a relevant person the court may have regard to:

(a)   any benefit; or

(b)   any detriment;

financial or otherwise, that may accrue to that person directly or indirectly in consequence of the arrangement.

In *W v M (APUM)*,[12] Laffoy J had regard to the principle in *In Re CL*[13] as to whether the relevant person would approve of the arrangement had she capacity to do so, and came to the conclusion that she would.

---

10.   *W v M* [2011] IEHC 217.
11.   *W v M (APUM)* [2011] IEHC 217.
12.   *W v M (APUM)* [2011] IEHC 217.
13.   *In re CL* [1969] I Ch 587.

Chapter 14

MISCELLANEOUS DECLARATIONS AND DIRECTIONS

PART I: COMMENTARY

[14.01] This chapter contains a selection of miscellaneous declarations that may be included in wills. Not all of them will be appropriate to every will, but regard might be had to them in the context of particular testators.

Declarations can appear at the end of the will or may be inserted in the will at other appropriate places. Draftspersons' attention is directed to the precedents of complete wills in **Ch 16** to see where some of the declarations have been incorporated into complete wills.

PART II: PRECEDENT CLAUSES

Declaration that a will is to apply only to property within the Republic of Ireland or to which Irish law applies

[14.02]

> **I HEREBY DECLARE** that this will shall only apply to property situate within the Republic of Ireland, or to which the law of the Republic of Ireland applies. For removal of all doubt, this declaration also applies to the revocation clause contained in this my will.

Declaration that the reference to children, grandchildren or issue in the will is to apply only to persons born in lawful wedlock, with provision for inclusion of adopted persons

[14.03]

> **I HEREBY DECLARE** that in this my will, any reference to my children, grandchildren or other issue shall be a reference only to children, grandchildren or issue born within lawful wedlock [and adopted pursuant to the provisions of the Adoption Acts or any Act amending or extending same], either before or after my death.

> (*Note*: under the Status of Children Act 1987, a reference to a child or any other person related to the testator shall include persons whether they are born in lawful wedlock or not. In order to exclude this aspect of the Status of Children Act 1987, it is necessary to include an express provision in the will.)

Declaration to exclude the operation of the Status of Children Act 1987 in respect of persons related to the testator

[14.04]

> **I HEREBY DECLARE** that in ascertaining the relationship of any person to me for the purposes of the person taking a benefit under this my will, my (executors and) trustees shall have regard to the marital relationships within the chain of that relationship and shall only confer a benefit on persons who have been born in lawful wedlock.

Declaration of renunciation of rights under the Succession Act 1965 by the spouse in a separation agreement as an explanation for no provision being made for the spouse*

[14.05]

> By Separation Agreement dated the *(insert date)* day of *(month)*, *(year)*, and made between myself and my spouse *(name)*, my said spouse renounced all his/ her rights to my estate under the Succession Act 1965 and I therefore confer no benefit in this my will on my said spouse.

Declaration of renunciation of rights under the Succession Act 1965 by the civil partner in an agreement as an explanation for no provision being made for the civil partner*

[14.06]

> By Agreement dated the *(insert date)* day of *(month)*, *(year)*, and made between myself and my civil partner *(name)*, my said civil partner renounced all his/her rights to my estate under the Succession Act 1965 and I therefore confer no benefit in this my will on my said civil partner.

Declaration in will where the spouse of the testator has renounced his or her rights in a separation agreement under Part IX of the Succession Act 1965 only*

[14.07]

> By Separation Agreement dated the *(insert date)* day of *(month)*, *(year)*, and made between myself and my spouse *(name)*, my said spouse renounced his/her rights pursuant to the provisions of Part IX of the Succession Act 1965 and my said spouse is therefore not entitled to a legal right share in my estate.
>
> *(Note*: some separation agreements only renounce the rights under Pt IX of the Succession Act 1965. This should be guarded against in separation agreements. Where only the rights under Pt IX of the Succession Act 1965 are renounced and a spouse dies intestate, the renunciation will have no effect as the rights under Pt IX of the Succession Act 1965 only arise where there is a will; the rights upon intestacy will remain intact.)

Declaration in will where the civil partner of the testator has renounced his or her rights in an agreement or unilateral renunciation under Pt IX of the Succession Act 1965 only*

[14.08] By Agreement/renunciation dated the *(insert date)* day of *(month)*, *(year)*, and made between myself and my civil partner *(name)*, my said civil partner renounced his/her rights pursuant to the provisions of Part IX of the Succession Act 1965 and my said civil partner is therefore not entitled to a legal right share in my estate.

Declaration in respect of renunciation by the spouse/civil partner of rights under the Succession Act 1965 where the renunciation was mutual*

[14.09]

By (Separation) Agreement dated the *(insert date)* day of *(month)*, *(year)*, and made between myself and my spouse/civil partner *(name)*, both myself and my spouse/civil partner mutually renounced all our rights pursuant to the provisions of the Succession Act 1965 to the estate of the other and for this reason I am making no provision for my spouse/civil partner in this my will.

(* In cases of a renunciation of rights by one or both spouses/civil partners, both parties must be independently advised. Under no circumstances should the same practitioner act for both parties.)

Declaration where a decree of divorce *a mensa et thoro* or judicial separation was obtained by the testator against his or her spouse

[14.10]

By order of High (or Circuit) Court, dated the *(insert date)* day of *(month)*, *(year)*, I obtained a decree of divorce *a mensa et thoro* against my spouse *(name)* [*or*, a decree of judicial separation under the Family Law (Judicial Separation) Act 1989 was made] and for this reason I am making no provision for my spouse in this my will.

Declaration where the spouse/civil partner is in desertion at the time the will is made

[14.11]

At the date of execution of this my will, my spouse/civil partner *(insert name)* is in desertion of me, which desertion has continued for a period of *(duration of desertion)* and for this reason I am making no provision for my said spouse/civil partner in this my will.

(*Note*: if the testator and his or her spouse enter into a separation agreement, this will terminate any desertion and the spouse will become entitled to a legal right share if no provision is made for him or her, unless the separation agreement contains a renunciation of the legal right share. Further, if the parties resume cohabitation prior to the death of the testator and the desertion is not continuing for a period of at least two years at the date of death of the testator, then the spouse may not be unworthy to succeed and may become entitled to claim the legal right share. The testator should be advised to revise his or her will if there is any reconciliation, even on a trial basis.)

Declaration that children have been properly provided for, in the view of the testator, and he or she is making no further provision for them in his or her will or is making no provision for them in the light of proper provision already having been made for them by the testator

[14.12]

I have properly provided for my children in accordance with my means and in accordance with my duty as a parent and for this reason I am making no further provision for them in this my will.

or

I have properly provided for my children in accordance with my means and notwithstanding that I have made such proper provision for my children in accordance with my means, I confer upon them the following bequests:

(*Set out bequests.*)

(*Note 1*: this second clause would be useful where a testator wishes to make a token bequest in favour of his or her children, notwithstanding that he or she has made proper provision for them.)

(*Note 2*: the opinion of the parent as to whether proper provision is made is not a decisive factor should the court be called upon to adjudicate upon a claim under s 117 of the Succession Act 1965. A statement to this effect by the testator may, however, be of assistance in refuting a claim that the testator has failed in his or her moral duty to make proper provision for a child in accordance with his or her means. It would be useful when drafting a will in which a statement like this is to be contained that the attendance in relation to the will would contain considerable detail as to what provision the testator had made for his or her children.)

Declaration excluding advancement under s 63 of the Succession Act 1965

[14.13]

In calculating the share of any beneficiary under any clause of this my will, no advancement made by me to the beneficiary within the meaning of advancement as defined in Section 63 of the Succession Act 1965 shall be brought into account and the provisions of Section 63 shall not apply to this my will.

(*Note*: that the Constitutionality of s 63 has be raised recently but Laffoy J did not comment upon same because the constitutional challenge had not been pleaded. Where the constitutionality of a statute is raised in proceedings it must be pleaded and the Attorney General must be a party to the proceedings.)

Declaration to exclude the operation of s 98 of the Succession Act 1965 to the will of the testator

[14.14]

The provisions of Section 98 of the Succession Act 1965 shall not apply to this my will and any bequest to a person who is my issue shall, if the beneficiary predeceases me, pass to the (spouse/civil partner) and (children) of the beneficiary in equal shares.

(*Note*: this general declaration can be used, but it is preferable and will give rise to less doubt if each bequest to which s 98 might potentially apply would contain an alternative disposition of the property in the event that the beneficiary who is issue predeceases the testator. If the testator is quite happy that the provisions of s 98 of the Succession Act 1965 would apply, then there would be no need for an alternative disposition or a declaration of this type. The provisions of s 98 are often misunderstood and care should be taken to read them carefully so that the effect of s 98 can be explained properly to the testator. Section 98 provides that where a bequest is made to a child or issue of the testator who predeceases him or her leaving children or issue, the child of the testator will be deemed to have survived him or her and died immediately after the testator. The bequest will fall into the estate of the predeceased child to be distributed in accordance with his or her will as the case may be.)

Declaration concerning simultaneous deaths – commorientes

[14.15]

In ascertaining the entitlement of any beneficiary under this my will, any beneficiary who dies in common calamity with me, who is not proved to have survived me, or does not survive me for a period of thirty days, shall be treated as having died before me.

(*Note*: s 5 of the Succession Act 1965 deals with the issue of *commorientes*. It provides that where persons die in circumstances rendering it impossible to ascertain which of them survived the other, they shall be deemed to have died simultaneously. The estate falls to be administered as if the particular person who dies simultaneously with the testator had predeceased the testator.)

Declaration to exclude the doctrine of satisfaction

[14.16]

None of the bequests contained in this my will is made in satisfaction or partial satisfaction of any debt or portion debt owed by me at the date of my death.

(*Note 1*: the doctrine of satisfaction is an operation of the equitable maxim, *equity imputes an intention to fulfil an obligation*. If the testator is indebted to a person at the date of his or her death and a bequest is given to that person, the question may arise as to whether the beneficiary is entitled to claim both the benefit conferred by the will and the debt. The presumption of satisfaction can be easily rebutted by showing that the benefit contained in the will and the debt are not of the same character, that the debt was not due and owing at the time the will was made, or that the benefit conferred by the will is less than the value of the debt.)

(*Note 2*: a testator may covenant to pay money to a child or a person to whom he or she stands *in loco parentis* giving rise to a portion debt. Again, the portion debt may be satisfied by a legacy contained in the will. If the testator does not intend this to be the case, then a declaration of this type will prevent the operation of the doctrine of satisfaction.)

(*Note 3*: the doctrine of satisfaction is dealt with in greater detail in the commentary to **Ch 8**.)

Declaration to exclude the operation of the doctrine of ademption, in the sense of a bequest being adeemed by a benefit conferred on the beneficiary during the lifetime of the testator

[14.17]

No benefit conferred by this my will shall be adeemed wholly or partially by any benefit conferred by me on a beneficiary in this my will during my lifetime, unless at the time when I confer the benefit in my lifetime I expressly declare in writing that I intend the benefit conferred by my will to be adeemed.

(*Note 1*: in this context, the doctrine of ademption referred to is the ademption of legacies by portions. The other context in which ademption is used is where a specific bequest is made to a beneficiary and the subject matter of the specific bequest is not available at the date of death of the testator. If the legacy is adeemed in this way, this clause will have no application.)

(*Note 2*: the doctrine of ademption is dealt with in greater detail in the commentary to **Ch 8**.)

Declaration to exclude the technical rules in relation to apportionment where the will creates a life interest

[14.18]

All income received after my death shall be treated from my estate regardless of the period to which it relates and the statutory rules concerning apportionment and the rules in *Howe v Dartmouth* and *Allhusen v Whittel* shall not be applied.

(*Note*: this clause is only required where the will creates a life estate.)

Direction concerning funeral and disposal of remains

[14.19]

I DIRECT that my executors should bury me with my parents/spouse/brother/sister at *(insert name of cemetery/graveyard)*.

Direction concerning cremation

[14.20]

> **I DIRECT** that my executors shall bury my remains and not cremate them.
>
> *Or*
>
> **I DIRECT** my executors to cremate my remains and to inter my ashes at *(insert name of cemetery or other place where the ashes are to he interred)* [*or,* scatter my ashes at *(insert location), or* scatter or inter my ashes as my executors in their discretion think fit].

Declaration concerning income and interest on bequests during the executors' year

[14.21]

> Any bequest contained in this my will, other than the bequest of the residue of my estate, shall not carry income or bear any interest until one year has expired from the date of my death and during that year my (executors and) trustees may at their absolute discretion:
>
> (i) Accumulate the income earned and hold same as part of the capital of the residue of my estate.
>
> (ii) Apply it in accordance with powers conferred upon my (executors and) trustees by statute, by general law, or by this my will.
>
> (iii) Pay it to the person entitled to the bequest in respect of which the income arises.

Declaration exonerating executors and trustees from any liability for loss

[14.22]

> Unless any executor or trustee of this my will be proved to have acted dishonestly or wilfully committed a breach of trust, none of my executors or trustees shall be liable for any loss incurred in the exercise by them of their powers conferred by this my will. Further, my executors and trustees shall be entitled to be indemnified out of the assets comprised in my estate in respect of all liabilities incurred by them in the *bona fide* execution of the duties and powers imposed and conferred upon them by statute, by general law, or by this my will.
>
> (*Note*: particularly where non-professional persons are asked to act in respect of trusts created by a testator's will, or where the trustees are members of the testator's family, it is important that a clause would be included exonerating them from liability, except where they are dishonest or wilfully commit a breach of trust. An executor is not allowed to profit from his or her office and the undertaking to act as a trustee is often an onerous obligation. The testator should consult with persons prior to asking them to act as executors or trustees, particularly if the administration of the estate is likely to be complicated or

protracted, eg, where there are minor children involved. The trustee is still expected to act *bona fide* in respect of the execution of his or her powers, but this clause will afford additional protection and comfort.)

Clause allowing professional executor or trustee to charge remuneration or fees for work done

[14.23] Any of my (executors and) trustees who is engaged in a profession may charge remuneration or fees for work done by him or her or by his or her firm (whether the work done is of a professional nature or not) on the same basis as if he or she were not one of my (executors and) trustees, but employed to carry out work on their behalf, and such remuneration or fees shall be paid in priority to all bequests under this my will.

(*Note 1*: as this clause is treated as a legacy, because an executor or trustee normally cannot profit from his or her office, the executor or trustee should not act as a witness and neither should the spouse of the executor or trustee, nor any member of a firm of which the executor or trustee is a member, act as a witness.)

(*Note 2*: if there is any question of abatement of legacies due to insufficient funds to pay them, then the clause should provide that the fees are to be paid in priority to all other bequests under the will, to avoid the charging clause abating either in whole or *pro rata* with other bequests.)

Chapter 15

ATTESTATION CLAUSES/TESTIMONIUMS

PART I: COMMENTARY

[15.01] Section 78 of the Succession Act 1965 expressly provides that a will shall not be invalidated by reason of the absence of an attestation clause or testimonium. However, if an attestation clause is not included, the Probate Office will seek evidence of due execution. This can give rise to difficulties, particularly where witnesses have become untraceable or have died, and if there is no direct evidence from an attesting witness or from some other person who was present at the execution of the will, the matter may be referred to the court. This will involve the estate in expense. It is, therefore, important that there be a proper attestation clause attached to the will.

In years gone by, attestation clauses were extremely verbose, but there was no necessity for such verbosity. Where there is a deviation from the norm in relation to due execution, such as where the testator signs the will by mark, or where the signature of the testator is feeble, or where there are double signatures, or the execution in some other way appears irregular, the Probate Office is at liberty to ask for an affidavit of attesting witness and usually does so. The Probate Office will usually seek an affidavit of attesting witness even where the attestation clause sets out fully that the provisions of the statute or general law were adhered to in relation to the unusual circumstances pertaining to the execution of the will. For this reason, it is advisable, even though the attestation clause may contain a full statement of what transpired at the due execution, to prepare at the time of the execution of the will an affidavit confirming that all relevant matters were attended to. Precedents for these affidavits are to be found in **Appendix 3**.

PART II: PRECEDENT CLAUSES

Simple form of attestation clause

[15.02] Signed by the testator in our presence, both present at the same time, and by us in the presence of the testator.

(*Note*: the Succession Act 1965 does not require witnesses to sign in each other's presence, but they must sign in the testator's presence. 'Presence' in this context has been held to mean visual presence and, therefore, a blind person cannot act as a witness to a will.)

Attestation clause where testator signs by mark, the will being read over to the testator by a third party prior to execution

[15.03]

Signed by the testator by making his/her mark, being unable to write due to illiteracy/physical debility, in our presence, both present at the same time, and by us in the presence of the testator, the will having first been read over to the testator in our presence by *(insert name of person who read over will)* and the testator appearing to understand the said will and he/she was at the time of execution of the said will of sound mind, memory and understanding.

Attestation clause where testator signs by mark, the will being read over by the testator him or herself

[15.04]

Signed by the testator by making his/her mark, being unable to write due to physical debility, in our presence, both present at the same time and by us in the testator's presence, the will having been first read over by the testator in our presence and he/she expressed him/herself satisfied with the said will and he/she was at the time of execution of the said will of sound mind, memory and understanding.

Attestation clause where testator is blind

[15.05]

Signed by the testator by making his/her mark, being unable to write due to blindness (he/she being blind), in our presence, both present at the same time and by us in the presence of the testator in such a position that had the testator been capable of sight, he/she would have been able to see us so sign.

Attestation clause where a signature is poorly formed or enfeebled

[15.06]

Signed by the testator in our presence, both present at the same time, and by us in the presence of the testator, the signature of the testator being enfeebled due to physical debility. Prior to the execution of the said will, the will was read over to the testator by *(insert name of person who read over will)* and the testator appeared to understand the same and was at the time of execution of sound mind, memory and understanding.

Attestation clause which includes reference to amendments or alterations in the will

[15.07]

Signed by the testator in our presence, both present at the same time, and by us in the presence of the testator, the figure '€1,000.00' being amended to read '€5,000.00' at line 5 of the will and the words 'my children' being deleted at line 10 of the will and the words 'my grandchildren' being interlined between lines 9 and 10 of the will in lieu thereof, such alterations being made prior to the execution of the said will by the testator.

Attestation clause where the will is on a number of single sheets of paper

[15.08]

Signed by the testator in our presence, both present at the same time, and by us in the presence of the testator, the said will having been written on *(insert number)* single sheets of paper, which said sheets of paper were all in the room at the time of execution of the will.

(*Note*: while the longer forms of attestation clause may not prevent and in many cases will not prevent the Probate Office seeking evidence from the attesting witnesses, if the witnesses prove untraceable or if their recollection is defective and the matter has to be referred to court, the longer forms of attestation clause will be useful in persuading the court that matters were attended to properly.)

In case of word-processor will, add on to all previous precedent attestation clauses

[15.09]

… this will having been printed on the front side only of the foregoing (*insert number*) sheets of A4 paper.

Chapter 16

COMPLETE WILLS AND CODICILS

PART I: COMMENTARY

Complete wills

[16.01] What follows may seem obvious to many. It is not included to give offence, but sometimes the most basic precepts can be overlooked. For that reason they need re-stating.

[16.02] None of the precedent wills and codicils in this chapter should be followed by any draftsperson slavishly. When preparing the first edition, I considered whether I would include complete wills in the book. It could encourage a tendency for persons drafting wills to simply identify the complete precedent, which he or she feels is as close as possible to what the testator requires, and to use it on a 'one size fits all' basis.

[16.03] Draftspersons should have regard to the earlier chapters of this book where the will is dealt with in its constituent parts and where various alternative clauses are explained and illustrated. In particular, **Ch 2** on the construction of wills should be read regularly and practitioners should keep abreast of any court decisions arising from constructional problems so they may be avoided.

[16.04] A person taking instructions for the drafting of a will should view every testator individually. Even where the testator is going to make a short, straightforward will, full instructions should be taken from the testator and the testator's intentions recorded faithfully in an attendance. This may seem to be statement of the obvious but often when problems arise, the attendances that I have seen fall far short of what one might expect.

[16.05] In *Curtin v O'Mahony*,[1] it was a cause of comment in both the High Court and Supreme Court that not only was there no attendance, but no one in the office where the will was drafted would own up to having drafted it. A very detailed will appeared to materialise without human intervention.

[16.06] The same care should be taken in relation to a testator who wishes to leave everything to his or her spouse/civil partner and appoint the spouse/civil partner executor as is adopted in relation to the person who requires to set up detailed and complicated provisions in relation to his or her will. The testator should be advised in relation to any moral obligation to a child, particularly in the case of civil partnerships or where there has been a second marriage. Full details should be recorded concerning the testator's estate. It should be recorded that the testator had capacity and, in the case of an old or infirm person, a medical report or affidavit of mental capacity might be obtained. It should be recorded that the testator was acting freely and voluntarily and free from influence.

---

1. *Curtin v O'Mahony* [1991] 2 IR 562.

[16.07] Persons seeking advice in relation to the making of their will may be nervous or reluctant to ask too many questions regarding making the will and may not be aware of the various options that might be open to them in the disposition of their property. The role of the practitioner is to explore with the testator what he or she may wish to achieve and to advise as to how that may happen or, alternatively, if it would give rise to problems, to point that out.

[16.08] The 'Frankenstein will' phenomenon, whereby a draftsperson takes bits and pieces from various precedents and welds them together into an incoherent whole, should be avoided. Regard should be had as to whether a particular declaration or provision in a will is apposite and regard should be had as to the function of particular provisions and declarations before inserting them into a will.

[16.09] In relation to the powers of executors and trustees, regard should be had as to what powers the executors and trustees might require in the fulfilling of their functions over and above statutory powers, and these powers should be included in the will. For example, there is little point in including a power to run the testator's business if the testator does not have a business.

Codicils

[16.10] A codicil should only be used where the changes in a will are to be minor, eg, to change appointment of executors, correct an error in the will, change the identity of a beneficiary or change the subject matter of a bequest. A large scale revision of a will should not be undertaken by codicil. A new will is preferable. While any number of codicils may be made, if there are more than three it might be better at that stage to consider a completely new will. A codicil may be a separate document or may be endorsed on the will where there is space so to do.

[16.11] The first codicil should not be referred to as such. If the first codicil is referred to as such and there transpires to be no further codicil, the Probate Office will require confirmation on affidavit that there is no other testamentary document in existence. Second and subsequent codicils can be described as such.

[16.12] If the testator has made a number of previous wills, care should be taken to refer to the correct will when identifying the last will in the codicil. Otherwise an earlier will may be accidentally revived or confusion may arise with the necessity of court intervention. I have seen a codicil refer inappropriately to the wrong will.

[16.13] Also, care should be taken to endorse the codicil on the correct will where the codicil is not to be a separate document.

If there is any dispute about the will to which the codicil relates, a court application will be necessary at first instance to the Probate Judge on the non-contentious probate side.

As a general rule, a will and codicil are regarded as one document and read together. However, where there are two bequests to the same beneficiary, one in the will and another in a codicil, they will be construed as separate documents in ascertaining whether the beneficiary is entitled to the benefit of both bequests. With clear drafting, such conundrums and potential applications to court can be avoided.

PART II: PRECEDENT CLAUSES

Complete wills

Will leaving entire estate to spouse of testator with spouse/civil partner of testator being appointed sole executor

[16.14]

THIS IS THE LAST WILL AND TESTAMENT OF *(insert name of testator)*, of *(address)*, made the *(date)* day of *(month)*, *(year)*. **I HEREBY REVOKE** all former wills and previous testamentary dispositions heretofore made by me.

I APPOINT my husband/wife/civil partner *(name)* as sole executor of this my will and **I DIRECT** him/her to pay all my just debts, funeral and testamentary expenses.

I GIVE, DEVISE AND BEQUEATH all my estate of every nature and description and kind, wheresoever situate, to my husband/wife/civil partner absolutely.

SIGNATURE OF TESTATOR:

SIGNED BY THE TESTATOR AS AND FOR HIS/HER LAST WILL AND TESTAMENT IN THE PRESENCE OF US, BOTH PRESENT AT THE SAME TIME, AND BY US IN HIS/HER PRESENCE.

Witness 1:

Address:

Witness 2:

Address:

Will leaving one-third of estate to spouse/civil partner of testator, being his or her legal right, with the remainder of the estate to the children of the testator, as tenants in common, with a substitutional provision in the event that any of the children predeceases the testator (avoiding s 98 of the 1965 Act)

[16.15]

THIS IS THE LAST WILL AND TESTAMENT OF *(insert name of testator)*, of *(address)*, made the *(date)* day of *(month)*, *(year)*. **I HEREBY REVOKE** all former wills and previous testamentary dispositions heretofore made by me.

I APPOINT *(name)*, of *(address)* and *(name)*, of *(address)*, as executors of this my will and **I APPOINT** trustees for the purposes of s 57 of the Succession Act 1965, the Land and Conveyancing Law Reform Act 2009 and the Conveyancing Acts 1881/1892*.

I APPOINT my executors as testamentary guardians of any child of mine who is under the age of eighteen at the date of my death.*

(*Consider the advisability of each of these additional appointments in the light of the facts of the particular case and whether executors and testamentary guardians should be the same person.)

I GIVE, DEVISE AND BEQUEATH one-third of my entire estate to my husband/wife/civil partner for his/her benefit absolutely, in satisfaction of his/her legal right share.

I GIVE, DEVISE AND BEQUEATH all the rest, residue and remainder of my property of every nature and description and kind, wheresoever situate, to my children *(name the children individually – or if the testator simply wants to leave to his/her children in the global sense, in case he/she might have further children, do not name them)* in equal shares.

If any of my children predeceases me leaving children, **I DIRECT** that the share to which that child would have been entitled shall pass to the children of that child in equal shares.*

(*This avoids s 98 but seek the testator's instruction.)

The provisions of s 63 of the Succession Act 1965 shall not apply to this my will and no child shall be required to bring any advancement into account in respect of the distribution of my estate.

SIGNATURE OF TESTATOR:

SIGNED BY THE TESTATOR AS AND FOR HIS/HER LAST WILL AND TESTAMENT IN THE PRESENCE OF US, BOTH PRESENT AT THE SAME TIME, AND BY US IN HIS/HER PRESENCE.

Witness 1:

Address:

Witness 2:

Address:

(Note 1: the testator may have reached an agreement with his or her spouse or civil partner that he or she would be left only his or her bare legal right share, but in cases where this might cause a difficulty for the spouse or civil partner in that he or she might be expecting more from the estate, it might be preferable that the spouse or civil partner not be one of the executors appointed. This is something that should be discussed with the testator. It might be better in this instance to appoint two of the testator's children (if they are of age) as executors or perhaps two independent persons.

This type of will may be prevalent where a testator perhaps remarries or enters into a civil partnership late in life and while he or she wishes to leave his or her new spouse or civil partner his or her statutory entitlement, he or she does not want to unduly affect the rights of inheritance that the children might have been expecting.)

(*Note 2*: if the children are minors and the estate includes real property then a trust of land within the meaning of Pt 4 of the 2009 Act arises and its provisions apply. Part 4 of the 2009 Act is set out in full in **Appendix 12, Pt 1**.)

(*Note 3*: consideration should be give to the appointment of testamentary guardians of any child who may be a minor at the date of death.)

(*Note 4*: if the spouse or civil partner is ordinarily resident in any dwelling forming part of the estate the right of appropriation under s 56 of the 1965 Act, as amended, will arise and may be availed of. The testator should be advised of this.)

Will leaving entire estate to spouse/civil partner for life, provided he or she survives the testator. Remainder over to the brothers and sisters of the testator jointly (he or she having no issue) living at the date of death of the spouse or civil partner and with the entire estate passing to the brothers and sisters of the testator jointly in the event that the spouse or civil partner predeceases the testator

[16.16]

THIS IS THE LAST WILL AND TESTAMENT OF *(insert name of testator)*, of *(address)*, made the *(date)* day of *(month)*, *(year)*.

I HEREBY REVOKE all former wills and previous testamentary dispositions heretofore made by me.

I APPOINT *(name)*, of *(address)* and *(name)*, of *(address)*, as executors and trustees of this my will. I appoint the said *(name)* and *(name)* as trustees for the purposes of Part 4 of the Land and Conveyancing Law Reform Act 2009.

Provided my husband/wife/civil partner *(name)* survives me, **I GIVE, DEVISE AND BEQUEATH** all of my property of every nature and description and kind, wheresoever situate, unto my husband/wife/civil partner for life, with remainder over on his/her death to such of my brothers and sisters as may be living at the date of death of my husband/wife/civil partner jointly.

All income received after my death shall be treated from my estate regardless of the period to which it relates and the statutory rules concerning apportionment and the rules in *Howe v Dartmouth* and *Allhusen v Whittel* shall not be applied.

In the event that my husband/wife/civil partner does not survive me then in that event **I GIVE, DEVISE AND BEQUEATH** all my estate of every nature and description and kind, wheresoever situate, to such of my brothers and sisters as survive me jointly.

SIGNATURE OF TESTATOR:

SIGNED BY THE TESTATOR AS AND FOR HIS/HER LAST WILL AND TESTAMENT IN THE PRESENCE OF US, BOTH PRESENT AT THE SAME TIME, AND BY US IN HIS/HER PRESENCE.

Witness 1:

Address:

Witness 2:

Address:

(*Note1*: this precedent assumes the testator has no children or any children were properly provided for in accordance with the testator's means.)

(*Note 2*: if the spouse/civil partner does survive the testator, it will be necessary for him or her to be put to his or her election *vis-à-vis* the legal right share and the benefit conferred by the will.)

(*Note 3*: if the spouse or civil partner is ordinarily resident in a dwelling, which forms part of the estate, at the date of death the right of appropriation under s 56 of the 1965 Act arises.)

(*Note 4*: the will creates a settlement; therefore, if there is land in the estate a trust of land arises under Pt 4 of the 2009 Act and its provisions apply. Part 4 of the 2009 Act is set out in **Appendix 4**.)

(*Note 5*: because of the life estate, the rules concerning apportionment of income should be excluded.)

(*Note 6*: as the gift over in remainder or the universal bequest, should it take effect, is left to the brothers and sisters jointly, there is no need for an alternative disposition in relation to any of the brothers or sisters predeceasing the testator as the right of survivorship will apply automatically.)

(*Note 7*: if the testator wishes his or her brothers and sisters to take as tenants in common the word 'jointly' should be replaced with words of severance, eg, 'share and share alike' or 'in equal shares'. The two types of co-ownership and their effect should be explained to the testator.)

Will making no provision for spouse/civil partner for a specified reason, with the entire estate being left to the children of the testator in equal shares, with no substitutional provision, so that the provisions of s 98 of the Succession Act 1965 will apply in the event that any child predeceases the testator

[16.17]

THIS IS THE LAST WILL AND TESTAMENT OF *(insert name of testator)*, of *(address)*, made the *(date)* day of *(month)*, *(year)*. **I HEREBY REVOKE** all former wills and previous testamentary dispositions heretofore made by me.

I APPOINT *(name)*, of *(address)* and *(name)*, of *(address)*, as executors and trustees of this my will. I appoint the said *(name)* and *(name)* as trustees for the purposes of the Settled Land Acts 1882–90 and the Conveyancing Acts 1881–92.

By Separation Agreement dated the *(date)* day of *(month)*, *(year)*, and made between myself and my spouse *(name)*, my said spouse renounced all his/her rights to my estate under the Succession Act 1965 and I therefore confer no benefit in this my will on my said spouse.

or

By Separation Agreement dated the *(date)* day of *(month), (year)*, and made between myself and my spouse *(name)*, my said spouse renounced his/her rights pursuant to the provisions of Part IX of the Succession Act 1965 and my said spouse is therefore not entitled to a legal right share in my estate.

By Agreement/Renunciation dated the *(date)* day of *(month), (year)* my spouse/civil partner renounced his/her entitlement to his/her legal right share pursuant to the provisions of Part IX of the Succession Act 1965 and by reason thereof he/she is not entitled to any legal right share in my estate.

or

By Separation Agreement dated the *(date)* day of *(month), (year)*, and made between myself and my spouse *(name)*, both myself and my spouse mutually renounced all our rights pursuant to the provisions of the Succession Act 1965 to the estate of the other and for this reason I am making no provision for my spouse in this my will.

or

By order of High (or Circuit) Court, dated the *(date)* day of *(month), (year)*, I obtained a decree of divorce *a mensa et thoro* against my spouse [*or,* a decree of judicial separation under the Family Law (Judicial Separation) Act 1989 was made] and for this reason I am making no provision for my spouse in this my will.

or

At the date of execution of this my will, my spouse/civil partner *(name)* is in desertion of me, which desertion has continued for a period of *(duration of desertion)* and for this reason I am making no provision for my said spouse in this my will.

I GIVE, DEVISE AND BEQUEATH all of my property of every nature and description and kind, wheresoever situate, unto my children living at the date of my death in equal shares.

SIGNATURE OF TESTATOR:

SIGNED BY THE TESTATOR AS AND FOR HIS/HER LAST WILL AND TESTAMENT IN THE PRESENCE OF US, BOTH PRESENT AT THE SAME TIME, AND BY US IN HIS/HER PRESENCE.

Witness 1:

Address:

Witness 2:

Address:

(*Note 1*: it would, of course, be open to the spouse/civil partner to challenge the reason stated in the will which could give rise to litigation but it is useful to have the reasons of the testator stated clearly in the will. The will should, of course, not include any defamatory or scandalous matter, which would be excised by the Probate Office from the will as proved. Full details of the spouse/civil partner's exclusion should be recorded in any attendance and any relevant court order should be obtained and perused.)

(*Note 2*: a decree of divorce *a vinculo* or dissolution of a civil partnership dissolves the union so it is not included as an alternative provision above. This is because spousal/civil partner rights will be dissolved with the dissolution of the marriage. I reiterate that the dissolution of a marriage or civil partnership does not revoke a will and any person who dissolves a marriage or civil partnership or is in the course of so doing should make a new will to take account of the changed circumstances.)

(*Note 3*: if the desertion terminates, the rights of the spouse/civil partner could be revived and the testator should be so advised. He or she should review his or her will if there is any reconciliation.)

(*Note 4*: if the children are minors, testamentary guardians might be appointed.)

Will leaving entire estate to the children of the testator (he or she being a widow, unmarried or not in a civil partnership) with provision for a gift over in favour of the children of any child who predeceases the testator

[16.18]

THIS IS THE LAST WILL AND TESTAMENT OF *(insert name of testator)*, of *(address)*, made the *(date)* day of *(month)*, *(year)*. **I HEREBY REVOKE** all former wills and previous testamentary dispositions heretofore made by me.

I APPOINT *(name)*, of *(address)* and *(name)*, of *(address)*, as executors and trustees of this my will. I appoint the said *(name)* and *(name)* (as trustees for of Section 57 of the Succession Act 1965, the Land and Conveyancing Law Reform Act 2009 and the Conveyancing Acts 1881–92*)

(**These appointments are only necessary if the children are minors.)*

I GIVE, DEVISE AND BEQUEATH all of my property of every nature and description and kind, wheresoever situate, unto my children living at the date of my death in equal shares. In the event that any child predeceases me leaving children then the share to which that child would have been entitled shall pass to the children of such child.

SIGNATURE OF TESTATOR:

SIGNED BY THE TESTATOR AS AND FOR HIS/HER LAST WILL AND TESTAMENT IN THE PRESENCE OF US, BOTH PRESENT AT THE SAME TIME, AND BY US IN HIS/HER PRESENCE.

Witness 1:

Address:

Witness 2:

Address:

(*Note1*: the gift over means that the provisions of s 98 of the Succession Act 1965 will not apply; this should be discussed with and explained to the testator and his or her instructions taken and recorded.)

(*Note 2*: if the children are minors, thought might be given to the appointment of testamentary guardians.)

(*Note 3*: where land is left to minors, it is held on a trust of land pursuant to the provisions of Pt 4 of the 2009 Act, hence the appointment of trustees.)

Will leaving one-third of estate to spouse/civil partner with remaining two-thirds to spouse /civil partner for his or her life with special power of appointment amongst the children of the testator and provision for gift over in the event of a default in the exercise of the power of appointment

[16.19]

THIS IS THE LAST WILL AND TESTAMENT OF *(insert name of testator)*, of *(address)*, made the *(date)* day of *(month)*, *(year)*.

I HEREBY REVOKE all former wills and previous testamentary dispositions heretofore made by me.

I APPOINT *(name)*, of *(address)* and *(name)*, of *(address)*, as executors and trustees of this my will. I appoint the said *(name)* and *(name)* as trustees for the purposes of Section 57 of the Succession Act 1965, the Land and Conveyancing Law Reform Act 2009 and the Conveyancing Acts 1881–92.

I GIVE, DEVISE AND BEQUEATH one-third of all of my property of every nature and description and kind, wheresoever situate, to my husband/wife/civil partner *(name)* absolutely.

I GIVE, DEVISE AND BEQUEATH the remaining two-thirds of all of my property of every nature and description and kind, wheresoever situate, to my husband/wife/civil partner *(name)* for life, with a special power of appointment of the said two-thirds share in favour of such one or more of my children as he/she may by deed or will appoint. In default of the exercise of the power, my children living at the date of death of my spouse/civil partner shall take the two-thirds share equally.

All income received after my death shall be treated from my estate regardless of the period to which it relates and the statutory rules concerning apportionment and the rules in *Howe v Dartmouth* and *Allhusen v Whittel* shall not be applied.

SIGNATURE OF TESTATOR:

SIGNED BY THE TESTATOR AS AND FOR HIS/HER LAST WILL AND TESTAMENT IN THE PRESENCE OF US, BOTH PRESENT AT THE SAME TIME, AND BY US IN HIS/HER PRESENCE.

Witness 1:

Address:

Witness 2:

Address:

(*Note 1*: if the spouse/civil partner is ordinarily resident at the date of the testator's death in a dwelling forming part of the estate, the right of appropriation under s 56 of the 1965 Act will arise.)

(*Note 2*: in the case of default of the exercise of a special power, the objects of the power take equally but the clause in this will makes clear what the testator intends.)

(*Note 3*: in view of the manner of the disposal of the estate, the advisability of appointing the spouse or civil partner as executor should be considered.)

(*Note 4*: if it is perceived that the spouse or civil partner might seek to challenge the will, full instructions should be taken so that any challenge can be defended. Should any allegation of lack of capacity or undue influence be possible, steps should be taken to seek to negative any such allegation.)

Will leaving entire estate to spouse/civil partner absolutely but in the event that he or she predeceases the testator to trustees upon a trust for sale and discretionary trust for the children of the testator until the youngest attains the age of 18 years (or 21 years if involved in full time education); appointing separate persons testamentary guardians; wide powers being given to the trustees, with charging clause and indemnity

[16.20]

THIS IS THE LAST WILL AND TESTAMENT OF *(insert name of testator)*, of *(address)*, made the *(date)* day of *(month)*, *(year)*. I HEREBY REVOKE all former wills and previous testamentary dispositions heretofore made by me.

I APPOINT *(name)*, of *(address)* and *(name)*, of *(address)*, as executors and trustees of this my will. I appoint the said *(name)* and *(name)* as trustees for the purposes of the Section 57 of the Succession Act 1965, the Land and Conveyancing Law Reform Act 2009 and the Conveyancing Acts 1881–92.

In the event that my husband/wife/civil partner *(name)* survives me, I GIVE, DEVISE AND BEQUEATH all my estate of every nature and description and kind to him/her absolutely.

In the event that my husband/wife/civil partner does not survive me or dies in common calamity with me, then I DIRECT that the following provisions shall take effect.

I APPOINT *(name)*, of *(address)* and *(name)*, of *(address)* as testamentary guardians of my children until they each attain the age of eighteen years.

I GIVE, DEVISE AND BEQUEATH all of my property of every nature and description and kind, wheresoever situate, to my executors and trustees upon trust for sale (with power to postpone such sale) and to hold the proceeds of the said sale or the assets of my estate for so long as they remain unsold for the benefit of my children until the last of them shall attain the age of eighteen years (or if involved in full-time education the age of twenty-one years) and when the last child attains the age of eighteen years (or if involved in full-time education the age of twenty-one years) to apply the said proceeds of sale, or the assets of my estate for so long as they remain unsold, or assets acquired by my executors and trustees in the exercise of the powers conferred by this my will for the benefit of my children in such share or in such proportion as they in their absolute discretion shall think fit.

In addition to the powers conferred upon them by statute and by general law, I confer the following powers upon my executors and trustees:

A.   The power to appoint new trustees under this my will shall be vested in my executors and trustees, or the survivor of them, and in exercising the power to appoint new trustees my executors and trustees shall have the power to appoint a professional trustee or a trust corporation upon such terms as to remuneration and otherwise as they in their absolute discretion shall think fit.

B.   The power on the realisation of any asset forming part of my estate, or with any moneys forming part of my estate, to acquire real property (leasehold and freehold) and to hold the said property upon the same trusts as my estate is held by them.

C.   To use the capital or income of my estate in the maintenance and/or improvement of any real property (whether freehold or leasehold) comprised in my estate or acquired by my executors and trustees after my death under the powers contained in this my will.

D.   To invest any asset forming part of my estate or the proceeds of sale thereof as if they were beneficially entitled to the said asset and this power, without liability for loss, includes the following rights:

    (i)   To invest in unsecured interest free loans to any beneficiary.

    (ii)   To invest in other non-income producing assets, including life assurance policies, with power to pay the premiums out of the income or capital of my estate.

    (iii)   To invest in the acquisition of a property or premises for the occupation of any beneficiary of this my will.

    (iv)   To hold investments in the name of any person or body as they think fit.

E.   To insure any asset forming part of my estate (or acquired by my trustees under the power conferred in this my will) upon such terms and upon such conditions as they in their absolute discretion shall think fit, and:

    (i)   To pay the premiums out of the income or capital of my estate, and

(ii) To use any moneys paid on foot of such insurance policy to restore the asset insured, or if this is not possible or not deemed expedient by my trustees as they in their absolute discretion shall think fit, to apply the moneys received on foot of such insurance policy as if it were proceeds of the asset's sale and hold the same upon the same trust as they hold my estate.

F. To carry on and continue any business I am engaged in at the date of my death for so long as my executors and trustees think fit and without prejudice to the generality of this power:

(i) To use in the running of the said business any assets comprised in my estate.

(ii) To become employed in the said business and to retain out of the profits of the said business reasonable remuneration.

(iii) To incorporate the said business or to form a company for the purposes of carrying on the said business.

(iv) To become a director of any company formed and to retain from the profits of the said business any reasonable remuneration for themselves.

(v) To be indemnified for any loss incurred in the running of the said business out of my estate.

G. To borrow from such person, institution or corporation, upon such terms and upon such conditions as they in their absolute discretion may think fit and to use the money borrowed for any purpose for which the assets comprised in my estate may be used and to furnish security for any money borrowed.

H. To sell any asset comprised in my estate at its full open market value to any one or more of my trustees *(or, if a particular trustee is to be named as the only person who can purchase an asset, name of that trustee).* Before selling any asset under this provision, my trustees shall obtain two independent valuations from reputable firms of valuers and shall sell the asset for the higher of the two valuations.

I. My executors and trustees may in their absolute discretion accumulate the income derived from my estate or apply the said income for the benefit of any beneficiary under the trust hereby created.

J. Where any beneficiary under the trust hereby created is under the age of eighteen years, my executors and trustees may pay any money from the income or capital of my estate to his or her parent and/or other legal or testamentary guardian for the benefit of the said beneficiary who is a minor and the receipt of the parent or legal or testamentary guardian shall be sufficient discharge to my executors and trustees in respect of such payment.

K.   While any of the beneficiaries under this trust are under the age of eighteen years, my executors and trustees may allow the said beneficiary to have the use of any personal chattel forming part of my estate to which he or she may become entitled.

L.   My executors and trustees may advance, for the benefit of any beneficiary under the trust hereby created, who is a minor, the whole or any part of the capital to which the beneficiary is entitled or may become entitled by paying the said income or capital to the parent or legal or testamentary guardian of the said beneficiary and the receipt of the parent or legal or testamentary guardian of the beneficiary shall be sufficient discharge to my executors and trustees.

M.   My executors and trustees shall have power to appropriate any asset forming part of my estate in accordance with the provisions of Section 55 of the Succession Act 1965 without the service of the notices required by that Section or the obtaining of the consents where required by that Section.

[Optional

I HEREBY DECLARE that in this my will, any reference to my children shall be a reference only to children born within lawful wedlock, [and adopted pursuant to the provisions of the Adoption Acts,] either before or after my death.

Or

I HEREBY DECLARE that in this my will, any reference to my children, shall include (*name(s)*) to whom I have stood *in loco parentis.**]

(**This may be necessary in the case of a civil partner who is not the biological parent of his or her partner's children but who wishes them to be included.*)

In calculating the share of any beneficiary under any clause of this my will, no advancement made by me to the beneficiary within the meaning of advancement as defined in Section 63 of the Succession Act 1965 shall be brought into account and the provisions of Section 63 shall not apply to this my will.

Unless any executor or trustee of this my will be proved to have acted dishonestly or wilfully committed a breach of trust, none of my executors or trustees shall be liable for any loss incurred in the exercise by them of their powers conferred by this my will. Further, my executors and trustees shall be entitled to be indemnified out of the assets comprised in my estate in respect of all liabilities incurred by them in the *bona fide* execution of the duties and powers imposed and conferred upon them by statute, by general law, or by this my will.

Any of my executors and trustees who is engaged in a profession may charge remuneration or fees for work done by him or her or by his or her firm (whether the work done is of a professional nature or not) on the same basis as if he or she were not one of my executors and trustees, but employed to carry out work on their behalf, and such remuneration or fees shall be paid in priority to all bequests under this my will.

SIGNATURE OF TESTATOR:

SIGNED BY THE TESTATOR AS AND FOR HIS/HER LAST WILL AND TESTAMENT IN THE PRESENCE OF US, BOTH PRESENT AT THE SAME TIME, AND BY US IN HIS/HER PRESENCE.

Witness 1:

Address:

Witness 2:

Address:

(*Note*: the powers of the trustees should be considered in each case individually and regard should be had to the provisions of Pt 4 of the 2009 Act, which is set out in full at **Appendix 12., Pt 1**)

Will leaving a number of pecuniary legacies (inflation proof), a demonstrative legacy (inflation proof), specific legacies, specific devises and charitable bequests, with residue to brothers and sisters of the testator jointly

[16.21]

THIS IS THE LAST WILL AND TESTAMENT OF *(insert name of testator)*, of *(address)*, made the *(date)* day of *(month)*, *(year)*. **I HEREBY REVOKE** all former wills and previous testamentary dispositions heretofore made by me.

I APPOINT *(name)*, of *(address)* and *(name)*, of *(address)*, as executors and trustees of this my will.

I GIVE the sum of €5,000.00 (five thousand euro) to my friends *(name)*, of *(address)* and *(name)*, of *(address)* jointly.

I GIVE the sum of €500.00 (five hundred euro) each to the children of my sister *(name)*, of *(address)*, to be paid to each of them on their eighteenth birthday.

I GIVE the sum of €1,000.00 (one thousand euro) to my god-daughter *(name)*, of *(address)*, such sum to be paid to her parent or guardian if she is under the age of eighteen years at my death and the receipt of such parent or guardian shall be sufficient discharge to my executors in the payment of this legacy.

I GIVE the sum of €5,000.00 (five thousand euro) to the treasurer for the time being at the date of my death of the Dublin Branch of the Samaritans at 112 Marlborough Street in the City of Dublin for the charitable purposes of the Samaritans, the receipt of the said treasurer or other proper officer of the Samaritans to be sufficient discharge to my executors in the payment of this legacy.

I GIVE the sum of €3,000.00 (three thousand euro) to my cousin *(name)*, of *(address)*, payable out of my account, number *(account number)*, with the

Governor and Company of the Bank of Ireland at its branch at *(address of branch).*

I GIVE each of the legatees in the preceding clauses the sum specified or such larger sum as my executors and trustees calculate to have the same value at the date of my death as the figure specified had at the date of my will.

I GIVE my motor car to my nephew, *(name), of (address).*

I GIVE my silver Victorian tea service to my sister *(name), of (address).*

I GIVE my stamp collection to my niece *(name), of (address),* daughter of my sister *(name).**

(*Where two nieces of the same name exist.)

I GIVE, DEVISE AND BEQUEATH my dwelling house at *(location of house; if registered give folio number and county)* to my executors upon trust for sale and to apply the proceeds of sale for the benefit of the Irish Society for the Prevention of Cruelty to Children, the receipt of the treasurer or other proper officer of the said society to be sufficient discharge to my executors and trustees in the payment of this bequest.

ALL THE REST, RESIDUE AND REMAINDER of my estate of every nature and description and kind and wheresoever situate **I GIVE, DEVISE AND BEQUEATH** to my brothers and sisters living at the date of my death in equal shares.

Unless any executor or trustee of this my will be proved to have acted dishonestly or wilfully committed a breach of trust, none of my executors or trustees shall be liable for any loss incurred in the exercise by them of their powers. Further, my executors and trustees shall be entitled to be indemnified out of the assets comprised in my estate in respect of all liabilities incurred by them in the *bona fide* execution of the duties and powers imposed and conferred upon them by statute and by general law.

Any of my executors and trustees who is engaged in a profession may charge remuneration or fees for work done by him or her or by his or her firm (whether the work done is of a professional nature or not) on the same basis as if he or she were not one of my executors and trustees, but employed to carry out work on their behalf, and such remuneration or fees shall be paid in priority to all bequests under this my will.

SIGNATURE OF TESTATOR:

SIGNED BY THE TESTATOR AS AND FOR HIS/HER LAST WILL AND TESTAMENT IN THE PRESENCE OF US, BOTH PRESENT AT THE SAME TIME, AND BY US IN HIS/HER PRESENCE.

Witness 1:

Address:

Witness 2:

Address:

Will conferring right of residence, maintenance and support on sister of testator with entire estate being left to a niece of the testator, with gift over to charity if niece predeceases the deceased

[16.22]

> **THIS IS THE LAST WILL AND TESTAMENT OF** *(insert name of testator)*, of *(address)*, made the *(date)* day of *(month)*, *(year)*. **I HEREBY REVOKE** all former wills and previous testamentary dispositions heretofore made by me.
>
> **I APPOINT** *(name)*, of *(address)* and *(name)*, of *(address)*, as executors and trustees of this my will. I appoint them trustees for the purposes of Part 4 of the Land and Conveyancing Law Reform Act 2009.
>
> **I GIVE, DEVISE AND BEQUEATH** all my estate of every nature and description to my niece *(name)*, of *(address)*, daughter of my brother *(name)*, subject only to a right of residence, maintenance and support for my sister *(name)* for her life on my farm house and lands comprised in Folio *(number)* of the Register County of *(county)*. During the period of enjoyment of the right of residence my said niece shall be entitled to reside in the said farm house with my said sister.
>
> In the event that my said niece predeceases me, **I GIVE, DEVISE AND BEQUEATH** all my estate (subject as aforesaid) to Church of Ireland Archbishop of Dublin for the benefit of the poor of the diocese of Dublin.
>
> SIGNATURE OF TESTATOR:
>
> SIGNED BY THE TESTATOR AS AND FOR HIS/HER LAST WILL AND TESTAMENT IN THE PRESENCE OF US, BOTH PRESENT AT THE SAME TIME, AND BY US IN HIS/HER PRESENCE.
>
> Witness 1:
>
> Address:
>
> Witness 2:
>
> Address:

Will dealing only with property in the Republic of Ireland and appointing firm of solicitors as executors leaving entire estate upon trust for sale for the benefit of specified charitable purposes

[16.23]

> **THIS IS THE LAST WILL AND TESTAMENT OF** *(insert name of testator)*, of *(address)*, made the *(date)* day of *(month)*, *(year)*. **I HEREBY REVOKE** all former wills and previous testamentary dispositions heretofore made by me.

I HEREBY DECLARE that this will shall only apply to property situate within the Republic of Ireland, or to which the law of the Republic of Ireland applies. For removal of all doubt, this declaration also applies to the revocation clause contained in this my will.

I HEREBY APPOINT the firm of solicitors practising under the style and title of *(name of firm),* of *(business address),* as executors and trustees of this my will, provided always that it shall be the partners of the said firm at the date of my death who shall be entitled to prove the said will and in the event that the said firm shall amalgamate with another firm under its own or a new name, or the said firm shall be incorporated into another firm of solicitors, the amalgamated firm of solicitors or the firm of solicitors into which the said firm shall be incorporated, shall be deemed to be executors and trustees of this my will. **I APPOINT** the said firm as trustees for the purposes of Section 57 of the Succession Act 1965, the Conveyancing Acts 1881–92 and the Land and Conveyancing Law Reform Act 2009.

The said firm of solicitors shall be entitled to charge professional fees for work done by it or its members in connection with my estate, whether or not the work is of a professional nature, on the same basis as if the said firm were not my executors and trustees but employed to carry out work on their behalf *and the fees so charged shall be paid in priority to all other bequests under this my will.* *

(* Delete italicised section if not required.)

I GIVE, DEVISE AND BEQUEATH all my estate of every nature and description to my executors and trustees upon trust for sale and to apply the proceeds of the said sale as they in their absolute discretion think fit for the benefit of charities having the following purposes or objects:

(a)   The education of persons for the priesthood of the Roman Catholic Church in Ireland.

(b)   The relief of poverty and distress of elderly people in the City and County of Cork.

(c)   The assistance of persons who are visually or aurally impaired or who suffer from both disabilities.

(d)   The welfare of animals in the Republic of Ireland.

The receipt of the treasurer or other proper officer of any charity which my executors and trustees in their discretion decide to benefit under this trust to be sufficient discharge to my executors in the payment of any benefit under this trust.

SIGNATURE OF TESTATOR:

SIGNED BY THE TESTATOR AS AND FOR HIS/HER LAST WILL AND TESTAMENT IN THE PRESENCE OF US, BOTH PRESENT AT THE SAME TIME, AND BY US IN HIS/HER PRESENCE.

Witness 1:

Address:

Witness 2:

Address:

Codicils

Codicil altering appointment of executors and confirming and republishing will

[16.24]

THIS IS A (SECOND) CODICIL to my last will dated the *(date)* day of *(month)*, *(year)*.

Whereas by the said will *(name)* of *(address)* was appointed [sole/one of the] executor(s) in my said will and has subsequently died **I HEREBY APPOINT** in his/her stead *(name)* of *(address)* as [sole/an] executor of my will.

Or

Whereas *(name)* of *(address)* was appointed [sole/one of the] executor(s) in my said will **I HEREBY REVOKE** the said appointment and **I APPOINT** in his/her stead *(name)* of *(address)* as [sole/an] executor of my will.

In all other respects I confirm and republish my said will.

Dated the *(date)* day of *(month)*, *(year)*.

SIGNATURE OF TESTATOR:

SIGNED BY THE TESTATOR AS AND FOR A (SECOND) CODICIL TO HIS/HER LAST WILL AND TESTAMENT DATED THE *(DATE)* DAY OF *(MONTH)*, *(YEAR)* IN THE PRESENCE OF US, BOTH PRESENT AT THE SAME TIME, AND BY US IN HIS/HER PRESENCE.

Witness 1:

Address:

Witness 2:

Address:

Codicil altering amount of pecuniary legacy and confirming and republishing will

[16.25]

THIS IS A (SECOND) CODICIL to my last will dated the *(date)* day of *(month)*, *(year)*.

Whereas by the said will I gave *(name)* of *(address)* the sum of ... *(amount in figures and words)* I now increase/decrease the said sum to ... *(new amount in figures and words)*.

In all other respects I confirm and republish my said will.

Dated the *(date)* day of *(month)*, *(year)*.

SIGNATURE OF TESTATOR:

SIGNED BY THE TESTATOR AS AND FOR A (SECOND) CODICIL TO HIS/HER LAST WILL AND TESTAMENT DATED THE *(DATE)* DAY OF *(MONTH)*, *(YEAR)* IN THE PRESENCE OF US, BOTH PRESENT AT THE SAME TIME, AND BY US IN HIS/HER PRESENCE.

Witness 1:

Address:

Witness 2:

Address:

Codicil revoking devise and devising property to a new beneficiary and confirming and republishing will

[16.26]

THIS IS A (THIRD) CODICIL to my last will dated the *(date)* day of *(month)*, *(year)*.

Whereas by the said will I devised my farm at *(location of farm)* to [my *(relationship to testator, if any)*] *(name)* of *(address)* I hereby revoke the said devise and leave the said farm to [my *(relationship to testator, if any)*] *(name)* of *(address)*.

In all other respects I confirm and republish my said will.

Dated the *(date)* day of *(month)*, *(year)*.

SIGNATURE OF TESTATOR:

SIGNED BY THE TESTATOR AS AND FOR A (THIRD) CODICIL TO HIS/ HER LAST WILL AND TESTAMENT DATED THE *(DATE)* DAY OF *(MONTH)*, *(YEAR)* IN THE PRESENCE OF US, BOTH PRESENT AT THE SAME TIME, AND BY US IN HIS/HER PRESENCE.

Witness 1:

Address:

Witness 2:

Address:

Codicil correcting error in will and confirming and republishing will

[16.27]

THIS IS A CODICIL to my last will dated the *(date)* day of *(month)*, *(year)*.

Whereas by the said will I gave the contents of my house to [my *(relationship to testator, if any)*] *(name)* of *(address)* and I intended to leave him/her my dwelling house and contents in order to correct the error appearing in the said will **I HEREBY GIVE, DEVISE AND BEQUEATH** my dwelling house and contents at *(location of dwelling house)* to [my said *(relationship to testator, if any)*] *(name)* of *(address)*.

In all other respects I confirm and republish my said will.

Dated the *(date)* day of *(month)*, *(year)*.

SIGNATURE OF TESTATOR:

SIGNED BY THE TESTATOR AS AND FOR A CODICIL TO HIS/HER LAST WILL AND TESTAMENT DATED THE *(DATE)* DAY OF *(MONTH)*, *(YEAR)* IN THE PRESENCE OF US, BOTH PRESENT AT THE SAME TIME, AND BY US IN HIS/HER PRESENCE.

Witness 1:

Address:

Witness 2:

Address:

Appendix 1

STATUTORY PROVISIONS OF THE SUCCESSION ACT 1965 RELATING TO WILLS

Part VII (ss 76–100) of the Succession Act 1965 lays down the statutory provisions in relation to wills as follows:

76. A person may by his will, executed in accordance with this Act, dispose of all property which he is beneficially entitled to at the time of his death and which on his death devolves on his personal representatives.

77. (1) To be valid a will shall be made by a person who—

(a)   Has attained the age of eighteen years or is or has been married, and

(b)   Is of sound disposing mind.

(2) A person who is entitled to appoint a guardian of an infant may make the appointment by will notwithstanding that he is not a person to whom paragraph (a) of subsection (1) applies.

78. To be valid a will shall be in writing and be executed in accordance with the following rules.

1. It shall be signed at the foot or end thereof by the testator, or by some person in his presence and by his direction.

2. Such signature shall be made or acknowledged by the testator in the presence of each of two or more witnesses, present at the same time, and each witness shall attest by his signature the signature of the testator in the presence of the testator, but no form of attestation shall be necessary nor shall it be necessary for the witnesses to sign in the presence of each other.

3. So far as concerns the position of the signature of the testator or of the person signing for him under rule 1, it is sufficient if the signature is so placed at or after, or following, or under, or beside, or opposite to the end of the will that it is apparent on the face of the will that the testator intended to give effect by the signature to the writing signed as his will.

4. No such will shall be affected by the circumstances—

(a)   That the signature does not follow or is not immediately after the foot or end of the will; or

(b)   That a blank space intervenes between the concluding word of the will and the signature; or

(c)   That the signature is placed among the words of the testimonium clause or of the clause of attestation, or follows or is after or under the clause of attestation, either with or without a blank space intervening, or follows or is after, or under, or beside the names or one of the names of the attesting witnesses; or

(d)   That the signature is on a side or page or other portion of the paper or papers containing the will on which no clause or paragraph or disposing part of the will is written above the signature; or

(e)   That there appears to be sufficient space on or at the bottom of the preceding side or page or other portion of the same paper on which the will is written to contain the signature; and

The enumeration of the above circumstances shall not restrict the generality of rule 1.

5. A signature shall not be operative to give effect to any disposition or direction inserted after the signature is made.

79. (1) An appointment made by will, in exercise of any power, shall not be valid unless it is executed in accordance with this Act. (2) Every will so executed shall, so far as concerns its execution and attestation, be a valid execution of a power of appointment by will, notwithstanding that it has been expressly required that a will made in exercise of such power shall be executed with some additional or other form of execution or solemnity.

80. Every will executed in accordance with this Act shall be valid without any other publication thereof.

81. If a person who attests the execution of a will is, at the time of execution, or at any time afterwards, incompetent to be admitted as a witness to prove the execution, the will shall not on that account be invalid.

82. (1) If a person attests the execution of a will, and any devise, bequest, estate, interest, gift, or appointment, of or affecting any property (other than charges and directions for the payment of any debt or debts) is given or made by the will to that person or his spouse or civil partner, that devise, bequest, estate, interest, gift, or appointment shall, so far only as concerns the person attesting the execution of the will, or the spouse or civil partner of that person, or any person claiming under that person or spouse, be utterly null and void. [As amended by the 2010 Act.]

(2) The person so attesting shall be admitted as a witness to prove the execution of the will, or to prove the validity or invalidity thereof, notwithstanding such devise, bequest, estate, interest, gift, or appointment.

(*Note*: by virtue of s 82(2), the fact that a beneficiary or a spouse/civil partner of a beneficiary may act as a witness does not invalidate the will itself; it only invalidates the particular bequest.)

83. If by will any estate is charged with any debt or debts, and a creditor, or spouse of a creditor, whose debt is so charged, attests the execution of the will, the creditor, notwithstanding such charge, shall be admitted a witness to prove the execution of the will, or to prove the validity or invalidity thereof.

84. A person shall not, by reason only of his being an executor of a will, be incompetent to be admitted a witness to prove the execution of the will, or a witness to prove the validity or invalidity thereof.

85. (1) A will shall be revoked by the subsequent marriage or entry into a civil partnership of the testator, except a will made in contemplation *of that marriage or civil partnership, whether so expressed in the will or not.* [As amended by the 2010 Act.] (Author's emphasis.)

(2) Subject to subsection (1), no will, or any part thereof, shall be revoked except by another will or codicil duly executed, or by some writing declaring an intention to revoke it and executed in the manner in which a will is required to be executed,

or by the burning, tearing, or destruction of it by the testator, or by some person in his presence and by his direction, with the intention of revoking it.

86. An obliteration, interlineation, or other alteration made in a will after execution shall not be valid or have any effect, unless such alteration is executed as is required for the execution of the will; but the will, with such alteration as part thereof, shall be deemed to be duly executed if the signature of the testator and the signature of each witness is made in the margin or on some other part of the will opposite or near to such alteration, or at the foot or end of or opposite to a memorandum referring to such alternation, and written at the end of some other part of the will.

87. No will or any part thereof, which is in any manner revoked, shall be revived *otherwise than* by the re-execution thereof or by a codicil duly executed and showing an intention to revive it; and when any will or codicil which is partly revoked, and afterwards wholly revoked, is revived, such a revival shall not extend to so much thereof as was revoked before the revocation of the whole thereof, unless an intention to the contrary is shown. (Author's emphasis.)

(*Note*: the revocation of a later will shall not revive an earlier will. If the earlier will is to be revived, it must be re-executed or confirmed by a later codicil.)

88. Where, subsequently to the execution of a will, a conveyance or other act is made or done relating to any estate comprised in the will, except an act by which the will is revoked, the conveyance or act shall not prevent the operation of the will with respect to any estate or interest in the property which the testator has power to dispose of by will at the time of his death.

89. Every will shall, with reference to all estate comprised in the will and every devise or bequest contained in it, be construed to speak and take effect as if it had been executed immediately before the death of the testator, unless a contrary intention appears from the will.

90. Extrinsic evidence shall be admissible to show the intention of the testator and to assist in the construction of or to explain any contradiction in, a will.

91. Unless a contrary intention appears from the will, any estate comprised or intended to be comprised in any devise or bequest contained in the will which fails or is void by reason of the fact that the devisee or legatee did not survive the testator, or by reason of the devise or bequest being contrary to law or otherwise incapable of taking effect, shall be included in any residuary devise or bequest, as the case may be, contained in the will.

92. A general devise of land shall be construed to include leasehold interests as well as freehold estates, unless a contrary intention appears from the will.

93. A general devise of land shall be construed to include any land which the testator may have power to appoint in any manner he may think proper, and shall operate as an execution of such power, unless a contrary intention appears from the will; and in like manner a general bequest of the personal estate (other than land) of the testator shall be construed to include any such estate which he may have power to appoint in any manner he may think proper, and shall operate as an execution of such power, unless a contrary intention appears from the will.

94. Where real estate is devised to a person (including a trustee or executor) without any words of limitation, the devise shall be construed to pass the whole estate or interest which the testator had power to dispose of by will in the real estate, unless a contrary intention appears from the will.

(*Note*: this is now echoed in the 2009 Act, which provides that words of limitation are no longer necessary in a conveyance.)

95. (1) An estate tail (whether general, in tail male, in tail female or in tail special) in real estate may be created by will only by the use of the same words of limitation as those by which a similar estate tail may be created by deed.

(2) Words of limitation contained in a will in respect of real estate which have not the effect of creating an estate fee simple or an estate tail shall have the same effect, as near as may be, as similar words used in a deed in respect of personal property.

(*Note*: the 2009 Act prohibits the creation of a fee tail, by any instrument, which includes a will.)

96. In a devise or bequest of real or personal estate, the words 'die without issue', or 'die without leaving issue,' or 'have no issue', or any other words which may import either a want or failure of issue of any person in his lifetime or at the time of his death, or an indefinite failure of his issue, shall be construed to mean a want or failure of issue in his lifetime or at the time of his death, and not an indefinite failure of his issue, unless a contrary intention appears from the will.

97. Where a person to whom real estate is devised for an estate tail or an estate in quasi entail dies in the lifetime of the testator leaving issue who could inherit under the entail, and any such issue is living at the time of the death of the testator, the devise shall not lapse, but shall take effect as if the death of that person had happened immediately after the death of the testator, unless a contrary intention appears from the will.

98. Where a person, being a child or other issue of the testator to whom any property is given (whether by a devise or bequest or by the exercise by will of any power of appointment, and whether as a gift to that person as an individual or as a member of a class) for any estate or interest not determinable at or before the death of that person, dies in the lifetime of the testator leaving issue, and any such issue of that person is living at the time of the death of the testator, the gift shall not lapse, but shall take effect as if the death of that person had happened immediately after the death of the testator, unless a contrary intention appears from the will.

99. If the purport of a devise or bequest admits of more than one interpretation, then, in case of doubt, the interpretation according to which the devise or bequest will be operative shall be preferred.

100. Where a person is entitled under a will to—

(a)   land for an estate in fee simple or for any lesser estate or interest not being an estate tail, or,

(b)   any interest in other property,

with an executory limitation over in default or failure of any of his issue, whether within a specified period of time or not, that executory limitation shall be or become void and incapable of taking effect, if and as soon as there is living any issue of the class in default or failure of which the limitation over was to take effect.

Appendix 2

DEFINITIONS CONTAINED IN THE SUCCESSION ACT 1965 TO WHICH REGARD SHOULD BE HAD

'**administration**' in relation to the estate of a deceased person means Letters of Administration, whether with or without a will annexed, and whether granted for special or limited purposes. **[s 3]**

'**administrator**' means a person to whom administration is granted. **[s 3(1)]**

'**advancement**' – for the purposes of s 63, 'advancement' is defined as follows:

> **advancement** means a gift intended to make permanent provision for a child and includes advancement by way of portion or settlement, including any life or lesser interest and including property covenanted to be paid or settled. It also includes an advance or portion for the purpose of establishing a child in a profession, vocation, trade or business, a marriage portion and payments made for the education of a child to a standard higher than that provided by the deceased for any other or others of his children. **[s 63(6)]**

'**assistant Probate Officer**' means the officer employed in the Probate Office who is next in rank to the Probate Officer and is qualified to be appointed to be Probate Officer. **[s 3(1)]**

'**child**' – for the purpose of s 63, 'child' is defined as follows:

> In this section '**child**' includes a person to whom the deceased was in loco parentis. **[s 63(10)]**

(*Note*: ror deaths after 14 June 1988 it would include a non-marital child – see the Status of Children Act 1987.)

'**conveyance**' includes a mortgage, charge, lease, assent, transfer, disclaimer, release and every other assurance of property by any instrument except a will. **[s 3(1)]**

'**the court**' shall be construed in accordance with s 6, which provides as follows:

> (1) The jurisdiction conferred on a Court by this Act may be exercised by the High Court.

> (2) Subject to subsection (3), the Circuit Court shall, concurrently with the High Court, have all the jurisdiction of the High Court to hear and determine proceedings of the following kinds:

> (a)   An action in respect of the grant or revocation of representation of the estate of a deceased person in case there is any contention in relation thereto;

> (b)   Proceedings in respect of the administration of the estate of a deceased person or in respect of any share therein;

> (c)   Any proceedings under section 56, 115, 117 or 121.

> (3) Unless the necessary parties to the proceedings in a cause sign, either before or at any time during the hearing, the form of consent prescribed by rules of court,

the Circuit Court shall not, by virtue of subsection (2), have jurisdiction where the estate of the deceased person, in so far as it consists of real estate, of which, at the time of his death, he was beneficially seized or possessed, exceeds the rateable valuation of £200.00.

(4) The jurisdiction conferred on the Circuit Court by this section shall be exercised by the judge of the circuit where the deceased, at the time of his death, had a fixed place of abode. **[s 6]**

(*Note*: the Circuit Court does not have any non-contentious probate jurisdiction; such jurisdiction is exercised by the High Court. The jurisdiction of the Circuit Court is unlimited in relation to personalty but in respect of realty the rateable valuation must be less than €254. The deceased should have a fixed place of abode at the date of his or her death within the jurisdiction of the particular Circuit Court. As probate matters are dealt with on the chancery or equity side there is no probate jurisdiction in the District Court.)

'devise or bequest' – for the purposes of s 115, 'devise' or 'bequest' is defined as follows:

In this section, but only in its application to a case to which subsection (1) of section 114 applies, **devise** or **bequest** means a gift deemed under that subsection to have been made by the will of the testator. **[s 115(6)]**

'die without issue'; **'die without leaving issue'**; **'have no issue'**:

In a devise or bequest of real or personal estate, the words **'die without issue'**, or **'die without leaving issue'**, or **'have no issue'**, or any other words which may import either a want or failure of issue of any person in his lifetime or at the time of his death, or an indefinite failure of his issue, shall be construed to mean a want or failure of issue in his lifetime or at the time of his death, and not an indefinite failure of his issue, unless a contrary intention appears from the will. **[s 96]**

'disposition' – for the purposes of s 121, 'disposition' is defined as follows:

In this section, **disposition** includes a *donatio mortis causa*. **[s 121(10)]**

'dwelling' – for the purposes of s 56, 'dwelling' is defined as follows:

dwelling means an estate or interest in a building occupied as a separate dwelling or a part, so occupied, of any building and includes any garden or portion of ground attached to and usually occupied with the dwelling or otherwise required for the amenity or convenience of the dwelling. **[s 56(14)]**

'estate' shall be construed in accordance with s 14. **[s 3(1)]**

Section 14 provides as follows:

References in the subsequent provisions of this Act and in any subsequent enactment to the **estate** of a deceased person shall, unless the contrary intention appears, *include references to both the real and personal estate of that deceased person*. (Author's emphasis.) **[s 14]**

'grant' means Grant of Representation. **[s 3(1)]**

'have no issue' – see 'die without issue'.

'heir or heirs' – s 15 provides as follows:

> (1) The word **'heir'** or **'heirs'**, used as words of limitation in any enactment, deed or instrument passed or executed either before or after the commencement of this Act, shall have the same effect as if this Act had not been passed.
>
> (2) The word **'heir'** or **'heirs'**, used as a word of purchase in any enactment, deed or instrument passed or executed *before* the commencement of this Act, shall bear the same meaning as if this Act had not been passed.
>
> (3) The word **'heir'** or **'heirs'**, used as a word of purchase in any enactment, deed or instrument passed or executed *after* the commencement of this Act, shall, unless the contrary intention appears, be construed to mean the person or persons, other than a creditor, who would be beneficially entitled under Part VI to the estate of the ancestor if the ancestor had died intestate.
>
> (4) Subject as aforesaid, references in any enactment, deed or instrument passed or executed either before or after the commencement of this Act to the heirs of any person shall be construed to refer to his personal representatives. (Author's emphasis.) **[s 15]**

'household chattels' – for the purposes of s 56, 'household chattels' are defined as follows:

> **household chattels** means furniture, linen, china, glass, books and other chattels of ordinary household use or ornament and also consumable stores, garden effects and domestic animals, but does not include any chattels used at the death of the deceased for business or professional purposes or money or security for money. **[s 56(14)]**

'infant' means a person under the age of [18] years. **[s 3(1)]**

'an intestate' means a person who leaves no will or leaves a will but leaves some beneficial interest undisposed of in his estate and 'intestate' shall be construed accordingly. **[s 3(1)]**

'land' – for the purposes of s 52, 'land' is defined as follows:

> References to **land** of a deceased person are references to land to which he was entitled or over which he exercised a general power of appointment by will. **[s 52]**

'legal right' means the right of a spouse or civil partner under s 111 and s 111A to a share in the estate of a deceased person. **[s 3(1)]** [As amended by the 2010 Act.]

'the Minister' means the Minister for Justice. **[s 3(1)]**

'pecuniary legacy' includes an annuity, a general legacy, a demonstrative legacy, so far as it is not discharged out of the designated property, and any other general direction by a testator for the payment of money, including all death duties free from which any devise, bequest or payment is made to take effect. **[s 3(1)]**

'per stirpes' shall be construed in accordance with s 3(3). **[s 3(1)]**

Section 3(3) provides as follows:

> Where a deceased person's estate or any share therein is to be distributed *per stirpes* among his issue, any issue more remote than a child of the deceased shall take through all degrees, according to their stocks, in equal shares if more than

one, the share which the parent of such issue would have taken if living at the death of the deceased, and no issue of the deceased shall take if the parent of such issue is living at the death of the deceased and so capable of taking. **[s 3(3)]**

'person entitled' – for the purposes of s 52, 'person entitled' is defined as follows:

> **Persons entitled** includes in relation to any estate or interest in land –
>
> (i) the person or persons (including the personal representatives of the deceased or any of them) who (whether by devise, bequest, devolution or otherwise) may be beneficially entitled to that estate or interest, and
>
> (ii) the trustee or trustees or the personal representative or representatives of any such person or persons. **[s 52(1)(e)]**

'personal representative' means the executor or the administrator for the time being of a deceased person. **[s 3(1)]**

'possession' includes the receipt of, or the right to receive, rents and profits, if any. **[s 3(1)]**

'probate' means probate of a will. **[s 3(1)]**

'property' includes all property, both real and personal. **[s 3(1)]**

'purchaser' means a grantee, lessee, assignee, mortgagee, chargeant or other person who in good faith acquires an estate or interest in property for valuable consideration. **[s 3(1)]**

'real estate' has the meaning assigned to it by s 4, which provides as follows:

> **real estate** includes chattels real and land in possession, remainder, or reversion, and every estate or interest in or over land (including real estate held by way of mortgage or security, but not including money to arise under a trust for sale of land, or money secured or charged on land). **[s 4(a)]**

'representation' means probate or administration. **[s 3(1)]**

'share' in relation to the estate of a deceased person includes any share or interest whether arising under a will, on intestacy or as a legal right and includes also the right to the whole estate. **[s 3(1)]**

'testamentary disposition' – for the purposes of Pt VIII, testamentary disposition is defined as follows:

> **testamentary disposition** means any will or other testamentary instrument or act. **[s 101]**

'trust corporation' has the meaning assigned to it by s 30(4), which provides as follows:

> In this Act, **'trust corporation'** means—
>
> (a) A corporation appointed by the High Court in any particular case to be a trustee;
>
> (b) A corporation empowered by its constitution to undertake trust business, and having a place of business in the State or Northern Ireland, and being—
>
> > (i) a company established by Act or charter, or

(ii)   an Associated Bank under the Central Bank Act, 1942, or

(iii)   a company (whether registered with or without limited liability) within the definition contained in the Companies Act, 1963, or within the meaning of the corresponding law of Northern Ireland, having a capital (in stock or shares) for the time being issued of not less than £250,000.00 of which not less than £100,000.00 has been paid up in cash, or,

(iv)   a company (registered without limited liability) within the definition contained in the said Companies Act or within the meaning of the said law of Northern Ireland, one of the members of which is a corporation within any of the previous provisions of this paragraph; or

(c)   A corporation which satisfies the President of the High Court that it undertakes the administration of any charitable, ecclesiastical or public trust without remuneration, or that by its constitution it is required to apply the whole of its net income for charitable, ecclesiastical or public purposes and is prohibited from distributing, directly or indirectly, any part thereof by way of profits, and is authorised by the President of the High Court to act in relation to such trusts as a trust corporation. **[s 30(4)]**

'**trustee**' – s 124 provides as follows:

Notwithstanding any rule of law, **trustee** in the Statute of Limitations, 1957, shall not include a person whose fiduciary relationship arises merely because he is in possession of property comprised in the estate of a deceased person in the capacity of bailiff for another person. **[s 124]**

'**valuable consideration**' means consideration in money or money's worth. **[s 3(1)]**

'**will**' includes codicil. **[s 3(1)]**

Appendix 3

AFFIDAVITS OF ATTESTING WITNESS THAT MAY BE SWORN AT THE TIME THE WILL IS EXECUTED AND LEFT WITH THE WILL WHERE THERE IS SOME UNUSUAL CIRCUMSTANCE PERTAINING TO THE EXECUTION OF THE WILL

1.   Affidavit of Attesting Witness where the will is signed by mark;

2.   Affidavit of Attesting Witness where signature of testator is feeble or poorly formed;

3.   Affidavit of Attesting Witness where signature is made twice;

4.   Affidavit of Attesting Witness where signature is made by a third party on behalf of the testator in his or her presence and at his or her direction;

5.   Affidavit of Attesting Witness of a blind testator where testator signs with ordinary signature;

6.   Affidavit of Attesting Witness of a blind testator where signature is poorly made or poorly formed;

7.   Affidavit of Attesting Witness where there are alterations to the will prior to execution;

8.   Affidavit of Attesting Witness where map or other document is attached to the will.

In a perfect world, all wills would be executed in the same way uniformly and without any question arising as to their due execution. It happens at times, however, that wills have to be drawn up as a matter of urgency when a person is ill and perhaps in danger of death. In such circumstances, difficulties may arise in relation to the execution of the will and it is a prudent course to adopt to swear an affidavit to be left with the will. The will may be drawn up in such a hurry that it may not be possible to get the will typed and bound and the will may be in a poor state of plight and condition at the time the will is executed, or may be on a number of sheets of paper.

The following precedents are aimed at assisting the practitioner in drafting affidavits to be left with the will that shall obviate difficulties when the will comes to be proved. Remember, attesting witnesses die, they forget, or they become untraceable, but if the affidavit of attesting witness is prepared at the time the will is executed and it is then sworn at the time of execution or shortly thereafter, it will be a more reliable piece of evidence.

In drafting the affidavit of attesting witness, it is useful to try to capture the circumstances surrounding the execution of the will and for that reason the precedents that are set out in this appendix indicate where the will was executed and the circumstances in which the attesting witness came to act as a witness. This is of assistance to the Probate Office in evaluating the affidavit of attesting witness.

It should be remembered that the Probate Office has authority to refer the matter to court in any case where it feels such a reference is warranted.

If the execution of the will is in order and there are no difficulties surrounding the execution of the will, but for some reason the plight and condition of the will is poor at the time of execution, any affidavit from an attesting witness must deal with due execution in addition to dealing with plight and condition. The Rules of the Superior Courts require that any affidavit from an attesting witness must also deal with due execution (see O 79, r 40).

1. AFFIDAVIT OF ATTESTING WITNESS WHERE THE WILL IS SIGNED BY MARK

THE HIGH COURT
(PROBATE)

IN THE MATTER OF THE WILL OF (*INSERT NAME OF TESTATOR*) OF
(*ADDRESS*), (*OCCUPATION/DESCRIPTION*)

AFFIDAVIT OF ATTESTING WITNESS

I, (*name of attesting witness*), of (*address of attesting witness*), (*occupation/ description*), aged eighteen years and upward make Oath and say as follows:

1. I make this affidavit on my own behalf from facts within my own knowledge save where otherwise appears and where so otherwise appears I believe those facts to be true.

2. I am one of the subscribing witnesses to the will of (*name of testator*), of (*address of testator*).

3. The said will was executed at (*location, eg, the offices of [name of firm of solicitors], at [address]; the home of the testator, at [address]; [name and address of hospital where will was executed]*).

4. I am a solicitor in the said firm of (*name of firm of solicitors*) [*or*, I am a neighbour/friend of the testator, *or*, I am a patient in the said hospital] and was asked by the testator [*or*, (*name of solicitor*)] to act as a witness to the will of the testator.

5. The said will was executed on the (*date*) day of (*month*), (*year*), by the testator by him/her affixing his/her mark at the foot or end thereof as the same now appears thereon, he/she being unable to write due to physical disability/illiteracy, in the presence of me and of (*name of other attesting witness*), both of us being present at the same time, and we then, in the presence of the testator, signed our names as witnesses to the said will.

6. Prior to the execution of the will as aforesaid, the will was read over to the testator by (*name of person who read the will over*) in my presence and the testator appeared fully to understand the same and was at the time of execution of the will of sound mind, memory and understanding.

    [*or*,

6. Prior to the execution of the said will as aforesaid, the will was read over by the testator him/herself in my presence and the testator fully understood the will and expressed him/herself to be satisfied with the same and was at the time of execution of the said will of sound mind, memory and understanding.]

    (*If necessary, deal with the plight and condition of the will, eg, where the will is drawn up in a hurry in a hospital and the sheet of paper upon which it is written is perhaps torn or in a poor state or condition or where the will is written on a number of sheets of paper.*)

7.   The said will was written out by *(name of solicitor)* on a single sheet of paper and the left hand edge of the paper is torn (serrated, perforated) as the paper was taken from a notepad or notebook and the will is in the same plight and condition as when executed by the testator and nothing of a testamentary nature was attached thereto.

[*or,*

7.   The said will of the testator was written on *(number)* sheets of paper. I can confirm that all sheets of paper were present in the room at the time the will was signed by the testator. Nothing further of a testamentary nature was attached to any of said sheets of paper.]

SWORN, ETC.

2. AFFIDAVIT OF ATTESTING WITNESS WHERE SIGNATURE OF TESTATOR IS FEEBLE OR POORLY FORMED

THE HIGH COURT
(PROBATE)

IN THE MATTER OF THE WILL OF (*INSERT NAME OF TESTATOR*) OF (*ADDRESS*), (*OCCUPATION/DESCRIPTION*)

AFFIDAVIT OF ATTESTING WITNESS

I, (*name of attesting witness*), of (*address of attesting witness*), (*occupation/ description*), aged eighteen years and upward make Oath and say as follows:

1. I make this affidavit on my own behalf from facts within my own knowledge save where otherwise appears and where so otherwise appears I believe those facts to be true.

2. I am one of the subscribing witnesses to the will of *(name of testator)*, of *(address of testator)*.

3. The said will was executed at (*location, eg the offices of [name of firm of solicitors], at [address]; the home of the testator, at [address]; [name and address of hospital where will was executed]*).

4. I am a solicitor in the said firm of *(name of firm of solicitors)* [*or*, I am a neighbour/friend of the testator, *or*, I am a patient in the said hospital] and was asked by the testator [*or, (name of solicitor)*] to act as a witness to the will of the testator.

5. The said will was executed by the testator on the *(date)* day of *(month)*, *(year)* by signing his/her name at the foot or end thereof in the presence of me and of *(name of other attesting witness)*, both of us being present at the same time, and we then, in the presence of the testator, signed our names as witnesses to the said will.

6. The signature of the testator as appears from the said will is enfeebled and/or poorly formed. This was because the testator was suffering from the after effects of a stroke and had lost some of the power in his/her right/left hand and was thus unable to make his/her signature properly.

    (*Note*: this paragraph can be adapted to fit the circumstances, eg, where the testator was in a greatly weakened physical state and was propped up in bed, thus unable to make the signature properly, or where the testator suffered from some condition, such as Parkinson's disease or a form of palsy, which rendered the hand of the testator shaky.)

7. Prior to the execution of the will as aforesaid, the will was read over to the testator by *(name of person who read the will over)* in my presence and the testator appeared fully to understand the same and was at the time of execution of the will of sound mind, memory and understanding.

    [*or*,

7. Prior to the execution of the said will as aforesaid, the will was read over by the testator him/herself in my presence and the testator fully understood the will and expressed him/herself to be satisfied with the same and was at the time of execution of the said will of sound mind, memory and understanding.]

    (*Note*: if necessary, deal with the plight and condition of the will, eg, where the will is drawn up in a hurry in a hospital and the sheet of paper upon which it is written is perhaps torn or in a poor state or condition or where the will is written on a number of sheets of paper.)

8. The said will was written out by *(name of solicitor)* on a single sheet of paper and the left hand edge of the paper is torn (serrated, perforated) as the paper was taken from a notepad or notebook and the will is in the same plight and condition as when executed by the testator and nothing of a testamentary nature was attached thereto.

    [*or*,

8. The said will of the testator was written on *(number)* sheets of paper. I can confirm that all sheets of paper were present in the room at the time the will was signed by the testator and nothing further of a testamentary nature was attached thereto.]

SWORN, ETC.

3. AFFIDAVIT OF ATTESTING WITNESS WHERE SIGNATURE IS MADE TWICE

THE HIGH COURT
(PROBATE)

IN THE MATTER OF THE WILL OF (*INSERT NAME OF TESTATOR*) OF
(*ADDRESS*), (*OCCUPATION/DESCRIPTION*)

AFFIDAVIT OF ATTESTING WITNESS

I, (*name of attesting witness*), of (*address of attesting witness*), (*occupation/ description*), aged eighteen years and upward make Oath and say as follows:

1.   I make this affidavit on my own behalf from facts within my own knowledge save where otherwise appears and where so otherwise appears I believe those facts to be true.

2.   I am one of the subscribing witnesses to the will of (*name of testator*), of (*address of testator*).

3.   The said will was executed at (*location, eg, the offices of [name of firm of solicitors], at [address]; the home of the testator, at [address]; [name and address of hospital where will was executed]*).

4.   I am a solicitor in the said firm of (*name of firm of solicitors*) [*or*, I am a neighbour/friend of the testator, *or*, I am a patient in the said hospital] and was asked by the testator [*or*, (*name of solicitor*)] to act as a witness to the will of the testator.

5.   The said will was executed on the (*date*) day of (*month*), (*year*) by the testator by him/her signing his/her name twice at the foot or end thereof as the same now appears thereon, once above the attestation clause and once below the attestation clause, in the presence of me and of (*name of other attesting witness*), both of us being present at the same time, and we then, in the presence of the testator, signed our names as witnesses to the said will.

6.   The two signatures appearing on the said will were made by the testator mistakenly. The testator first signed his/her name below the attestation clause in error and when the error was pointed out to him/her, he/she again signed his/her name above the attestation clause. I can confirm that both signatures were made in one continuous act of execution.

(*Note*: this paragraph made need to be altered to explain the circumstances of the double signature. The important thing is that the witness be able to say that both signatures were done in one continuous act of execution.)

7.   Prior to the execution of the will as aforesaid, the will was read over to the testator by (*name of person who read the will over*) in my presence and the testator appeared fully to understand the same and was at the time of execution of the will of sound mind, memory and understanding.

[*or*,

7.   Prior to the execution of the said will as aforesaid, the will was read over by the testator him/herself in my presence and the testator fully understood the will and expressed him/herself to be satisfied with the same and was at the time of execution of the said will of sound mind, memory and understanding.]

(*Note*: If necessary, deal with the plight and condition of the will, eg, where the will is drawn up in a hurry in a hospital and the sheet of paper upon which it is written is perhaps torn or in a poor state or condition or where the will is written on a number of sheets of paper.)

8.   The said will was written out by *(name of solicitor)* on a single sheet of paper and the left hand edge of the paper is torn (serrated, perforated) as the paper was taken from a notepad or notebook and the will is in the same plight and condition as when executed by the testator and nothing of a testamentary nature was attached thereto.

[*or,*

8.   The said will of the testator was written on *(number)* sheets of paper. I can confirm that all sheets of paper were present in the room at the time the will was signed by the testator and nothing further of a testamentary nature was attached thereto.]

SWORN, ETC.

4. AFFIDAVIT OF ATTESTING WITNESS WHERE SIGNATURE IS MADE BY A THIRD PARTY ON BEHALF OF THE TESTATOR IN HIS OR HER PRESENCE AND AT HIS OR HER DIRECTION

THE HIGH COURT
(PROBATE)

IN THE MATTER OF THE WILL OF (*INSERT NAME OF TESTATOR*) OF
(*ADDRESS*), (*OCCUPATION/DESCRIPTION*)

AFFIDAVIT OF ATTESTING WITNESS

I, (*name of attesting witness*), of (*address of attesting witness*), (*occupation/ description*), aged eighteen years and upward make Oath and say as follows:

1. I make this affidavit on my own behalf from facts within my own knowledge save where otherwise appears and where so otherwise appears I believe those facts to be true.

2. I am one of the subscribing witnesses to the will of (*name of testator*), of (*address of testator*).

3. The said will was executed at (*location, eg, the offices of* [name of firm of solicitors], *at* [address]; *the home of the testator, at* [address]; [*name and address of hospital where will was executed*]).

4. I am a solicitor in the said firm of (*name of firm of solicitors*) [*or*, I am a neighbour/friend of the testator, *or*, I am a patient in the said hospital] and was asked by the testator [*or*, (*name of solicitor*)] to act as a witness to the will of the testator.

5. The said will was executed on the (*date*) day of (*month*), (*year*) by (*name of person who made signature*) signing the name of the testator *or*, his/her own name) at the foot or end of the will at the direction of the testator and in the presence of the testator in lieu of the testator signing his/her own name, he/she being unable to write due to (*state reason*) in the presence of me and of (*name of other attesting witness*), both of us being present at the same time, and we then, in the presence of the testator, signed our names as witnesses to the said will.

6. Prior to the execution of the will as aforesaid, the will was read over to the testator by (*name of person who read the will over*) in my presence and the testator appeared fully to understand the same and was at the time of execution of the will of sound mind, memory and understanding.

   [*or*,

6. Prior to the execution of the said will as aforesaid, the will was read over by the testator him/herself in my presence and the testator fully understood the will and expressed him/herself to be satisfied with the same and was at the time of execution of the said will of sound mind, memory and understanding.]

   (*Note*: if necessary, deal with the plight and condition of the will, eg, where the will is drawn up in a hurry in a hospital and the sheet of paper upon which it is written is perhaps torn or in a poor state or condition or where the will is written on a number of sheets of paper.)

7.   The said will was written out by *(name of solicitor)* on a single sheet of paper and the left hand edge of the paper is torn (serrated, perforated) as the paper was taken from a notepad or notebook and the will is in the same plight and condition as when executed by the testator and nothing of a testamentary nature was attached thereto.

[*or,*

7.   The said will of the testator was written on *(number)* sheets of paper. I can confirm that all sheets of paper were present in the room at the time the will was signed by *(name of-person who made signature)* on behalf of the testator and nothing further of a testamentary nature was attached thereto.]

SWORN, ETC.

5. AFFIDAVIT OF ATTESTING WITNESS OF A BLIND TESTATOR WHERE TESTATOR SIGNS WITH ORDINARY SIGNATURE

THE HIGH COURT
(PROBATE)

IN THE MATTER OF THE WILL OF (*INSERT NAME OF TESTATOR*) OF
(*ADDRESS*), (*OCCUPATION/DESCRIPTION*)

AFFIDAVIT OF ATTESTING WITNESS

I, (*name of attesting witness*), of (*address of attesting witness*), (*occupation/ description*), aged eighteen years and upward make Oath and say as follows:

1. I make this affidavit on my own behalf from facts within my own knowledge save where otherwise appears and where so otherwise appears I believe those facts to be true.

2. I am one of the subscribing witnesses to the will of *(name of testator)*, of *(address of testator)*.

3. The said will was executed at (*location, eg, the offices of [name of firm of solicitors], at [address]; the home of the testator, at [address]; [name and address of hospital where will was executed]*).

4. I am a solicitor in the said firm of *(name of firm of solicitors)* [*or,* I am a neighbour/friend of the testator, *or,* I am a patient in the said hospital] and was asked by the testator [*or, (name of solicitor)*] to act as a witness to the will of the testator.

5. The said will was executed by the testator, who is blind, on the *(date)* day of *(month), (year),* by the testator signing his/her name at the foot or end thereof in the presence of me and of *(name of other attesting witness),* both of us being present at the same time, and we then, in the presence of the testator, signed our names as witnesses to the said will, and signed our names in such a position that had the testator been able to see, he/she would have been able to see us so sign.

6. Prior to the execution of the will as aforesaid, the will was read over to the testator by *(name of person who read the will over)* in my presence and the testator appeared fully to understand the same and was at the time of execution of the will of sound mind, memory and understanding.

    (*Note:* if necessary, deal with the plight and condition of the will, eg where the will is drawn up in a hurry in a hospital and the sheet of paper upon which it is written is perhaps torn or in a poor state or condition or where the will is written on a number of sheets of paper.)

7. The said will was written out by *(name of solicitor)* on a single sheet of paper and the left hand edge of the paper is torn (serrated, perforated) as the paper was taken from a notepad or notebook and the will is in the same plight and condition as when executed by the testator and nothing of a testamentary nature was attached thereto.

[*or,*

7. The said will of the testator was written on *(number)* sheets of paper. I can confirm that all sheets of paper were present in the room at the time the will was signed by the testator and nothing further of a testamentary nature was attached thereto.]

SWORN, ETC.

6. AFFIDAVIT OF ATTESTING WITNESS OF A BLIND TESTATOR WHERE SIGNATURE IS POORLY MADE OR POORLY FORMED

THE HIGH COURT
(PROBATE)

IN THE MATTER OF THE WILL OF (*INSERT NAME OF TESTATOR*) OF
(*ADDRESS*), (*OCCUPATION/DESCRIPTION*)

AFFIDAVIT OF ATTESTING WITNESS

I, (*name of attesting witness*), of (*address of attesting witness*), (*occupation/ description*), aged eighteen years and upward make Oath and say as follows:

1.   I make this affidavit on my own behalf from facts within my own knowledge save where otherwise appears and where so otherwise appears I believe those facts to be true.

2.   I am one of the subscribing witnesses to the will of (*name of testator*), of (*address of testator*).

3.   The said will was executed at (*location, eg, the offices of [name of firm of solicitors], at [address]; the home of the testator, at [address]; [name and address of hospital where will was executed]*).

4.   I am a solicitor in the said firm of (*name of firm of solicitors*) [*or, I am a neighbour/friend of the testator, or, I am a patient in the said hospital*] and was asked by the testator [*or, (name of solicitor)*] to act as a witness to the will of the testator.

5.   The said will was executed by the testator, who is blind, on the (*date*) day of (*month*), (*year*) by the testator signing his/her name at the foot or end thereof in the presence of me and of (*name of other attesting witness*), both of us being present at the same time, and we then, in the presence of the testator, signed our names as witnesses to the said will, and signed our names in such a position that had the testator been able to see, he/she would have been able to see us so sign.

       [*or,*

5.   The said testator signed his/her will by mark on the (*date*) day of (*month*), (*year*), he/she being blind from birth and being unable to make a signature [(*or*, by reason of physical disability, he/she having suffered from a stroke *or, (refer to other illness or condition)*.] [The said will was executed by the testator signing his name on the (*date*) day of (*month*), (*year*) in an enfeebled manner] at the foot or end thereof in the presence of me and of (*name of other attesting witness*), both of us being present at the same time, and we thereupon in the presence of the testator signed our names as witnesses to the will. The testator being blind, myself and the other attesting witness signed our names as witnesses in such position that had the testator been able to see, he/she would have been able to see us so sign. [The signature of the testator was enfeebled or poorly formed by reason of the testator being of advanced years (*or*, being unable to write due to his/her blindness *or, state other reason*).]

251

6.   Prior to the execution of the will as aforesaid, the will was read over to the testator by *(name of person who read the will over)* in my presence and the testator appeared fully to understand the same and was at the time of execution of the will of sound mind, memory and understanding.

(Note: if necessary, deal with the plight and condition of the will, eg, where the will is drawn up in a hurry in a hospital and the sheet of paper upon which it is written is perhaps torn or in a poor state or condition or where the will is written on a number of sheets of paper.)

7.   The said will was written out by *(name of solicitor)* on a single sheet of paper and the left hand edge of the paper is torn (serrated, perforated) as the paper was taken from a notepad or notebook and the will is in the same plight and condition as when executed by the testator and nothing of a testamentary nature was attached thereto.

[*or,*

7.   The said will of the testator was written on *(number)* sheets of paper. I can confirm that all sheets of paper were present in the room at the time the will was signed by the testator and nothing further of a testamentary nature was attached thereto.]

SWORN, ETC.

7. AFFIDAVIT OF ATTESTING WITNESS WHERE THERE ARE ALTERATIONS TO THE WILL PRIOR TO EXECUTION

THE HIGH COURT
(PROBATE)

IN THE MATTER OF THE WILL OF (*INSERT NAME OF TESTATOR*) OF (*ADDRESS*), (*OCCUPATION/DESCRIPTION*)

AFFIDAVIT OF ATTESTING WITNESS

I, (*name of attesting witness*), of (*address of attesting witness*), (*occupation/ description*), aged eighteen years and upward make Oath and say as follows:

1. I make this affidavit on my own behalf from facts within my own knowledge save where otherwise appears and where so otherwise appears I believe those facts to be true.

2. I am one of the subscribing witnesses to the will of *(name of testator)*, of *(address of testator)*.

3. The said will was executed at (location, eg, the offices of [*name of firm of solicitors*], at [*address*]; the home of the testator, at [*address*]; [*name and address of hospital where will was executed*]).

4. I am a solicitor in the said firm of *(name of firm of solicitors)* [*or*, I am a neighbour/friend of the testator, *or*, I am a patient in the said hospital] and was asked by the testator [*or, (name of solicitor)*] to act as a witness to the will of the testator.

5. The said will was executed by the testator on the *(date)* day of *(month)*, *(year)* by the testator signing his/her name at the foot or end thereof as the same now appears thereon in the presence of me and of *(name of other attesting witness)*, both of us being present at the same time, and we then, in the presence of the testator, signed our names as witnesses to the said will.*

   (* It may be necessary to insert in this precedent a paragraph from one of the other precedents if there are unusual circumstances surrounding the execution of the will, eg, where the testator is blind or where his or her signature is poorly formed.)

6. Prior to the execution of the said will as aforesaid, alterations were made to the will as follows:

   (*Set out in separate lettered sub-paragraphs the various alterations to the will, eg*:

   (a) *At line 10 of the said will, the figure €1,000.00 (one thousand euro) was amended to read €5,000.00 (five thousand euro).*

   (b) *At line 12 of the said will, the letter 's' was added to the words 'brother' and 'sister' so that the said words would read 'brothers' and 'sisters'.*

   (c) *At line 16 of the said will, the words 'my Volvo car, registration number ...' were deleted and the words 'any car I might own at the date of my death' were interlined between lines 15 and 16 in lieu of the deleted words.)*

7.   The said alteration to the said will [*or,* All of the said alterations to the said will] was/were made prior to the execution of the will as aforesaid.

[8.   The said alteration(s) was/were initialled by the testator in the presence of me and of *(name of other attesting witness)*, both of us being present at the same time, and we then attested by our initials the said alteration(s) in the presence of the testator.]

[9.   The said alteration(s) is/are referred to in the attestation clause and the attestation clause confirms that the said alteration(s) was/were made prior to the execution of the said will.]

(Note: if necessary, deal with the plight and condition of the will, eg, where the will is drawn up in a hurry in a hospital and the sheet of paper upon which it is written is perhaps torn or in a poor state or condition or where the will is written on a number of sheets of paper.)

10.   The said will was written out by *(name of solicitor)* on a single sheet of paper and the left hand edge of the paper is torn (serrated, perforated) as the paper was taken from a notepad or notebook and the will is in the same plight and condition as when executed by the testator and nothing of a testamentary nature was attached thereto.

[*or,*

10.   The said will of the testator was written on *(number)* sheets of paper. I can confirm that all sheets of paper were present in the room at the time the will was signed by the testator and nothing of a testamentary nature was attached thereto.]

SWORN, ETC.

8. AFFIDAVIT OF ATTESTING WITNESS WHERE MAP OR OTHER DOCUMENT IS ATTACHED TO THE WILL

THE HIGH COURT
(PROBATE)

IN THE MATTER OF THE WILL OF (*INSERT NAME OF TESTATOR*) OF
(*ADDRESS*), (*OCCUPATION/DESCRIPTION*)

AFFIDAVIT OF ATTESTING WITNESS

I, (*name of attesting witness*), of (*address of attesting witness*), (*occupation/ description*), aged eighteen years and upward make Oath and say as follows:

1.   I make this affidavit on my own behalf from facts within my own knowledge save where otherwise appears and where so otherwise appears I believe those facts to be true.

2.   I am one of the subscribing witnesses to the will of (*name of testator*), of (*address of testator*).

3.   The said will was executed at (location, eg, the offices of [*name of firm of solicitors*], at [*address*]; the home of the testator, at [*address*]; [*name and address of hospital where will was executed*]).

4.   I am a solicitor in the said firm of (*name of firm of solicitors*) [*or,* I am a neighbour/friend of the testator, *or,* I am a patient in the said hospital] and was asked by the testator [*or, (name of solicitor)*] to act as a witness to the will of the testator.

5.   The said will was executed by the testator on the (*date*) day of (*month*), (*year*) by the testator signing his/her name at the foot or end thereof as the same now appears thereon in the presence of me and of (*name of other attesting witness*), both of us being present at the same time, and we then, in the presence of the testator, signed our names as witnesses to the said will.*

(* It may be necessary to insert in this precedent a paragraph from one of the other precedents if there are unusual circumstances surrounding the execution of the will, eg, where the testator is blind or where his or her signature is poorly formed.)

6.   At the time of the execution of the said will, my attention was drawn to (*describe document to be incorporated in the will, eg, a list of bequests written on two sheets of A4 paper, white in colour, and signed at the end by the testator, or, a map upon which the testator had marked with the letter 'A' and signed his or her name and which myself and my co-witness signed for the purposes of identification and upon which a site being bequeathed to [name of beneficiary] was shown outlined in red*). I can confirm that the said (*describe document*) was in existence at the time the will was executed and that the document referred to in the will is the document now with the original will of the testator.

SWORN, ETC.

(Note: if the execution of the will is in order and there are no difficulties surrounding the execution of the will, but for some reason the plight and condition of the will is poor at the time of execution, any affidavit from an attesting witness must deal with due execution in addition to dealing with plight and condition. The Rules of the Superior Courts require that any affidavit from an attesting witness must also deal with due execution (see O 79, r 40).)

Appendix 4

AFFIDAVITS OF MENTAL CAPACITY TO BE PREPARED AT THE TIME THE WILL IS EXECUTED

The affidavits can be adapted to cases where the affidavit is required to be sworn after the death of the testator.

1. Affidavit of Mental Capacity where testator is of advanced years.

2. Affidavit of Mental Capacity where testator is in a greatly weakened physical state owing to illness, but of sound mind.

3. Affidavit of Mental Capacity where testator suffers from a psychiatric illness, but is making the will during a lucid interval.

4. Affidavit of Mental Capacity to be sworn by the solicitor or practitioner who draws up the will and attends to its execution, which might be sworn in addition to or in lieu of an affidavit from a medical attendant.

Where the testator is very advanced in years or perhaps where the testator has had a history of psychiatric illness or in any other case where a practitioner believes that the capacity of the testator might be called into question, it is prudent to have the testator examined at the time the will is executed so that a medical person can state that, in his or her view, the testator has testamentary capacity. It is even more prudent to have the medical attendant swear an affidavit to be left with the will so that if the testamentary capacity of the testator is questioned at a later date, sworn testimony to the effect that the testator did have capacity can be produced.

It is, of course, preferable that an affidavit of mental capacity be sworn by a doctor who is familiar with the testator, but in the absence of that, the testator can be examined by a doctor so as to satisfy him or herself that the testator does have testamentary capacity. In that regard, reference should be made to the test of testamentary capacity as laid down by *Banks v Goodfellow*,[1] which provides a threefold test:

(i) The testator must understand that he or she is executing a document which is his or her will, that is to say a document that will dispose of his or her property on death. It is not necessary that he or she understand its precise legal effect.

(ii) The testator must know the nature and extent of his or her property.

(iii) The testator must be able to have regard to the persons who might be expected to benefit from his or her estate and decide whether or not to benefit them.

It is useful when drafting the affidavit of mental capacity to try to capture the circumstances in which the affidavit of mental capacity came to be required and to give a well-rounded view, as opposed to an arid view, of the testamentary capacity of the testator.

---

1. *Banks v Goodfellow* (1870) LR 5 QB 549.

1. AFFIDAVIT OF MENTAL CAPACITY WHERE TESTATOR IS OF ADVANCED YEARS

THE HIGH COURT
(PROBATE)

IN THE MATTER OF THE WILL OF (*INSERT NAME OF TESTATOR*) OF
(*ADDRESS*), (*OCCUPATION/DESCRIPTION*).

AFFIDAVIT OF MENTAL CAPACITY

I, *(name of doctor)*, of *(address of doctor's practice or hospital to which he or she is attached)*, Medical Doctor/Psychiatrist/Geriatrician, aged eighteen years and upward make Oath and say as follows:

1.   I am a Medical Doctor in general practice and I make this affidavit from facts within my own knowledge save where otherwise appears and where so otherwise appears I believe those facts to be true.

     [or,

1.   I am a Psychiatrist attached to *(name of hospital or, if he or she is in private practice, name and address of practice)* and I make this affidavit on my own behalf from facts within my own knowledge save where otherwise appears and where so otherwise appears I believe those facts to be true.

     or,

1.   I am a Geriatrician specialising in Geriatric Medicine at *(name of hospital)* and I make this affidavit on my own behalf from facts within my own knowledge save where otherwise appears and where so otherwise appears I believe those facts to be true.]

2.   The testator *(name of testator)*, of *(address of testator)*, is a patient of mine and has been a patient of mine since in or about *(month)*, *(year)*.

     [or,

2.   The testator *(name of testator)*, of *(address of testator)*, is a patient in *(name of hospital)* and as a patient in the said hospital is under my care.

     or,

2.   The testator *(name of testator)* is a resident in *(name of nursing home or other residential care centre)* and has been under my care since in or about *(month)*, *(year)*.]

3.   I was advised by *(name of solicitor/practitioner/nurse/testator)* that the said *(name of testator)* wished to make his/her will and I was asked to examine the said testator for the purposes of ascertaining whether he/she had testamentary capacity.

4.   I carried out an examination of the testator on the *(date)* day of *(month)*, *(year)*, for the purposes of ascertaining his/her testamentary capacity. The examination took *(duration of examination)*.

5. During the course of my examination, I ascertained that the testator understood fully that he/she was executing a document which was a will and which would dispose of his/her property on his/her death. I questioned the testator about his/her property and he/she appeared to be fully conversant as to what property he/she had to dispose of. I also examined the testator as to who his/her next-of-kin were and he/she appeared to be fully aware of who his/her next-of-kin were and had views as to whether he/she should benefit them.

6. I also examined the testator generally in respect of current affairs, the day of the week, the year, and I asked the testator questions concerning current prominent personalities and he/she appeared to have a good knowledge of what was happening in the world.

7. The testator suffers from no illness that I can ascertain that would impair his/her cognitive functions.

8. The testator is at the time of execution of the will aged *(number)* years, but is of sound mind, memory and understanding and capable of making a will.

SWORN, ETC.

(*Note*: if the doctor is himself or herself an attesting witness, the affidavit should deal with due execution – see O 79, r 40 of the Rules of the Superior Courts.)

2. AFFIDAVIT OF MENTAL CAPACITY WHERE TESTATOR IS IN A GREATLY WEAKENED PHYSICAL STATE OWING TO ILLNESS, BUT OF SOUND MIND

THE HIGH COURT
(PROBATE)

IN THE MATTER OF THE WILL OF (*INSERT NAME OF TESTATOR*) OF
(*ADDRESS*), (*OCCUPATION/DESCRIPTION*)

AFFIDAVIT OF MENTAL CAPACITY

I, *(name of doctor)*, of *(address of doctor's practice or hospital to which he or she is attached)*, Medical Doctor/Psychiatrist/Geriatrician, aged eighteen years and upward make Oath and say as follows:

1. I am a Medical Doctor in general practice and I make this affidavit from facts within my own knowledge save where otherwise appears and where so otherwise appears I believe those facts to be true.

    [*or,*

1. I am a Psychiatrist attached to *(name of hospital or, if he or she is in private practice, name and address of practice)* and I make this affidavit on my own behalf from facts within my own knowledge save where otherwise appears and where so otherwise appears I believe those facts to be true.

    or,

1. I am a Geriatrician specialising in Geriatric Medicine at *(name of hospital)* and I make this affidavit on my own behalf from facts within my own knowledge save where otherwise appears and where so otherwise appears I believe those facts to be true.]

2. The testator *(name of testator)*, of *(address of testator)*, is a patient of mine and has been a patient of mine since in or about *(month)*, *(year)*.

    [*or,*

2. The testator *(name of testator)*, of *(address of testator)*, is a patient in *(name of hospital)* and as a patient in the said hospital is under my care.

    or,

2. The testator (name of testator) is a resident in (name of nursing home or other residential care centre) and has been under my care since in or about (month), (year).]

3. I was advised by *(name of solicitor/practitioner/nurse/testator)* that the said *(name of testator)* wished to make his/her will. The testator at the time of making the will was in a greatly weakened physical state owing to *(nature of condition that has weakened the testator)*.

4. From the point of view of mental capacity, however, the testator appeared to be fully alert.

5.   I carried out an examination of the testator on the *(date)* day of *(month)*, *(year)*, for the purposes of ascertaining his/her testamentary capacity. The examination took *(duration of examination)*.

6.   During the course of my examination, I ascertained that the testator understood fully that he/she was executing a document which was a will and which would dispose of his/her property on his/her death. I questioned the testator about his/her property and he/she appeared to be fully conversant as to what property he/she had to dispose of. I also examined the testator as to who his/her next-of-kin were and he/she appeared to be fully aware of who his/her next-of-kin were and had views as to whether he/she should benefit them.

7.   I also examined the testator generally in respect of current affairs, the day of the week, the year, and I asked the testator questions concerning current prominent personalities and he/she appeared to have a good knowledge of what was happening in the world.

8.   The testator suffers from no illness that I can ascertain that would impair his/her cognitive functions.

9.   The testator is suffering from physical weakness only and is at the time of execution of the will of sound mind, memory and understanding and capable of making a will.

SWORN, ETC.

(*Note*: if the doctor is himself or herself an attesting witness, the affidavit should deal with due execution – see O 79, r 40 of the Rules of the Superior Courts.)

3. AFFIDAVIT OF MENTAL CAPACITY WHERE TESTATOR SUFFERS FROM A PSYCHIATRIC ILLNESS, BUT IS MAKING THE WILL DURING A LUCID INTERVAL

THE HIGH COURT
(PROBATE)

IN THE MATTER OF THE WILL OF (*INSERT NAME OF TESTATOR*) OF (*ADDRESS*), (*OCCUPATION/DESCRIPTION*)

AFFIDAVIT OF MENTAL CAPACITY

I, *(name of doctor)*, of *(address of doctor's practice or hospital to which he or she is attached)*, Medical Doctor/Psychiatrist/Geriatrician, aged eighteen years and upward make Oath and say as follows:

1.   I am a Medical Doctor in general practice and I make this affidavit from facts within my own knowledge save where otherwise appears and where so otherwise appears I believe those facts to be true.

[*or,*

1.   I am a Psychiatrist attached to *(name of hospital or, if he or she is in private practice, name and address of practice)* and I make this affidavit on my own behalf from facts within my own knowledge save where otherwise appears and where so otherwise appears I believe those facts to be true.

or,

1.   I am a Geriatrician specialising in Geriatric Medicine at *(name of hospital)* and I make this affidavit on my own behalf from facts within my own knowledge save where otherwise appears and where so otherwise appears I believe those facts to be true.]

2.   The testator *(name of testator)*, of *(address of testator)*, is a patient of mine and has been a patient of mine since in or about *(month)*, *(year)*.

[*or,*

2.   The testator *(name of testator)*, of *(address of testator)*, is a patient in *(name of hospital)* and as a patient in the said hospital is under my care.

or,

2.   The testator *(name of testator)* is a resident in *(name of nursing home or other residential care centre)* and has been under my care since in or about *(month)*, *(year)*.]

3.   The testator has since or about *(month)*, *(year)*, suffered from a condition known as *(condition diagnosed, eg, Paranoid Schizophrenia)*. I was advised by *(name of solicitor/practitioner/nurse/testator)* that the said *(name of testator)* wished to make his/her will and by reason of the condition from which the testator suffers, I was asked to examine the said testator with regard to his/her mental capacity.

4.   I carried out an examination of the testator on the *(date)* day of *(month)*, *(year)*, for the purposes of ascertaining his/her testamentary capacity. The examination took *(duration of examination)*.

5.   I am of the view that although the testator suffers from the above stated condition, he/she is at the time of execution of the will perfectly lucid and alert and capable of making the will.

6.   I specifically examined the testator as follows: I ascertained that the testator understood fully that he/she was executing a document which was a will and which would dispose of his/her property on his/her death. I questioned the testator about his/her property and he/she appeared to be fully conversant as to what property he/she had to dispose of. I also examined the testator as to who his/her next-of-kin were and he/she appeared to be fully aware of who his/her next-of-kin were and had views as to whether he/she should benefit them.

7.   I also examined the testator generally in respect of current affairs, the day of the week, the year, and I asked the testator questions concerning current prominent personalities and he/she appeared to have a good knowledge of what was happening in the world.

8.   Despite the condition from which the testator suffers, I am satisfied that his/her cognitive function is not at the time of execution of the will impaired and that he/she is of sound mind, memory and understanding and capable of making a will.

SWORN, ETC.

(*Note*: if the doctor is himself or herself an attesting witness, the affidavit should deal with due execution – see O 79, r 40 of the Rules of the Superior Courts.)

4. AFFIDAVIT OF MENTAL CAPACITY TO BE SWORN BY THE SOLICITOR OR PRACTITIONER WHO DRAWS UP THE WILL AND ATTENDS TO ITS EXECUTION, WHICH MIGHT BE SWORN IN ADDITION TO OR IN LIEU OF AN AFFIDAVIT FROM A MEDICAL ATTENDANT

(*Note*: where, however, such an affidavit is being sworn in lieu of an affidavit being sworn by a medical attendant, a reason must be given as to why a medical attendant is not swearing an affidavit. In such cases, the Probate Office may refer the matter to court, notwithstanding the existence of the affidavit. It is preferable to have an affidavit from a medical attendant in addition to this affidavit.)

THE HIGH COURT
(PROBATE)

IN THE MATTER OF THE WILL OF (*INSERT NAME OF TESTATOR*) OF (*ADDRESS*), (*OCCUPATION/DESCRIPTION*)

AFFIDAVIT OF (*NAME OF SOLICITOR*)

I, *(name of solicitor),* of *(address),* aged eighteen years and upward make Oath and say as follows:

1.   I am a Solicitor in the firm of *(name of firm),* of *(address of firm)* and I make this affidavit from facts within my own knowledge save where otherwise appears and where so otherwise appears I believe those facts to be true.

2.   On or about the *(date)* day of *(month), (year),* I received instructions from *(name of testator or other person),* of *(address of testator or other person),* that the said testator *(name of testator),* of *(address),* wished to make his/her will.

3.   I attended on the testator at his/her home at *(address).*

        [*or,*

3.   I attended on the testator at *(name of nursing home),* at *(address of nursing home),* where the testator is currently resident.

        or,

3.   I attended on the testator at *(name of hospital)* where the testator is a patient.]

4.   I took instructions from the testator in relation to his/her will and he/she appeared to be fully lucid and alert and capable of giving me instructions.

5.   I specifically examined the testator as to:

        (a)   Whether he/she understood that he/she was executing a will and I am satisfied that the testator did understand that he/she was making his/her will and that this document would dispose of his/her property on his/her death.

        (b)   The nature and extent of the testator's property. The testator was able to tell me all of his/her assets, their current state of investment and the approximate value of his/her assets.

(c)   The persons whom the testator might be expected to benefit. The testator was able to tell me his/her next-of-kin and he/she had well formed intentions as to the persons whom he/she wished to benefit.

(*Note*: if the testator is going to disinherit someone, like perhaps a spouse or a child, an averment might be put in to the effect that the testator was advised as to the provisions of Pt IX of the Succession Act 1965 in relation to spouses or children as the case may be and an averment should be inserted to the effect that the testator appeared to fully understand his or her responsibilities in that regard. Similarly, if the testator is going to leave his or her property, say, to a stranger, and he or she has close relatives such as brothers and sisters who might more usually be expected to benefit, an averment might be put in as to why the testator decided to adopt the course he or she was adopting, eg, that his or her brothers and sisters never came to see him or her but that the beneficiary was particularly good to him or her over the years.)

6.   I was fully satisfied that the testator had testamentary capacity, notwithstanding his advanced years/that he was physically debilitated owing to a severe illness/ that I am informed that he has been diagnosed as suffering from *(state physical or mental illness)*.

7.   I beg to refer to the affidavit of Dr *(name of doctor)* in connection with the mental capacity of the testator when produced.

8.   I have no doubt that the testator was acting freely and voluntarily in relation to the making of his/her will. The testator was a long standing client of mine and I took instructions from him/her while we were alone and there was no other person present when instructions were being taken and the only persons present at the due execution of the will were myself and the attesting witnesses.

9.   I am satisfied therefore that at the time of execution of the will, the testator was of sound mind, memory and understanding and capable of making a will.

SWORN, ETC.

(*Note*: if the solicitor is himself or herself an attesting witness, the affidavit should deal with due execution – see O 79, r 40 of the Rules of the Superior Courts.)

Appendix 5

DISTRIBUTION OF ESTATES ON INTESTACY WHERE THE DECEASED DIES AFTER 1 JANUARY 1967 – TAKING INTO ACCOUNT AMENDMENTS WROUGHT BY THE 2010 ACT

Person(s) surviving the intestate	Entitlement
1. Spouse or civil partner only	The whole estate. **[s 67(1) as amended by the 2010 Act]**
2. Spouse or civil partner and issue	Spouse/civil partner takes two-thirds, children take one-third between them, with the issue of any predeceased child taking *per stirpes* their parent's share. **[s 67(2) and (4) as amended by the 2010 Act.]**
	(*Note*: under s 67A (as amended by the 2010 Act) the children of a deceased civil partner can apply to court to vary their entitlement on intestacy but they cannot receive more than their entitlement where their parent died without a civil partner. There is no jurisprudence on such applications to vary as yet.)
	(*Note*: that as civil partners will always be of the same sex only one partner can be the biological parent of any child being reared by the civil partners. There is no provision that a child to whom a civil partner is in *loco parentis* can apply for such variation. There is no provision for a civil partner to adopt the child of his or her civil partner.)
3. Issue only	Children share the estate between them, with the issue of any predeceased child taking *per stirpes* their parent's share. **[s 67(3) and (4)]**
4. No spouse/civil partner, no issue, but leaving parents	Parents take the whole estate equally. **[s 68]**
5. One parent only	Parent takes the whole estate. **[s 68]**
6. No spouse/civil partner, no issue, no parent, leaving brothers and sisters	Brothers and sisters share the estate between them, with the issue of any predeceased brother or sister taking *per stirpes* their parent's share. **[s 69(1)]**

Person(s) surviving the intestate	Entitlement
7. No spouse/civil partner, no issue, no parents, no brothers or sisters, leaving nephews or nieces	Nephews or nieces share the estate *per capita* according to their number. **[s 69(2)]**
8. No spouse/civil partner, no issue, no parents, no brothers or sisters, no nephews or nieces	Estate divided amongst the nearest next-of-kin *per capita* according to their number. **[s 70(1)]***

(* There is no *per stirpes* distribution except where there is issue surviving, in which case, the issue of predeceased issue will be admitted to taking *per stirpes* their parent's share and also in the case of brothers and sisters, where the issue of a predeceased brother or sister will share *per stirpes* their parent's share.)

RULES FOR ASCERTAINMENT OF NEXT-OF-KIN

Section 71 of the Succession Act 1965 provides as follows:

(1) Subject to the rights of representation mentioned in subsection (2) of section 70, the person or persons who, at the date of death of the intestate, stand nearest in blood relationship to him, shall be taken to be his next-of-kin.

(2) Degrees of blood relationship of a direct lineal ancestor shall be computed by counting upwards from the intestate to that ancestor and degrees of blood relationship of any other relative shall be ascertained by counting upwards from the intestate to the nearest ancestor common to the intestate and that relative and then downwards from that ancestor to the relative; but where a direct lineal ancestor and any other relative are so ascertained to be within the same degree of blood relationship to the intestate, the other relative shall be preferred to the exclusion of the direct lineal ancestor.

RELATIVES OF THE HALF-BLOOD

Section 72 of the Succession Act 1965 provides as follows:

Relatives of the half blood shall be treated as and shall succeed equally with relatives of the whole blood in the same degree.

(*Note*: stepchildren or stepbrothers and stepsisters who are not related in any way to the deceased person have no claim or entitlement to his or her estate. There must be a blood relationship in order for a person to be entitled to inherit, other than in the case of a spouse.)

STATE AS ULTIMATE INTESTATE SUCCESSOR

Section 73 of the Succession Act 1965 provides as follows:

(1) In default of any person taking the estate of an intestate, whether under this Part or otherwise, the State shall take the estate as ultimate intestate successor.

(2) The Minister for Finance may, if he thinks proper to do so, waive in whole or in part and in favour of such person and upon such terms (whether including or not including the payment of money) as he thinks proper having regard to all the circumstances of the case, the right of the State under this section.

(3) Section 32 of the State Property Act, 1954 (which provides for the disclaimer of certain lands devolving on the State by way of escheat or as bona vacantia) shall extend the grantee's interest under a fee farm grant and a lessee's interest where the State has a right to such interest as ultimate intestate successor.

THE STATUS OF CHILDREN ACT 1987

Since the coming into operation of the Status of Children Act 1987 on 14 June 1988, for all deaths after that date, all degrees of blood relationship where a person dies intestate are to be ascertained without regard to any marital relationship within the chain of relationship. Section 29(2) of the Succession Act 1965, however, states as follows:

Where a person, whose father and mother have not married each other, dies intestate, he shall be presumed not to have been survived by his father, or by any person related to him through his father, unless the contrary is shown.

This section appears to have been enacted for practical reasons, because in many instances fathers of non-marital children will not be traceable at the date of death of the non-marital child. To avoid the difficulties in relation to trying to trace the father of a non-marital child, this section was enacted. It does not, of course, preclude a father of a non-marital child from benefiting from the estate of the non-marital child, if the father can be easily ascertained and can be shown to have survived his child. But where the father of the non-marital child is not traceable, the presumption relieves the personal representative from trying to trace the father of a non-marital child or the persons claiming through him.

Section 3(1) of the Status of Children Act 1987 provides as follows:

In deducing any relationship for the purposes of this Act, or any Act of the Oireachtas passed after the commencement of this section, the relationship between every person and his father and mother (or either of them) shall, unless the contrary intention appears, be determined irrespective of whether his father and mother are or have been married to each other, and all other relationships shall be determined accordingly.

Section 29 of the Status of Children Act 1987 inserts a new section after s 4 in the Succession Act 1965, being s 4A. Section 4A(1) of the Succession Act 1965, as inserted by s 29 of the Status of Children Act 1987, provides as follows:

In deducing any relationship for the purposes of this Act, the relationship between every person and his father shall, subject to section 27(a) of this Act (inserted by the Act of 1987) be determined in accordance with section 3 of the Act of 1987 and all other relationships shall be determined accordingly.

ADOPTED PERSONS

Section 3(2) of the Status of Children Act 1987 provides that an adopted person shall be deemed from the date of the adoption order to be the child of the adopter or adopters and not the child of any other person or persons.

Section 3(2)(b) defines 'adopted person' as follows:

> **'adopted person'** means a person who has been adopted under the Adoption Acts 1952–1976 or where the person has been adopted outside the State whose adoption is recognised by virtue of the law for the time being in force in the State.

CIVIL PARTNERSHIP AND CERTAIN RIGHTS AND OBLIGATIONS OF COHABITANTS ACT 2010

The 2010 Act provided for the registration of a civil partnership, and where such is registered, the civil partner will have certain rights to a deceased civil partner's estate. Civil partners will always be of the same sex. This being so, only one party to the civil partnership can be the biological parent of any child being brought up within the civil partnership. The 2010 Act does recognise that the non-biological parent in the civil partnership may stand *in loco parentis* to any child or children. The 2010 Act does not recognise the position of the non-biological parent.

Where a civil partner dies intestate leaving a civil partner and children, *prima facie* the civil partner will take two-thirds of the estate and the child or children one-third. Section 67A of the 1965 Act, as inserted by the 2010 Act, provides that a child may apply to court to have his or her entitlement enlarged. The share of the child cannot be greater than he or she would receive had his or her parent died intestate without a civil partner. But given that a civil partner is likely perhaps to have only one child, that could be as much as the entire estate. There is no jurisprudence on such applications as yet.

The relevant provisions of the 2010 Act are as follows.

72. Amendment of section 67 of Act of 1965

Section 67 of the Act of 1965 is amended—

(*a*) in subsection (2)(*b*), by substituting "section 67B(2)" for "subsection (4)", and

(*b*) by repealing subsections (3) and (4).

73. Insertion of new sections in Act of 1965

The Act of 1965 is amended by inserting the following after section 67:

"67A. Shares of surviving civil partner and issue

(1) If an intestate dies leaving a civil partner and no issue, the civil partner shall take the whole estate.

(2) If an intestate dies leaving a civil partner and issue—

(a) subject to subsections (3) to (7), the civil partner shall take two-thirds of the estate; and

(b) the remainder shall be distributed among the issue in accordance with section 67B(2).

(3) The court may, on the application by or on behalf of a child of an intestate who dies leaving a civil partner and one or more children, order that provision be made for that child out of the intestate's estate only if the court is of the opinion that it would be unjust not to make the order, after considering all the circumstances, including—

(a)   the extent to which the intestate has made provision for that child during the intestate's lifetime,

(b)   the age and reasonable financial requirements of that child,

(c)   the intestate's financial situation, and

(d)   the intestate's obligations to the civil partner.

(4) The court, in ordering provision of an amount under subsection (3) shall ensure that—

(a)   the amount to which any issue of the intestate is entitled shall not be less than that to which he or she would have been entitled had no such order been made, and

(b)   the amount provided shall not be greater than the amount to which the applicant would have been entitled had the intestate died leaving neither spouse nor civil partner.

(5) Rules of court shall provide for the conduct of proceedings under this section in a summary manner.

(6) The costs in the proceedings shall be at the discretion of the court.

(7) An order under this section shall not be made except on an application made within 6 months from the first taking out of representation of the deceased's estate.

67B. Share of issue where no surviving spouse or surviving civil partner

(1) If an intestate dies leaving issue and no spouse or civil partner, the estate shall be distributed among the issue in accordance with subsection (2).

(2) If all the issue are in equal degree of relationship to the deceased the distribution shall be in equal shares among them; if they are not, it shall be *per stirpes*."

Appendix 6

RIGHTS OF SURVIVING SPOUSES AND CIVIL PARTNERS

1. LEGAL RIGHT SHARE

The legal right share of the spouse/civil partner is established by Pt IX of the Succession Act 1965. Section 111 of the Act and s 111A (as inserted by the 2010 Act) provides as follows:

> (1) If the testator leaves a spouse/civil partner and no children, the spouse shall have a right to one-half of the estate.

> (2) If the testator leaves a spouse/civil partner and children, the spouse shall have a right to one-third of the estate.

If the spouse/civil partner is not, therefore, provided for in the will, he or she will have a right to either:

(a)   one-half of the estate if there are no children or

(b)   one-third of the estate if there are children.

The estate must be administered accordingly. It has been held in *O'Dwyer and Another v Keegan and Others*,[1] that the legal right share established by s 111 vests in the spouse on death and he or she does not have to take any step to claim the right. This case involved spouses but the same reasoning would now apply to civil partners. The right of the spouse/civil partner to enforce the legal right share will be statute barred six years after the date on which the right to receive it accrued. This will usually be the date of death but in the case where there an election is required it would be six years from the date of election (s 126 of the 1965 Act substituting a new s 45 in the Statute of Limitations 1957).

If the spouse/civil partner is considered by the executors or legal personal representatives to be unworthy to succeed by virtue of the provisions of s 120 of the Succession Act 1965, then it is for the executors or legal personal representatives to bring the matter before the court to have the spouse/civil partner declared unworthy to succeed (see **Appendix 8**). That is unless the spouse/civil partner accepts his or her unworthiness to succeed.

Section 112 of the Succession Act 1965, as amended by the 2010 Act, provides as follows:

> The right of the spouse/civil partner under section 111/section 111A (which shall be known as a legal right) shall have priority over devises, bequests and shares on intestacy.

---

1.   *O'Dwyer and Another v Keegan and Others* [1997] 2 IR 585, V ITR 367.

Section 113 of the Succession Act 1965, as amended by the 2010 Act, provides as follows:

> The legal right of a spouse/civil partner may be renounced in an ante-nuptial/civil partnership contract made in writing between the parties to intended marriage/ civil partnership or may be renounced in writing by the spouse/civil partner after marriage/civil partnership and during the lifetime of the testator.

Section 114 of the Succession Act 1965, as amended by the 2010 Act, provides as follows:

> (1) Where property is devised or bequeathed in a will to a spouse or civil partnership and the devise or bequest *is expressed in the will* to be in addition to the share as a legal right of the spouse or civil partner, the testator shall be deemed to have made by the will a gift to the spouse or civil partner consisting of
>
>> (a) The sum equal to the value of the share as a legal right of the spouse or civil partner and
>>
>> (b) The property so devised or bequeathed.
>
> (2) In any other case, a devise or bequest in a will to a spouse or civil partner shall be deemed to have been intended by the testator to be in satisfaction of the share as a legal right of the spouse or civil partner. (Author's emphasis.)
>
> (*Note*: therefore, if a spouse/civil partner is leaving a bequest in his or her will which he or she intends to be in addition to the legal right of the spouse or civil partner, he or she should expressly state that. Otherwise, under s 114(2), it will be deemed to be in satisfaction of the share as a legal right of the spouse or civil partner – see precedent clauses in relation to legacies, devises and residuary bequests in **Chs 6, 7** and **10** respectively.)

Section 115 of the Succession Act 1965, as amended by the 2010 Act, provides as follows:

> (1) (a) Where, under the will of a deceased person who dies wholly testate, there is a devise or bequest to a spouse or civil partner, the spouse or civil partner may elect to take either that devise or bequest or the share to which he is entitled as a legal right.
>
>> (b) In default of election, the spouse or civil partner shall be entitled to take under the will; he shall not be entitled to take any share as a legal right.
>
> (2) (a) Where a person dies partly testate and partly intestate, the spouse or civil partner may elect to take either—
>
>> (i) *His share as a legal right, or,*
>>
>> (ii) *His share under the intestacy, together with any devise or bequest to him under the will of the deceased.*
>
>> (b) In default of election, the spouse or civil partner shall be entitled to take his share under the intestacy, together with any devise or bequest to him under the will and he shall not be entitled to take any share as a legal right.
>
> (3) A spouse or civil partner, in electing to take his share as a legal right, may further elect to take any devise or bequest to him, less in value than the share, in partial satisfaction thereof.

(4) It shall be the duty of the personal representative to notify the spouse or civil partner in writing of the right of election conferred by this section. The right shall not be exercisable after the expiration of six months from the receipt by the spouse or civil partner of such notification, or one year from the first taking out of representation of the deceased's estate, *whichever is the later.*

(5) Where the surviving spouse or civil partner is a person of unsound mind, the right of election conferred by this section, may, if there is a committee of the spouse's or civil partner's estate, be exercised on behalf of the spouse or civil partner by the committee by leave of the Court which has appointed the committee, or if there is no committee, be exercised by the High Court, or, in a case within the jurisdiction of the Circuit Court, by that Court.

(6) In this section, but only in its application to a case in which subsection (1) of section 114 applies, a 'devise or bequest' means a gift deemed under that subsection to have been made by the will of the testator.

(Author's emphasis.)

(*Note 1*: the right of election only arises where there is a provision for the spouse or civil partner in the will of the testator.)

(*Note 2*: it has been held that the right of election is personal to the spouse and cannot be exercised by his or her legal personal representative after his or her death (see *In Re Urquhart;*[2] *Reilly v McEntee*[3]). The cases involved spouses but the same would now apply to a surviving civil partner. If, therefore, a right of election arises and the spouse/civil partner is infirm, the election that is most beneficial to him or her should be made. It is not necessary to receive the notification prior to making such election. I take the view, though it is not yet tested, that if it is unclear as to whether the benefit under the will or the legal right share is more beneficial it is permissible to elect to take the more valuable of the two. The important thing would be to make the election where the spouse or civil partner is in any way in danger of death.)

(*Note 3*: there is a mandatory duty upon the personal representative to notify the spouse or civil partner of the right of election. Time will not begin to run against the spouse or civil partner in respect of the right of election until six months has elapsed from the date of notification or one year from the first taking out of representation in relation to the deceased's estate, whichever is the later. Where a spouse or civil partner dies *wholly testate* and makes provision for a spouse or civil partner in his or her will and the spouse or civil partner does not elect within the requisite period or dies without electing, then the spouse or civil partner shall take the benefit conferred by the will and *shall lose the legal right.* See note 2 above.)

(*Note 4*: where a testator dies *partly intestate,* the spouse/civil partner may elect to take either:

(a)   the legal right share, *or,*

---

2.   *In Re Urquhart* [1974] IR 197.
3.   *Reilly v McEntee* [1984] ILRM 572.

(b)   the share that the spouse or civil partner is entitled to under the partial intestacy (which would be the entire of the property passing under the partial intestacy if there are no children and two-thirds of it if there are children) together with the devise or bequest passing under the will.

In default of electing, the spouse or civil partner shall take the benefit under the will and the share on intestacy and *shall lose the legal right.*)

(*Note 5*: the spouse or civil partner can elect to take the legal right share but also choose to take the benefit conferred by the will in part satisfaction of that legal right share.)

2. TRANSITIONAL PROVISION

Section 116 of the Succession Act 1965 provides as follows:

(1) Where a testator, during his lifetime, has made permanent provision for his spouse, whether under a contract or otherwise, all property which is the subject of such provision (other than periodical payments made for her maintenance during his lifetime) shall be taken as given in or towards satisfaction of the share as a legal right of the spouse.

(2) The value of the property shall be reckoned as of the date of the making of the provision.

(3) If the value of the property is equal to or greater than the share of the spouse as a legal right, the spouse shall not be entitled to take any share as a legal right.

(4) If the value of the property is less than the share of the spouse as a legal right, the spouse shall be entitled to receive in satisfaction of such share so much only of the estate as when added to the value of the property is sufficient, as nearly as can be estimated, to make up the full amount of that share.

(5) *This section shall only apply to a provision made before the commencement of this Act.* (Author's emphasis.)

(*Note*: as this section only applies to provisions made prior to 1 January 1967, it is not now likely to be of relevance in relation to estates currently being administered, but its provisions should nevertheless be borne in mind. It essentially introduces the hotchpot provisions contained in s 63 of the Act in relation to children regarding provisions made by spouses, but only in respect of provisions made by spouses prior to the coming into operation of the Succession Act 1965.)

3. THE RIGHT OF APPROPRIATION

This right does not arise simply in relation to benefits conferred by wills, but applies to all benefits to which a spouse or civil partner may be entitled on the death of his or her spouse or civil partner, ie, under a will, on intestacy or as a legal right.

Section 56 of the Succession Act 1965 (as amended by the 2010 Act) provides as follows:

> (1) Where the estate of a deceased person includes a dwelling in which, at the time of the deceased's death, the surviving spouse or civil partner was ordinarily resident, the surviving spouse or civil partner may, subject to subsection (5), require the personal representative in writing to appropriate the dwelling in section 55 in or towards satisfaction of *any* share of the surviving spouse or civil partner. (Author's emphasis.)

(*Note 1*: the dwelling must form part of the estate of the deceased – see definition of dwelling at s 56(14) and see also the limitations on appropriation in s 56(6).)

(*Note 2*: the surviving spouse/civil partner must be ordinarily resident in the dwelling at the date of death of the deceased.)

(*Note 3*: appropriation can be in respect of *any share* of the surviving spouse/civil partner, which includes a share on intestacy, a share as a legal right, or under the will of the deceased.)

> (2) The surviving spouse or civil partner may also require the personal representative in writing to appropriate the household chattels in or towards satisfaction of any share of the surviving spouse or civil partner.

(*Note*: see definition of household chattels at s 56(14).)

> (3) If the share of a surviving spouse or civil partner is insufficient to enable an appropriation to be made under subsection (1) or (2), as the case may be, the right conferred by the relevant subsection may also be exercised in relation to the share of any infant for whom the surviving spouse or civil partner is a trustee under section 57 or otherwise.

(*Note 1*: an infant will be a person under the age of 18.)

(*Note 2*: in order for the spouse/civil partner to appropriate the share of the infant, he or she must be a trustee under s 57 or otherwise (eg, under the will) of the infant's share. An appointment of the spouse/civil partner as trustee under s 57 and Pt 4 of the 2009 Act, therefore, may be necessary.)

(*Note 3*: the share of the infant is of course held upon trust by the spouse for the infant.)

> (4) It shall be the duty of the personal representative to notify the surviving spouse or civil partner in writing of the rights conferred by this section.

> (5) A right conferred by this section shall not be exercisable
>
> (a) After the expiration of six months from the receipt by the surviving spouse or civil partner of such notification or one year from the first taking out of representation to the deceased's estate, whichever is the later, or,
>
> (b) In relation to a dwelling, in any of the cases mentioned in subsection (6), unless the Court, on application made by the personal representatives or surviving spouse or civil partner, is satisfied that the exercise of that right is unlikely to diminish the value of the assets of the deceased, other than the dwelling, or to make it more difficult to dispose of them in due course of the administration and authorises its exercise.

(*Note 1*: the period of notification is similar to the notification period under s 115 involving the right of election. There is a mandatory duty of the personal representative or the executor to notify the spouse or civil partner of his or her rights. Time will not begin to run against the spouse or civil partner in respect of the right of appropriation until six months has elapsed from the date of notification or one year from the first taking out of representation in relation to the deceased's estate, whichever is the later.)

(*Note 2*: subsection (5) makes provision for a delay in the exercise of the right of appropriation consequent on the bringing of proceedings under s 56(6) by providing that the right to appropriate can proceed if the court decides that it is proper to proceed, notwithstanding the provisions of s 56(6) and further notwithstanding that the period for the appropriation has expired.)

(6) Part (b) of subsection (5) and paragraph (d) of subsection (10) apply to the following cases:

(a) Where the dwelling forms part of a building and the estate or interest in the whole building forms part of the estate;

(b) Where the dwelling is held with agricultural land, an estate or interest in which forms part of the estate;

(c) Where the whole or part of the estate was, at the time of death, used as a hotel, guest house or boarding house;

(d) Where part of the dwelling was, at the time of death, used for purposes other than domestic purposes.

(*Note*: where any of these circumstances pertain, appropriation *may* not be allowed unless a court is satisfied that there will be no diminution in the value of the assets of the deceased, other than the dwelling, by the exercise of the right of appropriation.)

(7) Nothing in subsection (12) of section 55 shall prevent the personal representatives from giving effect to the rights conferred by this section.

[Section 55(12) provides: 'The personal representative shall, in making the appropriation, have regard to the rights of any person who may thereafter come into existence, or who cannot, after reasonable enquiry, be found or ascertained at the time of appropriation and any other person whose consent is not required by this section.']

(8) (a) So long as the right conferred by this section continues to be exercisable, the personal representatives shall not, without the written consent of the surviving spouse or civil partner or leave of the Court given on the refusal of an application under paragraph (b) of subsection (5), sell or otherwise dispose of the dwelling or household chattels except in course of administration owing to want of other assets.

(b) This section shall not apply where the surviving spouse or civil partner is a personal representative.

(c) Nothing in this section shall confer any right on the surviving spouse or civil partner against a purchaser from the personal representative.

(*Note 1*: this subsection requires the personal representatives to retain the dwelling house until the rights in relation to the appropriation have been ascertained, unless the sale of the dwelling house is necessary in due course of the administration of the estate of the deceased.)

(*Note 2*: if, however, the legal personal representatives do sell the dwelling house in contravention of this subsection, the surviving spouse/civil partner shall have no rights against the purchaser from the personal representatives and any action on the part of the spouse would be against the personal representatives themselves.)

(9) The rights conferred by this section on a surviving spouse or civil partner include a right to acquire appropriation partly in satisfaction of a share in the deceased's estate and partly in return for a payment of money by the surviving spouse or civil partner on the spouse's or civil partner's own behalf and also on behalf of any infant for whom the spouse or civil partner is trustee under section 57 or otherwise.

(*Note*: if there is a shortfall between the value of the spouse's or civil partner's share in the estate of the deceased and the value of the dwelling being appropriated, then the spouse or civil partner will be required to make up the difference. Due allowance can be made for any share of an infant which the spouse or civil partner is entitled to appropriate as a trustee under s 57 or otherwise by virtue of s (56)(3).)

(10)(a) In addition to the rights to acquire appropriation conferred by this section, the surviving spouse or civil partner may, so long as the right conferred by this section continues to be exercisable, apply to the Court for appropriation on the spouse's or civil partner's own behalf and also on behalf of any infant for whom the spouse or civil partner is a trustee under section 57 or otherwise.

(b) On any such, application, the Court may, if of opinion that, in the special circumstances of the case, hardship would otherwise be caused to the surviving spouse or civil partner, or to the surviving spouse or civil partner and any such infant, order that appropriation to the spouse shall be made without payment of money provided for in subsection (9) or subject to the payment of such amount as the Court considers reasonable.

(c) The Court may make such further order in relation to the administration of the deceased's estate as may appear to the Court to be just and equitable, having regard to the provisions of this Act and to all the circumstances.

(d) The Court shall not make an order under this subsection in relation to a dwelling in any of the cases mentioned in subsection (6) unless it is satisfied that the order would be unlikely to diminish the value of the assets of the deceased, other than the dwelling, or to make it more difficult to dispose of them in due course of administration.

(*Note 1*: this subsection allows a spouse or civil partner to apply to the court in relation to an appropriation where the appropriation is on the spouse's or civil partner's own behalf or on behalf of any infant. The subsection principally arises where hardship would accrue to the surviving spouse or civil partner or the surviving spouse or civil partner and infant if they were required to pay money into the estate to make up the difference between the value of the share of the spouse or civil partner, or the spouse or civil partner and the infant, and the value of the dwelling being appropriated. The court can order that the appropriation proceed without any payment by the spouse or civil partner, or the spouse or civil partner and infant, or on foot of such payment as to the court may seem just.)

(*Note 2*: the court is also empowered under s 56(10)(c) to make such further order in relation to the administration of the deceased's estate as may appear to the court to be just and equitable, having regard to the provisions of the Act and to all the circumstances of the case.)

(11) All proceedings in this section shall be heard in chambers.

(*Note*: the proceedings will be held *in camera*.)

(12) Where the surviving spouse or civil partner is a person of unsound mind, a requirement or consent under this section may, if there is a committee of the spouse's estate, be made or given on behalf of the spouse or civil partner by the committee by leave of the Court which has appointed the committee, or if there is no committee, be given or made by the High Court, or in a case within the jurisdiction of the Circuit Court, by that Court.

(13) An appropriation to which this section applies shall, for the purposes of succession duty, be deemed to be a succession derived from the deceased.

(*Note*: succession duty or estate duty has now been replaced by inheritance tax and as matters stand there is no inheritance tax payable as between spouses/civil partners.)

(14) In this section—

'dwelling' means an estate or interest in a building occupied as a separate dwelling or a part so occupied of any building and includes any garden or portion of ground attached to and usually occupied with the dwelling or otherwise required for the amenity or convenience of the dwelling;

'household chattels' means furniture, linen, china, glass, books, or other chattels of ordinary household use or ornament and also consumable stores, garden effects and domestic animals, but does not include any chattels used at the death of the deceased for business or professional purposes, or money or security for money.

4. THE RIGHT OF FORMER SPOUSES UNDER S 18 OF THE FAMILY LAW (DIVORCE) ACT 1996

Section 18 of the Family Law (Divorce) Act 1996 provides as follows:

(1) Subject to the provisions of this section, where one of the spouses in respect of whom a decree of divorce has been granted dies, the court on application to it in that behalf by the other spouse ('the applicant') not more than 6 months after representation is first granted under the Act of 1965 [the Succession Act 1965] in respect of the estate of the deceased spouse, may by order make such provision for the applicant out of the estate of the deceased spouse as it considers appropriate, having regard to the rights of any other person having an interest in the matter and specifies in the order if it is satisfied that proper provision in the circumstances was not made for the applicant during the lifetime of the deceased spouse under section 13, 14, 15, 16 or 17 for any reason (other than conduct referred to in subsection (2)(i) of section 20 of the applicant).

(*Note*: s 20(2)(i) requires the court to have regard to 'the conduct of each of the spouses, if that conduct is such that in the opinion of the court it would in all the circumstances of the case be unjust to disregard it'.)

(2) The court shall not make an order under this section in favour of a spouse who has remarried since the granting of the decree of divorce concerned.

(3) In considering whether to make an order under this section, the court shall have regard to all the circumstances of the case including

(a) Any order under paragraph (c) of section 13(1) or a property adjustment order in favour of the applicant, and

(b) Any devise or bequest made by the deceased spouse to the applicant.

(4) The provision made for the applicant concerned by an order under this section, together with any provision made for the applicant by an order referred to in subsection (3)(a) (the value of which for the purposes of this section shall be at the value on the date of the order) shall not exceed in total the share (if any) of the applicant in the estate of the deceased spouse to which the applicant was entitled, or (if the deceased spouse died intestate, as to the whole or part of his or her estate) would have been entitled under the Act of 1965 if the marriage had not been dissolved.

(5) Notice of an application under this section shall be given by the applicant to the spouse (if any) of the deceased spouse concerned and to such (if any) other persons as the court may direct and, in deciding whether to make the order concerned and in determining the provisions of the order, the court shall have regard to any representations made by the spouse of the deceased spouse and any other persons as aforesaid.

(6) The personal representative of a deceased person in respect of whom a decree of divorce has been granted shall make a reasonable attempt to ensure that notice of his or her death is brought to the attention of the other spouse concerned and, where an application is made under this section, the personal representative of the deceased shall not, without leave of the court, distribute any of the estate of that spouse until the court makes or refuses to make an order under this section.

(7) Where the personal representative of a deceased spouse in respect of whom a decree of divorce has been granted gives notice of his or her death to the other spouse concerned ('the spouse') and—

(a) The spouse intends to apply to court for an order under this section

(b) The spouse has applied for such an order and an application is pending, or

(c) An order has been made under this section in favour of the spouse,

the spouse shall, not later than one month after the receipt of the notice, notify the personal representative of such intention, application or order as the case may be and, if he or she does not do so, the personal representative shall be at liberty to distribute the assets of the deceased spouse, or any part thereof, among the parties entitled thereto.

(8) The personal representative shall not be liable to the spouse for the assets or any part thereof so distributed unless, at the time of such distribution, he or she had notice of the intention, application or order aforesaid.

(9) Nothing in subsection (7) or (8) shall prejudice the right of the spouse to follow any such assets into the hands of any person who may have received them.

(10) On granting a decree of divorce or at any time thereafter, the court, on application to it in that behalf by either of the spouses concerned, may during the lifetime of the other spouse or as the case may be, the spouse concerned, if it considers just to do so, make an order that either or both spouses shall not, on the death of either of them, be entitled to apply for an order under this section.

A number of points need to be noted:

(a)   In subs (10) of s 18, the court, when making the decree of divorce *a vinculo matrimonii*, can include a provision in its order that an application under this section may not be brought in the future. This is something that should be considered if a testator is applying for a divorce and if such an order is made, it would be useful to refer to such order in the will of the testator.

(b)   The limitation period for bringing an application under s 18 is six months from the date on which representation is first granted. However, the legal personal representative is required to 'make a reasonable attempt' to ensure that notice of the death is brought to the attention of the 'other spouse concerned'. Presumably this would require the personal representative to send notice of the death to the 'other spouse concerned' at his or her address, or, if the precise whereabouts of the spouse is unknown, to advertise appropriately the death of the testator in a newspaper circulating where the 'other spouse concerned' is now believed to be living.

(c)   If notice of the death is given to the 'other spouse concerned', the 'other spouse concerned' must within one month give notice to the personal representative:

   (i)   of an intention to apply for an order under s 18;

   (ii)   that an application has been made under the section and is pending;

   (iii)   that an order has been made under the section.

If the 'other spouse concerned' fails to give such notice within the one-month period, then the personal representative may distribute the assets to the persons entitled thereto and the personal representative will not be liable to the 'other spouse concerned', but he or she is not precluded from following assets into the hands of other beneficiaries, provided that the application for relief under the section is brought within the limitation period of six months from the date of issue of the grant.

(d)   Notice of the application must be given to any spouse of the deceased spouse if the deceased spouse has remarried and to any other person who might be affected by the order that the court might make and those persons are entitled to make representations to the court and the court is required to have due regard to the representations made in that behalf.

(e)   The right to bring an application under s 18 is completely barred if the 'other spouse concerned' has remarried following the decree of divorce *a vinculo matrimonii*.

(f)   The court will not make an order under s 18 unless it is satisfied that the deceased spouse has failed to make proper provision for the 'other spouse concerned' during the course of his or her life. What 'proper provision' might be would presumably vary from case to case, depending on the deceased spouse's means and resources. The onus of establishing that proper provision was not made would rest upon the applicant spouse (the 'other spouse concerned'). The court in this context would have regard to any order made under s 13 of the Family Law (Divorce) Act 1996 with regard to property adjustments and further to any devise or bequest contained in the will of the deceased spouse to the 'other spouse concerned'.

(g)   The court, in making any provision for the former spouse of the deceased under s 18, would have to have regard to the legal right share of any new spouse of the testator. Section 112 of the Succession Act 1965 provides that the legal right share of a surviving spouse (in this context the new spouse) has priority over all other devises and bequests and shares on intestacy. It would, therefore, have to have priority over any order that the court might make under s 18 of the Family Law (Divorce) Act 1996.

(h)   Section 15A of the Family Law Act 1995, as inserted by s 56(g) of the Family Law (Divorce) Act 1996, allows the court to make orders when granting a decree of divorce *a vinculo matrimonii* similar to orders made pursuant to s 14 of the Family Law Act 1995 to block such applications of this nature (see **Appendix 8**).

For a fuller discourse on these spousal/civil partnership rights see Spierin, *The Succession Act 1965 and Related Legislation, A Commentary* (4th edn, Bloomsbury Professional, 2011).

Appendix 7

RIGHTS OF SURVIVING CHILDREN WHERE THERE IS A WILL

Unlike a surviving spouse/civil partner, the children of the testator have no right to a defined share in the estate of a testator where the testator dies wholly testate. They instead have a right to apply to court if they believe that their parent has failed in his or her moral duty to make proper provision for them in accordance with his or her means, and if the court finds that this is so, the court has an absolute discretion to make such provision for the child as it considers just.

It is outside the scope of this book to include a full commentary on this, probably the most litigated section in the Succession Act, and the reader is referred to Spierin, *The Succession Act 1965 and Related Legislation, A Commentary* (4th edn, Bloomsbury Professional, 2011).

SECTION 117 OF THE SUCCESSION ACT 1965 – AS AMENDED BY THE 2010 ACT

Section 117 of the Succession Act 1965 provides as follows:

> (1) Where, on the application by or on behalf of the child of a testator, the Court is of opinion that the testator has failed in his moral duty to make proper provision for the child in accordance with his means, *whether by his will or otherwise*, the Court may order that such provision shall be made for the child out of the estate as the Court thinks just. (Author's emphasis.)

(*Note*: the court is not simply concerned with the provisions made by the testator in his or her will, but also provision made for the child by the testator during his or her lifetime.)

> (2) The Court shall consider the application from the point of view of a prudent and just parent, taking into account the position of each of the children of the testator and any other circumstances which the Court may consider of assistance in arriving at a decision that will be as fair as possible to the child to whom the application relates and the other children.

> (3) An order under this section *shall not affect* the legal right of a surviving spouse or, if the surviving spouse or *is the mother or father of the child*, any devise or bequest to the spouse or any share to which the spouse is entitled on intestacy. (Author's emphasis.)

> (3A) An order under this section shall not affect the legal right of a surviving civil partner unless the court, after consideration of all the circumstances, including the testator's financial circumstances, including the testator's financial circumstances and his or her obligations to the surviving civil partner, is of the opinion that it would be unjust not to make the order.

(*Note 1*: by this subs (3), the legal right share of the spouse is immune from interference under s 117. Further, if the surviving spouse is the mother or father of the child making the claim, the court cannot interfere with any devise or bequest or any share under any partial intestacy to which the spouse is entitled. So if a testator in his or her will leaves all of his or her property to the mother or father of a claiming child, the claim cannot succeed because the court cannot interfere with the devise or bequest made to that spouse. In other words, the court has no jurisdiction to entertain the claim. The reasoning behind this is perhaps that the surviving spouse who is the mother or father of the child concerned will in due course make provision for the child in accordance with his or her means and if he or she fails to do so, then the child can bring an application under s 117.)

(*Note 2*: by subs (3A), the situation concerning a civil partner is not as fully protected as a spouse and is more nuanced. The court must consider the obligations of the testator to the civil partner and consider whether it would be unjust not to make an order under s 117. Even the legal right of a civil partner is not ring-fenced in the same manner as that of a spouse. It will remain to be seen whether a court would hold that such discrimination would be constitutionally justified should there be a challenge to subs (3A). It should be remembered that in a civil partnership only one partner will be the biological parent of the child so that it is only in respect of the estate of that partner that an application under s 117 would lie. The Act of 2010 does not appear to have grappled fully with the difficulty of children being brought up by civil partners.)

(4) Rules of Court shall provide for the conduct of proceedings under this section in a summary manner.

(*Note*: in the High Court, such proceedings are brought by way of special summons grounded on affidavit. In the Circuit Court, where that court has jurisdiction, proceedings are brought by way of succession law civil bill.)

(5) The costs of the proceedings shall be at the discretion of the Court.

(6) An order under this section shall not be made except on application made within [six] months from the first taking out of representation of the deceased's estate.

(*Note 1*: the limitation period, initially 12 months in s 117 as originally enacted, was reduced to *six months* by s 46 of the Family Law (Divorce) Act 1996.)

(*Note 2*: in relation to the limitation period, it has been held by Carroll J, in the High Court, that the limitation period is a jurisdictional limit and that the court cannot entertain proceedings at all once the period of limitation has expired. It would appear, therefore, that there is no extension of the time limit allowed if the person is a minor or is of unsound mind (see *MPD v MD*[1]).)

(*Note 3*: I take the view that in the absence of a duty on the part of the personal representative at a minimum to notify the child of even the death of his or her parent or to make efforts to locate a child, that the very short time limit in s 117, which goes to the very jurisdiction of the court, may offend against the provisions of the Constitution. It is not inconceivable in modern times that the personal representative may be the step-parent or person in *loco parentis* of a child with a potential claim under s 117. There

---

1.   *MPD v MD* [1981] ILRM 179.

may be an incentive not to have a claim brought on the child's behalf should the child be a minor. An unadopted non-marital child may not have been in touch with the testator but his whereabouts might be capable of being ascertained. There is an incentive in the section to take out the grant, wait for the six months for the time limit to expire, at which point the child's claim will be completely barred, even though he or she did not know it existed in the first instance. Given that the section is founded on a 'moral failure' on the part of the parent, if the child is in need of provision this seems morally indefensible. In line with the reasoning of the Supreme Court in *O'Brien v Keogh*,[2] therefore, I feel there is an argument, in an appropriate case, for the subsection to be ruled unconstitutional. In relation to spouses, civil partners, and former spouses, the personal representative has to take some step to locate the person concerned and at a minimum notify him or her of the death and at the other end of the scale (spouses and civil partners) notify them mandatorily of their rights. It is curious that there is no similar requirement in relation to a child. The recent (31st) amendment of the Constitution creating children's rights may strengthen the basis for alleging unconstitutionality of the subsection. (The subsection, of course, enjoys a presumption of constitutionality.)

Guidelines for consideration of cases under s 117

> 'It seems to me that the existence of a moral duty to make proper provision by will for a child must be judged by the facts existing *at the date of death* and must depend upon (a) the amount left to the surviving spouse or the value of the legal right if the survivor selects [*sic*] to take this, (b) the number of the testator's children, their ages and the positions in life at the date of the testator's death, (c) the means of the testator, (d) the age of the child whose case is being considered and his or her financial position and prospects in life, (e) whether the testator has already in his lifetime made proper provision for the child.' (Author's emphasis.)

These guidelines were laid down by Kenny J in *EM v TAM*[3] (see p 87 of the report) and have been universally applied in cases since. They were endorsed by the Supreme Court in *In Re IACC and F v WC and TC*,[4] subject to the qualification that Finlay CJ stated that there is 'a relatively high onus of proof' resting on the applicant seeking relief under s 117 and he stated (at p 819):

> 'It is not apparently sufficient from these terms in the section to establish that the provision made for a child was not as great as it might have been or that compared with generous bequests to other children or beneficiaries in the will, it appears ungenerous. The Court should not, I consider, make an order under this section merely because it would on the facts proved have formed different testamentary dispositions. A positive failure in moral duty must be established.'

Kenny J's guidelines have most recently been approved by the Supreme Court in *EB v SS and Another*.[5]

---

2.   *O'Brien v Keogh* [1972] IR 144.
3.   *EM v TAM* (1970) 106 ILTR 82.
4.   *In Re IACC and F v WC and TC* [1989] ILRM 815.
5.   *EB v SS and Another* [1998] 4 IR 527.

In *Re ABC decd, XC & Ors v RT & Ors*,[6] Kearns J (as he then was) took the opportunity to distil the principles that had been established up to that date. This restatement is a very useful touchstone for a person drafting a will and advising a parent in relation to his or her moral duty having regard to the individual testator's circumstances.

Counsel on both sides were agreed that the following relevant legal principles can, as a result of these authorities, be said to derive under s 117:

(a)   The social policy underlying s 117 is primarily directed to the protection of those children who are still of an age and situation in life where they might reasonably expect support from their parents, against the failure of persons who are unmindful of their duties in that area.

(b)   What has to be determined is whether the testator, at the time of his death, owes any moral obligation to the children and if so, whether he has failed in the obligation.

(c)   There is a high onus of proof placed on an applicant for relief under s 117, which requires the establishment of a positive failure in the moral duty.

(d)   Before a court can interfere, there must be clear circumstances and a positive failure in moral duty must be established.

(e)   The duty by s 117 is not absolute.

(f)   The relationship of parent and child does not, itself and without regard to other circumstances, create a moral duty to leave anything by will to the child.

(g)   Section 117 does not create an obligation to leave something to each child.

(h)   The provision of an expensive education for a child may discharge the moral duty as may other gifts or settlements made during the lifetime of the testator.

(i)   Financing a good education so as to give a child the best start in life possible and providing money, which, if properly managed, should afford a degree of financial security for the rest of one's life, does amount to making 'proper provision'.

(j)   The duty under s 117 is not to make adequate provision but to make proper provision in accordance with the testator's means.

(k)   A just parent must take into account not just his moral obligations to his children and to his wife, but all his moral obligations, eg, to aged and infirm parents.

(l)   In dealing with a s 117 application, the position of any applicant child is not to be taken in isolation. The court's duty is to consider the entirety of the testator's affairs and to decide upon the application in the overall context. In other words, while the moral claim of a child may require a testator to make a particular provision for him, the moral claims of others may require such provision to be reduced or omitted altogether.

(m)   Special circumstances giving rise to a moral duty may arise if a child is induced to believe that by, for example, working on a farm, he will ultimately become the owner of it, thereby causing him to shape his upbringing, training and life accordingly.

(n)   Another example of special circumstances might be a child who had a long illness or exceptional talent which it would be morally wrong not to foster.

---

6.   *Re ABC decd, XC & Ors v RT & Ors* [2003] IR 250 p 262.

(o)   Special needs would also include physical and mental disability.

(p)   Although the court has very wide powers both as to when to make provision for an applicant child and as to the nature of such provision, such powers must not be construed as giving the court a power to make a new will for the testator.

(q)   The test to be applied is not which of the alternative courses open to the testator the court itself would have adopted if confronted with the same situation but, rather, whether the decision of the testator to opt for the course he did, of itself and without more, constituted a breach of moral duty to the plaintiff.

(r)   The court must not disregard the fact that parents must be presumed to know their children better than anyone else.

The Status of Children Act 1987

Section 117 of the Succession Act 1965 was amended by s 31 of the Status of Children Act 1987 to allow non-marital (formerly illegitimate) children to make application under s 117 of the Succession Act 1965. The relevant date for considering whether the non-marital child has a right to apply is 14 June 1988. Where the testator died after that date (the operative date of Pt V of the Act), the non-marital child will have a right to bring an application under s 117 of the Succession Act 1965. The date of the making of the testator's will is irrelevant *vis-à-vis* the date of the application. The relevant date is the date of death. Section 31 of the Status of Children Act 1987 amended s 117 of the Succession Act 1965 as follows:

Section 117 of the Act of 1965 is hereby amended by the insertion of the following subsection after sub-s (1):

'(1A)

(a)   An application made under this section by virtue of Part V of the Status of Children Act, 1987 shall be considered in accordance with subsection (2) irrespective of whether the testator executed his will before or after the commencement of the said Part V.

(b)   Nothing in paragraph (a) shall be construed as conferring a right to apply under this section in respect of a testator who dies before the commencement of the said Part V.'

The new s 27A in the Succession Act 1965 is inserted by s 30 of the Status of Children Act 1987 and provides as follows:

For the purposes of the application of section 26 or 27 in respect of the estate of a deceased person, the deceased shall be presumed, unless the contrary is shown, not to have been survived by any person related to him whose parents have not married each other or by any person whose relationship with the deceased is deduced through a person whose parents have not married each other.

Under s 27(A), therefore, in applying for a grant of representation to the estate of a deceased person where the existence of a non-marital child or other non-marital relative is unknown, it is presumed that the deceased was survived by no such person for the purposes of making an application for a grant of representation under s 26 or 27 of the Succession Act 1965.

It is to be noted that an apparent anomaly may arise in respect of non-marital children *vis-à-vis* marital children. As we have seen, s 117 of the Succession Act 1965 precludes a child whose father or mother is taking a devise or bequest or share on intestacy from the estate of a deceased spouse from interfering with that spouse's devise or bequest or share on intestacy. Therefore, if a testator makes a will leaving everything to his or her spouse, a child of that spouse cannot bring a s 117 application. If, however, the testator had a non-marital child who is not the child of the surviving spouse, the non-marital child could bring an application under s 117, notwithstanding that all of the estate has been left to the testator's spouse.

The apparent anomaly is, however, justifiable on the basis that the spouse who is the parent of the child who cannot bring the claim will be expected in due course to make provision for that child and if he or she fails to do so, the child can bring s 117 proceedings. The surviving spouse, however, who is not the parent of the non-marital child would owe no duty to that child and, therefore, it is proper that the non-marital child could bring a claim against the estate in those circumstances.

SECTIONS 118 AND 119 OF THE SUCCESSION ACT 1965

Section 118(1) of the Succession Act 1965 provides:

> Property representing the share of a person as a legal right and property which is the subject of an order under section 117 shall bear their due proportions of estate duty payable on the estate of the deceased.

Estate duty has now been replaced by inheritance tax under the Capital Acquisitions Tax Act 1975 and s 118 applies accordingly. As of now, there is no tax as between spouses; therefore, there would be no tax payable on a legal right share.

Section 119 of the Succession Act 1965 provides that all proceedings in relation to this Part shall be heard in chambers. Therefore proceedings in relation to the legal right share of the spouse and in relation to the rights of the children shall be heard *in camera*. This is in common with proceedings in relation to the appropriation of the dwelling under s 56(11), proceedings in relation to unworthiness to succeed under s 120, and proceedings under s 121 (dispositions intended to disinherit spouse or children).

For a fuller discourse on this topic see Spierin, *The Succession Act 1965 and Related Legislation, A Commentary* (4th edn, Bloomsbury Professional, 2011).

Appendix 8

PROVISIONS IN RELATION TO UNWORTHINESS TO SUCCEED AND DISINHERITANCE WITH PRECEDENT AFFIDAVIT

Section 120 of the Succession Act 1965, as amended by the 2009 Act, provides for persons being unworthy to succeed in certain circumstances. The section (as amended), *inter alia*, provides as follows:

> (1) A sane person who has been guilty of the murder, attempted murder or manslaughter of another shall be precluded from taking any share in the estate of that other, except a share arising under a will made after the act, constituting the offence, and shall not be entitled to make an application under section 117.

> (2) A spouse against whom the deceased obtained a decree a mensa et thoro, a spouse who failed to comply with a decree for restitution of conjugal rights obtained by the deceased and a spouse guilty of desertion which has continued up to the death for two years or more shall be precluded from taking any share in the estate of the deceased as a legal right or on intestacy.

> (2A) A deceased's civil partner who has deserted the deceased is precluded from taking any share in the estate of the deceased as a legal right or on intestacy if the desertion has continued for a period of two years up the date of death or more.

(*Note*: this section provides for three different circumstances in which a spouse may be deemed unworthy to succeed:

1. Where a decree of divorce *a mensa et thoro* has been obtained against that spouse. In order for the section to operate, the spouse being deemed unworthy to succeed must be the blameworthy party in the proceedings giving rise to the action for a decree of divorce *a mensa et thoro.*

2. Where a spouse fails to comply with a decree for restitution of conjugal rights obtained by the deceased.

3. Where a spouse or civil partner is guilty of desertion, and the desertion has continued for a period of two years or more up until the date of death of the deceased.

Spouses who come within these conditions (or a civil partner who has deserted) are unworthy to succeed *vis-à-vis* any share as a legal right or on intestacy. They are not, however, precluded from taking a benefit under the will of the testator made after the act giving rise to the unworthiness to succeed.

In the case of desertion, it is important to note that the desertion must be for a period of two years or more and must continue up until the date of death. Generally speaking, in separation agreements the persons agree to live separate and apart. If there is such agreement, any desertion that existed prior to the date of the separation agreement is set aside. Therefore, if the separation agreement makes no other provision in relation to rights under the Succession Act 1965, a spouse or civil partner who was unworthy to succeed by virtue of desertion may be rendered worthy again by the entering into a separation agreement.

Similarly, of course, a reconciliation between the parties prior to the death whereby the parties resume cohabitation would normally render the spouse once again worthy to succeed.)

> (3) By virtue of subsections (3) and (3A) A spouse or civil partner who is guilty of conduct which justifies the deceased in separating and living apart from him shall be deemed to be guilty of desertion within the meaning of subsection (2) and subsection (2A)

(*Note*: this imports into the Succession Act 1965 the concept of constructive desertion. Therefore, if the spouse who actually deserted was justified in leaving the other spouse, the spouse who remained shall be deemed to have constructively deserted the spouse who left. It can often be difficult to prove that a desertion was not justified if it is alleged that the deceased spouse was guilty of conduct which justified the surviving spouse deserting where that allegation is made. A key witness, the deserted spouse, will be dead. So, if acting for someone who has been deserted, it would be wise to take a very full statement or even affidavit as to his or her side of the story. This last state of affairs would also apply to civil partners.)

> (4) A person who has been found guilty of an offence against the deceased, or against the spouse, or any child of the deceased (including a child adopted under the Adoption Acts, 1952 and 1964 and a person to whom the deceased was in loco parentis at the time of the offence), punishable by imprisonment by a maximum period of at least two years or by a more severe penalty, shall be precluded from taking any share of the estate as a legal right or from making an application under section 117.

(*Note*: this subject applies to civil partners, spouses and children. The subsection relates only to the legal right share and s 117 claims by a child. It does not appear to exclude such a person taking a benefit under an intestacy or a benefit conferred by a will. In cases where a person has been guilty of such an offence, the will of the testator should be revised.)

> (5) Any share which a person is precluded from taking under this section shall be distributed as if that person had died before the deceased.

ANCILLARY ORDERS MADE ON FOOT OF DECREE OF JUDICIAL SEPARATION, DIVORCE *A VINCULO MATRIMONII* AND ON DISSOLUTION OF A CIVIL PARTNERSHIP

By virtue of s 14 of the Family Law Act 1995, the court is empowered to make the following orders, ancillary to a decree of judicial separation, which may have a bearing on succession rights and which a person drafting a will should bear in mind.

The court may extinguish the legal right share of the spouse or a spouse's rights on intestacy where:

(i)   it is satisfied that adequate and reasonable financial provision exists or can be made under ss 8, 9, 10(1)(a), 11, 12 or 13 of the Family Law Act 1995 for the spouse whose succession rights are in issue ('the spouse concerned'); or,

(ii)   'the spouse concerned' is a spouse in relation to whom the court refused to make a support order under ss 8, 9, 10(1)(a), 11, 12 or 13 of the Family Law Act 1995; or,

(iii)   it is satisfied that 'the spouse concerned' is not a spouse for whose benefit the court would, if an application were made to it in that behalf, make an order under ss 8, 9,10(1)(a), 11, 12 or 13 of the Family Law Act 1995.

The court, in making such an order, is obliged to consider 'all the circumstances' of the case and whether it is 'in the interests of justice' to make the order.

Section 15A of the Family Law Act 1995, as inserted by s 56(g) of the Family Law (Divorce) Act 1996, permits the court to make similar orders where a decree of divorce *a vinculo matrimonii* is granted in that s 18 of the Family Law (Divorce) Act 1996 allows a former spouse in certain circumstances to seek provision from the estate of the other former spouse who is deceased.

Section 127 of the 2010 Act contains a similar provision permitting a civil partner to apply for provision from a deceased civil partner's estate but s 127(11) provides that the court, on granting a decree of dissolution, can provide that either or both civil partners can be precluded from bringing an application under s 127.

FOREIGN DIVORCE

If the testator has obtained a foreign divorce, the question of the recognition of the foreign divorce under Irish law should be considered. A foreign divorce will be recognised under Irish law (whenever granted) if it was granted in the court of the domicile of one of the parties to the marriage. (See the Domicile and Recognition of Foreign Divorces Act 1986, Brussels II and recent case law all of which is dealt with in detail in **Ch 1** of this book.)

For a fuller discourse on this topic see Spierin, *The Succession Act 1965 and Related Legislation, A Commentary* (4th edn, Bloomsbury Professional, 2011).

AFFIDAVIT BY TESTATOR CONCERNING SPOUSE'S/CIVIL PARTNER'S UNWORTHINESS TO SUCCEED

IN THE MATTER OF THE LAST WILL AND TESTAMENT OF ME *(INSERT NAME OF TESTATOR)* OF *(ADDRESS OF TESTATOR).*

AFFIDAVIT OF (*NAME OF TESTATOR*)

I, *(name of testator)*, of *(address of testator)*, aged eighteen years and upwards make Oath and say as follows:

1.　I make this affidavit from facts within my own knowledge save where otherwise appears and where so appears I believe those facts to be true.

2.　I was married to *(name of spouse)* at *(location of marriage)* on the *(date)* day of *(month), (year)* and I beg to refer to a certificate of my marriage upon which marked with the letter 'A' I have signed my name prior to the swearing hereof.

   [*Or*

2.　I entered into a Civil Partnership with on the date day of month, year and I beg to refer to a Certificate of Registration of the Civil Partnership upon which marked with the letter 'A' I have signed my name prior to the swearing hereof.]

3.　I have made my will on the *(date)* day of *(month), (year)* and in the said will I have made no provision for my said spouse/civil partner.

4.　I am advised by my Solicitor *(name)* that by virtue of the provisions of Part IX of the Succession Act 1965 my spouse/civil partner could seek to claim one-half/ one-third* of my estate as a legal right.

   *(*One-half of estate where there are no children; one-third where there are children.)*

5.　I am further advised by my Solicitor of the terms of Section 120 of the Succession Act 1965 concerning the worthiness of a spouse/civil partner to succeed to a deceased person's estate.

6.　I believe my husband/wife/civil partner is unworthy to succeed because he/she has been in desertion of me since in or about the month of *(month)* of *(year)* without any just cause and the desertion is continuing.

   [*or,*

6.　I believe my husband/wife/civil partner is unworthy to succeed because although I have been in desertion of him/her since in or about the month of *(month)* of *(year)* I was caused to desert him/her by reason of his/her unreasonable and intolerable conduct as follows *(describe conduct sufficient to show constructive desertion).*

   or,

6.　I obtained a decree of divorce *a mensa et thoro (or,* decree of judicial separation) against him/her on the *(date)* day of *(month), (year)* on the grounds of his/her adultery/physical/mental cruelty and I beg to refer to refer to the said decree when produced.

or,

6.   My spouse/ civil partner was found guilty of ... against me or my child ... or ... to whom I stand *in loco parentis* (*state nature of offence*) which offence is punishable by a maximum term of two years or greater penalty and I beg to refer to the order and conviction when produced.]

7.   I make this affidavit for the benefit of my executors and the court in the event of my spouse seeking to make a claim against my estate.

SWORN, ETC.

Appendix 9

PROVISIONS RELATING TO DISPOSITIONS MADE FOR THE PURPOSES OF DISINHERITING A SPOUSE OR CHILDREN

Section 121 of the Succession Act 1965 makes provision for the setting aside of certain dispositions made for the purposes of disinheriting a spouse/civil partner or children. The application of the section is reasonably limited and attention is particularly directed to s 121(7). Also, it would appear that the primary intention of the person making the disposition must be to disinherit the spouse and children (see *MPD v MD*[1]).

Section 121 of the Succession Act 1965, as amended by the 2010 Act, provides as follows:

> (1) This section applies to a disposition of property (other than a testamentary disposition or a disposition to a purchaser) under which the beneficial ownership of the property vests in possession in the donee within three years before the death of the person who made it, or on his death, or later.
>
> (2) If the Court is satisfied that a disposition to which this section applies was made for the purpose of defeating or substantially diminishing the share of the disponer's spouse or civil partner, whether as a legal right or on intestacy, or the intestate share of any of his children, or leaving any of his children insufficiently provided for, then, whether the disponer died testate or intestate the Court may order that the disposition shall, in whole or in part, be deemed for the purposes of Parts VI and IX to be a devise or bequest made by him by will or to form part of his estate and to have had no other effect.
>
> (3) To the extent to which the Court so orders, the disposition shall be deemed never to have had effect as such and the donee of the property, or any person representing or deriving title under him, shall be a debtor of the estate for such amount as the Court may direct accordingly.
>
> (4) The Court may make such further order in relation to the matter as may appear to the Court to be just and equitable, having regard to the provisions and spirit of this Act and to all the circumstances.
>
> (5) Subject to subsections (6) and (7), an order may be made under this section—
>
> (a)   In the interest of the spouse or civil partner on the application of the spouse, civil partner or personal representative of the deceased made within one year from the first taking out of representation.
>
> (b)   In the interest of a child on an application under section 117.
>
> (6) In the case of a disposition made in favour of the spouse or civil partner of the disponer, an order shall not be made under this section on the application by or on behalf of the child of the disponer who is also a child of the spouse or civil partner.

---

1.   *MPD v MD* [1981] ILRM 179.

(7) An order shall not be made under this section affecting a disposition made in favour of any child of the disponer, if,

(a)   The spouse or civil partner of the disponer was dead when the disposition was made, or,

(b)   The spouse or civil partner was alive when the disposition was made but was a person who, if the disponer had then died, would have been precluded under any of the provisions of section 120 from taking a share in his estate, or,

(c)   The spouse or civil partner was alive when the disposition was made and consented *in writing* to it.

(Author's emphasis.)

(8) If the donee disposes of the property to a purchaser, this section shall cease to apply to the property and shall apply instead to the consideration given by the purchaser.

(9) Accrual by survivorship on death of a joint tenant of a property shall, for the purpose of this section, be deemed to be a vesting of the beneficial ownership of the entire property and the survivor.

(10) In this section disposition includes a *donatio mortis causa*.

Section 122 of the Succession Act 1965 provides as follows:

All proceedings in relation to this Part shall be heard in chambers.

For a fuller discourse on this topic see Spierin, *The Succession Act 1965 and Related Legislation, A Commentary* (4th edn, Bloomsbury Professional, 2011).

Appendix 10

VALIDITY AS TO FORM OF FOREIGN TESTAMENTARY DOCUMENTS

Section 101 of the Succession Act 1965 provides as follows:

> In this Part 'testamentary disposition' means any will or other testamentary instrument or act.

Section 102 of the Act lays down the criteria for the recognition of foreign testamentary dispositions with regard to form only. The section provides as follows:

> (1) A testamentary disposition shall be valid as regards form if its form complies with the internal law—
>
> (a)   Of the place where the testator made it, or,
>
> (b)   Of a nationality possessed by the testator, either at the time when he made the disposition or at the time of his death, or,
>
> (c)   Of a place in which the testator had his domicile, either at the time when he made the disposition or at the time of his death, or,
>
> (d)   Of the place in which the testator had his habitual residence, either at the time when he made the disposition or at the time of his death, or,
>
> (e)   So far as immovables are concerned, of the place where they are situated.
>
> (2) Without prejudice to subsection (1), a testamentary disposition revoking an earlier testamentary disposition shall also be valid as regards form if it complies with any one of the laws according to the terms of which, under that subsection, the testamentary disposition that has been revoked was valid.
>
> (3) For the purpose of this Part, if a national law consists of a non-unified system, the law to be applied shall be determined by *the rules in force in that system* and, failing any such rules, by the most real connexion which the testator had with any one of *the various laws within that system.*
>
> (4) Determination of whether or not the testator had his domicile in a particular place shall be governed by *the law of that place.* (Author's emphasis.)

Section 103 provides as follows:

> Without prejudice to section 102, a testamentary disposition made on board a vessel or aircraft shall also be valid as regards form if its form complies with the internal law of the place with which, having regard to its registration (if any) and any other relevant circumstances, the vessel or aircraft may have had the most real connexion.

Section 104 provides as follows:

> (1) Without prejudice to section 102, a testamentary disposition shall also be valid as regards form so far as it exercises a power of appointment if its form complies with the law governing the essential validity of the power.

(2) A testamentary disposition so far as it exercises a power of appointment shall not be treated as invalid as regards form by reason only that its form is not in accordance with any formal requirements contained in the instrument creating the power.

Section 105 provides as follows:

This Part shall also apply to the form of testamentary dispositions made by two or more persons in one document.

Section 106 provides as follows:

(1) For the purpose of this Part, any provision of law which limits the permitted forms of testamentary dispositions by reference to the age, nationality or other personal conditions of the testator, shall be deemed to pertain to matters of form.

(2) The same rule shall apply to the qualifications that must be possessed by witnesses required for the validity of a testamentary disposition and to the provisions of section 82.

(*Note*: this does not apply to restrictions in relation to mental capacity.)

Section 107 provides as follows:

(1) The construction of a testamentary disposition shall not be altered by reason of any change in the testator's domicile after the making of the disposition.

(2) In determining whether or not a testamentary disposition complies with a particular law, regard shall be had to the requirements of that law at the time of making the disposition, but it shall not prevent account being taken of an alteration of law affecting testamentary dispositions made at that time if the alteration enables the disposition to be treated as valid.

Section 108 provides as follows:

A testamentary disposition which under this Part is valid as regards form shall have the same effect as if it were a will executed in compliance with Part VII.

For a fuller discourse on this topic see Spierin, *The Succession Act 1965 and Related Legislation, A Commentary* (4th edn, Bloomsbury Professional, 2011).

Appendix 11

DISCLAIMER

A beneficiary who has obtained a benefit under the will of a testator, or as a legal right share, or under an intestacy, may disclaim the benefit conferred or accruing to him or her. The legal effect of the disclaimer will differ, however, with the circumstances.

1. DISCLAIMER OF GENERAL, DEMONSTRATIVE OR SPECIFIC LEGACY OR DEVISE UNDER A WILL

Where a testator by his or her will makes a general, demonstrative or specific bequest in favour of a named beneficiary or class of beneficiaries, the beneficiary or member of the class of beneficiaries may disclaim the benefit conferred.

Where a sole beneficiary is entitled to the benefit and he or she disclaims a general, demonstrative or specific legacy or devise, the subject matter of the bequest will fall into the residue of the estate to be distributed in accordance with the residuary bequest contained in the will (see s 91 of the Succession Act 1965).

Where a member of a class of beneficiaries disclaims a benefit conferred upon him or her, the effect of the disclaimer will depend on whether the benefit is conferred upon the class as joint tenants or tenants in common. Where the benefit is conferred upon the class as joint tenants, then the remaining members of the class will take the benefit of the disclaimed interest. Where, however, the benefit is conferred upon the class of beneficiaries as tenants in common, the share of the beneficiary who has disclaimed will fall into the residue of the estate of the deceased under s 91 of the Succession Act 1965.

2. DISCLAIMER OF RESIDUARY BEQUEST

Where the benefit disclaimed is contained in a residuary bequest and the person disclaiming is the sole residuary legatee and devisee named in the will, then this will give rise to a partial intestacy with regard to the subject matter of the residue. The subject matter of the residuary bequest would then fall to be distributed amongst the deceased's next-of-kin in accordance with the rules on intestacy – s 74 of the 1965 Act (see **Appendix 5**).

If the bequest of the residue is to a class of persons and the residue is left to the class of residuary legatees and devisees as joint tenants, then on the disclaimer of one of them, the benefit disclaimed will pass to the remaining residuary legatees and devisees.

If, on the other hand, the residuary bequest is to the residuary legatees and devisees as tenants in common, the share of the beneficiary who disclaims will pass on a partial intestacy to the next-of-kin of the deceased in accordance with the rules on intestacy (see **Appendix 5**).

3. DISCLAIMER OF LEGAL RIGHT SHARE

Where the spouse/civil partner of a testator becomes entitled to a legal right share and no benefit is conferred upon the spouse/civil partner in the will of the testator, then no question of an election on the part of the spouse/civil partner arises and the beneficial entitlement to the legal right share of either one-half or one-third of the estate of the testator vests in the surviving spouse/civil partner. If he or she decides to disclaim the legal right share, then the estate will be administered in accordance with the terms of the will of the testator as if the legal right share did not arise.

A disclaimer of the legal right share where there is a benefit conferred upon a spouse/civil partner in a will shall hardly arise, as the spouse/civil partner will be required to elect between the legal right share and the benefit conferred by the will. If the spouse/civil partner elects to take under the will, then presumably he or she will take the benefit contained in the will, and if he or she elects not to take the legal right share and additionally decides to disclaim the benefit contained in the will, then the effect of the disclaimer of the benefit conferred by the will would be precisely the same as a disclaimer by any other beneficiary (see above).

4. DISCLAIMER ON INTESTACY

The law in relation to disclaimer on intestacy was amended by the Family Law (Miscellaneous Provisions) Act 1997. It applies to cases where the disclaimer is made after the date of passing of that Act, being 5 May 1997.

Prior to the enactment of s 6 of this Act, which inserted s 72A into the Succession Act 1965, where a person disclaimed on intestacy, the effect under Irish law was unclear.

It is not possible for a person to disclaim in favour of another person. The result of a disclaimer takes effect by operation of law and is independent of the intention of the person disclaiming.

Under the Succession Act 1965, prior to the enactment of the Family Law (Miscellaneous Provisions) Act 1997, where a benefit was disclaimed on intestacy, there was not authority in Ireland as to the effect of such disclaimer. Under the law of England and Wales, by virtue of the decision in the case of *In Re Scott Widows v Friends of the Clergy Corporation*,[1] it was decided that where a member of a class of persons entitled on intestacy disclaimed, the benefit disclaimed passed to the remaining members of the class and if the class was exhausted by the disclaimer, it would pass to the next class of persons entitled. Generally speaking in Irish law, the Revenue Commissioners appear to have adopted that approach, although there was no Irish decision to that effect.

It was academically argued most cogently in the March 1992 *Irish Tax Review* that, by virtue of the wording of s 73 of the Succession Act 1965 under which the State takes as ultimate intestate successor, which is different to the equivalent section in the Administration of Estates Act 1925 under which the Crown in England and Wales takes *bona vacantia,* where a benefit was disclaimed on intestacy, it did not pass to the remaining members of the class, or to the next class if the initial class was exhausted, but rather passed to the State as ultimate intestate successor.

---

1.   *In Re Scott Widows v Friends of the Clergy Corporation* [1975] 2 All ER 1033.

Section 73(1) of the Succession Act 1965 provides as follows:

> In default of any person taking the estate of an intestate, whether under this Part *or otherwise*, the State shall take the estate as ultimate intestate successor. (Author's emphasis.)

It is argued that the words 'or otherwise' envisage a situation such as disclaimer and not merely a failure of persons entitled to inherit.

Section 6 of the Family Law (Miscellaneous Provisions) Act 1997 amended the law by the insertion of a new s 72A into the Succession Act 1965. Section 6 provides as follows:

> The Succession Act 1965 is hereby amended by the insertion after section 72 of the following section:
>
> '72A Where the estate, or part of the estate, as to which a person dies intestate is disclaimed after the passing of the Family Law (Miscellaneous Provisions) Act, 1997 (otherwise than under section 73 of this Act), the estate, or part, as the case may be, shall be distributed in accordance with this Part—
>
> (a)   as if the person disclaiming had died immediately before the death of the intestate, and
>
> (b)   if that person is not the spouse or a direct lineal ancestor of the intestate, as if that person had died without leaving issue.'

The section has not been judicially interpreted, but I would feel that the reference to 'the estate or part of the estate' makes reference to whether the deceased died wholly or partially intestate. It does not allow for disclaimer of part of the benefit conferred upon the person disclaiming. The person disclaiming must disclaim the whole of the benefit or take the whole of the benefit. It is, of course, open to a beneficiary to disclaim for valuable consideration.

The effect of the person disclaiming is that the person is treated as if he or she had died immediately before the deceased. However, except in cases of a spouse/civil partner or a direct lineal ancestor, the person disclaiming is to be deemed as dying without leaving issue.

It would seem, therefore, that if a spouse/civil partner disclaims, the share of the spouse/civil partner disclaimed will pass to the issue of the intestate (if any) because the spouse/civil partner will be treated as dying immediately before the intestate and he or she is not presumed to have died without issue.

Similarly, in cases where the parent or parents of an intestate disclaim, the interest of the parent or parents would pass either to the other surviving parent, or, if there is only one parent or both parents disclaim, would pass to the brothers and sisters of the intestate because the parent or parents disclaiming would be treated as dying immediately before the intestate, but would not be deemed to have died without issue.

On the other hand, if the persons entitled to the benefit on the whole or partial intestacy are other than a parent or lineal ancestor, eg, a brother or sister, the person who disclaims will be deemed to have died before the intestate without leaving issue and the benefit disclaimed should, therefore, pass to the remaining brothers or sisters of the intestate and any issue of a predeceased brother or sister, but excluding the issue, if any, of the person who disclaimed.

The operation of the section, therefore, would seem to bring into effect largely the same result as the English decision of *In Re Scott Widows* in respect of all disclaimers after 5 May 1997.

This interpretation of the section, however, is subject to the caveat that it has not been as yet judicially interpreted.

For a fuller discourse on this topic see Spierin, *The Succession Act 1965 and Related Legislation, A Commentary* (4th edn, Bloomsbury Professional, 2011).

PRECEDENT DEED OF DISCLAIMER

THIS DEED OF DISCLAIMER made the *(date)* day of *(month)*, *(year)* by *(name of beneficiary)* of *(address of beneficiary)* (hereinafter called 'the Beneficiary').

WHEREAS:

1. By will dated the *(date)* day of *(month)*, *(year)* (hereinafter called 'the Will') *(name of testator)* (hereinafter called 'the Testator') late of *(late address)* bequeathed to the Beneficiary *(describe bequest)* (hereinafter called 'the Bequest').

2. The Testator died on the *(date)* day of *(month)*, *(year)* without having revoked or altered his/her said will.

3. By this Deed the Beneficiary **HEREBY DISCLAIMS** the entire of the benefit of the Bequest and the Beneficiary **HEREBY CONFIRMS** that he/she has not entered into possession of the Bequest nor done any other act or thing which would constitute an acceptance of the Bequest.

4. The Beneficiary has been invited to take independent legal advice prior to the signing of this Deed of Disclaimer and has had the benefit of such advice/has declined to do so.

Signed, sealed and delivered

by *(name of beneficiary)*

in the presence of:

Appendix 12

DEFINITIONS RELEVANT TO DRAFTING WILLS

Part 1

• Land and Conveyancing Law Reform Act 2009

Part 2

• Rules of the Superior Courts (Land and Conveyancing Law Reform Act 2009) 2010
(SI 149/2010)

• Circuit Court Rules (Land and Conveyancing Law Reform Act 2009) 2010
(SI 155/2010)

PART 1

LAND AND CONVEYANCING LAW REFORM ACT 2009

3 Interpretation generally

'In this Act, unless the context otherwise requires—

"Act of 1957" means the Statute of Limitations 1957;

"Act of 1963" means the Companies Act 1963;

"Act of 1964" means the Registration of Title Act 1964;

"Act of 1965" means the Succession Act 1965;

"Act of 1976" means the Family Home Protection Act 1976;

"Act of 1988" means the Bankruptcy Act 1988;

"Act of 1989" means the Building Societies Act 1989;

"Act of 1995" means the Family Law Act 1995;

"Act of 1996 " means the Family Law (Divorce) Act 1996;

"Act of 2000" means the Planning and Development Act 2000;

"Act of 2005" means the Interpretation Act 2005;

"Act of 2006" means the Registration of Deeds and Title Act 2006;

"assent" has the meaning given to it by section 53 of the Act of 1965;

"consent" includes agreement, licence and permission;

"conveyance" includes an appointment, assent, assignment, charge, disclaimer, lease, mortgage, release, surrender, transfer, vesting certificate, vesting declaration, vesting order and every other assurance by way of instrument except a will; and "convey" shall be read accordingly;

"the court" means—

(a)   the High Court, or

(b)   the Circuit Court when exercising the jurisdiction conferred on it by the Third Schedule to the Courts (Supplemental Provisions) Act 1961;

"covenant" includes an agreement, a condition, reservation and stipulation;

"deed" has the meaning given to it by section 64(2);

...

"disposition" includes a conveyance and a devise, bequest or appointment of property by will and "dispose" shall be read accordingly;

...

"fee farm grant" means any—

(a)   grant of a fee simple, or

(b)   lease for ever or in perpetuity,

reserving or charging a perpetual rent, whether or not the relationship of landlord and tenant is created between the grantor and grantee, and includes a sub-fee farm grant;

"freehold covenant" has the meaning given to it by section 48;

"freehold estate" has the meaning given to it by section 11(2);

"housing loan" has the meaning given to it by section 2(1) of the Consumer Credit Act 1995, as substituted by section 33 of, and Part 12 of Schedule 3 to, the Central Bank and Financial Services Authority of Ireland Act 2004 and "housing loan mortgage" means a mortgage to secure a housing loan;

"incumbrance" includes an annuity, charge, lien, mortgage, portion and trust for securing an annual or capital sum; and "incumbrancer" shall be read accordingly and includes every person entitled to the benefit of an incumbrance or to require its payment or discharge;

"instrument" includes a deed, will, or other document in writing, and information in electronic or other non-legible form which is capable of being converted into such a document, but not a statutory provision;

...

"land" includes—

(a)   any estate or interest in or over land, whether corporeal or incorporeal,

(b)   mines, minerals and other substances in the substratum below the surface, whether or not owned in horizontal, vertical or other layers apart from the surface of the land,

(c)   land covered by water,

(d)   buildings or structures of any kind on land and any part of them, whether the division is made horizontally, vertically or in any other way,

(e)   the airspace above the surface of land or above any building or structure on land which is capable of being or was previously occupied by a building or structure and any part of such airspace, whether the division is made horizontally, vertically or in any other way,

(f)   any part of land;

"Land Registry" has the meaning given to it by section 7 of the Act of 1964;

...

"legal estate" has the meaning given to it by section 11(1);

"legal interest" has the meaning given to it by section 11(4);

...

"Minister" means the Minister for Justice, Equality and Law Reform;

"mortgage" includes any charge or lien on any property for securing money or money's worth;

"mortgagee" includes any person having the benefit of a charge or lien and any person deriving title to the mortgage under the original mortgagee;

"mortgagor" includes any person deriving title to the mortgaged property under the original mortgagor or entitled to redeem the mortgage;

"notice" includes constructive notice;

"personal representative" means the executor or executrix or the administrator or administratrix for the time being of a deceased person;

...

"possession" includes the receipt of, or the right to receive, rent and profits, if any;

"prescribed" means prescribed by regulations made under section 5;

"property" means any real or personal property or any part or combination of such property;

"Property Registration Authority" has the meaning given to it by section 9 of the Act of 2006;

"purchaser" means an assignee, chargeant, grantee, lessee, mortgagee or other person who acquires land for valuable consideration; and "purchase" shall be read accordingly;

"registered land" has the meaning given to it by section 3(1) of the Act of 1964;

"Registry of Deeds" has the meaning given to it by section 33 of the Act of 2006;

"rent" includes a rent payable under a tenancy or a rentcharge, or other payment in money or money's worth or any other consideration, reserved or issuing out of or charged on land, but does not include interest;

"rentcharge" means any annual or periodic sum charged on or issuing out of land, except—

(a)   a rent payable under a tenancy, and

(b)   interest;

"right of entry" means a right to take possession of land or of its income and to retain that possession or income until some obligation is performed;

"right of re-entry" means a right to forfeit the legal owner's estate in the land;

"strict settlement" has the meaning given to it by section 18(1)(a);

...

"trust corporation" has the meaning given to it by section 30(4) of the Act of 1965;

"trust of land" has the meaning given to it by section 18(1);

"unregistered land" has the meaning given to it by section 3(1) of the Act of 1964;

"valuable consideration" does not include marriage or a nominal consideration in money;

"will" includes codicil.'

PART 3
Future Interests

15 Operation of future interests in land

(1) Subject to subsection (2), all future interests in land, whether vested or contingent, exist in equity only.

(2) Subsection (1) does not apply to—

(a)   a possibility of reverter, or

(b)   a right of entry or of re-entry attached to a legal estate.

16 Abolition of various rules

Subject to section 17, the following rules are abolished:

(a)   the rules known as the common law contingent remainder rules;

(b)   the rule known as the Rule in *Purefoy v Rogers*;

(c)   the rule known as the Rule in *Whitby v Mitchell* (also known as the old rule against perpetuities and the rule against double possibilities);

(d)   the rule against perpetuities;

(e)   the rule against accumulations.

17 Scope of section 16

Section 16 applies to any interest in property whenever created but does not apply if, before the commencement of this Part, in reliance on such an interest being invalid by virtue of the application of any of the rules abolished by that section—

(a)   the property has been distributed or otherwise dealt with, or

(b)   any person has done or omitted to do any thing which renders the position of that or any other person materially altered to that person's detriment after the commencement of this Part.

PART 4
Trusts of Land

18 Trusts of land

(1) Subject to this Part, where land is—

[SLA 1882, ss 2, 59, 60]

(a)   for the time being limited by an instrument, whenever executed, to persons by way of succession without the interposition of a trust (in this Part referred to as a "strict settlement"), or

(b)   held, either with or without other property, on a trust whenever it arises and of whatever kind, or

(c)   vested, whether before or after the commencement of this Part, in a minor,

there is a trust of land for the purposes of this Part.

(2) For the purposes of—

(a)   subsection (1)(a), a strict settlement exists where an estate or interest in reversion or remainder is not disposed of and reverts to the settlor or the testator's successors in title, but does not exist where a person owns a fee simple in possession,

(b)   subsection (1)(b), a trust includes an express, implied, resulting, constructive and bare trust and a trust for sale.

(3) Subject to this Part, a trust of land is governed by the general law of trusts.

(4) Conversion of a life estate into an equitable interest only does not affect a life owner's liability for waste.

[LEA 1695]

(5) Where, by reason of absence from the State or otherwise, it remains uncertain for a period of at least 7 years as to whether a person upon whose life an estate or interest depends is alive, it shall continue to be presumed that the person is dead.

(6) If such presumption is applied to a person but subsequently rebutted by proof to the contrary, that person may bring an action for damages or another remedy for any loss suffered.

(7) In dealing with an action under subsection (6), the court may make such order as appears to it to be just and equitable in the circumstances of the case.

(8) Any party to a conveyance shall, unless the contrary is proved, be presumed to have attained full age at the date of the conveyance.

(9) This Part does not apply to land held directly for a charitable purpose and not by way of a remainder.

19 Trustees of land

(1) The following persons are the trustees of a trust of land—

[SLA 1882, ss 38, 39]

(a)   in the case of a strict settlement, where it—

    (i)   exists at the commencement of this Part, the tenant for life within the meaning of the Settled Land Act 1882 together with any trustees of the settlement for the purposes of that Act,

    (ii)   is purported to be created after the commencement of this Part, the persons who would fall within paragraph (b) if the instrument creating it were deemed to be an instrument creating a trust of land,

(b)   in the case of a trust of land created expressly—

    (i)   any trustee nominated by the trust instrument, but, if there is no such person, then,

    (ii)   any person on whom the trust instrument confers a present or future power of sale of the land, or power of consent to or approval of the exercise of such a power of sale, but, if there is no such person, then,

    (iii)   any person who, under either the trust instrument or the general law of trusts, has power to appoint a trustee of the land, but, if there is no such person, then,

    (iv)   the settlor or, in the case of a trust created by will, the testator's personal representative or representatives,

(c)   in the case of land vested in a minor before the commencement of this Part or purporting so to vest after such commencement, the persons who would fall within paragraph (b) if the instrument vesting the land were deemed to be an instrument creating a trust of land,

(d)   in the case of land the subject of an implied, resulting, constructive or bare trust, the person in whom the legal title to the land is vested.

(2) For the purposes of—

(a)   subsection (1)(a)(ii) and (1)(c), the references in subsection (1)(b) to "trustee" and "trustee of the land" include a trustee of the settlement,

(b)   subsection (1)(b)(iii) a power to appoint a trustee includes a power to appoint where no previous appointment has been made.

(3) Nothing in this section affects the right of any person to obtain an order of the court appointing a trustee of land or vesting land in a person as trustee.

20 Powers of trustees of land

(1) Subject to—

(a)   the duties of a trustee, and

(b)   any restrictions imposed by any statutory provision (including this Act) or the general law of trusts or by any instrument or court order relating to the land,

a trustee of land has the full power of an owner to convey or otherwise deal with it.

(2) The power of a trustee under subsection (1) includes the power to—

(a)   permit a beneficiary to occupy or otherwise use the land on such terms as the trustee thinks fit,

(b)   sell the land and to re-invest the proceeds, in whole or in part, in the purchase of land, whether or not situated in the State, for such occupation or use.

21 Overreaching for protection of purchasers

(1) Subject to subsection (3), a conveyance to a purchaser of a legal estate or legal interest in land by the person or persons specified in subsection (2) overreaches any equitable interest in the land so that it ceases to affect that estate or interest, whether or not the purchaser has notice of the equitable interest.

(2) For the purposes of subsection (1), the "person or persons specified"—

(a)   shall be at least two trustees or a trust corporation where the trust land comprises—

(i)   a strict settlement, or

(ii)   a trust, including a trust for sale, of land held for persons by way of succession, or

(iii)   land vested in or held on trust for a minor,

(b)   may be a single trustee or owner of the legal estate or interest in the case of any other trust of land.

(3) Subsection (1) does not apply to—

(a)   any conveyance made for fraudulent purposes of which the purchaser has actual knowledge at the date of the conveyance or to which the purchaser is a party, or

(b)   any equitable interest—

(i)   to which the conveyance is expressly made subject, or

(ii)   protected by deposit of documents of title relating to the legal estate or legal interest, or

(iii)   in the case of a trust coming within subsection (2)(b), protected by registration prior to the date of the conveyance or taking effect as a burden coming within section 72(1)(j) of the Act of 1964 (or, in the case of unregistered land, which would take effect as such a burden if the land were registered land).

(4) In subsection (3)(b)(iii), "registration" means registration in the Registry of Deeds or Land Registry, as appropriate.

(5) Where an equitable interest is overreached under this section it attaches to the proceeds arising from the conveyance and effect shall be given to it accordingly.

(6) Nothing in this section affects the operation of the Act of 1976.

22 Resolution of disputes

(1) Any person having an interest in a trust of land, or a person acting on behalf of such a person, may apply to the court in a summary manner for an order to resolve a dispute between the—

(a)   trustees themselves, or

(b)   beneficiaries themselves, or

(c)   trustees and beneficiaries, or

(d)   trustees or beneficiaries and other persons interested,

in relation to any matter concerning the—

(i)   performance of their functions by the trustees, or

(ii)   nature or extent of any beneficial or other interest in the land, or

(iii)   other operation of the trust.

(2) Subject to subsection (3), in determining an application under subsection (1) the court may make whatever order and direct whatever inquiries it thinks fit in the circumstances of the case.

(3) In considering an application under subsection (1)(i) and (iii) the court shall have regard to the interests of the beneficiaries as a whole and, subject to these, to—

(a)   the purposes which the trust of land is intended to achieve,

(b)   the interests of any minor or other beneficiary subject to any incapacity,

(c)   the interests of any secured creditor of any beneficiary,

(d)   any other matter which the court considers relevant.

(4) In subsection (1), "person having an interest" includes a mortgagee or other secured creditor, a judgment mortgagee or a trustee.

(5) Nothing in this section affects the jurisdiction of the court under section 36 of the Act of 1995.

PART 5
Variation of Trusts

23 Interpretation of Part 5

In this Part—

"appropriate person", in relation to a relevant trust, means—

(a)   a trustee of, or a beneficiary under, the trust, or

(b)   any other person that the court, to which the application concerned under section 24 is made, considers appropriate;

"arrangement", in relation to a relevant trust, means an arrangement—

(a)   varying, revoking or resettling the trust, or

(b)   varying, enlarging, adding to or restricting the powers of the trustees under the trust to manage or administer the property the subject of the trust;

"relevant person", in relation to a relevant trust, means—

(a)   a person who has a vested or contingent interest under the trust but who is incapable of assenting to an arrangement by reason of lack of capacity (whether by reason of minority or absence of mental capacity),

(b)   an unborn person,

(c)   a person whose identity, existence or whereabouts cannot be established by taking reasonable measures, or

(d)   a person who has a contingent interest under the trust but who does not fall within paragraph (a);

"relevant trust"—

(a)   subject to paragraph (b), means a trust arising, whether before, on or after the commencement of this section, under a will, settlement or other disposition,

(b)   does not include—

(i)   a trust created for a charitable purpose within the meaning of the Charities Acts 1961 and 1973 and the Charities Act 2009,

(ii)   an occupational pension scheme within the meaning of the Pensions Act 1990 established under a trust,

(iii)   a trust created by a British statute,

(iv)   a trust created by a Saorstát Éireann statute, or

(v)   a trust created by an Act of the Oireachtas, whether passed before, on or after the commencement of this section.

24 Jurisdiction of court to vary, etc, trusts

(1) An appropriate person may make, in respect of a relevant trust, an application to the court for an order to approve an arrangement specified in the application for the benefit

of a relevant person specified in the application if the arrangement has been assented to in writing by each other person (if any) who—

(a)   is not a relevant person,

(b)   is beneficially interested in the trust, and

(c)   is capable of assenting to the arrangement.

(2) The court shall not hear an application made to it under subsection (1) in respect of a relevant trust unless it is satisfied that the applicant has given notice in writing of the application—

(a)   to the Revenue Commissioners, and

(b)   to such persons as may be prescribed by rules of court,

at least 2 weeks before the hearing of the application.

(3) The court may hear an application made to it under subsection (1) otherwise than in public if it considers that it is appropriate to do so.

(4) The court shall determine an application made to it under subsection (1) in respect of a relevant trust—

(a)   subject to paragraph (b), by making an order approving the arrangement specified in the application if it is satisfied that the carrying out of the arrangement would be for the benefit of—

    (i)   the relevant person specified in the application, and

    (ii)   any other relevant person,

(b)   by refusing to make such an order in any case where—

    (i)   the court is not satisfied as referred to in paragraph (a), or

    (ii)   the Revenue Commissioners have satisfied the court that the application is substantially motivated by a desire to avoid, or reduce the incidence of, tax.

(5) In determining under subsection (4) whether an arrangement would be for the benefit of a relevant person, the court may have regard to any benefit or detriment, financial or otherwise, that may accrue to that person directly or indirectly in consequence of the arrangement.

(6) Nothing in this section shall be construed as derogating from or affecting the operation of—

(a)   the Charities Acts 1961 and 1973 and the Charities Act 2009,

(b)   any power of a court, whether under an enactment or rule of law, to—

    (i)   vary, revoke or resettle a trust (including a relevant trust), or

    (ii)   vary, enlarge, add to or restrict the powers of the trustees under a trust (including a relevant trust) to manage or administer the property the subject of the trust, or

(c)   any rule of law relating to the termination or revocation of a trust (including a relevant trust).

PART 2

RULES OF THE SUPERIOR COURTS (LAND AND CONVEYANCING LAW REFORM ACT 2009) 2010 (SI 149/2010)

We, the Superior Courts Rules Committee, constituted pursuant to the provisions of the Courts of Justice Act 1936 , section 67, and reconstituted pursuant to the provisions of the Courts of Justice Act 1953, section 15, by virtue of the powers conferred upon us by the Courts of Justice Act 1924, section 36, and the Courts of Justice Act 1936, section 68 (as applied by the Courts (Supplemental Provisions) Act 1961, section 48), and the Courts (Supplemental Provisions) Act 1961, section 14, and of all other powers enabling us in this behalf, do hereby make the following Rules of Court.

Dated this 3rd day of December, 2009.

John L Murray

Nicholas Kearns

William McKechnie

Elizabeth Dunne

Patrick O'Connor

Paul McGarry

Noel Rubotham

Maeve Kane

I concur in the making of the following Rules of Court.

Dated this 12th day of April, 2010.

DERMOT AHERN,

Minister for Justice, Equality and Law Reform.

1. Subject to paragraph 2, these Rules shall come into operation on the 10th day of May 2010.

2. Any application for registration of a lis pendens containing the particulars required by law before 1 December 2009 for such registration which is received after 1 December 2009 and prior to the date mentioned in paragraph 1 shall be deemed to comply with the requirements for registration of a lis pendens in accordance with section 121 of the Land and Conveyancing Law Reform Act 2009.

3. These Rules shall be construed together with the Rules of the Superior Courts 1986 to 2010 and may be cited as the Rules of the Superior Courts (Land and Conveyancing Law Reform Act 2009) 2010.

4. The Rules of the Superior Courts are amended:

(i)   by the substitution for paragraph (3) of Order 3 of the following paragraph:

"(3) The payment into Court of any money in the hands of executors, administrators or trustees, or the payment into Court in respect of prior incumbrances by a mortgagee in accordance with the Land and Conveyancing Law Reform Act 2009, section 107(1)(a).";

(ii)   by the insertion immediately following paragraph (9) of Order 3 of the following paragraph:

"(9A) An order under the Land and Conveyancing Law Reform Act 2009, section 31, section 49(5), section 50(1), section 68, section 97(2), section 100(3) or both section 97(2) and section 100(3).";

(iii) by the substitution for paragraphs (11) and (12) of Order 3 of the following paragraphs:

"(11) The appointment of a trustee (including a trustee mentioned in the Land and Conveyancing Law Reform Act 2009, section 19) or a new trustee with or without a vesting or other consequential order; or a vesting order or other order consequential on the appointment of a new trustee, whether the appointment is made by the Court or out of Court; or a vesting or other consequential order in any case where a judgement or order has been given or made for the sale, conveyance or transfer of any land or stock; or a vesting order under the Trustee Act 1893, section 39; or an order directing a person to convey.

(11A) An order to resolve a dispute mentioned in the Land and Conveyancing Law Reform Act 2009, section 22.

(11B) An order to approve an arrangement specified in an application under the Land and Conveyancing Law Reform Act 2009, section 24.

(12) The determination of any question under the Land and Conveyancing Law Reform Act 2009, section 55.";

(iv)   by the substitution for paragraph (15) of Order 3 of the following paragraphs:

"(15) Sale, delivery of possession by a mortgagor, or redemption; reconveyance, or delivery of possession by a mortgagee, otherwise than under the Land and Conveyancing Law Reform Act 2009.

(15A) An action by a mortgagor to which the Land and Conveyancing Law Reform Act 2009, section 94, applies.

(15B) An order on an application by a judgment mortgagee under the Land and Conveyancing Law Reform Act 2009, section 117.";

(v)   by the substitution for paragraph (c) of sub-rule (2) of rule 4 of Order 5 of the following paragraph:

"(c)   the redemption of mortgages;";

(vi)   by the substitution for rule 31 of Order 15 of the following rule:

"31. Wherever—

(a)   any order has been made under section 31 of the Land and Conveyancing Law Reform Act 2009, or

(b)   in any action for the administration of the estate of a deceased person, or the execution of the trusts of any deed or instrument, or for the partition or sale of any hereditaments, a judgment or order has been pronounced or made—

(i)   for an account; or

(ii)   under Order 33; or

(iii)   affecting the rights or interests of persons not parties to the action;

the Court may direct that any person affected by the order under section 31 of the said Act or interested in the estate or under the trust or in the hereditaments shall be served with notice of the judgment or order; and after such notice such persons shall be bound by the proceedings in the same manner as if they had originally been made parties and shall be at liberty to attend the proceedings under the judgement or order. Any person so served may, within one month after such service, apply to the Court to discharge, vary or add to the judgment or order.";

(vii)   by the insertion immediately following rule 11 of Order 33 of the following rule:

"12. References in this Order to incumbrances include references to judgment mortgages, and cognate words shall be construed accordingly.";

(viii) by the insertion in rule 3 of Order 51 immediately following the words "In all cases where a sale" of the words "(including a sale directed under section 94(2) of the Land and Conveyancing Law Reform Act 2009)";

(ix)   by the substitution for rule 3 of Order 54 of the following rule:

"3. Any mortgagee or mortgagor, whether legal or equitable, any person entitled to or having property subject to a legal or equitable charge, or person having the right to redeem any mortgage, whether legal or equitable, may take out a special summons for relief of the nature or kind specified in Order 3(15), (15A) or (15B).";

(x)   by the substitution for paragraph (29) of rule 1 of Order 63 of the following paragraph:

"(29) An order to vacate a lis pendens on an application under section 123 of the Land and Conveyancing Law Reform Act 2009.";

(xi)   by the insertion immediately following Order 72 of the following Order:

"Order 72A
Land and Conveyancing Law Reform Act 2009

1 In this Order:

"the Act" means the Land and Conveyancing Law Reform Act 2009 and any reference in this Order to a section shall, unless the context otherwise requires, be deemed to be a reference to a section of the Act;

2. (1) Proceedings for the following reliefs under the Act shall be commenced by special summons in accordance with Order 3:

(a)   an order to resolve a dispute mentioned in section 22;

(b)   an order to approve an arrangement specified in an application under section 24;

(c)   an order under section 31;

(d)   an order under section 49(5);

(e)   an order under section 50(1);

(f)   an order under section 68.

(2) The following proceedings under the Act may be commenced by plenary summons in accordance with Order 1, rule 2:

(a)   an action for damages in accordance with section 18(6);

(b)   an action in which an order is sought under section 35(2);

(c)   an application for damages in accordance with section 84(8).

(3) Applications for the following reliefs under the Act shall be brought by motion on notice in the proceedings before the Court to which the application relates, grounded upon an affidavit sworn by or on behalf of the moving party:

(a)   an order under section 98, where the Court is already seised of an application or proceedings relating to the mortgaged property;

(b)   an order under section 112(3)(d) in an action relating to the mortgaged land.

3. (1) The register of lis pendens referred to in section 121 (in this rule, the "register") shall be maintained in a book to be kept for that purpose in the Central Office. The register shall be arranged, in alphabetical order, according to the surname of the person whose estate is intended to be affected by each lis pendens. The book kept for that purpose in accordance with section 10 of the Judgments (Ireland) Act 1840 immediately before 1 December 2009 shall, until replaced, and with such modifications as may be necessitated by this rule, continue to be the register.

(2) To register a lis pendens in the register, the plaintiff or his solicitor shall provide to the proper officer, in respect of each person whose estate is intended to be affected by the lis pendens:

(a)   a memorandum in duplicate in the Form No. 31 in Appendix C containing the particulars specified in sub-rule (3) of the action or proceedings mentioned in section 122, and

(b)   a copy of the originating document,

and shall on request produce to the proper officer the sealed originating document.

(3) The particulars to be entered in the register are:

(a)   the name and the usual or last known place of residence (or in the case of a company, the registered office) and description of the person applying for registration, and the name and place of business of his solicitor, if any;

(b)   the name and the usual or last known place of residence (or in the case of a company, the registered office) and description of the person whose estate is intended to be affected by the registration;

(c)   the Court in which, and date on which the action was, or the proceedings were, commenced, and the title and record number of the action or proceedings.

4. (1) The consent referred to in paragraph (a) of section 122 shall be in the Form No. 32 in Appendix C.

(2) The requirement in paragraph (b) of section 122 for lodgement in the Central Office of a notice of an order under section 123 shall be satisfied by lodging an attested copy of the order of the Court or, as the case may be, of the Circuit Court, in the Central Office.

5. The proper officer shall, on request, issue a certificate of the registration of a lis pendens in the form included in Form No. 31 or, as the case may be, of the cancellation of an entry on the register in Form No.33.";

(xii)   by the substitution for rule 14 of Order 96 of the following rule:

"14. Procedure by special summons shall be adopted in the case of an application to the Court, under the Registration of Title Act 1964, section 62(7), by an owner of a charge created before 1 December 2009 for possession of registered land, and the foregoing rules of this Order shall not apply to such proceedings."; and

(xiii)   by the insertion of the forms in the Schedule in Appendix C, immediately following Form No. 30 in that Appendix.

O 72A rule 3(2)

SCHEDULE No. 31.

HIGH COURT

APPLICATION FOR THE REGISTRATION OF A LIS PENDENS

I request that you enter the following particulars in the register of lis pendens in accordance with section 121 of the Land and Conveyancing Law Reform Act 2009.

Name and address of applicant for registration:

Name:

Address:

Solicitor for applicant:

Name:

Address:

Court in which the action was, or the proceedings were, commenced:

High Court/Circuit Court, ... Circuit, County of

Date on which the action was, or the proceedings were, commenced: 20..........

Title and record number of the action or proceedings:

High Court (or, Circuit Court)

Between Plaintiff

And Defendant

Record No.

Name and the usual or last known place of residence (or in the case of a company, the registered office) and description of the person whose estate is intended to be affected by the registration

Name:

Address:

Description

(for office use only)

CERTIFICATE OF REGISTRATION OF A LIS PENDENS

I CERTIFY that the lis pendens particulars of which are set out in the above memorandum was duly registered in the Central Office on .... 20...... (in Book ...., Page ......).

Dated: .... 20......

Registrar

O 72A rule 4(1)

No. 32. HIGH COURT

CONSENT TO CANCELLATION OF AN ENTRY OF A LIS PENDENS

I ...., applicant for registration of the lis pendens particulars of which are set out below, hereby consent to cancellation of the entry in respect of it on the register of lis pendens in accordance with paragraph (a) of section 122 of the Land and Conveyancing Law Reform Act 2009.

Name and address of applicant for registration:

Name:

Address:

Solicitor for applicant:

Name:

Address:

Particulars of lis pendens to be cancelled

Date of entry in the register of lis pendens:

Court in which the action was, or the proceedings were, commenced:

High Court/Circuit Court, ... Circuit, County of

Title and record number of the action or proceedings:

High Court (or, Circuit Court)

Between Plaintiff

And Defendant

Record No.

Name and the usual or last known place of residence (or in the case of a company, the registered office) and description of the person whose estate was intended to be affected by the registration

Name:

Address:

Description

O 72A rule 5

No. 33. HIGH COURT

CERTIFICATE OF CANCELLATION OF ENTRY OF A LIS PENDENS

I CERTIFY that the entry of a lis pendens, particulars of which are set out below, was cancelled on the register of lis pendens in accordance with section 122 of the Land and Conveyancing Law Reform Act 2009

*[with the consent, given in the prescribed manner, of [XY] on whose application it was registered]

*[upon the lodgement in the Central Office of a notice, given in the prescribed manner, of an order of the .... Court dated the ...... day of .... 20...... under section 123 of the Land and Conveyancing Law Reform Act 2009 vacating the lis pendens]

Particulars of entry of lis pendens cancelled

Date of entry in the register of lis pendens:

Court in which the action was, or the proceedings were, commenced:

High Court/Circuit Court, ... Circuit, County of

Title and record number of the action or proceedings:

High Court (or, Circuit Court)

Between Plaintiff

And Defendant

Record No.

Name and the usual or last known place of residence (or in the case of a company, the registered office) and description of the person whose estate was intended to be affected by the registration

Name:

Address:

Description

* delete as appropriate

EXPLANATORY NOTE

(This does not form part of the Instrument and does not purport to be a legal interpretation.)

These rules effect various amendments to the Rules of the Superior Courts, including the insertion of a new Order 72A, to facilitate the operation of the Land and Conveyancing Law Reform Act 2009.

Circuit Court Rules (Land and Conveyancing Law Reform Act 2009) 2010 (SI 155/2010)

We, the Circuit Court Rules Committee, constituted pursuant to the provisions of section 69 of the Courts of Justice Act 1936, and section 12 of the Courts of Justice Act 1947, by virtue of the powers conferred on us by section 66 of the Courts of Justice Act 1924 and section 70 of the Courts of Justice Act 1936, (as applied by section 48 of the Courts (Supplemental Provisions) Act 1961) and section 27 of the Courts (Supplemental Provisions) Act 1961, and of all other powers enabling us in this behalf, do hereby, with the concurrence of the Minister for Justice, Equality and Law Reform, make the annexed Rules of Court.

Dated this 8th day of December 2009.

(Signed): Matthew Deery

(Chairman of the Circuit Court Rules Committee)

Alison Lindsay

Tony Hunt

Joe Deane

Ronan Boylan

I concur in the making of the above Rules of Court.

Dated this 15th day of April 2010.

Signed: DERMOT AHERN,

MINISTER FOR JUSTICE, EQUALITY AND LAW REFORM.

Circuit Court Rules (Land and Conveyancing Law Reform Act 2009) 2010

(SI 155/2010)

1. These Rules, which may be cited as the Circuit Court Rules (Land and Conveyancing Law Reform Act 2009) 2010, shall come into operation on the13th day of May 2010.

2. These Rules shall be construed together with the Circuit Court Rules 2001 to 2010.

3. The Circuit Court Rules are amended:

(i)   by the substitution for the definition of "Equity Suit" and "Equity Proceeding" in the Interpretation of Terms provisions of the following definition:

" "Equity Suit" and "Equity Proceeding" includes:

(a)   any proceedings mentioned in the Third Schedule of the Courts (Supplemental Provisions) Act 1961 at reference numbers 17 to 23 inclusive, 24 (so far as it relates to proceedings for the care of minors' estates) and 25 to 28 inclusive, and

(b)   so far as not mentioned at paragraph (a) or otherwise provided for in these Rules, any proceedings mentioned in section 33 of the County Officers and Courts (Ireland) Act 1877;";

(ii)   by the substitution for paragraph (xxiv) of rule 1 of Order 18 of the following paragraph:

"(xxiv)An order to vacate a lis pendens on an application under section 123 of the Land and Conveyancing Law Reform Act 2009.";

(iii) by the substitution for rule 2 of Order 43 of the following rule:

"2. Where a sale, mortgage, partition or exchange is ordered, or an order is made under section 31 or section 94 of the Land and Conveyancing Law Reform Act 2009, the Court, in addition to the powers already existing, may authorise effect to be given to its order:

(a)   by laying proposals before the Court for its sanction; or

(b)   by proceedings out of Court, and any moneys produced thereby shall be paid into Court, or to trustees, or otherwise dealt with as the Court orders;

provided always that the Judge shall not authorise a sale out of Court unless and until he is satisfied that all persons interested in the land are before the Court, or are bound by the order.";

(iv)   by the substitution for the title and rule 1 of Order 46 of the following title and rule:

**"Order 46
Proceedings by Equity Civil Bill**

"1. The following proceedings shall be commenced by issuing an Equity Civil Bill in accordance with Form 2B of the Schedule of Forms, entitled in the matter of the Act under which the proceeding is taken and, where relevant, of the trust or settlement, as the case may be:

(a)   proceedings under section 33(i) or (k) of the County Officers and Courts (Ireland) Act 1877,

(b)   proceedings under the Trustee Acts (other than for payment into Court by trustees),

(c)   any other proceedings required or permitted by these Rules to be commenced by Equity Civil Bill.";

(v)   by the insertion immediately following Order 46 of the following Order:

"Order 46A
Land and Conveyancing Law Reform Act 2009

1. In this Order:

"the Act" means the Land and Conveyancing Law Reform Act 2009 and any reference in this Order to a section shall, unless the context otherwise requires, be deemed to be a reference to a section of the Act;

2. (1) Proceedings for the following reliefs under the Act shall be commenced by Equity Civil Bill in accordance with Order 46:

(a)   an order to resolve a dispute mentioned in section 22;

(b)   an order to approve an arrangement specified in an application under section 24;

(c)   an order under section 31;

(d)   an order under section 50(1);

(e)   an order under section 68.

(2) The following proceedings under the Act may be commenced by Ordinary Civil Bill in accordance with Order 1, rule 2:

(a)   an action for damages in accordance with section 18(6);

(b)   an action in which an order is sought under section 35(2);

(c)   an action for damages in accordance with section 60(2);

(d)   an application for damages in accordance with section 84(8);

(e)   proceedings in which a remedy in damages is sought in accordance with section 105(2).

(3) Applications for the following reliefs under the Act shall be brought by motion on notice in the proceedings before the Court to which the application relates, grounded upon an affidavit sworn by or on behalf of the moving party:

(a)   an order under section 98, where the Court is already seised of an application or proceedings relating to the mortgaged property;

(b)   an order under section 112(3)(d) in an action relating to the mortgaged land.

(vi)   by the substitution for sub-rule (33) of rule 4 of Order 59 of the following rule:

"33. The plaintiff in proceedings wherein it is sought to have a conveyance declared void pursuant to the provisions of section 3 of the Family Home Protection Act 1976 (as amended by section 54 of the Family Law Act 1995) (which said proceedings shall be instituted by way of Equity Civil Bill seeking declaratory relief) shall forthwith and without delay following the institution of such proceedings cause relevant particulars of the proceedings to be entered as a lis pendens upon the property and/or premises in question under and in accordance with section 121 of the Land and Conveyancing Law Reform Act 2009.", and

(vii)   by the substitution for rule 27 of Order 66 of the following rule:

"27. For the purpose of the taxation or measurement of costs, any proceedings mentioned in the Third Schedule of the Courts (Supplemental Provisions) Act 1961 at reference numbers 17 to 28 inclusive shall be deemed to be Equity proceedings."

EXPLANATORY NOTE

(This does not form part of the Instrument and does not purport to be a legal interpretation.)

These rules effect various amendments to the Circuit Court Rules, including the insertion of a new Order 46A, to facilitate the operation of the Land and Conveyancing Law Reform Act 2009.

Appendix 13

RELEVANT PROVISIONS OF THE CHARITIES ACT 2009

2 Interpretation

(1) In this Act—

"Act of 1962" means the Street and House to House Collections Act 1962;

"Act of 1998" means the Education Act 1998;

"Act of 2001" means the Criminal Justice (Theft and Fraud Offences) Act 2001;

"Authority" has the meaning assigned to it by section 13;

"body" includes, in relation to a trust in respect of which there is only one trustee, that trustee;

" charitable gift " means a gift for charitable purposes;

"charitable organisation" means—

(a)   the trustees of a charitable trust, or

(b)   a body corporate or an unincorporated body of persons—

    (i)   that promotes a charitable purpose only,

    (ii)   that, under its constitution, is required to apply all of its property (both real and personal) in furtherance of that purpose, except for moneys expended—

        (I)   in the operation and maintenance of the body, including moneys paid in remuneration and superannuation of members of the staff of the body, and

        (II)   in the case of a religious organisation or community, on accommodation and care of members of the organisation or community,

    and

    (iii)   none of the property of which is payable to the members of the body other than in accordance with section 89,

but shall not include an excluded body;

"charitable purpose " shall be construed in accordance with section 3;

"charitable trust" means a trust—

(a)   established for a charitable purpose only,

(b) established under a deed of trust that requires the trustees of the trust to apply all of the property (both real and personal) of the trust in furtherance of that purpose except for moneys expended in the management of the trust, and

(c) none of the property of which is payable to the trustees of the trust other than in accordance with section 89;

"charity trustee" includes—

(a) in the case of a charitable organisation that is a company, the directors and other officers of the company, and

(b) in the case of a charitable organisation that is a body corporate (other than a company) or an unincorporated body of persons, any officer of the body or any person for the time being performing the functions of an officer of the body,

and references to a charity trustee of a charitable organisation shall be construed as including references to a trustee of a charitable trust;

"chief executive" has the meaning assigned to it by section 19;

"company" means a company established under the Companies Acts;

"constitution" means the rules (whether in writing or not) governing the administration and control of a charitable organisation and that regulate its activities, and includes—

(a) in the case of a charitable organisation consisting of trustees of a charitable trust, the deed of trust establishing the charitable trust,

(b) in the case of a charitable organisation that is a company, the memorandum and articles of association of the company,

(c) in the case of a charitable organisation that is a body corporate other than a company, the charter, statute or other like instrument by which it is established, and

(d) in the case of a charitable organisation that is an unincorporated body of persons, the rules of the body,

but does not include any enactment or rule of law applicable to the carrying on of the activities of the organisation;

"dissolved body" has the meaning assigned to it by section 81;

"education body" means—

(a) a vocational education committee established by section 7 of the Vocational Education Act 1930,

(b) a recognised school within the meaning of the Act of 1998,

(c) a management committee established for the purposes of section 37 of the Act of 1998,

(d) a parents' association established in accordance with section 26 of the Act of 1998,

(e)   a student council established in accordance with section 27 of the Act of 1998,

(f)   an institution of higher education within the meaning of the Higher Education Authority Act 1971 (amended by section 52 of the Institutes of Technology Act 2006), or

(g)   a body established solely for the purpose of funding not more than one such institution of higher education;

"EEA Agreement" has the same meaning as it has in the European Communities (Amendment) Act 1993;

"EEA state" means—

(a)   a member state of the European Communities (other than the State), or

(b)   a state (other than a member state of the European Communities) that is a contracting party to the EEA Agreement;

"establishment day" shall be construed in accordance with section 12;

"excluded body" means—

(a)   a political party, or a body that promotes a political party or candidate,

(b)   a body that promotes a political cause, unless the promotion of that cause relates directly to the advancement of the charitable purposes of the body,

(c)   an approved body of persons within the meaning of section 235 of the Taxes Consolidation Act 1997,

(d)   a trade union or a representative body of employers,

(e)   a chamber of commerce, or

(f)   a body that promotes purposes that are—

       (i)   unlawful,

       (ii)   contrary to public morality,

       (iii)   contrary to public policy,

       (iv)   in support of terrorism or terrorist activities, whether in the State or outside the State, or

       (v)   for the benefit of an organisation, membership of which is unlawful;

"judicial office in the Superior Courts" means the office of judge of the High Court or the office of judge of the Supreme Court;

"local authority" has the same meaning as it has in the Local Government Act 2001;

"material interest" shall be construed in accordance with section 2(3) of the Ethics in Public Office Act 1995;

"Minister" means the Minister for Community, Rural and Gaeltacht Affairs;

"personal connection" shall be construed in accordance with subsection (2);

"prescribed" means prescribed by regulations made by the Minister;

"public benefit" shall be construed in accordance with section 3;

"record" includes, in addition to any record in writing—

(a)   a plan, chart, map, drawing, diagram, pictorial or graphic image,

(b)   a disc, tape, soundtrack or other device in which information, sounds or signals are embodied so as to be capable (with or without the aid of some other instrument) of being reproduced in legible or audible form,

(c)   a film, tape or other device in which visual images are embodied so as to be capable (with or without the aid of some other instrument) of being reproduced in visual form, and

(d)   a photograph;

"register" has the meaning assigned to it by section 39, and "registered" shall be construed accordingly;

"registered charitable organisation" means—

(a)   a charitable organisation that is registered in the register, or

(b)   a charitable organisation that, by virtue of section 40, is deemed to be registered in the register;

"registration number" has the meaning assigned to it by section 40(6)(e);

"Tribunal" has the meaning assigned to it by section 75.

(2)

(a)   For the purposes of this Act—

    (i)   a person is connected with an individual if that person is a parent, brother, sister, spouse, grandparent or grandchild of the individual or a child of the spouse of the individual,

    (ii)   a person, in his or her capacity as a trustee of a trust, is connected with an individual if that individual, or any of that individual's children, or any body corporate that that individual controls is a beneficiary of the trust,

    (iii)   a person is connected with any person with whom he or she is in partnership,

    (iv)   a person is connected with any person by whom he or she is employed under a contract of service,

    (v)   a body corporate is connected with another person if that person has control of it or if that person and persons connected with that person together have control of it, and

    (vi)   any two or more persons acting together to secure or exercise control of a body corporate shall be treated in relation to that body corporate as

> connected with one another and with any person acting on the directions of any of them to secure or exercise control of the body corporate.

(b)   In this subsection "control" has the meaning assigned to it by section 11 of the Taxes Consolidation Act 1997, and cognate words shall be construed accordingly.

3 Charitable purpose

(1) For the purposes of this Act each of the following shall, subject to subsection (2), be a charitable purpose:

(a)   the prevention or relief of poverty or economic hardship;

(b)   the advancement of education;

(c)   the advancement of religion;

(d)   any other purpose that is of benefit to the community.

(2) A purpose shall not be a charitable purpose unless it is of public benefit.

(3) Subject to subsection (4), a gift shall not be of public benefit unless—

(a)   it is intended to benefit the public or a section of the public, and

(b)   in a case where it confers a benefit on a person other than in his or her capacity as a member of the public or a section of the public, any such benefit is reasonable in all of the circumstances, and is ancillary to, and necessary, for the furtherance of the public benefit.

(4) It shall be presumed, unless the contrary is proved, that a gift for the advancement of religion is of public benefit.

(5) The Authority shall not make a determination that a gift for the advancement of religion is not of public benefit without the consent of the Attorney General.

(6) A charitable gift for the purpose of the advancement of religion shall have effect, and the terms upon which it is given shall be construed, in accordance with the laws, canons, ordinances and tenets of the religion concerned.

(7) In determining whether a gift is of public benefit or not, account shall be taken of—

(a)   any limitation imposed by the donor of the gift on the class of persons who may benefit from the gift and whether or not such limitation is justified and reasonable, having regard to the nature of the purpose of the gift, and

(b)   the amount of any charge payable for any service provided in furtherance of the purpose for which the gift is given and whether it is likely to limit the number of persons or classes of person who will benefit from the gift.

(8) A limitation referred to in subsection (7) shall not be justified and reasonable if all of the intended beneficiaries of the gift or a significant number of them have a personal connection with the donor of the gift.

(9) There shall be no appeal to the Tribunal from a determination of the Authority to which subsection (5) applies.

(10) For the purposes of this section, a gift is not a gift for the advancement of religion if it is made to or for the benefit of an organisation or cult—

(a)   the principal object of which is the making of profit, or

(b)   that employs oppressive psychological manipulation—

    (i)   of its followers, or

    (ii)   for the purpose of gaining new followers.

(11) In this section "purpose that is of benefit to the community" includes—

(a)   the advancement of community welfare including the relief of those in need by reason of youth, age, ill-health, or disability,

(b)   the advancement of community development, including rural or urban regeneration,

(c)   the promotion of civic responsibility or voluntary work,

(d)   the promotion of health, including the prevention or relief of sickness, disease or human suffering,

(e)   the advancement of conflict resolution or reconciliation,

(f)   the promotion of religious or racial harmony and harmonious community relations,

(g)   the protection of the natural environment,

(h)   the advancement of environmental sustainability,

(i)   the advancement of the efficient and effective use of the property of charitable organisations,

(j)   the prevention or relief of suffering of animals,

(k)   the advancement of the arts, culture, heritage or sciences, and

(l)   the integration of those who are disadvantaged, and the promotion of their full participation, in society.

7 Exemption from liability to pay tax

(1) Nothing in this Act shall operate to affect the law in relation to the levying or collection of any tax or the determination of eligibility for exemption from liability to pay any tax.

(2) The Revenue Commissioners shall not be bound by a determination of the Authority as to whether a purpose is of public benefit or not in the performance by them of any function under or in connection with—

(a)   section 207, 208 or 609 of the Taxes Consolidation Act 1997,

(b)   section 17 or 76 of the Capital Acquisitions Tax Consolidation Act 2003, or

(c)   section 82 of the Stamp Duties Consolidation Act 1999.

11 Repeals

The Charities Act 1961 is repealed to the extent specified in column (2) of Schedule 2.

SCHEDULE 2

Repeals

Section 11

Short Title (1)	Extent of Repeal (2)
Charities Act 1961	Chapter I of Part II (other than sections 11(2) and 17) and sections 26 and 45.
	In section 23(1), by the deletion of the words ", with the previous consent of the Attorney General,".
	In section 24, by the deletion of the words "without obtaining the consent of the Attorney General".
	In section 25, by the deletion of the words "other than the Attorney General,".
	In section 53, by the deletion of the words "except the Attorney General".

INDEX

Instruction-taking (contd)
foreign divorce, 1.26–1.28
generally, 1.01
grounds for non-recognition, 1.31–1.33
jurisdiction to grant divorce, separation
or nullity, 1.30
legacies and legatees
abatement, 1.48
ademption, 1.47
generally, 1.45–1.46
manslaughter, 1.37
marital status, 1.16
married persons
additional considerations, 1.62–1.85
tax considerations, 1.86
murder, 1.37
non-marital children, 1.59–1.60
nullity
generally, 1.43
jurisdiction to grant, 1.30
principles for recognition, 1.31–1.33
pecuniary legacies and legatees, 1.45
principles for recognition, 1.31–1.33
property outside of Ireland, 1.103–
1.105
residuary estate, 1.52–1.55
revocation of earlier wills and
dispositions, 1.57
separation
generally, 1.24
jurisdiction to grant, 1.30
principles for recognition, 1.31–1.33
specific legacies and legatees, 1.46
tax considerations
all testators, 1.58
civil partners, 1.86
married persons, 1.86
testators with property outside of
Ireland, 1.105
unmarried persons not in civil
partnership or cohabiting, 1.61
testamentary capacity, 1.02–1.15
testamentary freedom, 1.17–1.18
testators who are civil partners
children of civil partner under s 117,
1.93
children of civil partner who dies
intestate, 1.88–1.92

generally, 1.87
testators who are cohabiting with
another person, 1.94–1.102
testators with property outside of
Ireland
generally, 1.103–1.104
tax considerations, 1.105
undue influence, 1.19–1.20
unmarried persons not in civil
partnership or cohabiting, 1.59–1.60
unworthiness to succeed, 1.34–1.41

Insuring assets forming part of estate
executor and trustee powers, and, 12.38

Intention of testator
principles of drafting and construction,
and, 2.04

Interlineations
due execution of wills, and, 1.113

Interpretation of wills
colloquial words, 2.04
duty of care to beneficiaries, 2.11
extrinsic evidence, 2.03
general principles, 2.01–2.10
intention of testator, 2.04
legal meaning, 2.04
popular words, 2.04
'property', 2.08
special 'lexicon' of meanings, 2.05
technical meaning, 2.04
void conditions, 2.09

Introductory clauses
alias used by testator, where, 3.03
alteration of name by marriage, deed
poll or otherwise, where, 3.04
colloquial name used, where, 3.06
executor powers, and
executors and trustees are different
persons, where, 12.32
executors and trustees are same
persons, where, 12.31
identification of testator, 3.01
informal name used, where, 3.06
more than one address, where, 3.07
name usually used is different from
birth certificate, where, 3.05
normal clause, 3.02